D0966932

A FORWARD STRATEGY FOR AMERICA

A FOREIGN POLICY RESEARCH INSTITUTE BOOK

HARPER & BROTHERS, PUBLISHERS, NEW YORK

A FORWARD STRATEGY FOR AMERICA

BY ROBERT STRAUSZ-HUPÉ, WILLIAM R. KINTNER

AND STEFAN T. POSSONY

With Alvin J. Cottrell, James E. Dougherty, Richard B. Foster, Walter F. Hahn, Robert C. Herber, Francis P. Hoeber, Robert L. Pfaltzgraff, Jr., and Donovan Yeuell, Jr.

A FORWARD STRATEGY FOR AMERICA

Printed in the United States of America

FIRST EDITION

A-L

Library of Congress catalog card number: 61-6199

CONTENTS

PREFACE

In May, 1959, *Protracted Conflict*, a study prepared by the Foreign Policy Research Institute of the University of Pennsylvania, was published. An analysis of communist strategy, it examined the principles guiding communist conflict management and the techniques and stratagems of the Cold War.

The public response to *Protracted Conflict* suggested a prescriptive treatment of the problems posed. The following pages are addressed to the necessities which urge upon the United States a strategy beyond survival, and set forth the general concepts for such a strategy.

For several years, the United States and the Free World have steadily lost ground in the international struggle with communism. If this process continues, it may, within the foreseeable future, become irreversible. The resources of the Free World, both physical and spiritual, far outweigh those of the communist bloc. If they were fully mobilized, the communists could not hope to prevail. Yet, the communists are confident, as the fascists were, that the great Western democracies are doomed by the inexorable laws of history—if not by their propensity for doing too late what need be done. The communists are convinced of the inevitability of *their* ultimate victory. The burden of the following pages is that the struggle hangs in the balance. There is no assurance that we shall confound the all-too-obvious purpose of the communists unless we and the peoples on our side join in an effort in the cause of freedom much greater than we have thought thus far worth our while. The present study, starting with the premises developed in the analysis of *Protracted Conflict*, seeks to trace the unitary pattern of the many and varied measures which must go into the design of a Forward Strategy for America.

We are well aware of the ambitious nature of the task we set ourselves. Because this book covers the full range of our foreign policy problems, its conclusions rest upon the findings of many men. We, the three principal authors, have presided over a prolonged and, we trust, systematic process of synthesis. The organization of this study was facilitated by the fact that many of those who participated in it, or who were consulted in the course of its preparation, had served in responsible positions of government in areas concerned with both policy and strategy. Hence, we were able to draw upon many years of accumulated firsthand experience and study. Each chapter was drafted many times and subjected to intensive criticism by knowledgeable experts.

In the process of writing this volume, we consulted many academic institutions, research organizations and governmental agencies. Although the final product represents the views of the three authors, it is based on a synthesis of ideas gathered in extensive discussions and conferences in which Institute representatives sought the advice and counsel of their colleagues.

One of the most useful conferences held in connection with the preparation of this book was the three-day meeting in mid-June, 1960, at the Foreign Service Institute of the Department of State. A first draft of several of the chapters of the book was reviewed on this occasion by the staff and members of the Senior Officers Seminar. Other meetings and discussions, held during the spring and summer of 1960, include a conference with Governor C. Canby Balderston of the Federal Reserve Board and members of the Board's staff; an all-day seminar with representatives of the staff of the Stanford Research Institute at Menlo Park, California, and a meeting with Director Ellis A. Johnson and staff members of the Operations Research Organization in Washington. Numerous meetings were called to review individual chapters with groups of experts. Many of the ideas presented in this book were discussed in national-strategy seminars held in a number of cities throughout the country. Outstanding in this connection was the National Strategy Seminar, organized by the United States Sixth Army and conducted at the Asilomar, California, April, 1960, by the Stanford Research Institute. The Defense Strategy Seminar, organized under the auspices of the

Joint Chiefs of Staff, at the National War College in July, 1960, proved to be a particularly useful forum for discussion of some of the national security problems examined in this book. The Foreign Policy Research Institute assisted in preparing the curriculum and providing course direction for this seminar.

Although many chapters of this study represent a collective effort, the three principal authors are alone responsible for the final integration of the materials. They are directly responsible for the final form of the study. In the drafting of certain chapters, the following have contributed most importantly: Chapter 3, "Building the Free World": Robert L. Pfaltzgraff, Jr., and Robert C. Herber; Chapter 4, "The Technological Factor": Donovan Yeuell, Jr., Richard B. Foster and Ralph Sanders; Chapter 5, "Military Strategy, Power and Policy": Alvin J. Cottrell, Richard B. Foster and Donovan Yeuell, Jr.; Chapter 7, "Diplomatic Arm of Strategy": Walter F. Hahn; Chapter 8, "Psychological Operations": Robert C. Herber, Vladimir Petrov and Paul M. A. Linebarger; Chapter 9, "Security Through Arms Control?": James E. Dougherty; Chapter 10, "Strategy of Ways and Means": Francis P. Hoeber, James E. Dougherty and Ralph McCabe; Chapter 11, "Structure for Strategy": Edwin F. Black.

Alvin J. Cottrell and Walter F. Hahn have since joined the Institute for Defense Analyses. Their work was completed prior to assuming their new duties. Richard B. Foster and Francis P. Hoeber are members of the Stanford Research Institute. Their participation in this study was on a personal basis, and in no way implies endorsement of the book by the Stanford Research Institute.

Throughout its preparation, the study derived benefit from discussions with the associates of the Institute: William Yandell Elliott, Harvard University; Field Haviland, Brookings Institution; Hans Kohn, College of the City of New York; and Norman D. Palmer, Froelich G. Rainey and Arthur P. Whitaker, University of Pennsylvania.

Aside from the research assistants of the Foreign Policy Research Institute included in the above list, the authors wish to express their gratitude to Erasmus H. Kloman, Keith Wheelock, J. Roffe Wike and James F. McGarry. Mr. Kloman assisted the authors both administratively and in various research assignments.

Our special thanks go to Regina Eldor, research assistant to Dr. Stefan T. Possony; and to Joy Cottrell; Joanne Walter; Jacqueline

Ketcham; Margaret Capotrio; Diane Kressler and Kay Christiansen, whose painstaking task it was to type and proofread the several working drafts of each chapter and the final manuscript.

The Institute owes a special debt to George C. Reinhardt, RAND Corporation, who was particularly helpful with respect to Chapter 6, "Economic Framework of Strategy," and Chapter 10, "Strategy of Ways and Means"; to E. Bruce Glenn, who assisted in drafting Chapter 8, "Psychological Operations"; to Joseph Z. Kornfeder, for his contributions to Chapter 2 and Chapter 8; and to Cass Canfield, Jr., for his editorial advice.

The authors met with numerous representatives of United States governmental agencies, both in Washington and abroad. Much valuable counsel was obtained through such consultation.

Others whom the authors wish to thank most warmly are:

Brigadier General Donald Armstrong
Frank R. Barnett
Anthony T. Bouscaren
Brutus Costa
John Cushman
Colonel Ralph Devine
Earl De Long
Tibor Eckhardt
Robert Ekvall
Theodore Geiger
Major Abbott C. Greenleaf, USAF
Lorna H. Hahn
Stuart L. Hannon
Rear Admiral Edwin B. Hooper
E. Gordon Keith
Fritz G. A. Kraemer
Charles A. Malik
William Platt
Brigadier General Robert C. Richardson, III, USAF
Hamlin Robinson
Alexander Sachs
Ralph Sanders
Colonel Richard G. Stilwell, USA
Herbert E. Striner
Anwar Syed
Captain Brown Taylor, USN
George Taylor
Donald Treadgold
Brigadier General Clifton Van Kann, USA
Richard L. Walker
Nathaniel Weyl
Karl Wittfogel

While acknowledging our indebtedness to the contributions made by many incisive minds, the principal authors are alone responsible for the conceptual framework of this book and for the specific views advanced.

ROBERT STRAUSZ-HUPÉ
WILLIAM R. KINTNER
STEFAN T. POSSONY

November, 1960

CHAPTER 1 THE SETTING

The greatness of a nation lies neither in the abundance of its possessions nor in the strength of its arms. A people finds greatness in its response to the historical challenge—by how it manages to harness its strivings to the aspirations of the age. Thus, to be great is to fulfill a promise that surpasses the national interest. Rome extended the lawful order of the city to the entire ancient world. Britain's victory over Napoleon opened an era of a hundred years of peace and progress for all of mankind. Rome and Britain attained, within the limits of the techniques of their day, predominant power—military, political and economic. Each wedded power to a noble idea of community. Greatness lies in the creative use of power and not in its denial.

Like Rome and Britain, each in her day, America stands at a turning point in history. The felt necessities of the times strain toward a new order. The decline and fall of old empires and the calamities of two world wars wrenched the state system of the nineteenth century—the century of peace and progress—from its moorings. The great problem of our times is to wrest a new order from disorder.

The United States is confronted by environmental changes which are perceptible now. Their consequences are, to some extent, predictable: Of the many forces spurring the world's systemic revolution, scientific-technological advance and the population increase are the most powerful. In the foreseeable future many states will be able to develop nuclear weapons and to exploit their possession for policy purposes which, while perhaps more limited than those of the U.S., Great Britain and the Soviet Union, may collectively and cumulatively alter the world political situation. The diffusion of nuclear military power will take place concurrently with a formidable increase in population pressure. More likely than not, the population explosion may shape the history of this century as fatefully as any other event—as fatefully even as the release of atomic energy, the two world wars, the Bolshevik Revolution and the exploration of space.

Many of the great political and social issues of the twentieth century have been largely determined or powerfully influenced by accelerating rates of population growth. These rates have been rising since the beginning of the nineteenth century. In many places, population densities and rates of increase now are straining to the breaking point traditional institutions. Within the next few decades, the population problem will have reached critical proportions not only for such countries as India and China, but, because of its sheer magnitude, for the world community as a whole.

Within the next fifteen years the population of India, for example, will have grown by more than one-half of its present size. Conceivably, the world demographic problem is soluble globally since croplands can probably be increased by some 50 per cent. Yet, it is unlikely that this rate of increase can be attained within the boundaries of those very states that must anticipate the largest increase of population and where demands for rapidly rising living standards are voiced most stridently. Hence the gap between the standards of living of the haves and the have-nots will widen farther and, at some level of population density, national and international social conflict will wax more intense. That level will vary with culture, economic resources and circumstance. In Oriental societies, long accustomed to higher population densities and lower standards of life, tolerable levels are high, and seem to be higher than elsewhere. The Sino-Soviet bloc countries may be able to deal more efficiently than the West with rapid rates of population increase and excessive crowding. The regime of the ant heap and the communist system have not a few features in common.

The incipient, world-wide population crisis confronts the West with political, economic, social and military problems unprecedented in history—unprecedented in statistical magnitude and geographical scope. As the growth of population presses upon the political system, governments will rely increasingly on force in order to maintain order. Unless men learn to exercise restraint on governments, the state will assume ever greater powers over men's lives. At the limit, as in China, an entire society might seek to survive by total and permanent regimentation. Population growth may so exacerbate social conflict that states will seek to "export" their domestic crisis and launch upon foreign wars.

The grave problems posed by the proliferation of nuclear power centers and the increase of population pressures will be aggravated by the birth of additional new nation-states. The newcomers will press home their claims to an independent say in world politics. They will seek to acquire the instruments of power needed to enforce these claims. Thus the world is confronted with a series of problems that will call for ever closer administrative and purposive integration and co-operation. Yet the essentially divisive nature of the nation-state system and the thrust of new nationalisms point toward a dramatic increase of political friction and conflict.

In all past ages, tendencies of this kind have led to social and international conflicts, revolutions and wars. Reduced to the simplest formula, American policy should seek to forestall a catastrophe which is now in the making and to promote a new international system which will accommodate technological acceleration (including the spread of nuclear power), increased world population and the revolutionary aspirations of mankind.

No blame attaches to the communists for the intrusion of nuclear weapons and population pressure into world politics. Neither the industrial-scientific revolution nor the political revolution that shakes the nation-state system are of the communists' making. But the problems posed by these two permanent and universal revolutions are immensely complicated by the hostility of the communists to any and all forces of order which they do not control. The ideologies and social systems of the Free World and the communist bloc are locked in conflict over the new world order. This protracted conflict is global and of indefinite duration, multidimensional and dialectic.

As for guiding strategic concepts, the Western nations have until now unsuccessfully pitted a narrow, primarily military strategy against a much broader, much more total strategy developed by Lenin and Stalin, Khrushchev and Mao. The spectrum of weapons employed by the communists is not confined to force, but brackets all possible relationships between states and social groups—ideological, political, economic, psychological, cultural, technological and military. Activities which Western peoples have looked upon as pursuits of peace, such as diplomacy, education, trade, cultural exchange and scientific research, are regarded by the communists as tools of strategy. The ability to beat plowshares into swords—a concept repellent to the Western mind—has characterized the communist movement ever since Lenin placed his indelible imprint upon it.

The communists have grasped more firmly than have we the meaning of time as a strategic fourth dimension. Whereas everything in our cultural tradition and our psychology prompts us to yearn for the decisive encounter ("to take up arms against a sea of troubles, and by opposing end them"), the communist strategists avoid skillfully head-on encounters until the achievement of final victory has become feasible. Convinced that time is on their side, they are quite content to avoid the frontal assault and to measure their challenges to a calculus of intermediate risks until the supremacy of power has been gained and technological advantage has shifted overwhelmingly to their side. The indirect approach, at which they excel, is not difficult to practice in the nuclear-missile age, when both sides appear to recognize the risk of excessive military involvement, and in an international environment which furnishes abundant opportunities for exploiting troublesome crises. The communists have been able to carry the fight against the West through a variety of auxiliaries and proxies—local communist parties, satellite governments, partitioned states, neutrals, nationalists, anticolonialist and pacifist movements, guerrilla armies and sundry front organizations. Thus they have maintained a relentless pressure against the West without presenting that ultimate challenge—the *casus belli*—which historically has proved indispensable to provoke Western nations into going to war against the major adversary.

"Protracted conflict" is a generic term describing a world situation in which two power blocs are fighting each other over a long period of time, one to achieve global supremacy, the other to preserve the basic freedoms of individuals and nations. The strategy of protracted conflict aims at conclusive victory by increments of subsidiary wars and nonviolent campaigns. Yet, total war is an element within protracted conflict. Sooner or later, one protagonist in the protracted conflict will conclude that he has been outmaneuvered decisively. He will be left the option to launch a nuclear war and thus spoil the victory of the opponent or to accommodate himself to the latter's design for a new order.

The nuclear balance is unstable. It can be upset *at any moment* by the changes in the relative effectiveness of delivery and interception systems. Basic shifts in technology, force levels and moral climate may terminate abruptly a situation of apparent stalemate or, in turn, may change the quasi stalemate to such a degree that the would-be aggressor finds it advisable to attack. *Hence, the various techniques of protracted conflict are not predicated on the perpetuation of a hypothetical thermonuclear stalemate; indeed, their primary objective is to change the strategic balance in such a way that either the aggressor can risk the plunge or, conversely, the defender is successful in maintaining the power to deter the would-be aggressor.*

Given the unpredictable vagaries of political life, technological breakthroughs and other contingent events, it is entirely possible that, at one time or another, a unique opportunity may present itself for waging total nuclear war under optimum conditions for the aggressor. According to communist doctrine, the taking of unnecessary risks—risks which far exceed possible gains—is considered "adventurism" and is taboo. By the same token, however, failure to take advantage of great opportunities which might never recur is, too, one of the mortal sins of communist doctrine. Given the favorable opportunity, a would-be world conqueror obviously would be foolish if he did not take advantage of the occasion to terminate the struggle once and for all on his own terms.

It has been argued, fallaciously, that since in all likelihood the protracted conflict is to be fought primarily by limited means of conflict, much of our efforts and resources should be devoted to this type of struggle. In fact, the protracted conflict could be decided with considerable finality were the United States to lower its defenses against nuclear surprise attack. It has been argued, no less fallaciously, that concentration upon efforts designed to deter a general nuclear war will provide not only the necessary but also the sufficient basis of our national security and that the total strategy of protracted conflict is but the icing of the national security cake.

The reality of our age is, however, that the most important battles may not be fought by exchanges of nuclear firepower, but, like the conflicts of the sixteenth and seventeenth centuries, will consist of maneuvers and diversions designed to achieve a decisive advantage by one side or the other.

There is no reason, subjective or objective, why the United States cannot develop and pursue a unified and total strategy of its own —run the race for technological supremacy and at least maintain the nuclear balance, *and*, at the same time, press for the transformation of the societies under communist rule. Both tasks are intimately linked to the mandate of the systemic revolution: the unification of the globe. The communists are prepared to execute this mandate; their doctrine tells them what the new order should be and how to create it. The American people, by force of circumstance, must seek to make the settlement of the twentieth century systemic revolution *their* mission, for only thus can they create the universal order that insures the survival of American society—an open society —in contradistinction to a hive of human beings, objects of a sociological experiment designed by the rulers of a closed society. The alternatives are stark—as stark as the strategic confrontation.

We may assume, for the sake of argument, that the Communist Party of the Soviet Union will compromise between Marxist-Leninist dogma and the material aspirations of the Soviet masses, between a cherished doctrine of conflict and the human, all too human, longing for surcease from strife and the costly sacrifices for the sake of strife. It is, to say the least, improbable that the Communist Party will abdicate its absolute, unchallenged power over the Soviet masses—barring a shattering defeat in war and a subsequent revolution. No matter the changes in the domestic and international climate—an effective ban on nuclear testing, the settlement of such critical issues as, for example, the status of Berlin, and vastly increased cultural exchanges with the noncommunist world—the Party leadership will still remain in control of a formidable engine of destruction. The temptation to use it will remain as strong as the chances of using it with impunity will appear to be good.

We are aware that the current international situation lends itself to varying interpretations. Many factors must be taken into account, some good, some bad, some of debatable meaning. Among the heartening developments, for example, are these: the emergence of Western Europe as a politically stable and economically powerful force in the world; the efforts of Britain and France to work out new partnerships with the Africans; the emergence of West Germany as a strong and friendly nation; the halting of communist expansion by violent means in most of the peripheral areas during recent years; the noticeable economic and social progress made by many underdeveloped countries; the growing suspicion of Soviet and Chinese imperialism in some of the Afro-Asian states; the successful stands of the United States since 1957 in crises in the Middle East, the Far East, and Berlin.

Disturbing signs, on the other hand, include the following: deepening divisions of opinion within the Atlantic Alliance over economic integration, summit diplomacy and nuclear strategy; a shift in the scene of social conflict and anti-Western agitation from Asia to Africa and Latin America; the visible headway of communist efforts to transform Japan into a quasi-neutral nation; the growth of Soviet nuclear-missile power and the improved use by the communists of nonmilitary methods of conflict; the increase of Soviet bloc capabilities for conducting economic warfare and political penetration, and the over-all industrial and technological programs of the U.S.S.R. and Communist China.

There are several factors which are difficult to assess at the present time: for example, a strong probability that other states will enter the ranks of the nuclear powers in the 1960's; the relations between the Soviet Union and Red China; and the nature of the changes which are taking place inside the Soviet Union.

The last is the most crucial problem to be considered. Western opinion is badly divided regarding the "modernization" of the Soviet Union. Some hold that communism, like all revolutionary movements known to history, is beginning to lose its initial fervor. They argue that both as ideology and as an organization it is undergoing rapid modification in an era of profound technological change—that communist leadership, realistic as always, is gradually adjusting to the hard facts of a pluralistic world even while continuing to pay lip service to the idea of universal mission.

According to other analysts, whatever "relaxation" has occurred since the death of Stalin should be construed as a sign of enhanced self-confidence, not ideological weakening, on the part of the communists. The time has come when more can be gained by carefully lifting totalitarian controls than by retaining them in all their vigor. The struggle for survival is over; the struggle for victory has begun. Lenin's effort to give Marx's "inevitable historic process" a badly needed push has finally succeeded. From now on it is only a matter of time before the communists inherit the earth. The changed psychological atmosphere which has so impressed Western visitors to the Soviet Union is not something which has been forced upon the Party against its will. The Party is still in control of the environment, mental as well as material.

It is most unlikely that any categorical conclusions can be drawn concerning the turn of world events. Ambiguity is rooted in the very structure of the current international situation.

We need not, and should not, commit ourselves to any specific analysis of Soviet intentions. As we see it, the most prudent policy—and indeed the only safe policy—for the next decade will be to be prepared for continued conflict along a wide spectrum. The United States will have to develop greater strength in all areas of international power and influence and, at the same time, encourage all objective developments which contribute to a genuine rather than a superficial relaxation of international tension.

The real issues at stake between the West and the communist bloc are more complicated than Premier Khrushchev would have us believe. If the struggle were in fact merely a clash between two economic systems, then its solution would be infinitely easier than it is. When we say that Soviet society must undergo a change, we do not refer to a change in its economic organization or method. A free, capitalist system can coexist with a planned, socialist one. This has been amply demonstrated within the West itself, where diverse economic systems not only coexist but co-operate intimately.

The real issue is not economic but political—totalitarianism versus the open, liberal, democratic society, and the approaches adopted by each in its relations with other states. Different political systems can exist side by side, but not when one system is aggressive, geared to conflict and bent upon conquest. The nature of the Soviet system exacerbates the problem of arriving at a settlement, because the communists can appear to renounce aggression for a few years in order to lull the West to sleep. In short, the communist system itself is the most disturbing and dangerous source of world tensions.

The Soviet system, irrespective of its domestic popularity, is not a legitimate, constitutional government in the Western sense of the term. Its concept of treaty obligations is based on entirely different assumptions from those which underlie the Western legalist approach to international relations. So long as the succession of leadership power in the Soviet Union continues to hinge upon the crudest type of conspiratorial politics within the party hierarchy, the United States cannot enter into any agreement with the Soviets which might lead to the unilateral weakening of the American military posture. Even conceding for the sake of the argument that one communist leader or dominant faction may earnestly desire peace with the West on mutually beneficial terms, there is no way of knowing what will be the attitude of their successors. A totalitarian system is capable of rapid reversals of policy. Its political lead-time problems are much less formidable than those of democratic societies, where basic policy shifts occur very slowly and only after a great deal of governmental debate and public discussion.

If our analysis has any validity, then it should be profitable for us to examine the emerging world picture from that unified viewpoint and suggest the outlines of a forward United States strategy to counter the communist conflict pattern. Perhaps in this way we can put ourselves on guard against the possibility that some of the policies which we are now tempted to espouse may play into the Soviets' hands and contribute to the further success of their strategy. Such an analysis might also enable us to discern the broad outlines of what our policies—both functional and regional—should be in the years ahead. It could furnish some valuable criteria by which the appropriateness and consistency of actual U.S. policies and programs might be measured in terms of basic Free World goals.

America has the men and the tools wherewith to fashion the instruments of victory. American society—the open society—has brought forth an idea of order and a style of life that appeal to many peoples. America has loyal allies. The question is thus not one of means or ideas or friends. Specifically, the question is as to whether the people of the U.S. can shake off that chronic apathy which seems to afflict all Western democratic peoples when they think themselves at peace while in fact the aggressor moves stealthily to destroy them.

We must bear the burden of the past—irretrievable errors, missed opportunities and, least avoidably, the ravages of time. Its weight enters into the calculation of where and how far we can go. We cannot recapture the spring of American power in the 1940's. Today, the terrain upon which we must measure ourselves against the Soviets is not so favorable as that we could have chosen during the years of American pre-eminence, 1945-1950. Popular preconceptions notwithstanding, the kind of international conflict democracies know how to wage best is military conflict. In war, the call for discipline and sacrifice is unambiguous. In apparent peacetime, the inclination of democratic peoples toward partisanship and self-indulgence is apt to prevail. Despotic rulers, especially those armed with a militant ideology, find it much easier in peacetime to keep their peoples on a war footing. Despite several shifts of policy, apparent or real, the Soviet rulers have been able to maintain a tight discipline over the Soviet masses. More important still, iron will has shaped Soviet policy, and a unitary control presides over its execution. Hence, in the light of the history of democratic-totalitarian confrontations, it is not surprising that most of the significant encounters of the Cold War should have been won by the Soviets.

We can design the positive policies that will render secure the position of the West and place the communists on the defensive; but these policies and the concomitant means must be devised now. The task of rallying the scattered forces of the West is difficult because we have suffered defeats, and, for a while at least, some of these cannot be reversed. Fortunately, we have all the building blocks needed to devise a strategy that aims at turning lost battles into a victorious campaign.

It would be comforting to believe that all of the social, economic and ethical problems posed by the technological-scientific revolution can be solved rationally and humanely. It would be comforting to believe that we have the time, two or three generations at least, to put the affairs of mankind in order, so that by the year 2000, let us say, the most dangerous cliffs of readjustment will have been rounded and orderly, peaceable progress will henceforth be assured.

Unfortunately, alleviation of the perplexing problems of the systemic revolution is rendered more difficult by the power struggle which the communists have imposed on us. The requirements of foreign policy are to assert authority, to enhance prestige, to stand firm, to face down threats, to take risks, to stand by one's allies, to punish one's enemies and, whenever pursuing these tasks calls for the use of force, to use force. The single-mindedness and intransigence of the communist bid for world power leave us no other choice but to think soberly about force and to accept the ever-present contingency that force will be used against us and that we will have to counter it in kind. Our essentially "other-directed" foreign policy has not only failed to alter the international equation in our favor, but has also managed to deceive our own people about the grim, the true nature of the struggle.

Compassion and generosity are not alternatives for resolution in taking the risks and bearing the sacrifices with which the use of power is fraught. If men of good will, when they confront the challenge of the aggressor, shirk the use of power, they court not only their own defeat but also the defeat of those humane causes which they seek to further. The issue before us is not the future of mankind in some ideal state of harmony, but how to assure mankind a future under freedom. The communists charge that the cry for freedom is merely a pretense; that democracy itself is a form of special privileges; that the democratic nations, having acquired by force a major portion of the world's wealth, and having set up a controlling power over the world, have used that power to exploit other peoples for their own advantage, and are now fighting to retain these superior benefits.

Communist rule is government by power above any law, human or divine. Yet, government is legitimate and genuine only so far as its ruling end is the protection of human freedom. Foremost in the mind of every legitimate ruler must be the desire to protect the freedom of those whom he governs. For the sake of this end he must continually restrain his own will and subordinate it to the rule of law. Hence, if we are to assure the future of mankind morally, we must break communist power.

To do this we might pursue alternative strategies. The question might well be as to whether we should strive to root out communist power where it now holds sway, or contain it in such a way that it can no longer wreak evil upon the Free World. Whichever of the two strategies we adopt, however, neither can be carried farther than the reach of our power. They can each be pursued by many different means, but they must always be dependent upon our willingness and capability to use force whenever the nature of the communist challenge leaves us no other choice.

to do business with the victor. If the physical occupation of the United States by Soviet ground forces, or vice versa, proves impossible, the nuclear strike must be followed by political conquest or revolution. In this sense, therefore, protracted conflict techniques are the indispensable prerequisites for victory in "contracted" war.

The foregoing propositions for the waging of conflict in the thermonuclear age apply to both contestants. We turn now to the characteristics of the communist protagonist.

Three distinct but related strategic tasks confront the United States: (1) to seek a more effective partnership with those nations in Europe and elsewhere who share its political values and cultural heritage; (2) to find a new basis for mutual respect and co-operation with nations of Asia, the Middle East, Africa and Latin America; and (3) to frustrate communist plans to establish the emerging world order in the image of communist society. The first two tasks require carefully conceived measures of co-operation which are discussed in the subsequent chapter. The last calls for engagement in protracted conflict. Since the success of the first two tasks requires the successful conduct of the third, let us consider the range of feasible policy choices before us in preventing communist expansion.

The selection of American policy with respect to the Sino-Soviet challenge requires examination of the communist bloc and its worldwide offshoots. The communist world is not a monolithic entity. The three major components of the communist bloc, namely the Soviet Union, Communist China and the East European satellites, differ widely in acceptance of communism, in cultural background and industrial status. The communist parties in other countries—a global fifth column—differ widely in strength but are willing to comply with Moscow's general directions, although Peking is believed to play the guiding role with respect to a few of them.

Since 1945, the power position of communism has been strengthened in areas of critical importance. The Soviets, by dint of relentless concentration on the military sector of their economy, have achieved a formidable nuclear and missile capability. Secondly, in the post-Stalin era, Soviet leadership has increased its freedom of action, for domestic policies have won it greater popular acquiescence. Thirdly, Red China has become one of the major powers of East

It is necessary to speak clearly on the use of power. Our friends must be certain that we will not desert them in the hour of supreme test. If that certainty is not given we will have no friends. Then all talk about American leadership is mere exercise in rhetoric. Then we will not be able to lead in building the community of freedom that will stand as the true monument of our greatness.

As the systemic revolution approaches a climax, both the communists and we are faced with imperatives: to grasp the meaning of conflict in the nuclear age and to master the forces of systemic change. The communists, informed by a theory of history, spurred by commitment and armed with their doctrine of protracted conflict, have integrated nuclear weapons into a comprehensive strategy of world conquest. The United States cannot let the decision go to Sino-Soviet leadership by intellectual and moral default. The United States, on its part, must design a Forward Strategy that accords with the logic of the systemic revolution and the dynamics of nuclear power. The lead-time of survival is short.

CHAPTER 2 THE CHOICES OF POLICY

National strategy is both a redoubtable and sophisticated agent of policy. It deals in hard but complicated choices. It sets the direction of national effort, marshals national resources and plans operations necessary for the attainment of national political objectives. Its formulation is based on estimates of the international situation.

A policy to extend freedom must deal with such varied forces as the following: (1) communist expansionism; (2) the proliferation of technology in its military and peaceful applications, and the impact of both on the world political order; (3) the population explosion; (4) the "revolution of rising expectations" now rampant in many of the underdeveloped areas—expectations that are not likely to be fully satisfied over the next generation and hence will give rise to frustration and political disorders; (5) ideological and sociological obstacles to international co-operation, such as tradition, nationalism, racialism, isolationism, neutralism and cultural collisions resulting from the growing proximity of diverse peoples; (6) governmental inefficiency and the "business as usual" mentality.

The advent of thermonuclear weapons and global delivery systems is altering drastically all established relations between states. The fact that a large part of humanity could be wiped out in a few hours is certainly the most awesome and probably the central issue around which the world political struggle now revolves. As Charles de Gaulle observed, there is "no territorial disagreement or ideological dispute that has any importance by comparison." The advent of nuclear military power has given rise to many questions for which few satisfactory answers have yet been found. The horrendous prospects of large-scale nuclear warfare have had an almost paralyzing effect on the thinking of even the most seasoned military professionals and civilian military experts. *The net result has been an irrational aberration from the traditional purpose of military power.* Thus far the U.S. has failed to discover a rational formula for integrating nuclear weapons and other technological paraphernalia into a constructive strategy. The Soviets appear to have accomplished this task almost simultaneously with their technological-military achievements.[1]

Therefore a realistic consideration of American policies and their attendant strategies must begin with a clarification of the new dimensions which global-range nuclear weapons have introduced in the measurement of the international power balance.

Total nuclear war is more than just the most massive among the individual instruments of protracted conflict. Potentially, it could be the climax of the over-all conflict. Even if a total war will never be fought, the necessities and risks of total nuclear war influence and, in many instances, determine alternative policies and strategies. The logic of total nuclear war predominates throughout the entire conflict spectrum in the same manner as the law of gravity influences physical events.

Protracted conflict and total war are dialectically related to one another. This relationship may be expressed in the following propositions:

1. For the first time in history there exist weapons permitting a technologically armed superpower to conquer the entire world. The master method of world conquest is a surprise attack utilizing nuclear explosives of high yield designed to destroy the competing superpower's military force. The attacker must, however, succeed in annihilating or neutralizing the defender's strategic nuclear forces *without, in the process, exposing his own nuclear strength and the basis of his military power for retaliatory destruction.* If he attains this objective, he has achieved military supremacy and, since his weapons systems have intercontinental range, he can subject to his writ the entire globe. This potentiality is inherent in nuclear explosives and global-range delivery systems and constitutes a fundamentally new development in world affairs.

[1] See Chapter 5, "Military Strategy, Power and Policy."

2. As technology progresses, *more and more weapons systems, i.e., delivery systems and nuclear applications, are coming into existence.* This proliferation of weapons systems orders the strategic choices of a would-be world conqueror. Nuclear weapons and global delivery systems were invented after Mao Tse-tung had formulated the doctrine of protracted conflict. Although the new technology is entirely in line with the notions of Marx and Engels, who envisaged the world revolution as taking place in one fell swoop, it does not invalidate Mao's concept. *The techniques of protracted conflict are designed either to prepare for the climax of the decisive battle or to render this battle altogether superfluous.*

3. In the Cold War, the Soviet Union has one overriding advantage, namely, its freedom to opt for a sudden surprise attack. The United States, on its part, has deliberately rejected this option for moral reasons and has done so despite the enormous military disadvantages which that rejection entails. American strategy—a strategy dictated by moral considerations—facilitates a Soviet strategy of all-out war. But it does not ease necessarily the over-all strategic problem of the Soviets. If the Soviet Union were to rely on a strategy of piecemeal conquest, the very success of Soviet "nibbling" could push the United States into a nuclear conflict at *some* point where its vital interests left no other choice. Unless the United States could be induced to surrender or be subverted by an internal revolution, both of which contingencies are most unlikely, a reversal of American strategy toward pre-emption may, sooner or later, be in order. *Precisely because of the devastating power of nuclear weapons and because the United States continues to be the only other major nuclear power besides the Soviet Union, a reversal of U.S. strategy remains possible almost to the last minute.* Even at a moment when the United States faces defeat because, for example, Europe, Asia and Africa have fallen to communist domination, a sudden nuclear attack against the Soviet Union could at least avenge the disaster and deprive the opponent of the ultimate triumph. While such a reversal at the last moment almost certainly would result in severe American casualties, it might still nullify all previous Soviet conquests.

A communist strategy of world conquest would be made increasingly difficult by the spreading of nuclear weapons, for the proliferation of nuclear powers not only would complicate the problems of piecemeal conquest and increase the danger of American intervention, but it would also compel the Soviets to neutralize, in the last phase of the conflict, all those nuclear forces which may exist in addition to those of the United States.

4. *Even if the United States chose not to avenge a disaster which its isolation would entail, the communists must still seek to render impotent American retaliatory power.* The communists cannot stop short, in prudence, of the total emasculation of American power. Here the fight between Rome and Carthage provides the apposite historic model: The struggle ends only with the total destruction of the weapons of one or the other contestant.

5. *Under modern conditions, the significance of what could be called technological positions has become overwhelming.* Historically, the objective of war and accumulation of power was seizure of territories. Consequently, the growth of empires could be measured in terms of square miles and increments of populations and industries. This type of calculation is still valid, but it is no longer decisive. Thus, the fall of, let us say, India or the Middle East to communism would be disastrous; but the effective conquest by the communists of the space between the earth and the moon might prove an even more painful defeat for the United States. On the other hand, an advance in military technology might compensate for spatial retreat. The loss of India or the Middle East might be balanced by our development of nuclear-propelled forces such as aircraft or space ships, and of antimissile defenses. This does not mean that geographical-positional strategy must now yield its historic place to a new strategy of means. It is necessary, however, to recognize clearly the characteristics of a conflict based on technology and nuclear weapons, and to analyze the conflict as a *whole.*

6. In foreign policy, the American people have not infrequently displayed a somewhat excessive fondness for utopian solutions. Yet on most occasions they have managed to conduct their foreign affairs soberly and realistically. Consequently, neither Americans nor communists can assume that, as the conflict progresses, all the initiatives will remain in communist hands. In fact, they never did. The military weakness of the United States is partly a derivative of its decision not to strike the first nuclear blow. But were there no practical alternatives left and were communist aggression to render a pre-emptive retaliatory American strike both morally defensible

and militarily mandatory, American military power would increase—and increase suddenly—by virtue of this one decision alone. Therefore, the dogmatic adherence by the communists to an unending strategy of piecemeal conquest would not be altogether dissimilar to the labors in Hades of Sisyphus, whose job it was to roll a rock up to the top of the mountain, but who always was forced to do the job all over again because, just before reaching the peak, the rock invariably rolled backward. *Each communist success, and especially each territorial conquest, brings with it the risk of a strong American reaction, including the quickening of arms preparation in general and the acceleration of weapons programs suitable to balance or partly compensate for the loss suffered in particular.* From the communist point of view, this danger must be added to that of retaliation. To put it differently, a continued success by piecemeal conquest could render more difficult a victory in the decisive encounter.

A strategy of limited operations in the nuclear age is not inherently a strategy of military world conquest. Even if it gains for the aggressor overwhelming preponderance of force, its final success depends upon destroying the will-to-resist of the principal opponent so that he lays down his arms for total war. Each war between minor nations or, for that matter, each upheaval—such as anarchy in the Congo—requires policy decisions by the great powers, including, possibly, intervention. Thus an aggressive state such as the Soviet Union may, because of accidents and prestige considerations, trigger or intervene in limited wars. Yet from the point of view of a strategy aiming at ultimate victory such actions may not always be expeditious.

7. *Changes in force relationships, as they bear on the strategy of total war, bear directly and significantly on protracted conflict strategy.* For example, the initial penetrations into space did not upset the military balance. Certainly, their significance in terms of limited war was negligible. These penetrations constituted, however, a major change in the over-all balance inasmuch as they altered the psychological climate, disclosed technological capabilities and opened new fronts of conflict. Hence the importance of space, in terms of the protracted conflict, has been immense and will continue to grow. Initially, the launching of space satellites favored the Soviet Union. Sputnik I demonstrated that the Soviet Union had become a first-rate technological power, a fact which up to that

time was doubted by many. In the future, however, space systems are likely to benefit the Free World because, first, they diminish the effectiveness of one of the basic props of communist power, namely the Iron Curtain; and, second, they complicate the problem of nuclear surprise attack. By weakening what are basically the strongest elements in Soviet strategy, they will weaken the over-all potential of Soviet conflict management.

8. *A thermonuclear exchange could be the climactic phase of the protracted conflict.* This phase is fraught with prohibitive risks so long as the defender is strong, vigilant, resolute and capable of retaliating with devastating force. Consequently, it is necessary to use the means, especially the nonviolent means, of protracted conflict strategy designed to degrade the defender's force levels and technological strength. As long as the defender maintains strong military force, it will be necessary to weaken his warning and recuperation systems, and to undermine his will to resist so that in the end total nuclear war need not be waged physically, but can be won psychologically through the inducement of surrender.

Protracted conflict, possibly including limited war, would serve to carry on the struggle despite mutual deterrence. Its purpose would be to change the "nuclear stalemate" in favor of one or the other competitor. In such a situation, there is a good chance that limited conflict would remain limited, unless one or the other of the two camps was willing to risk enlargement of the contest. By the same token, however, gains would remain limited. In the past, the problem of a stalemate did not arise because, before the early 1960's, the Soviet Union lacked a weapons system through which it could destroy the United States so rapidly and so conclusively as to preclude its own destruction. The continuation of the so-called "nuclear stalemate" will depend on many factors, of which the foremost is the maintenance of the American retaliatory capacity sufficient to deter any potential aggression.

9. *Protracted conflict serves to create the conditions in which the aggressor can risk the attack or issue the ultimatum for surrender, without exposing his own power base to devastation and destruction.* Obviously, these efforts must be combined with direct preparations for the general nuclear war. But protracted conflict methods will serve to train and utilize insurgent and revolutionary forces in the target country to seize power and install a new government willing

Asia. Fourthly, the communists have moved beyond the natural boundaries of their geographical base and, as events in Cuba, Africa and Southeast Asia bear witness, now challenge European and American influence in these regions.

Present-day Russia and China, the two chief pillars of communism, are at different levels of historical development. Soviet society, now the second generation after the Bolshevik Revolution, is passing through a novel experience; some relaxation of discipline goes hand in hand with a nominal increase in consumer goods. The Chinese communists, by contrast, have set out on the same forced march toward internal consolidation and economic development on which Russia launched herself many years ago.

The Chinese communists, however, are dependent upon the Soviet Union for the realization of their ambitious plan of industrial development. The Soviets stand thus at the fountainhead of Chinese power. The Soviet Union supplies China with all capital goods, 85 per cent of its foreign trade, and skilled technicians. Lack of capital, equipment, skilled labor and proven basic resources will limit the Chinese economy for years to come. In the process of becoming a modern state, China must look to outside help for at least a generation.

As those who accompanied Mao on the Long March pass on, friction among the newly emerging leaders can be expected. Moreover, the Communist Party must absorb and perhaps purge its new members before it can discharge competently its function as organizational overseer. An easy acceptance of regimentation and self-criticism, a strong nationalist spirit and the substantial success recorded to date give Chinese leaders cause for guarded optimism for the future. At the same time, however, constant change—the mounting pressures of industrialization—will produce continual internal strains and tensions. While the events of recent years suggest that the regime is firmly entrenched, disastrous failures at home or abroad or a split between power groups could touch off with explosive fury a struggle for political leadership.

The status of communist control in Eastern Europe differs widely from that in the U.S.S.R. or Red China. Full Soviet control over the satellites will never be an easy task. Local nationalisms will continue to spark antagonism against Soviet domination. Communist ideology has failed to capture the people of Eastern Europe. Although open revolt against Soviet rule would appear futile, Russia must always be apprehensive lest the forces of rebellion in Eastern Europe, now chained by Soviet military power, are again unleashed. Hostility to the Soviet Union and the communist system is not a fleeting phenomenon. It is the most profound fact of life in Central and Eastern Europe. A perceptive correspondent of the *New York Times*, A. M. Rosenthal, wrote: "Westerners may forget, but Eastern Europeans never do, that communism in Eastern Europe exists only because of the Soviet Union. In the true meaning of the word, Eastern Europe is a captive to foreign power."

Other astute American observers of the East European scene have given testimony to the same effect. Stewart Alsop, for instance, after a tour of all the captive countries, concluded that "the revolutions in Eastern Europe were not made in the countries of Eastern Europe. They were imposed on those countries by Russia. That is a simple, obvious fact which is nevertheless often overlooked. . . ." John Scott, of *Time* magazine, a seasoned observer of Soviet affairs, summed up his impression gleaned from an extended visit to the captive countries as follows: "The Soviet Union took East Europe by military conquest. Military occupation, or the threat of military occupation, remains today the ultimate and ever present *sine qua non* of Soviet control over the satellites, as well as of the maintenance of power by local communist parties and governments."

The rift that separates the overwhelming majority of the East European peoples from the peoples of Soviet Russia can only be closed by the disappearance of the communist regimes, symbols of foreign conquest. Soviet communism is a standing offense to the peoples of Eastern Europe because it does violence to spiritual and emotional values deeply rooted in history. The conflict, therefore, cannot be composed by marginal improvements, be they economic or political, which a totalitarian regime can afford to grant without imperiling its very existence.

The rulers of Soviet Russia and Communist China hold in common —or believe that they hold in common—the same ideological doctrine: the teachings of Marx and Lenin, which purport to hold the "scientific" and "universal" truths about man, his history, his economics and his salvation. In addition, they share a specific set of operating principles and conflict techniques which make up the operational code for seizure of power, the destruction of free societies and the consolidation of communist power.

Ideology has been essential in providing a unifying mystique for the international communist movement—the communist world party. "Stripped of the Marxist justifications, the masters of the Soviet Union would stand before history, at best, as only the last of the long succession of cruel and wasteful Russian rulers who relentlessly forced the country on to ever newer heights of military power in order to guarantee the security of their internally weak regimes."[2]

Nationalism, to be sure, remains a powerful force in Russia. The communist leaders of the Soviet Union have maneuvered easily between now curbing and then exciting the spirit of Russian nationalism, just as they have sought to divert or suppress the nationalistic aspirations of the many other peoples who comprise the Soviet empire. It matters little, however, as to whether the mass of peoples living under communism are indifferent to or content with its doctrines. For the moral commitment and fervor of their leaders infuses the movement with an *élan* and magnetism noticeably lacking in the West.

Ideological uniformity has been more difficult to maintain after the brief flush of "national communism" and after Communist China staked her claims to the ideological co-leadership of world communism. The long-range significance of polycentric communism is, as yet, uncertain. Soviet and Chinese collaboration in Cuba, for example, makes it difficult to judge who are the more doctrinaire revolutionaries of the communist bloc. The Chinese communists, despite their consistent support of many aspects of Stalinism, have developed national variations of their own in the application of Marxist-Leninist ideology. Red ideological rifts came into the open during 1959 and 1960. As in the past, these were resolved in Moscow's favor at the 1960 conclave of communist leaders in Moscow.

Despite the divisive doctrinaire factors present within the communist world, one must be wary in assessing their importance. The communists must shroud their totalitarian rule in an ideology. Thus, ideological differences may often be sublimated in order to maintain the united front of the communists. This also explains the communist proclivity toward "reinterpretations" rather than the flat

[2] George Kennan, quoted in *The Forrestal Diaries*, Walter Millis, editor, New York: Viking, 1951, p. 147.

repudiation of previous doctrines. Moreover, the consistency of communist actions transcends the level of ideological debate. Communist operational principles are steeped in three basic tenets of Marxism: (1) the dominance of material factors; (2) the inevitability of the triumph of the "socialist" camp; and (3) the dialectical process. These provide a broad foundation for the communist system.

Of late, not a few Western experts on Soviet Russia and China have given currency to the idea that the two communist powers are falling out, ideologically speaking, over the issue of war in the nuclear age.

Both Moscow and Peking agree that the world is divided into two camps, one representing declining capitalism and the other rising socialism; and these two camps are pitted against each other in a fundamental and inevitable conflict. The Kremlin no longer regards as inevitable an all-out battle—provided the Free World ends its resistance to communist advances. The Soviet leaders would prefer to exploit politically whatever military superiority they may possess without resorting to force, taking advantage of the many factors working in their favor. The Soviets will, when occasion favors such a course, pursue policies designed to encourage relaxation of Western military efforts. But the Soviet leaders cannot foresee how successful their temporizing tactics will be. Largely because of this uncertainty they may veer toward the alternative of nuclear attack as a means of securing objectives which future developments beyond their control may otherwise render unattainable. The Chinese, so we are told, are even more disposed than the Russians to press conflict to the point of nuclear war and might even be willing to instigate a war which would result in a Soviet-American nuclear exchange. Controversy though there may be, communist ideological arguments are, nevertheless, over means, not ends—a discussion between gravediggers over which shovel to use in burying us.

Chinese and Soviet leaders both claim that they are moving with the "inexorable" forces of history and that communisim is the "wave of the future." Any rupture in Sino-Soviet relations could cause serious loss of political prestige and power for both parties, and its impact on world communism could be profound. The communists, more loquacious than in the past, have made some of their differences public. Available evidence suggests, however, that the two communist powers still maintain firm agreement on fundamental communist principles.

Not a few Western observers believe that the ideological bonds which now tie the communist world together will one day be shattered by obdurate nationalism.[3] General de Gaulle, for example, expressed this view in his press conference of November 10, 1959: "No doubt Soviet Russia, in spite of having aided communism to take root in China, recognizes that nothing can change the fact that she is Russia, a white nation of Europe which has conquered part of Asia, and is, in sum, richly endowed with land, mines, factories and wealth, face to face with the yellow masses of China, numberless and impoverished, indestructible and ambitious, building through trial and hardship a power which cannot be measured and casting her eyes about her on the open spaces over which she must one day spread."

Nationalism is, of course, a powerful force with which to reckon. Khrushchev may worry over the industrialization of China even though he himself is building and monitoring it. The Chinese communists are trying to take advantage of the Russians at every turn. The Soviets are not acceding so readily to every Chinese request as they did five years ago.

Their mutuality of interests—based on past history, vested interests, economic relations, common ideology, and especially the tremendous stake in the unity and infallibility of both partners—will probably arrest the growth of frictions short of a break. It would be imprudent, however, to overlook the degree of tension and difference which could develop, given the long history of Russian-Chinese controversies, the extreme nationalism on both sides, the ambitions of leaders, and the fact that the Chinese do not encounter in great numbers citizens of other countries while the Soviets—probably to Chinese chagrin—have been placed in the position of speaking for Red China in world councils.

A series of events has been building up for over a year indicating that, in many respects, the United States policy, consciously adopted or not, of pushing the two partners as tightly into each other's embrace as possible is beginning to pay dividends. Certainly a major

[3] An analysis of this point of view is contained in John E. Tasjean, *Where China Meets Russia: An Analysis of Dr. Starlinger's Theory,* Washington: Central Asia Collectanea, 1959.

factor in the Sino-Soviet riddle is the personality and role of Mao Tse-tung, the Chinese leader. In view of his limited knowledge of the external world and increasing inclination toward irrational actions, we should not rule out a Chinese-Soviet break brought about by accident rather than calculation. Some examples of recent differences and tensions between the two partners include: the cool reception of Khrushchev in Peking in October, 1959; the failure of one of the top Chinese leaders to greet the new Soviet ambassador, Chervonenko, when he arrived in Peking in November, 1959; the failure of any one of the big three Chinese leaders (Mao, Chou En-lai or Liu Shao-ch'i) to attend the Bolshevik Revolution anniversary celebrations held in Peking, November 7, 1959; the theoretical differences aired in the early months of 1960 by both sides; the conspicuous absence from the Twenty-fifth International Congress of Orientalists in Moscow, August 9-16, 1960, of a Chinese delegation.

What all of these straws in the wind add up to is not easy to ascertain. They surely point toward jealousy, distrust and mutual irritation. Mao, who has become increasingly convinced of his omniscience, undoubtedly resents Khrushchev's caustic comments about his pet scheme, the "people's communes." With passing years, it seems highly likely that the outside world will have the opportunity of enjoying the wholesome spectacle of the two leadership groups pecking lustily at one another.

At the very least, the Russians and the Chinese may find it necessary to define separate spheres of national influence more clearly than they have done to date. Already the Soviets have made considerable concessions to China. Manchuria now is within the Chinese sphere; Port Arthur has been relinquished; and, in deference to Chinese nationalist feelings, the Soviets have sought to avoid frictions over common borders by narrowing their own sphere of influence. In return, the Chinese have conceded little. Some observers believe that, in view of China's rapidly expanding population, resettlement in border areas such as Siberia and Outer Mongolia might be a future bone of Sino-Soviet contention. At best, however, these areas could offer China but marginal relief. The more natural area for massive Chinese resettlement would be Southeast Asia, with its large overseas Chinese communities and its rich surpluses of rice, rubber, tin and petroleum.

The Soviets and the Chinese are still joined by overriding common interests in foreign policy. Mao acknowledges the existence of only two world camps, the camp of the imperialists and the camp of the "socialists"; and his allegiance to the "socialist" camp is unequivocal. Moreover, China benefits greatly from the Soviet Union's global position. The Chinese communists need the Soviet Union to underpin their military might with nuclear power.

China, unless the Soviets provide the skills and tools, cannot challenge a nuclear superpower like the U.S. along the periphery of Asia. At the same time, Russia would be sorely troubled if a hostile China would face her across her Far Eastern border. It seems unlikely that this alliance will be split over territorial disputes.

According to one observer:

> There are Russians who share Western prejudices against the "yellow race" and imagine the Chinese to be more cruel or ferocious than white men. But there is no sense of fear in Moscow today that the rapidly growing nation of 650,000,000 Chinese might some day be a threat to the Soviet Union, with its only moderately expanding population of 215,000,000.
>
> Russians smile when they hear a suggestion of this threat from Western acquaintances. With Premier Khrushchev they think that science will solve the Chinese food problem. Often they quip that direct conflict might, indeed, develop—"when all our problems with the capitalists are over."[4]

There is no way of telling whether or not a fundamental split will ever divide Communist China and the Soviet Union. For the time being, their goals and general policies are set on parallel lines. The Moscow-Peking alliance is the territorial, military and ideological base for a world-wide movement which is far more powerful today than it was before the Chinese communists conquered China.

Russia and Communist China recognize the great strength which derives from their joint control over the bulk of the Eurasian land mass. Yet, full harmony does not necessarily reign within the communist bloc. Consequently, our policy and strategy should be designed to take advantage of every latent discord. Opportunities of manipulating the balance of power may beckon us in the future. For the time being, they appear slim. Despite the obvious signs of dis-

[4] Max Frankel, *New York Times,* September 13, 1960, p. 12.

unity within the communist empire the West will be well advised not to wait supinely for communism to fall apart, rent by "internal contradictions." Communism is a dynamic force. It feeds on success. Our best hope for bringing about the dissolution of communist bloc unity will lie in a soundly conceived and well-executed Forward Strategy which will deny the forces of world communism the stimulus of further external successes.

Let us now examine a range of possible policies the United States might pursue toward the communist bloc and its world-wide appendages, together with the assumptions on which they are based.

Policy One

ASSUMPTION: The major threat to the major industrialized nations of the Western world, including the U.S.S.R., is the militant nationalism of Asia and Africa. The Soviet Union recognizes that this threat is particularly embodied in the growing power of Red China and is, therefore, anxious to make an early settlement with the U.S.

Under this assumption the U.S. should seek an alliance with the U.S.S.R. and an agreement on spheres of influence. Obviously, such an argument presupposes fundamental changes in our foreign policy. Upon such a drastic reorientation the U.S. would be in a position to negotiate seriously with the U.S.S.R. The first step would be to ban nuclear testing under the combined auspices of the four nuclear powers, Britain, France, the U.S. and the U.S.S.R. This step would be followed by serious disarmament discussions with the Russians, based upon the recognition that neither side wishes nor can achieve total disarmament—that, rather, a co-ordinated armaments policy (with a Soviet-American alliance in prospect) can increase the safety of the industrialized world at less cost to all nations, including Russia.

Under this policy, the leadership of the Western world would pass to Moscow, and the United States would surrender its political birthright. Not so surprisingly, this would be acceptable to Moscow. This alternative is seriously advocated by a few Americans and most plausibly by those who regard the long-range potential threat of an industrialized and aggressive Red China with greater trepidation than the present Soviet challenge.

Policy Two

ASSUMPTION: The communist bloc poses no real threat to the United States in the Western Hemisphere, and the sole cause of world tensions is the unnecessary involvement of the United States in other continents.

Under this assumption the United States should seek security in isolation and base its defense on the North American Continent. For numerous military reasons, this arrangement would prove unworkable. It would be tantamount to turning over Asia, Europe, Africa and, possibly, Latin America to the communists. Ultimately, an encircled United States would face either destruction or capitulation on communist terms.

Policy Three

ASSUMPTION: The containment of the communist world within the existing frontiers over a prolonged period of time will sap communist fervor and ease the peaceful resolution of great power conflicts.

Under this assumption we should pursue a defensive strategy in alliance with a smaller or larger number of overseas countries. Obviously, an alliance system is necessary if the glacis of our defense is to extend well beyond North America. Essentially, American policy, up until now, fits this general description. A strategy of containment leaves the initiative to the enemy. It is a strategy of the *status quo* as contrasted with the communist strategy of revolution and conquest. This is its congenital fault.

Under such a strategy, the communists are free to strengthen their own internal capabilities, penetrate more deeply into Asia, Africa and Latin America, and undermine, more or less at will, the solidity and effectiveness of the Free World alliance system. To put it in other terms, this strategy allows the communists to devote full time to the job of aggression. It is permissive. It is a deceptively "safe" solution. It implies resignation to the inevitable and for this reason alone weakens the morale of the Free World. A containment strategy, however, provides the foundation for other and more ambitious action. A strong defense posture and effective alliances are the essential ingredients of any strategy. But defensive measures by themselves can never assure victory in the protracted conflict.

Policy Four

ASSUMPTION: The U.S. must seize initiatives to open up the closed societies under communist control and defeat the communist movement outside the Iron Curtain as the first step in assuring the survival of free societies.

A policy compatible with this assumption aims at one principal objective: The communist world must be drawn into the "war zone" of the protracted conflict. To make this purpose stick, the U.S. must achieve an advantageous military posture vis-à-vis the communist bloc and launch a psychological, ideological and political offensive to exploit the explicit contradictions within the communist orbit.

There are many possibilities to enlarge the pressures on the communist bloc. For example, higher Western armament levels, tightened trade restrictions and stepped-up political warfare could increase unrest and, under favorable circumstances, force the Soviets to divert strength from other areas. In its early phases, this strategy could not forestall all communist initiatives. Gradually, however, the scales of power would be tipped decisively to the Western camp. The communist regime, put on the defensive first by ideological-psychological pressures from without and then by the onslaught of opposition forces from within the communist bloc, will eventually have to yield its stranglehold on its own peoples, turn its back on its designs for world conquest and, ultimately, surrender its power to a successor government responsive to legitimate Russian aspirations. This strategy aims forthrightly at the eradication of communist influences now operating within the Free World. It seeks to detach Eastern Europe from the communist bloc and to create a united Europe possessing geographical depth and all the other prerequisites of an independent power center. The threat of the Soviet Union, deprived of its advanced bridgehead, East Germany and the Danube Valley, and of the resources of Eastern Europe, which constitute one-third of its economic power, would become more manageable. Europe, her eastern marches liberated and manned by peoples alert both to Soviet Russian imperialism and its communist Trojan horses, could defend herself by her own resources and efforts. Thus, an effective and credible counterweight would balance the vast nonnuclear military forces of the Soviet Union.

Soviet diplomacy persistently seeks to wrest from the Western powers the admission that the present arrangement in Central and Eastern Europe is permanent. In Eastern Europe, the Soviet rulers have sought to cow the peoples into a resigned acceptance of communist domination. An active American and Western policy toward Eastern Europe would require that we (a) refrain from any action that could be construed by the people of Eastern Europe as a ratification of their present fate, and (b) demonstrate, Soviet contentions to the contrary, that the balance of power remains favorable to the West.

A positive Western policy in Eastern Europe, it is argued, will prevent the Soviets from aligning themselves with the West in the event of a serious split with Communist China. Yet China will be a threat to Russia only if Russia is relatively weakened. The Soviets, should they gain the coveted prize of Western Europe, would be able to deal at leisure with China. Indeed, the Soviet Union, flanked on the West by a united Europe, might seek, in time, a genuine accommodation in order to face down a hostile China in the East. In extremes, the Soviet Union, to gain European allies or, at least, to secure its rear, might be brought to the supreme sacrifice: the immolation of communist doctrine on the altar of Russian national security.

It might be argued that liberation movements within the communist bloc, triggered by the assurance of American military help, might drive the communists to preventive war. The answer as to whether the Kremlin would accept peaceably such major reverses is to be found in history and in the record of the men who have shaped the thinking of the communist elite—Lenin, Stalin and Mao Tse-tung. History tells us of many conflicts between powers of disparate strength which were settled by concessions made by the weaker power rather than by war. This was particularly the case whenever the stronger power presented its demands piecemeal and consented to face-saving devices. The weaker power would thus be led to make concessions that did not appear to involve survival or the sacrifice of vital interests in preference to the forbidding prospect of defeat in war. Communist doctrine cautions against accepting an external challenge at the time and place chosen by the enemy.

It prescribes ways and means of inhibiting the will of a superior enemy. But it also makes provision for tactical retreats. Lenin's description of the Brest Litovsk Treaty as a tactical move designed to "trade space" (that can be recovered later) "against time" to assure political survival (which if lost cannot be retrieved) and the desperate attempt of Stalin to forestall, as late as June 12, 1941, nazi military attack by a public display of his willingness to "negotiate differences" best illuminate the communist concept of "tactical retreat."

We cannot tell whether, in the future, the communists will see the wisdom of prudent retreat. Consequently, we must weigh against the clearly discernible adverse consequences of a purely defensive policy the risks involved in a policy of pressure. It seems to us that granting the Soviet Union time to overcome its deficiencies and vulnerabilities and eventually to neutralize the mainstay of West European defense involves risks of incomparably greater magnitude than challenging the Soviet rulers at times and places favorable to the West.

The far-reaching consequences that would flow from the establishment of a safe balance of power in Continental Europe are incalculable. Soviet freedom of action in the Middle East would be greatly curtailed. The image of a "winning" Soviet Union and the myth of the communist "wave of the future" would be shattered. Without these props, the Soviet Union would have little chance to draw to its side the geographically remote, uncommitted nations of Asia and Africa, or penetrate into Latin America.

Policy Five

ASSUMPTION: Communism will never voluntarily relinquish its hold over territories it now controls and, therefore, wars of liberation will be essential elements of any plan to open up closed societies.

Implicit in this assumption is the adoption of a strategy of liberation by means of peripheral wars. Such a strategy could be opportunistic in the sense that the West would await future uprisings in the style of Hungary, 1956, before calling upon the Free World to intervene in favor of the insurgents. On the other hand, it could be part of a calculated offensive. A Western nation might launch a military attack against a communist satellite, provided over-all

Western military strength were sufficient to provide cover for such a limited war.

A calculated war of liberation would be extremely costly in terms of the political cohesion of the Free World. It might subject the solidarity of our alliance system to intolerable strains. Then, too, there is the question as to whether the deliberate resort to wars of liberation is morally justified. On the other hand, it might be asked whether acquiescence in a system which deprives about one billion humans of their rights of freedom and withholds the rights of self-determination from numerous nations is morally defensible. The permanent rejection of this course of action depends on the degree of optimism with which we appraise the evolution of communism and, specifically, the intentions of communist leadership with respect to the Free World.

Policy Six

ASSUMPTION: The communist bloc will endeavor to destroy the United States by any feasible means at the earliest possible time and, consequently, the United States, in order to survive, must launch a preventive war.

If the first part of this assumption holds, the United States, together with the Free World, could not help but prepare for preventive war. This strategy would be consistent with the argument that, since an annihilating attack by the aggressor sooner or later will be inevitable, he should be struck down before he can launch a war under conditions which, from his point of view, are the most favorable. In the nuclear age, the argument for preventive war is stronger than ever because the attacker gains enormous military advantages through a first nuclear strike. At the same time, however, the very destructiveness of nuclear weapons has strengthened arguments against preventive war. There are many uncertainties: Can the enemy not be deterred or persuaded by means short of total conflict? Furthermore, can it ever be certain that the enemy really intends to launch a full-fledged attack? If it is not, should we risk the devastations of nuclear contest simply because a pessimistic appraisal of the enemy's intentions appears more plausible than an optimistic one?

We reject the strategy of preventive war. The unacceptability of preventive war is one of the axioms on which rests the moral superiority of democratic societies. We reject the assumption that if we do not strike the communists first they will one day destroy us. The renunciation of preventive war does not signify a strategic bargain. The strategy of the second strike which we have chosen is a costly strategy. We can risk it only if we be stronger than the U.S.S.R. in all essential categories of military strength. The United States, however, cannot wage a conflict (which, for that matter, it cannot shirk) by placing a taboo upon the objective analysis of the implications of this essentially moral position. A moral policy of "no preventive war" is reasonable *provided* we pay for its military and political costs. We believe that it would be prudent for the United States to advise the communists that our reluctance to initiate war holds only so long as we still believe that they likewise will not choose armed conflict. We will be compelled to reconsider our basic concept if we should ever become convinced that our forbearance will avail us nothing and, in fact, may only contribute to our undoing. We should make clear in this fashion that our opposition to initiating war does not give a blank check to the Kremlin.

During the past fifteen years the United States has clearly rejected both of the extreme policies we have examined in the preceding pages. At the same time, we have failed to decide which of the intermediate policies should be pursued consistently.

The following propositions weigh heavily in the consideration of alternative policies:

1. The widespread opinion that a fundamental amelioration in the relationship between the communist world and the Free World is in sight, and will occur spontaneously, is erroneous. Though many things change and will change in the communist world, as they are wont to do everywhere, the constancy of communist rule and ideology is not likely to change within the foreseeable future.

Whether we call the present state of things Cold War, Peaceful Coexistence, or Protracted Conflict is immaterial. These are names for the same thing. The conflict that started in 1917 is still the same conflict today.

2. Although we should work for and hope for a possible fundamental transformation in Communist Russia, we cannot relax our

efforts until it comes to pass. We must work toward such a fundamental transformation while being fully aware of the formidable obstacles that block the achievement of such a goal. The mark of such a fundamental transformation will be the free movement of peoples and ideas across the communist frontiers. A Moscow-Peking rift, which will weaken the communist posture, may open in the fullness of time. We must not ignore the irrational forces that move all men, communists included. But we must not wager our fortunes on what one clique of communists may or may not do to the other.

3. It is neither wise nor warranted by the evidence on hand to exaggerate communist efficiency and power. We have gone from one extreme to the other. We underestimated communist prowess in 1941 and again in 1946; we have stood in awe of communist achievement ever since the launching of the Sputnik. Exaggerating Soviet strength and belittling the might of the democratic powers will play into the hands of Soviet propaganda. A similar loss of judgment helped to build up the chimera of Hitlerian might.

4. It follows that we must remain, for the foreseeable future, well armed and vigilant. As long as we keep the trigger cocked and the powder dry, the Cold War can be kept cold, or, to put it differently, a precarious peace can be maintained. The age of protracted conflict does not vouchsafe our generation a more reposeful condition.

5. We have to learn, therefore, to live with the realities of the Cold War. Communism retains its appeal particularly for some intellectuals and politicians who are seeking power in Africa, Asia, and Latin America. Against the multibased and many-pronged communist offensive, no simple and conclusive riposte is possible, whether we bank on the hope for reconciliation or on our power to confound an irreconcilable adversary.

6. The communists claim (and not a few voices in the democratic corner concur) that the majority of the peoples in the Soviet Union and China would subscribe voluntarily to the form of government under which they live. There is, however, considerable evidence to the contrary. Both governments were installed, after long and bloody civil wars, by force. Both governments employ oppressive police power and saturation propaganda against the people they govern.

Both governments are not governments by consent. If political stability is ever to bless this planet, open societies must one day flourish everywhere. The obstacles to the march of freedom must not deter us from the attempt to advance it everywhere. But whether we attempt to contain or to advance, conflict between freedom and communism seems inescapable.

Theoretically, our conflict with the communist-dominated areas might be resolved by: (1) eliminating the causes of the conflict, i.e., inducing one side by genteel persuasion or brutal pressure to accept the basic political philosophy and the political system of the other; (2) accepting the *status quo* with clearly defined spheres of influence; (3) engaging in an all-out war, at the end of which the winner dictates his terms to the loser; (4) maneuvering one protagonist by stratagems of political warfare, re-enforced by military and economic pressures, into a settlement.

Sir Winston Churchill once described the conflict between communist materialism and the Christian-humanist ethos of the West as the most rending ever to confront humanity. In the past, any two irreconcilable societies that were physically accessible to one another engaged invariably in conflicts leading to the destruction of one or the other. Now deep hostility is matched by global access to the respective centers of hostile power: the respective centers of the Free World and communist power are capable of reciprocal destruction.

With regard to these alternatives, we cannot ignore the possibility that a calculated or irrational decision can ignite a nuclear war. The Soviet calculus may differ from our own; the Soviets may see an opening where we would not. But as long as the United States meets the conditions for keeping nuclear exchanges out of bounds, the conspicuous hostilities of the protracted conflict are likely to shift more than ever into the political, psychological and economic fields of battle. Yet, it is Soviet military power that bestows freedom of action upon communist policy.

We hold that permanent coexistence between systems so fundamentally opposed as closed societies and open societies is impossible—that the tightly shrunken world of tomorrow can no more bear the indefinite separation by Iron and Bamboo Curtains than could the American Union of Lincoln's day endure half-slave and half-free. This grim axiom is sustained by fundamental sociological, psychological and military considerations—and the dialectic of fear. The communists propose to "bury us." No matter how we interpret their intent, the intent is redolent of finality. The ultimate objective of the strategy for freedom, therefore, must be the devolution of communist totalitarian governments and their replacement by governments by consent. Our quarrel is not with the peoples dominated by communist power elites; it is with the elites themselves.

The issue is the open versus the closed society. First things must come first: The target is the societies under communist domination. We hold that, over time, the struggle between freedom and communist statism—and, for that matter, the world struggle as a whole—can be won by the conduct of an adroitly integrated strategy which exploits, politically and psychologically, the possession of military power, a progressive technology and a healthy economy.

If the American purpose is the expansion of the open society, America should offer a standing invitation to all peoples, including those now under communist domination, to join the community of open societies. Ultimate victory does hinge on the accommodation, however distant, of new elites that one day must burst the hard chrysalis of totalitarian rule and lead their peoples onto the path of freedom. Such accommodation can only be contrived—enforced, if you will—by the wise exercise of the Free World's aggregate strength, material, moral and intellectual.

A Forward Strategy, designed to put ultimately the Free World on a secure basis, regardless of the changes in the nuclear power equation, was once the declared policy of the United States.

President Eisenhower, a few months before assuming office, made this statement:

> Today, this world dwells in a twilight zone between peace and war—a zone we call "cold war." . . . What courses of action lie before us in shaping national policy?
>
> One is to appease. This is a proven folly.
>
> A second course would be to adopt a stupidly aggressive attitude and so markedly increase the risk of global war. Modern war is not a conceivable choice in framing national policy. War would do unthinkable damage to every moral and material value we cherish.
>
> War is the last desperate resort when freedom itself is at stake.

The third course is to prosecute the "Cold War" in which we now find ourselves with vigor and wisdom.[5]

The operational policy of the United States and that of its principal allies never responded to this call for action. Of the many factors which account for this failure of the West to pursue a Forward Strategy, the more important will be briefly enumerated here.

The first and major factor is the *defensive* psychology of the West and the moral aversion of the free nations to employ force for purposes other than defense against physical aggression.

The second factor is the strange reluctance of the West to face the plain fact that the goals of the enemy are as fixed as his methods are flexible. At times, the understanding of this basic truth is forced upon the West by communist action. Then again communist legerdemain raised unrealistic hopes of a change of heart in the communist camp.

The third factor is the residual complacency regarding the security of our defenses, now nurtured by the belief that a nuclear stalemate has made war "unthinkable."

The fourth factor is the failure of the West to calculate correctly both the military power of the Soviet Union and the extent to which its rulers are prepared to assume the risks of a showdown. Thus, during the mid-fifties the West was still thinking in terms of containing the Soviet Union, when, in reality, the Soviet Union was undermining Western power.

The fifth factor has been the military weakness of Western Europe and its corollary, namely, the fear that a bold American policy would invite a Soviet invasion.

The sixth factor has been—except during the Hungarian Revolution—Western underestimation of the strength of the anticommunist sentiment within the communist bloc.

The seventh factor is the erroneous notion that the so-called noncommitted areas hold the balance of power and, therefore, claim the highest priority in Western policy. In the long run, the uncommitted nations may well tip the scale of world power. But the overriding issue of the coming decade is the confrontation of Western and com-

[5] Excerpt from General Eisenhower's Foreign Policy Speech in San Francisco, Thursday, October 8, 1952 (as quoted by the *New York Times*, October 9, 1952).

munist power. We seek to preserve the opportunity of peoples to choose freedom. Therefore, the security of the central bastion of freedom—the Atlantic world—alone guarantees the freedom of the uncommitted peoples as well as our own.

The execution of Policy Four will involve selecting broad national objectives and the design of a unified and coherent Forward Strategy to achieve them. The essential characteristics of the Forward Strategy can be summarized in the following basic propositions:

A Forward Strategy is, by definition, a strategy of active pressures directed against the communist bloc. It is designed not only to contain communism but to emasculate its disruptive power. We have always lived at peace with the great peoples of Russia and China. Their estrangement has not been of our doing. It is the communist leaders, not they, who are our enemies. It is against these leaders that we conduct our Forward Strategy.

We should proclaim by word and confirm by deed that freedom *within* Soviet Russia and China and the independence of the captive nations are American political objectives to be pursued by *all legitimate* means. Mere occasional statements of sympathy with the plight and aspirations of the peoples living under communism are empty propaganda gestures.

The pursuit of the strategic aims we advocate will inevitably entail risks and setbacks. Nonetheless, there is more risk in inaction than in well-conceived action. Acceptance of calculated risk is a far sounder practice than foolhardy or panicky reaction to an unforeseen crisis.

Grand strategy is still "the art of the possible." Ultimate goals must be reached step by step. But the possible must not be conceived as merely what exists, and the scope of action must be bold and imaginative. Faith and commitment to a large purpose are the catalyst of any grand strategy. In a game over great stakes, will power, endurance and constancy are decisive.

It is not beyond our powers of articulation to put the meaning of grand strategy into words that those who must carry it out can understand beyond a shadow of a doubt. Explicitly, the United States must take the lead in consolidating the Free World and exposing the communist experiment to the test of freedom.

The communist threat is the principal concern of Western strategy.

There are, however, other pressing problems with which the Forward Strategy must deal concurrently. The United States cannot attempt to "go it alone." The strength of our allies is part of our strength. We must learn to play simultaneously on several boards and not just on one. We must seek to orient toward the West the unstable but politically important uncommitted peoples of the globe. To this end, we should work through the UN except when the idiosyncrasies of that organization frustrate the quest for order and freedom. At the same time, we should use force when we must, to limit communist aggression and keep irresponsible elements from plunging the Free World into anarchy.

We need not strain our imagination to envisage the horrors of a global nuclear war. Nevertheless, U.S. national and Free World strategy must rest on the people's will to face up to the possibility of total war and their readiness to marshal the efforts that will assure them victory in such a conflict. The security of the United States and the rest of the world stands in inverse relationship to the strength and influence of international communism. Hence the reduction of the ruthless power elite and the elimination of its apparatus for world-wide conflicts are the only permanent guarantees of our security.

We know that the communist world has been rent by internecine conflicts, purges and struggles for power both *within* communist countries—most notably the Soviet Union—and *among* communist countries, e.g., the Soviet Union and Yugoslavia. The eruption of serious trouble between China and the Soviet Union lies, therefore, within the range of the possible. Pressing as are the reasons for maintaining the Sino-Soviet partnership, they do not lay to rest the schismatic ghost. If a conflict breaks out, its impact on world communism will be shattering. It will necessitate a significant adjustment and, perhaps, a thorough reorientation of Free World strategy. The possibility of such developments requires careful and continued examination of Sino-Soviet relations. For the present, however, the Free World should view the partnership as if it were indissoluble, keeping in mind that a time-bomb may be ticking even now. Only when it goes off will it alter the shape of world politics.

For the time being there is little we can do to influence directly the course of events in Communist China. There is more hope for beneficial evolution, however halting and oblique, inside the Soviet system. Yet present policies do not disclose a specific stratagem for achieving this desirable result.

A Forward Strategy should be a strategy of clarification not only for the benefit of the Free World but also for that of the peoples and the nations within the Soviet Union. They should be told that the present system is not the only one which suits their conditions—that a better system is theirs for the asking, and that such a system can be built. Russian and non-Russian leadership and intellectual groups, if they work hard on reforming their system, can spare themselves a bloody revolution and, possibly, another world war. The West has always been the source of political innovation in Russia. The co-operation of Western intellectuals and their Russian colleagues culminated in the collapse of the Czarist regime. It is imperative now that this exchange be resumed. Denied the diversions of continued expansion, Soviet citizens and leaders will be led to examine practical alternatives to the present regime. If adopted, they could be achieved through nonviolent methods of political change. Unless the Forward Strategy is successful enough to pose realistically these alternatives, the present world crisis is likely to lead to war.[6]

The fortunes of Eastern Europe are inseparable from those of the communist bloc and the Free World. Some Western statesmen who look toward an inevitable Sino-Soviet split hold that we must not press for the liberation of Eastern Europe and thus bar a Russian rapprochement with Europe. We reject this thesis. Whatever we do, we should continue to reject the finality of the East European *status quo*. Such a policy will help to keep alive the hope of the captive nations for freedom. It would deny the Soviet Union a firm base for further communist expansion westward. Such a policy, reinforced by *efforts to pierce the psychological Iron Curtain,* might foster an evolutionary process in the direction of greater political freedom. Refusal to endorse the present political status of the captive nations is a beginning; it cannot be the end of Western efforts to dissolve the not-so-monolithic Soviet empire. The self-determination of the many nationalities now under Soviet Russian rule is a long-term goal consistent with a strategy for freedom—if not today, then tomorrow, and if not tomorrow, then next year.

[6] Alternate solutions for communist society are discussed in Chapter 8.

The argument that the captive peoples or the Free World would benefit from a relaxation of international tensions is contradicted by incontrovertible facts. Whatever gains toward greater freedom the peoples of Eastern Europe have made have been the result of internal and external pressures. The Soviet and satellite rulers seek relaxation of tensions—a term of communist coinage—as a means of relaxing Western pressures. Relaxation of tensions—the flagging of Western will and vigilance—demoralizes all peoples opposed to communism. When the external and internal pressures are thus relieved, the Soviet and satellite rulers are free to exert whatever degree of coercion they deem expedient.

The first requirement for the reduction of communist power is to restore and maintain a comprehensive military advantage over the Sino-Soviet bloc. Concurrently, we must check the initiative of communism in the areas most vulnerable to communist influence. Once this process has begun, then the positive pressures—direct and indirect—can come into play. The operational detail of these measures necessarily must be left to governments. We can, however, draw here the broad outline of such a campaign, which, in essence, will be a plan for political warfare.

Political warfare embraces diplomacy, international commerce, information, military action and other activities, governmental and nongovernmental. Yet the meaning of these terms is twisted by the dynamism and the intense hostility and competition of the protracted conflict. Let us use more accurate terms: for diplomacy, political action; for commerce, economic warfare; and for information, psychological warfare. We must extend the term "military action" beyond its traditional scope to include, for example, aid to friendly populations threatened by guerrilla warfare.

The West, in its dictionary of political terms, tends to associate political warfare with a shooting war. Since the protracted conflict is all-embracing, the sum total of a nation's power does not repose in its government. That is to say, a nation is much more than a hierarchy of officials; into the national reservoir of power flows the strength of social, economic, and political subgroupings—political parties, associations, labor unions, religious groups, educational institutions—each influencing and being influenced by massive sociopolitical trends and important governmental decisions. It follows, then, that we should exploit all the instruments of power available to a state—diplomacy, psychological warfare and economic warfare. It follows, too, that we must use these instruments to influence directly or indirectly the components of the adversary's sociopolitical fabric. Political warfare thus is tantamount to manipulation of the competing groups which compose the target nation, shaping their world view and, through them, the policies of the adversary. This has been the practice of communist political warfare against the West. But the tools of political warfare are ethically neutral. They fit the hand of freedom as well as they fit the hand of tyranny.

The employment of the various instruments of political warfare should be guided by certain basic principles. The conduct of political warfare requires in the first place a firm ideological position. This is as true for our political warfare as for that of the communists. The ideology of the communist leaders is supported by an integrated doctrine of action. This marriage of ideology and doctrine of action has borne fruit in a vast accumulation of power. Since they have proved their practical worth, the communists see no reason to discard their ideology and operational code. A communist may be smitten with doubts about certain tenets of ideology; but the communist (who, just like a Christian sectarian, may question a credo without putting his entire faith in question) finds the general Marxist-Leninist prescription convincing. Not only has it proved successful; it is essential to the communist, since he cannot maintain the integrity of his personality without faith in the myths of Marxism.

The most fundamental obstacle to the prosecution of political warfare by the United States and its allies is the unwarranted hope that a general settlement with the communists may be achieved. Such hopes are inspired by two mistaken beliefs: one, that we can encourage the emergence of new, moderate and tractable leaders and groups within the upper circles of communism; the other, that the Kremlin leaders basically think as we do. The first of these ideas does not jibe with the evidence: The occasional moderation of communist leaders resembles closely temporary "retreat," a tactical response to opposing pressure, rather than a change in over-all intent. The retreat-advance pattern of Soviet behavior is illustrated by the Korean Armistice, the Soviet backdown at Quemoy in 1958, and the end of the 1948-49 Berlin Blockade, on one hand, and the aggressive Soviet penetration of the Middle East following the Geneva Conference in 1955 on the other. As regards the second idea, it has always been a stratagem of the communists to foster the illusion that they do indeed think as we do—which, as communists, they do not and cannot do.

Another handicap to American political warfare is our failure to "see the big picture." By tradition, Americans "think big" only about economic problems. In matters political, we tend to conservatism and caution. Nathan Leites has pointed out that when faced with a new problem, the Russian communist tends to consider the extreme alternatives first, while we concentrate on weighing "middle" or compromise solutions.[7]

Examples of the Soviet tendency to "think big" are many—not alone in the field of economics, but in science, military matters and politics as well. Their political proposals and actions are timed to direct Western attention now to the Far East, now to Europe, and now to the Middle East. Their initiatives are phased to shift the West's focus of attention first to military challenges, then to economic competition, and then to political gambits. Communist political warfare gambits are designed to keep our policy-makers off balance and too preoccupied to plan initiatives of their own.

A Forward Strategy must rest upon a clear theory of action based on an understanding of the basic communist conflict doctrine. Such an understanding could provide us with the insights necessary to counter and overcome the communist challenge. Furthermore, it would make apparent the need for co-ordinated and dynamic use, on the scale appropriate to the challenge, of the instruments of political warfare.

What then are our basic requirements if we are to meet the challenge of our age? We need to accept wholeheartedly the fact that we are now in a total, permanent struggle against a force unparalleled in history, a force which combines a militant ideology with powerful instruments of military-political warfare, in a drive for world conquest.

Against this force stands the United States, the bulwark and the prime defender of the Western idea of freedom. We cannot shirk

[7] Nathan Leites, *The Operational Code of the Politburo*, New York: McGraw-Hill, 1951, p. 85.

the task which history has conferred upon us. The Premier of the Soviet Union expressed his confidence that our grandchildren will grow up under communism. Unless we confound his purpose, they will. Edmund Burke said: "All that is required for the forces of evil to win is for good men to do nothing."

CHAPTER 3 BUILDING THE FREE WORLD

The present nation-state system—a sprawling jungle of national sovereignties—can no longer meet the complex problems facing humanity. The issue now before mankind is the political organization of the globe. The crucial question is who will provide a design for the future. Two forces contest the future planetary order: Western democracy and Soviet-Chinese communism. Neither in the Marxist-Leninist utopia nor in Soviet practice is there a place for individual man. The issue before the West is the creation under its leadership of a world community in which free men make their own laws and live by them in peace. Whether the West accomplishes this task will determine the survival of free mankind.

The leaders of communism project forcefully their pattern of society wherever a political vacuum exists. The United States, in marked contrast, has failed to convey to other peoples an image which conforms to the needs of free societies. The communist view of history serves as a guide for the foreign policy of the Sino-Soviet bloc. The United States, lacking a world view of history and not having embraced explicitly a mission beyond its borders, has entered the world struggle of our times at a decided disadvantage. Without seeking to impose our system on others, we need not shirk comparison. The measure of our own past may fall wide of what other peoples can and will achieve. Nevertheless, even the communists pay us the compliment of envy and imitation. They reach eagerly for what our system has to give in wealth and power; they inveigh against the political and social institutions that have presided over our material progress. But the attempt to separate one side of the coin from the other betrays the communist dilemma.

The great challenge to the United States is to adapt democracy and the Western concept of human dignity to new environments. Our institutions and political processes reflect the struggles and insights of many generations of peoples in Western Europe and North America. Within the United States itself the story is one of the evolution from the English heritage through the first attempts at federation, and the making of the Constitution, on to the rise of modern urban-industrial society. It is, indeed, a story still being written. And so is the story of democracy elsewhere.

Because the democratic concept is undogmatic and its origins are rooted in many civilizations, it *is* adaptable to societies at various stages of economic and cultural development. This is part of its strength.

Americans are committed temperamentally, if not philosophically, to the open-ended, pragmatic search for solutions to world problems. Americans reject ideological panaceas. Yet out of the depth of their experience, they believe and have always believed that the United States can make a unique contribution toward the formation of the world of the future. Perhaps their most important contribution is a permanent quest for a consensus of values which will necessarily incorporate the tenets of other peoples, remote from us by virtue of their ethical and historical formation. Such a synthesis should be a transcendent goal of American statecraft. This goal is a distant and a difficult one, but does not lie beyond the range of our national experience. Though lofty, this goal is not unrealistic. For only the establishment of a wider consensus can put life into old institutions and create new and efficient ones that are equal to the necessities of the times. It is in keeping with our own federative philosophy that the order be pluralistic and that it be composed of individual states retaining their own ways of life, but that it be also united by the mutual exchange of peoples, goods and ideas and the common defense of a just peace.

In its broadest sense the term "Free World" denotes the society of those countries which have not been subjected to the domination of communism. In the Free World nations may forge their destinies within wide limits of discretion more or less as they desire. In place of doctrinal conformity, the Free World embraces a vast array of nation-states pursuing often divergent goals in an environment of political, economic and cultural diversity. The freedoms enjoyed by the citizens of the various member states are by no means identical or equal. In some the dignity and freedom of the individual are indeed subordinated either to a dominant minority or to an authoritarian leadership. Nevertheless, the principal member nations of the Free World are pledged to democratic principles, to guard fundamental human rights and the rights of minorities.

We need not vaunt the efficacy of our institutions. We are not the one and only people who have reconciled freedom with responsibility, unity with toleration of diversity. But among the leading nations of history we have gone farthest along this road.

The task for American leadership is to foster co-operation with other countries of the Free World who share or who aspire to share our political values and heritage. This not only should include political and military affairs, but also should embrace economic and cultural matters. Nations must take counsel together; but it is even more important that they begin to act together. Admittedly, the task of convincing the American people themselves, not to mention those in other countries whose support we seek to enlist, of the need for common action will be immensely difficult. Yet, as will be shown in this and in subsequent chapters, the success of a Forward Strategy will depend, in large measure, upon America's ability to harness and utilize the resources of other free nations to deal with common problems.

While the notion of a universal political order is both utopian and debatable at this stage of human development, the necessity for better co-operation between nations is obvious. There is little uniformity between the many nation-states that comprise the world political community. Many of the newer ones are nations by international courtesy rather than by ethnic or cultural unity. Yet we must work with the materials at hand: nations must be the building blocks of any conceivable international order.

The great American contribution to political thought, the federative principle, offers mankind a vehicle for moving the nation-state system toward a more logical political organization. Federating is a voluntary process. Nations federate by virtue of agreement on a common need or advantage. In the absence of such free agreement, "federation" is but the other name for imperial domination. Federation is no more durable a state form than any other. Its defects are no secret. Americans know a good deal about them—to their own sorrow. All we can now see is that the federative process can lead today's nation-states and, most importantly, their individual citizens, least painfully out of an obsolescent and dangerous system into a new and better one.

Nationalism, then, presents two specific problems for an American foreign policy seeking to strengthen the Free World. The first is that of leading the already developed nation-states of the world into higher forms of international organization. The second is that of strengthening the national cohesiveness of the newly created states of Africa and Asia and finding more durable forms of political organization in those continents. Success in these endeavors would help thwart the further expansion of existing empires such as that of the Sino-Soviet bloc, and the development of potential empires elsewhere.

The first problem of nationalism—leading the already developed nation-states into a more advanced co-operative relationship—confronts, in the first instance, the North Atlantic peoples. Federative institutions within Western Europe would, in the estimation of many European leaders, enable that continent to exercise greater influence in Western counsels. The federative process has as its goal the achievement of a better and more secure life for the individual citizens of the European countries.

The problems facing the Afro-Asian states are far different from those confronting Western Europe.

American policy must be tailored to fit the individual case. Not all existing states represent, within their present boundaries, viable national structures. In short, the United States must steer between two extremes: that of encouraging a Balkanization in Africa, the Middle East and in Asia which must lead to rending internecine strife, and that of acquiescing in the efforts of local leaders to fashion new empires at the expense, and against the will, of the inhabitants of autonomous territories.

In Europe and the Atlantic region the federative pull has already loosened the nation-state system. Many new organizational devices are being tried. As yet no grand design exists, but the embryo of a grand design can be detected in the variety of federative experience around us. The economic inter-dependence of nations is forcing coalition. The new European organizations for functional co-operation are fusing themselves into a single complex. So are regional alliances. The economic resources of Latin America complement those of the North Atlantic Community. The Organization of American States strategically backstops NATO. Since the United States is the kingpin of OAS, NATO and SEATO, these three organizations are in effect linked.

In the midst of the systemic revolution we cannot yet discern the exact shape of the institutions which will finally emerge. The statesman's wisdom lies in recognizing forces stronger than mere politics. His task now is to reconcile the conflict of forces which the federative urge has released. Perhaps the greatest obstacle he must overcome is the regressive traditions of the nation-state. The indispensable attribute of the nation-state has been geographical. Yet, as in the European Coal and Steel Community, a new kind of federal state—specialized or functional—can be based on production instead of geography. If the federative experience of the West teaches anything, it teaches that there is not one sure formula for federation. There are many, and none is simple, for the basic concept presupposes the reconciliation of many views. To federate is to strike a balance between a high degree of local option and solidarity in the execution of specific tasks. History shows that a federation at its inception may be relatively loose. The federative concept embraces specialized functional and political regionalism, both of which in differing ways serve to broaden people's sense of community. It is the former, however, which seems more likely at this point in time to pave the way toward higher forms of international life. All successful federations have grown slowly; the way of empire is quick and usually short. Again, we hasten to concede, American federative experience does not offer a model for universal application. Yet, on a continental scale, it is the best available. It comes close enough to setting a standard which other peoples can, by appropriate modification, make their own. We need not, and should not, try to press our experiences upon others. We have the results of one experiment to offer. We keep on working on this, our own national experiment. We invite others to improve on it and to enrich the fund of federative knowledge by their own trials and errors.

The nation-state system was never—and is less today than ever—fully identical with a system of nations, i.e., discrete units of culture and history. American federative leadership must therefore aim not at the unmaking of national diversities but at the transformation of an international political system that has yoked the idea of national freedom with the increasingly awkward burden of national sovereignty.

In the historical perspective of tomorrow we can first foresee alignments of regional alliances; then within these alliances increasing political and economic co-operation; next, the proliferation of functional federations and their association in larger complexes; finally, the coalition of multiple federations, some military-political, some economic-functional. For a long time the system remains loose and untidy. Trial and error precede formal constitution. The West now leads in ingenuity and variety of federative techniques. In particular, the strength of the federative process in Western Europe attests to the continual vitality of the West in the practice and development of modern political concepts.

The North Atlantic Community

Soviet strategy is based on the assumption that divisive tendencies in the West are inevitable and can be exploited successfully. Soviet leadership assumes that whatever unity the West possesses can be sundered and that the influence of a divided West in the uncommitted countries can be eroded by purposeful communist action. In point of fact, Western strength can only be increased by greater unity within the Atlantic Community. Western influence in the underdeveloped countries must be nourished by Western unity in purpose and action. A united West has much to offer the world. A divided West may not be able to insure its own survival, not to speak of assisting the rest of the world to grow more prosperous and secure.

The Atlantic Alliance[1] is the core of the West's federative powers and its mightiest bulwark against communist expansion. The basis for community among the Atlantic peoples is present in their common strategic interests, their economic and social interdependence, and their shared cultural heritage. This does not mean that the West, no matter how strong its common bonds, can thrive in isolation, nor

[1] See Chapter 7 for a fuller discussion of the measures required to strengthen the Atlantic Community.

that the United States can cold-shoulder its friends in Asia, Africa and Latin America and renounce making new friends. To the contrary, the United States does and must pursue policies which will ease the transition of former colonial areas to independence and responsible statehood. But national sovereignty would avail the emancipated peoples little if the communists were to prevail over the West and were thus left free to impose upon mankind their "federation" experiment—the monolithic communist state in the sheep's clothing of "people's democracy."

The North Atlantic area possesses an expanding industrial base which can sustain increasingly complex programs of military and industrial technology both to thwart the challenge of communism and to assist emergent countries in their quest for political and economic development. The North Atlantic nations in partnership could aid the development of other areas of the Free World far more effectively than can the individual North Atlantic states by themselves. A working community of the North Atlantic peoples could provide the leadership for bringing the underdeveloped areas through the difficult transitional period which lies before them.

As a reservoir of skilled manpower, as a center of great industrial production and technological and scientific development, and as an intellectual fountainhead, Western Europe is for the communists the tempting prize of the protracted conflict. Conversely, Western Europe is an integral part of the base from which the United States can lead the Free World in a Forward Strategy. Although the United States cannot afford to lose any region of the world to the Sino-Soviet bloc, Western Europe is the one center outside the United States which is most essential to the cause of freedom.

Western Europe's growing prosperity, the result of technological advances, economic growth and functional integration, redounds not only to its own strength but also to that of the Free World as a whole. West European industrial productivity has increased at a rate which, in combination with that of the United States, will enable the Free World to retain a significant lead in total economic capacities over the Sino-Soviet bloc. The probability that the Soviet Union and Communist China will continue to expand ever more vigorously their productive power gives significance to Western Europe in the world balance.

It is in the North Atlantic Community that the most modern forms of political, social and economic organization have been developed and tested. Many of the ideas and practices which have evolved in the North Atlantic area have sparked the revolutions which are sweeping most of the underdeveloped world. The North Atlantic Community represents the first open society in history. The great strength of the Atlantic idea is the universal appeal of the basic world values and way of life which all Atlantic peoples share. Our civilization is open to all nations wishing to belong, without regard to race or creed. The limits of this community are fixed by attitudes of mind rather than by geographic boundaries. The idea of progress is an idea of Atlantic civilization. Modern science and technology sprang from the minds of Atlantic peoples. The "revolution of rising expectations" is a response to the world-wide diffusion of Atlantic ideas and techniques.

The West has failed to make effective use of the vast potential inherent in the universal appeal of North Atlantic civilization. By default, it has allowed the communists to propagate the myth that they are the harbingers of a new freedom and the "wave of the future." Paradoxically, the stock of Western ideals is falling most disastrously throughout the world at the very moment when the non-Western peoples are about to transform radically their respective societies with the help of Western techniques. The process of Westernization in Asia and Africa appears to run its course at the expense of Western political and cultural influence. To underdeveloped peoples the benefits of Western civilization have sometimes appeared to be the luxuries of a privileged minority of the world's population. Yet there is no reason (in mental and material endowment) why the people of Asia, Africa and Latin America cannot make these benefits their own. Some have done so already; some will do so in time—by sound planning, hard work and cooperation with North Atlantic countries. As a matter of fact, this has been the established pattern of progress in the underdeveloped world. In some places the advance has been slow; in many others it has been considerable. The West's material contribution has not always been made wisely, on an adequate scale or with disinterested motives. But compared with the contribution of the West, that of the communists has been minuscule, cunningly contrived and always laced with ulterior motives. Yet some peoples appear ready to entrust their future to communist methods and largesse.

The successes of the communists and the decline of Western influence throughout the non-Western world has been abetted by several factors, of which the most important one is the persistence of Western disunity. The day of Western dominance in the nineteenth-century style is ended. The Western peoples, if they are true to the spirit of their civilization, will not mourn the passing of this era. But they have still an enormous stake, moral and material, in the rest of the world. If they let this stake go, their power to influence the making of the future world order will then stand for nought. To defend their stake they must first learn to see it as a common one. The isolation of the West is not foreordained. The fortunes of Western unity are tied to the future of the Atlantic Alliance.

Modern Western civilization faces two major problems, each no less difficult than those posed a generation ago by the First World War and its revolutionary aftermath. The first is the transcendence of self-centered nationalism within the North Atlantic Community itself; the second, the rapid transition to freedom and equality of former dependencies. No other civilization in the past has set out upon so formidable a task; no other civilization has gone farther on the way of achieving successfully the transition from one state system to another by the voluntary devolution of empires. These difficult tasks demand the closest collaboration of all North Atlantic countries. In the last resort, it is they alone who can assure liberty to the less developed countries, for it is they who have advanced farthest toward the realization of an open society and of a federative community.

It is the fundamental unity of the North Atlantic Community which determines the range of choices available to American policy. Conceivably, it could be argued on a purely technical premise that the United States has a wider military choice: continued American presence in Europe or withdrawal to Fortress America. The latter alternative has been explored by some strategic experts in the light of ICBM capabilities. Until the present it has been rejected consistently. Conceivably, the United States might be defended by forces based exclusively in the Western Hemisphere. But were the communists to occupy Western Europe, then the survival of citadel America would be meaningless politically and economically. As long as American policy is predicated upon the existence and preservation of the Free World, American involvement in Europe remains a constant in the equation of American foreign policy.

There are no road maps showing the most direct, or the least hazardous, course of United States policy. There are, for example, many alternate routes which might lead toward close Atlantic co-operation—toward the making of a more viable NATO, or toward the creation of another system that would either absorb or replace NATO. There are two general types of approaches to Atlantic unity: first, to build up and strengthen the strictly transatlantic ties, and, second, to strengthen Europe as an equal partner in the community. Within the context of the first alternative, it is again possible to envisage alternative courses: first, the expansion of NATO through the implementation of Article 2[2] of the North Atlantic Pact; second, the expansion of European arrangements for economic co-operation into an Atlantic economic organization; and third, the creation of a federative structure that would either be superimposed on NATO or supersede it.

The second major alternative, in order to conform to American national interests, may be premised on the assumption that a partnership of equals is a necessary condition of United States–European co-operation. Here again it is possible to project alternative approaches: first, the integration of Western Europe around the core of the Six who have banded together in the European Coal and Steel Community and in the Common Market; second, a larger, albeit looser European grouping—a solution which, in the last resort, must be based upon the recognition of the historic position of Great Britain on the one hand, and on the novel approach of the major Continental powers, Germany and France, on the other hand.

These two major alternatives do not cancel out one another, but are rather aspects of one and the same process. In the past, American policy has been guided by the recognition that they complement one

[2] Article 2 of the North Atlantic Treaty provides that: "The parties will contribute toward the further development of peaceful and friendly international relations by strengthening their free institutions, by bringing about a better understanding of the principles upon which these institutions are founded, and by promoting conditions of stability and well-being. They will seek to eliminate conflict in their international economic policies and will encourage economic collaboration between any or all of them."

another. Ever since World War II the United States has taken the initiative in consolidating Atlantic ties, as well as supporting Western Europe's own efforts toward integration. To be sure, a policy that aims at the restoration of West European power as the prerequisite of a powerful Atlantic Community is not without risks. To some measure, it is an act of faith—faith in the organic wholeness of the North Atlantic Community. To give greater unity to the policies and actions of the North Atlantic nations, it is necessary to take concrete steps to strengthen the spirit and forms of their co-operation. These we discuss in Chapter 7.

The Developing Nations

The systemic revolution of our times gives urgency to the need for a new relationship between the Atlantic Community and the remainder of the Free World. The decline and dissolution of colonial empires and the emergence of new states pose critical problems for all Atlantic countries, colonial and noncolonial powers alike. Most newly independent countries possess neither the economic resources, the trained people, nor the social cohesion essential for the development of modern states. Close collaboration among members of the North Atlantic peoples is imperative if they are to assure the gradual and peaceful integration of the emergent nations into the Free World and to secure for them the economic and political benefits which, of the two great power blocs, the Atlantic Community is far better able to provide.

A paradoxical feature of the systemic revolution has been the decline of the nation-state in its birthplace, Western Europe, side by side with the rise of new states in Asia and Africa, each stridently affirming the prerogatives of national sovereignty. With few exceptions, the new nation-states of Asia and Africa are politically unstable and economically weak. In almost all of them, internal tensions, generated by racial, tribal and religious frictions, are being increased by population pressure. If massive forces are not brought to bear from outside, most of them will fall apart. The signs of dissolution are plainly visible in many areas of the globe. Great transformations are sweeping the Afro-Asian countries, as well as Latin America. The fragments, the remains of these changes, will be the bones of contention in tomorrow's conflicts. Traditional social structures are crumbling under the impact of Western ideas and techniques. This disintegration will be hastened by the collapse of state structures, some derived from Western, others from Soviet, political philosophy, and some from the ephemeral settlements of the two world wars. The ensuing catastrophes can but unleash still more violent revolutionary movements.

Throughout the Afro-Asian world, and also in Latin America, a "new order" has already come to power or will in the coming decade assume control of the destinies of millions of people. The new leaders in many areas are far less sympathetic to Western objectives and interests than were the rulers of the "old order." In fact, the political, social, psychological and economic turbulence engendered by the systemic revolution has spurred nationalist movements charged with anticolonial and anti-Western fervor. Nationalism in most underdeveloped areas has been in large measure the ideological contrivance of a small—and, in some places, tiny—native minority demanding opportunities and rewards equal to those of the European. It would be indeed an extraordinary telescoping of a long historical process if, overnight, the vast masses of people in the underdeveloped countries were to become aware of national belonging. The likelihood that local leaders will resort to force as the lever of nation-making is great. It is in the United States' interest to prevent the use of force wherever possible. The United States Civil War was fought with little interference from outside powers. But civil wars in the new countries of Asia and Africa, or between them, cannot be insulated from world politics. Internal conflict invites great power intervention. Under present conditions, the shadow of total war falls over every civil war.

Communist strategy has always been partial to the use of proxies. The communists are alert to the ideological aspiration and political configuration of all active groups in the new countries of Asia and Africa. Whether or not these groups and their leaders lean toward communism or diverse Marxist heresies—which many do—they are, in the eyes of the Soviet Union, useful pawns in its larger struggle with the West. Indeed, the West has waged a none too successful delaying action against the twin forces of fierce nationalism and dogmatic collectivism that are sweeping the underdeveloped world. Nowhere has it recovered ground once it has been lost to anti-Western chauvinism and to that propensity for nationalization which seems to vent its rage chiefly on Western property. The communists have been the gainers not only because the ejection of Western influence creates a power vacuum that they may fill, but also because the victory of nationalist collectivism is tantamount to the rejection of Western democratic ideals.

In dealing with new states, the United States should make its concepts of political development understood. Merely giving economic or military aid without relating it closely to long-range political goals only eases the way for Soviet penetration. To be sure, the United States cannot expect to impose upon others its federal system, its "way of life" or its institutions; but it can disseminate its ideas and organizational methods and show their relationship to its highly developed economic and political life.

The struggle with international communism over the allegiance of the underdeveloped and uncommitted peoples resolves itself in a competition of models of economic growth and political integration. Hence the achievements of the Atlantic Community should be translated into terms which will be comprehensible and serviceable to other peoples. Only thus will other countries remember or begin to see the relationship between the political systems and ideals of the West and its economic strength and technological proficiency.

Because our commitment is to the open society, we must reject dogmatism in politics; we cannot speak meaningfully of "blueprints" or "world orders" in any but a loose sense. Communism purports to offer the exact specifications of a future perfect society. The making of this perfect society requires but one single alteration of the present state of things: the abolition of private property. This is about as satisfactory a diagnosis of social evolution as is the explanation of death as a consequence of the heart having stopped beating. Communism is fundamentally in error because it reduces all social problems to one, namely, the economic one.

The open society admits any solution which holds promise, but at the same time, it stands ready to reject solutions which have proved to be false. This is its virtue. Communist thought is still imprisoned in the history of the early nineteenth century. It proves attractive to peoples and persons whose thought processes have remained "underdeveloped." Communist ideology is, in fact, prerailroad as well as preairplane and prespace. We should not attempt to argue with such an archaic ideology on its own terms.

In other words, we should not "blueprint" a future order but seek it by trial and error. We should not go to other nations and tell them that, because we have created a "perfect" society, we have a solution to offer to all of their problems. We should merely tell them that we have been trying some of the methods which seem conducive to social improvements; that we have found that social improvements need not be paid for by the enormous hardships which communist societies have suffered, let alone civil wars and terror; that there are tested ways of distinguishing good from bad solutions; that nations mature by shedding demagogic ideologies and by thinking rationally about politics; that the individual solution to a problem will differ from society to society; that most reforms should be effected gradually; that we are ready to share with other peoples our experiences as well as to profit from their experiences; and that all of us have still a great deal to learn about the technique of reform and progress. We need not affect a humility which, as a people, we do not feel anyway, and which is misunderstood by many recently emancipated peoples as a case of Western bad conscience.

It seems almost certain that no people will begin to develop the Good Society until they have experienced their share of twentieth-century social change. We may hope to help them in this process. We will expect them to create political institutions most attuned to their cultural heritage. For those in early and difficult stages of development, our own concepts of political democracy will generally be too advanced. But we can help these peoples to find a concept of political development of their own consistent with concepts of a free society. The task may absorb their energies for generations—yet they have already launched themselves upon the sea of change; they will turn either to us or the communists for guidance.

Ideas, even more than guns or money, sway men. Modern man will find eventually his place in one or the other of the great political orders now bidding for his allegiance. We should not, and cannot, deny the so-called uncommitted peoples the right to pursue independent policies and to search their ancient philosophies for answers to the political and social problems of statehood and economic development. For all we know, their search may be rewarded with discoveries that will benefit all of us. But, in the foreseeable future, it is unlikely that they can reconcile the two competing orders with one another or by their own efforts dissolve either or both.

Many of them profess to find the stark alternatives—democracy and communism—distasteful. Distasteful or not, the dialectic of the Cold War may sooner or later make the choice for them.

We are being reminded by many anguished voices of how uncertain are America's goals and how single-mindedly she pursues the gratification of materialistic desires at the expense of avowed ethical precepts. There is no complete definition of freedom. If there were, men would have stopped thinking about it and it would cease to exist. Similarly, "American goals," either national or international, cannot be nailed down for good. Such goals are inherently, properly and forever changing—the aggregate expression of the national purpose under specific circumstances. So far, our basic goals have not been evoked so convincingly as to inspire the American people to plunge wholeheartedly into the most challenging venture: the extension of the frontiers of freedom.

Individual freedom of choice is the fundamental aspiration of human life. This axiom is at the heart of democratic belief. In consequence, the well-being of the individual rather than the aspirations of politically organized society must always command our highest attention. The concept of individual freedom is anathema to the communist power elite, who wish to force all humanity into their impersonal conditioning mold. In the world outside their sphere, the actual degree of freedom which various nations accord their citizens varies widely—but nowhere in the Free World has the very idea of freedom altogether lost its luster.

The contrast between the two types of society and between the world view of the West and that of the communists is revealed most clearly in their respective approaches to the underdeveloped nations. The communists treat the process of domestic change in transitional societies as a part of a program of political development leading to a new world order. Whatever they say and do in the underdeveloped world is made to appear as the word or the word-made-manifest of communist dogma. We, on our part, are loath to discuss the relationship between our political values and our economic and technical help. We contemplate uneasily the great material gap between the underdeveloped countries and ourselves. We shrink from stating values and objectives. Hence we confine ourselves to discussions of technical matters—and leave politics to the tender care of the communists. The question is not whether the West shall help the backward peoples to deal with the age-old problems of misery, but whether it shall seek to advance a conception of man which gives its material achievements meaning and purpose.

Developing the Free World is the weaving together of many strands—man's hopes and fears, cultural traditions and new techniques, politics and economics, religion and science, faith and fact. The design of the pattern will be determined by factors such as these: the basic ideals of the individual's role in diverse societies; the translation by institutional means of those ideals into meaningful terms; the ways in which the U.S. and the "have" nations of the Free World can help to fulfill the aspirations of individual men and women throughout the underdeveloped lands; the reconciliation of nationalism with federative regionalism; the strengthening of the Free World strategic defenses against communism; and the determination of the contribution which each of the Free World peoples can make toward the ultimate triumph of freedom. These questions cannot be answered all at once, and certainly not by ourselves alone.

The term "freedom" comes to life in politics. Without political freedom all the other freedoms—economic, cultural and religious—are so many hostages to be recalled at will by arbitrary governments. The basic guarantees of freedom are the right to organize opposition parties, the right to vote, the rights and immunities of our Bill of Rights. But freedom as a human condition does not derive from these rights alone. It draws concrete meaning from education, discipline, morality, motivation, moderation, ability to reason and discuss, sense of responsibility, literacy and access to information. To insist on "freedom" will not help where, as, for example, in parts of Africa, the precipitate rush into democracy will lead to general disorder, the ideal precondition for a communist takeover.

Some of the conditions which the U.S. envisions for a free society anywhere are absolutes, impervious to differences in status, social contribution or personal resources: the freedom of the individual member of a society to have the family he wants and to profess the religious faith of his choice; equality and equal justice under law; the basic rights of free press, free speech and free association; the right to change political authority; the right to own property; the public protection of personal safety; and the opportunity to make, according to choice and ability, individual social and economic contributions. These rights have become commonplace in the Atlantic world; they are still far from being universally accepted. Yet the values which they incorporate have universal appeal. These values should be our contribution to the development and the extension of free institutions everywhere. It is they which bend material progress to the well-being of the individual.

Charles Malik wrote:

> Western civilization is doomed until, jolted out of its complacency, self-satisfaction and sense of apartness, it rediscovers and reaffirms what is genuinely human and universal in its own soul. This means not only economic and technical sharing with Asia and Africa, but intellectual, moral, and spiritual sharing.
>
> What is supremely good must be good for all. Those who keep on repeating, as though they discovered a transcendental wisdom, that their ideas, their way of life, their civilization are "not for export," but only their industrial products, do not know that they are thereby digging the grave of their civilization and the grave of their way of life. . . .
>
> A civilization in which the human and universal has atrophied can relate itself to others only through force; and force is not an enduring mode of relation, and it can always be broken by force.
>
> . . . a civilization is doomed if it is not creatively conscious of something universal and human it can and must give . . . Western civilization need not be doomed because no civilization conceived and developed the human and universal more than it did.
>
> Most certainly it is not a question of "imposing" anything on anybody. What is genuinely human and universal is never imposed, it is awaited, welcomed and embraced.[3]

The criteria of institutional and procedural reforms are subject to debate. Governments of free societies subscribe to a certain ethos of political action. The purpose of free government is not the aggrandizement of the state or collective, but the enhancement of the individual in the undisturbed enjoyment of his rights.

If we try to compete with the communists for the allegiance of the Free World by matching their slogans with ours—an ideological tournament—we might gain some initial temporary successes but lose the game in the end. The spirit of freedom comes to life in workaday institutions rather than rhetoric. Since it cannot be poured into obsolete vessels, our task is to help in creating institutions that can receive and nourish it.

[3] *U. S. News and World Report,* July 4, 1960, p. 59.

A world environment in which freedom can flourish must one day be embodied in institutions. We cannot draw, *a priori,* their exact outlines. We believe, however, that the United States has a unique contribution to make toward promoting a consensus of values on which the structure of a future world order can securely rest. We reaffirm our conviction that the great American contribution to political thought—the federative principle—provides the bridge between the anarchy of the moribund nation-state system and a world order based on universal values that, over the centuries, have developed in the Atlantic world.

The values and methods which we have considered here provide the political and moral foundations of a Forward Strategy.

CHAPTER 4 THE TECHNOLOGICAL FACTOR

The rapid acceleration of scientific learning and technological achievement and the speed-up in the dissemination of information are transforming not only the daily lives of individuals, but also the international political order. A discussion of their nature and their ubiquitous impact should precede treatment of the established instruments of strategy.

Technology, along with economic and industrial strength, provides a versatile tool for the making of strategy. Technology has entered the life of every human being who has been remotely touched by Western civilization. It has been a principal cause of the world-wide systemic revolution. The technologies that have grown out of modern science are affecting human values and relationships at a rate both exhilarating and breath-taking. As we live in fear of nuclear destruction, we draw hope from the bright prospects that science unfolds.

The speed and variety of technological advance raise grave doubts about man's capacity to deal with its pervasive social and political, economic and cultural consequences. Technology places not only unprecedented strains on the human intellect, but challenges to the utmost man's moral fiber, his philosophical concept and his psychological stamina. Unless the techno-scientific tide is harnessed to the purpose of creating that good society that elevates man rather than dwarfs him, there is an ominous and real chance that man will collapse under the weight of his tools.

The following treatment of the technological factor is concerned mainly with the management of science and technology as an instrument of national policy and a tool of strategic planning and action.

The particulars that comprise the vast field of technological activity in the 1960's cannot be covered comprehensively here; they could not be compressed into a thousand volumes.

Technology is the systematic application of scientific knowledge, technical skill and productive method in the creation and exploitation of human and natural resources for the purposes of man. Technology thus extends from the mind of the scientist at work on basic research, through various stages of research and development, into production and the actual utilization of goods, services and techniques for bettering and controlling human life. The technological cycle "feeds back" into the system and provides a basis for further development.

What has been described as the fourth great stage of human culture is upon us. Prehistoric man's passage through the first stage—the use of primitive tools and fire—continued until about the sixth millennium B.C., when the advent of man-grown food opened the second or agricultural stage. No major technological changes then occurred until the beginning of the nineteenth century, when, with the conversion of heat into power, the third stage was ushered in as great new sources of energy became available and production rose astronomically in industrial societies. The start of the fourth era can be placed at about 1940-1945, when nuclear energy, electronics and cybernetics unfolded radically new potentials.

Standing at the threshold of this great new stage of technological promise, man now has at his disposal the means of ridding himself of want, toil and misery. The material burdens of existence may be rendered inconsequential through the intelligent technological application of nature's resources to man's needs and desires. But the human race has also acquired the means of destroying itself and of altering life in novel, inhuman ways. Within limits of the measurable, there seems to be almost nothing that is "impossible" if technology is appropriately exploited. The main obstacles to human progress through technology will be the irrationalities of human behavior, preconceptions and institutions.

Technology has indeed few absolute or rational limitations for the betterment of mankind—provided it is *exploited* toward the right purposes and controlled so as not to get out of hand. It can also be turned against man—as it was in Nazi Germany and prewar Japan, and is today in the Soviet Union and Red China. Through the automation of work and the simplification of the use of knowledge, technology may tempt man to neglect his moral and spiritual faculties and abandon his responsibility for seeking ever more diligently the enhancement of human values and individual fulfillment.

The United States has already demonstrated its ability to exploit vigorously, and with marvelous results, the potentialities of applied science. Henceforth, we must link technology with philosophical and moral values beyond the increase of national power or the expansion of material comforts, and marshal soberly and sanely the untold potentialities at our command. Whether the systemic world revolution ends in chaos or in a new universal tyranny, or whether the aspirations of free men ultimately prevail, will depend in very large measure upon how the United States and her industrialized partners manage the leviathan of technology. The outcome will hinge on intelligent decisions.

To communists, science and technology are principal instruments for designing a world order drawn to their specifications. The Free World, because it fails to put technological progress high enough in its work agenda, may lose its over-all advantage to its adversaries.

Technology as a strategic element encompasses so broad a range of activities that it cannot be categorized as a substrategy in the same way one speaks of the more clearly definable, functional aspects of strategy—i.e., the military, economic, political, diplomatic and psychological plans and programs of a nation or a coalition. The variegated nature of technology cannot be squeezed into such tight compartments. It is more meaningful to speak of the *technological factor* in a particular phase of over-all strategy than it is to attempt to draw a clear parallel between, say, military strategy and technological endeavor.

Scientific study has been concerned mainly with the detached pursuit of truth and knowledge. Today, however, the scientist, the engineer, the industrial producer and the technical specialist are cast in an unfamiliar role: As a result of their labors, they bear responsibility for the social and political consequences of their achievements.

Technology has dragged its progenitor, modern science, from its ivory tower and made it a captive of politics. Consequently, it challenges political man to reappraise his values and responsibilities to civilization.

Crucial as technology has been throughout history, and tremendous though its present impact may be, technological innovation per se has never been decisive. It has been the manner in which a technological advantage has been used that has affected human destiny. The excellence of strategy, tactics and leadership has won the campaigns and battles more often than weaponry. The wisdom and foresight of rulers, rather than a superior technology, built enduring and healthy societies. It is high purpose and spiritual toughness as well as the technological genius that have turned the experiment into a successful going concern. It has been human choice and pursuit of human values that have governed the role of technology. But can these historical insights be extrapolated toward the future?

It remains to be seen whether the advent of nuclear weapons and space exploration has or has not precipitated man into an age that cannot draw useful analogies from the past. Indeed, there has evolved a new school of thought that would substitute technological causation—the "ultimate reality"—for any previous brand of determinism. This sort of technological determinism prevails not only in the Soviet Union and Communist China, where technology has assumed almost deistic stature, but also has won converts among large numbers of intelligent members of Western society.

To "take things as they are" in order to master them is to sever oneself from creation—its mystery, its drama and its joy. To substitute "know-how"—skill in the management of things—for the best we know of truth and its application to life is to strip existence of adventure, meaning, responsibility and conscience.

In substance, then, the unbridled march of technocracy—the cult of technology—flaunts human dignity and freedom. So complete has been its triumph in some totalitarian countries that technocracy is almost synonymous with the state. In particular, Soviet man, as well as the new man of Red China, has become technological man, not because he is more efficient technologically than man in a free society, but because he is led to cherish few if any values outside of technological progress.

Man's search for the ultimate reality will not be any more conclusive in the contemporary technological revolution than it was in the Age of Reason, although the difficulty of the quest has certainly become heightened. Man will come closer to that reality only through the pursuit of freedom, and not by surrender to a process which he feels to be within his power to control.

It stands to reason that care must be taken not to abdicate to a technological elite the decisions which control our destiny merely because familiar social functions and political relationships have been complicated by scientific and technological developments. It is fashionable to inveigh against the "arrogant scientist" who has seized the power of decision-making, and to deplore the "ignorant policy-maker" who has become the slave of technocracy. There has, in fact, been a tendency to magnify science and technology beyond their proper place in human affairs. But we need also to beware of the decision-maker who arrogantly slights expert advice.

The technological revolution bears strangely mixed blessings that should be received with both caution and open-mindedness. The same technology which is creating these problems is also capable of producing means toward their solution. For example, the data-gathering processes and the electronic computers will give us partial answers to complex human, physical and operational relationships. Likewise, television, high-speed printers and space communication-relays point the way to a broadening of the process of popular understanding. The resources that are made available by technology include methods of mastering it.

Technology and Strategic Posture

Technology is distinguished by a characteristic unique in the field of strategic conflict: Its development as an arm of strategy is relatively within our own control. Unlike the diplomatic, economic, military and psychological arms of strategic action, the technological aspects of United States strategy are little susceptible to interference by external pressures. This relative freedom imposes the vexing responsibility of making sound decisions. But it also holds out great advantages to be won by technological selectivity and boldness. In this one field most of the choice is, relatively speaking, our own.

Though a nation's relative power cannot be measured accurately by technological achievement alone, this criterion is becoming ever more significant. Our pluralistic and fragmented approach to technology tends to obstruct a cool-headed appraisal of just "how are we doing." The Soviets are in deadly earnest about outstripping us in this key field of endeavor. This is not merely a race for marginal advantages, but rather a ruthless competition for the wherewithal and know-how to gain the upper hand in the protracted conflict.

American technology is at work far and wide in both the public and the private sector. A profusion of agencies and many billion dollars are devoted to research and development undertakings which, not many years ago, could count their resources in relatively few millions of dollars. It is difficult indeed to see just where the United States does stand. One could hardly expect to find unanimity of opinion on so elusive a subject. It is possible, however, to assemble a fair estimate of our status. Notwithstanding repeated official assurances that the U.S. need not fear being left behind in the technological race, the independent analyses reach conclusions that are not entirely comforting. The findings of a group composed of scientists, business executives, trade union leaders and personalities in public life offer the following representative conclusion on the status of American military technology:

> . . . all is not well with present U. S. [military policy]. The over-all U. S. strategic concept lags behind developments in technology and in the world political situation. Defense organization is unrelated in major ways to critically important military missions. Systems of budgets, appropriations, and financial management are out of gear with the radically accelerating flow of military developments. . . . The United States is rapidly losing its lead in the race of military technology.[1]

This conclusion was reached in 1957; late in 1960 the situation had hardly improved. At the end of World War II it seemed unbelievable to thinking Americans that the United States could ever lose the industrial and technological superiority which had just been a decisive factor in victory. Today, barely fifteen years later, a new opponent has drawn abreast of us in some fields and is challenging our waning superiority in others.

How did we lose so great a preponderance in so short a time? The answer is as complex as the topic to which it is addressed. We can, however, point to several conspicuous factors.

For one thing, the Free World, and notably the United States, has harmed itself and given comfort to the communists by self-defeating policies on technological secrecy. The U.S. appears smitten with schizophrenia: It gives away great masses of knowledge in techno-

[1] *National Security—the Military Aspect* by the Rockefeller Brothers Fund, January, 1958, page 62.

logy[2] that might better be kept under cover, while it withholds, on rather shaky grounds of "security," important information from the public at large and the technological community in particular. Rapid technological advance is made by building on all that is known about a given subject. Unfortunately, the Soviets benefit from their own investigations, as well as most of ours. We are more ignorant of communist technology than we need to be, and partial censorship often denies our own scientists and engineers access to adequate data regarding a specific technical problem.

The Soviets appear to be more rational and selective in this respect. What they really consider should be kept secret, or otherwise hard for outsiders to come by, is quite inaccessible to the noncommunist world. But technology is moving so fast that secrecy is becoming less important than communicating its advances to the various elements of the communist elite, and Soviet open literature is bulging with data to a degree that would have been inconceivable a few years back.

The entire U.S. approach to this problem needs to be reappraised. In its present uneven form, it seems to confuse those who should be enlightened and inform those who should be kept guessing.

Whereas the U.S. has no peer in the production of goods and services for any purposes, civilian or military, the Soviets are generally superior in the organization and management of their technological resources. The Soviet objective—to achieve technological-industrial parity with, and eventually clear-cut superiority over, the United States—has been pursued relentlessly under centralized direction. In the postwar period, the Soviets poured vast efforts into the expansion and improvement of their military technology. This is the part of the race that must command our special attention. The communist scheme of things allots a much smaller place to the improvement of the average standard of living. It is probable that during the next five to ten years, the communist empire will achieve, in some key technological areas, substantial equality with the United States and, in other fields, superiority. In this contest the role of Red China and the European satellites may be secondary, but it nonethe-

[2] *Atomic Energy for Military Purposes* (The Official Report on the Atomic Bomb under the Auspices of the United States Government), 1940-45, Henry deWolf Smythe, Princeton: Princeton University Press, 1945. This report is borne out by other recent appraisals. The issue was brought to light during the debate on the so-called missile gap in 1959-60.

less supports the main effort. Whenever the Soviet Union has concentrated its resources, effective new weapons systems have rolled off the production line in remarkably short times; in a few critical fields, the quality of these weapons equals our own.

Many Americans discount the possibility that the Soviets might "win" the race. Even the furor caused by the Sputniks and the Lunik was only momentary. American rocketry and space technology have, indeed, some remarkable achievements to their credit. Yet, serious concern has been voiced in many competent quarters over what should be done to improve our over-all technological position.

Before seeking to answer the question of how best to employ our technological resources, let us survey briefly some of the major technological activities that bear either directly or indirectly on grand strategy. Those touched upon below are selected mainly to illustrate the diversity of technological activities that in one way or another impinge on our strategic posture.

The Variety of Technological Activity

The military implications of modern technology are obviously in the forefront of all considerations of protracted conflict strategy. It is not, however, our purpose to compile a catalogue of military research and development projects, nor to assess the virtues or defects of particular "hardware" or weapons systems.

Toward the close of World War II, the U.S. made a choice among several conceivable military strategies. "Strategic air power" virtually subordinated the development of "mixes" of other technologies and military forces as means of American strategy. Our technological advance and strategic posture have been largely conditioned by this basic choice. The task now is to build on this base and to exploit additional technologies so as to insure, as best we can, a military posture in keeping with our political aims.

The military developments clustered around general nuclear war are of paramount importance to American security. We still have much to learn and do about "clean" bombs, radiation weapons, a greater variety of warheads, and the reduction in costs of nuclear warheads and delivery systems. We particularly need to perfect nuclear warheads of such yields and characteristics as are appropriate to strictly "military targets." We need to develop further nuclear propulsion systems for subsurface, surface and atmospheric uses as well as for military penetration into space and for defense against military threats from space. *Unless really satisfactory arms control can be achieved without delay, these considerations call peremptorily for further nuclear testing.*

Within the past years, two divergent trends in nuclear weaponry have become apparent. One points to a galaxy of relatively small but potent intercontinental missiles. The second leads to the development of relatively few so-called Doomsday weapons possessing destructive power so vast as to stagger the imagination—the ominous "begaton" and "gigaton" bombs. These trends flow from scientific and engineering advances which only a few years ago appeared beyond the range of the possible, if not imaginable. The terrifying speed of these developments adds new dimensions of uncertainty and increases the gravity of the already complex problem of United States security. These developments will have an important bearing on the question of allocation of resources which we discuss elsewhere.[3] The final decision, whatever it is, will impinge on currently held concepts of military strategy; it will influence our policy on the issue of arms control and security.

Let us first turn to the possibility of developing a new family of smaller, but deadly intercontinental ballistic missiles. This alternative flows from technological breakthroughs in solid-state physics, solid-propellant rockets, and metallurgy, as well as important advances that have been made in increasing yield-weight ratios in nuclear warheads and in overcoming, for all intents and purposes, the problems posed by friction-induced heat at the re-entry of intercontinental ballistic missiles into the earth's atmosphere. New developments in solid-state physics will permit miniaturization of electronic components required for missile guidance and other purposes. The advance is roughly of the same order of magnitude as that attained when transistors replaced the vacuum tube. Electronics required in intercontinental ballistic missiles may eventually be fitted into or contained in a volume not much larger than a cigar box. Even without further testing, existing nuclear warheads can be reduced in size and still produce far greater devastation. With adequate testing it is conceivable that the size of nuclear warheads can be substantially reduced while their destructive power is increased. The increase in their yield-to-weight ratio would approxi-

[3] Cf. Chapter 10, "Strategy of Ways and Means."

mate ten to one. Because of improvements in heat-resistant materials, the size of the protective cone now required to prevent destruction of the missile or the warhead may be greatly reduced. Currently each missile must carry a protective cone, which makes up a considerable portion of the weight of the missile. This can be cut down to much less than a tenth of the total weight of the payload. Added to these developments, improvements in solid-fuel propellants may make possible the development of an intercontinental ballistic missile of a total weight not much greater than ten thousand pounds, packing considerable destructive power.[4]

If these technological breakthroughs were pushed and incorporated in the development of a new family of small but potent missiles it is quite conceivable that the unit cost of each missile could be greatly reduced. If so, major powers like the United States or the Soviet Union could conceivably produce, without straining their resources, ten to twenty to thirty thousand missiles. A defense against such missiles, particularly if they were fired in volleys, would be difficult to mount. Furthermore, they could be so dispersed that they would be almost invulnerable to a counterforce strike. Moreover, it is quite possible that many small countries, once they have trained competent scientists and engineers, will be able to enter the missile race, which at present is limited almost entirely to the United States and the Soviet Union.

Let us now consider, at the other end of the scale, the Doomsday weapons. The American press, on September 4, 1960, disclosed that, within the next five years, both the United States and the Soviet Union may be able to produce weapons of an explosive force of a thousand million tons of TNT.[5] Theoretically, fifteen of these great "begaton" weapons, exploded over the United States and European Russia, could devastate both countries by cremating everything and everybody within a radius of five hundred miles. According to experts, the "begaton" weapon could be built from devices now on the drawing board. Beyond the begaton, some scientists are looking toward a gargantuan explosive device called "gigaton." One of these weapons, it is said, would be sufficient to knock out a continent. Furthermore, it is conceivable that either of these Doomsday wea-

[4] *Aviation Week*, June, 1960, p. 26.
[5] *Washington Star*, September 4, 1960, p. 1.

pons could be placed in permanent and sustained orbit around the earth.

The likelihood that such weapons *can* be produced raises the question as to whether they *will* be produced. Khrushchev's statements in 1960 about "fantastic" new weapons suggest that the Soviet Union proposes to produce something like them.[6] It is conceivable that the Soviets, were they to succeed in their endeavors, would try to blackmail America into surrender and thus gain political domination of the globe. We, in turn, might resist such blackmail only if we had comprehensive systems for wiping out much of the Soviet Union, whether we employed begaton weapons or not. There are some, apprehensive of this trend toward ever more frightful weapons, who advocate that the only recourse is to proceed, with least delay, to an arms control agreement with the communists. The communists may not be so inclined, particularly if they could hope to disarm us by begaton blackmail before we have acquired these weapons ourselves. Unwilling to stay in the bidding, we might accept some form of accommodation with the communist world even at the jeopardy of our political values. In short, failure to forge these weapons might spell our conclusive defeat in the Cold War. The decision to develop them along with other weapons that would permit us to engage in an effective offensive-defensive strategy would doubtless prove costly. But the alternative may be more distasteful than the expenditure of cash and energy.

In less esoteric areas of weaponry, the Soviets have kept pace with and, in some cases, surpassed the United States. They have exploited boldly their achievements, especially since the first Sputniks were put into orbit. Brandishing spectacular technological devices has become part and parcel of Soviet foreign policy. While the U.S. can hardly avoid participating in this space age vaudeville show, it should not permit propaganda objectives to smother hard-headed military requirements.

The employment of nuclear weapons for strategic air and naval strikes and air defense has come to be accepted as a matter of

[6] In an open letter to both Senator John F. Kennedy and Vice President Richard M. Nixon, former Atomic Energy Commissioner Thomas E. Murray deplored the United States moratorium on atomic tests as permitting the Soviets to gain tremendous advantage with "fantastic third generation nuclear weapons." Murray's letters were reported in the *Washington Post,* November 1960.

course. Yet, there remains a strong psychological block to our willingness to use them in land warfare even though they have been fully integrated into our field forces. Despite this paradox, nuclear weapons have become indispensable to NATO's defense. The technological facts do not support the widely held opinion that there is little difference between "a small nuclear weapon and a very large one."

In the non-nuclear fields, too, advance is stymied either by indifference or mistaken notions about modern war. Many military professionals believe that great improvements in "conventional" munitions are possible and should be pushed; very little has been actually accomplished in this direction. It is perplexing that, in the midst of the nuclear age, the U.S. still underplays chemical and biological weapons in its arsenal. The fact that they have been incorporated by our opponents into their arsenal should persuade us to continue the development of the same or better weapons, particularly the uniquely "humane," non-lethal agents. From the over-all standpoint of land-air combat, it appears certain that the United States has not taken advantage of the available technology. Had the United States done so and applied greater resources to exploit it, the Free World's position vis-à-vis the communist armies facing both East and West might be considerably more favorable than it is.

The operation of naval forces has been greatly complicated by technological developments. Advanced methods of antisubmarine warfare are vitally important for the United States and its allies. A more mundane naval deficiency, which can be partially remedied by technology, is the inadequacy of really up-to-date amphibious and oceangoing transports for men and matériel.

In the development of an effective air defense, technology is probably the determining factor. Although perfect results cannot be expected in this field any more than in any other military field, there is ample scope for technological improvement in the air defenses of North America, Western Europe and Japan. For some years to come, the United States and its allies may find themselves virtually defenseless against Soviet ballistic missiles. The blame for this sorry state lies with incorrect technological decisions, poor allocation of resources and political confusion, compounded by the counsel of vested military interests. U.S. technology, more properly utilized, could go a long way toward blocking a Soviet missile attack.

Another gap in our defense posture, which technology could readily fill, is our deficiency in equipment for strategic and tactical airlift. Because of the lack of funds, the U.S. trails in the competition for high-performance aircraft. Limitations on funds for the B-70 supersonic bomber may leave the U.S. behind the Soviets in the field of long-range aircraft. Such large and fast planes could, for instance, carry troops to exploit a nuclear attack.

The use of manned aircraft, as a carrier of people and matériel, has increased greatly in importance. During the next decade improved aircraft of all types—tactical and strategic, troop carrier and cargo lift—will be needed for more varied functions than ever before. Although the helicopter may have reached the limits of its development potential, there is still ample room for the further development of low-flying inexpensive vehicles as, for example, the "flying jeep," and of vertical and short take-off-and-landing aircraft.

It is unlikely that missiles will completely replace aircraft defense and delivery systems in the foreseeable future. Manned aircraft offer advantages which the missile does not possess. Relative slowness becomes less significant as aircraft speeds move into the range of 2 to 3 Mach.[7] Aircraft are still the most suitable weapon for second-strike missions and attacks on mobile sites. As we adopt more mobile missile systems, the Soviets will need to rely on aircraft to seek out and attack our delivery bases; the converse applies to us. Target detection, reconnaissance and surveillance, and damage assessment are all functions for which, other developments notwithstanding, manned aircraft remain essential.

The complexities of technological-military developments are typified by the problem of dispersal posed by immensely greater firepower. New requirements arise for mobility, communications and methods of controlling military operations. These are pressing needs and not marginal ones. Technology has to be put to work to solve the military problems that it has helped to create. Our failure to utilize technology effectively to meet our military needs accounts in large measure for the relative deterioration of America's power position in recent years.

This situation is exacerbated by a factor alluded to earlier—

[7] Mach = speed of sound.

namely, the barriers to a free exchange of technical information which have been erected between the U.S. and some of its principal allies in the mutual exploitation of military technology. Pointless technological isolation mars our policies governing the release of restricted atomic data. This policy virtually forced the British and, particularly, the French into developing their own nuclear weapons to the detriment of NATO defense and of political relations. Nor has this dog-in-the-manger attitude by any means faded from the day-to-day relationships in many lesser technological phases of interallied dealings. Can technology be a major source of strength to a coalition when the senior member withholds knowledge that may be essential to the defense of all members and, for good measure, appears to justify his reticence by the not-so-tacit presumption that only he is above collusion with the enemy? If the U.S. does not proceed on the basis that trust begets trust, the hopes for a common victory in the protracted conflict and collaboration in peace may evaporate together with a dissolving alliance. Technology in general—and this point stands out in especially bold relief in military matters—must serve the common cause of freedom through co-operative venture. If the U.S. continues to withhold its technological treasures from its allies —and especially from the technologically advanced ones—it may end up poorly armed as well as alone in the power struggle.

Despite the somber aspects of modern military technology, many persons hope that technology may one day succeed where politics has failed: in abolishing war. Yet the assumption that a "balance of terror" automatically produces a stable nuclear stalemate is dangerous. Incessant technological change deals harshly with preconceptions of strategic permanence. Mutual deterrence need not be an exception to the rule. As long as scientists and technologists persist in looking for "breakthroughs," they will come up with the most disconcerting military surprises.

No less exciting technological developments in areas other than the military are about to change the world we now know. There are many other uses, in addition to nuclear energy, for the atom.

We are living in a period of rapidly expanding supplies of energy. In the United States, nuclear-fission reactors are not yet competitive with hydrocarbon power sources. They are, however, more than competitive in many places abroad because of higher fuel prices.

In another decade, the economic characteristics of reactors will probably surpass by far those of the present.

Nuclear energy now appears to be the primary source of energy in nature. Yet "fission" is not nature's normal way of releasing energy. In the long run, systematic industrial experimentation with, and exploitation of, nuclear energy may gradually develop procedures more naturally and effectively adjusted to nuclear energy. Consequently, in a few decades, energy may become far cheaper than it is today—with coal and oil used mainly as raw materials for organic chemical synthesis, to which their properties are best suited.

It appears that in the near future another major source of energy will be the sun itself. In recent years, several types of solar furnaces have been built to produce temperatures nearly two-thirds as hot as the sun's surface. These furnaces concentrate the sun's rays by optical mirrors and convert thermal into mechanical energy through steam-generating and other systems. Temperatures as high as nine thousand degrees Fahrenheit have been reached. These furnaces can fuse and produce minerals at temperatures above those attainable in conventional open hearth, electric or blast furnaces; furthermore, they furnish "pure" heat, uncontaminated by gaseous by-products such as result from heat created by fuels.

It has been discovered that the chemical elements, selenium, silicon, copper and certain others, when joined in thin layers with their oxides or other pure metals, produce upon exposure to sunlight an electric current. This property has been put to use in the production of several types of solar batteries, operating from the sun's radiant energy. In commercial application, solar-powered telephone and radio equipment has already been developed, and portable sun-powered battery units offer a valuable expedient for emergency and military use. Their most publicized use so far has been in the earth satellite program.

Recent research has shown that the use of heat from the sun to distill salt water holds the promise of economical, large-scale, fresh-water production. This technique may open to cultivation such dry areas as the Southwestern part of the United States, the Middle East and other deserts of the earth where solar intensities are high.

During the next several decades, research and development in this field is likely to transform solar energy into an abundant source of energy, not only for industrial, military and communications purposes, but also for the heating and electrification of homes.

Isotope research forms yet another promising area for American scientific advances. American industry now saves roughly $500 million each year by using isotopes. Isotopes are now employed in agriculture, industry and medical diagnosis and therapy.

Isotopes applied to biological processes may unlock many secrets of the human body. Since accurate knowledge of the functional interrelationships of our organs—a knowledge which we do not yet possess—is the very foundation of all effective prophylaxis, diagnosis and therapy, it is hard to conceive of any information of greater importance to mankind. Thus far we have concentrated on arming the medical profession with isotopes to preserve life. While we have succeeded in lengthening life, we have not extended the span of man's productive years. Little is known about the biological degenerative processes. Through isotope research, new answers can be expected in geriatrics, the study of the aging process.

In the next decade or two, science may well give us considerable control over the weather. Advances made toward control of the amount of rainfall seem to indicate that this aim is an attainable one. The problem of climate control has challenged scientific investigation. It is likely that man will be able to control to some extent the amount of solar energy absorbed by land, sea and atmosphere, and thus to exercise a degree of control over all major weather phenomena. The major difficulty lies in predicting in detail the effects of a drastic intervention in climate. Nevertheless, the instruments of systematic atmospheric and climatic intervention lie within our grasp. They will influence all phases of human, animal and plant ecology. The impact of such a scientific and technological advance might be fraught with greater consequence than recent or possible future wars.

The continuous, dynamic drive of modern science to pierce the secrets of nature spurs modern technology on to ever greater and more fantastic achievements. It is the catalytic effects of science, rather than science itself, which stand out in public view. But science is not a mere grab bag from which technology pulls its gadgets. Science, pure as well as applied, holds a high place in the strategic complex.

Until recently, the physical sciences have held the limelight in technological progress. It seems probable that the greatest advances will henceforth be made in the life sciences and ultimately in the social sciences. The biological sciences are revealing unexpected relationships with physics and mathematics; and the latter enter increasingly close relationships with chemistry and neurophysiology. The trends of scientific inquiry are leading toward deeper knowledge of life. Radiation medicine, which may well prove crucial in nuclear warfare, was badly neglected for some years; steps which are being taken now to intensify research in this field need even greater support and emphasis. Psychochemicals have yet to be sufficiently explored as tools of peace and weapons of war. The study of neuropsychology and cybernetics—the use of knowledge and the control of human behavior—is linked to the development of computing machines and, ultimately, of "thinking machines."

The Soviets are known to be intensely aware of the new technological vistas and may well have begun to march toward them as vigorously as toward their goal of surpassing the United States in military power and economic strength. The main interest of the communist hierarchy is in the control of men, machines and society. If the Soviets should learn to employ cybernetics and arm themselves with a special technology for the purpose of pressing their own society and others into the mold of effective conformity, they will have gained an immeasurable advantage in the protracted conflict.

The foregoing selection of technological problems and prospects, though far from exhaustive, serves to illustrate the variety and depth of the problems with which technology confronts the strategic planner and decision-maker.

The Technological Process

Our main concern here is the effective use of technology as a tool of grand strategy. The technological process is governed by choices which determine not only how it is to be exploited but also how it is to be controlled. The intelligent handling of new knowledge in relation to old practices is the main junction where decisions must be made.

Significant advances in knowledge and skill are achieved through sustained methodical effort, contemplation and concentration, and through insight, intuition and fruition. The word "breakthrough" does not quite accurately describe this process. The great bulk of scientific and technological discovery and invention results from long and arduous work. Chance and accident have played important roles in discovery and invention, but, as Pasteur said, chance helps those who are prepared for it. Moreover, discovery is the response not only to one man's effort but also to the historical climate. Historically, it was the benevolent attitude of governments toward science or the widespread and insistent pragmatic demand for technological advance which fostered an efflorescence of discovery.

The exploitation of basic scientific research and technological empiricism impinges upon every phase of world affairs: Agriculture is being revolutionized by advances in chemistry, farm tools and irrigation; industrial productivity everywhere is being raised by progress in machine tools, automatic data processing and transportation systems; the dimensions of military power are being raised by improvements in metallurgy, electronics, mechanics and meteorology.

The control of technology—to make it serve rather than dictate the development of man and society—is by all odds the most important of the issues raised by technology. Control is largely a matter of selecting from a wide range of choices those technological programs to which resources shall be applied. Specific technological decisions determine strategy, a fact not infrequently overlooked in practice. A striking case in point is the American decision to proceed, though not without considerable delays, with the development of thermonuclear weapons. This decision undoubtedly kept the U.S. military posture far stronger than it would have been if these weapons were missing from our arsenal or had been developed first by the Soviets. Although legitimate differences of opinion must always be expected to beset decision-making, all too often the wrong decisions are made simply because the decision-maker is ignorant of the technological process. The technological choices available for a given purpose are derived from highly complex technical and scientific research, exploration and development. A working knowledge of the interactions and feedbacks is invaluable to the high-level decision-maker, although he need not be any more an expert than the manager of a large industry need be personally proficient in the detailed knowledge of production. What matters is that the decision-maker, who is usually a generalist rather than a specialist, be sufficiently aware of the technological process to form a judgment by combining his own knowledge and intuition with the advice of the "experts."

Growth Curves[8]

The growth of many technologies can be represented graphically. The growth curves of technologies provide valuable insights into the problems of decision-making. The hypothesis underlying growth curves is that knowledge does not increase at random. Instead, it appears to obey a general, "natural law" of growth. Scientists have evolved mathematical models that describe the growth not only of organisms, but of human population, economic and social institutions *and technology*. From what has been determined so far, one of the most important characteristics of the technological growth trend is that the rate of increase during youth and early maturity seems to accelerate in a geometric progression—a pattern represented in aggregated series by an exponential curve.

The best way to explain growth curves is by a concrete example, e.g., the increase in the speed of manned aircraft in the first sixty years of this century. The over-all speed trend has been determined by the growth pattern of two major subtechnologies—piston-driven and jet aircraft, plotted on Chart 1.

If one were to plot the same data on a ratio scale they would appear as a sloping logarithmic curve. Depicting the rate of growth rather than the amount, the ratio curve reveals a falling off in the rate of growth, i.e., the marginal utility of the technology is diminishing.

Chart 2 also illustrates that the development of the jet engine and the rocket introduced *quantum jumps* into the over-all technology of flight. A quantum jump occurs when a new technology's performance exceeds that of an old one by a whole order of magnitude at less cost per unit. Ratio curves tell the decision-maker that, as he approaches the end of a profitable development, he should shift his emphasis from quantitative improvements of an existing technology to a new technology which can effect a major qualitative change.

All technologies—material manifestations of knowledge—do not, of course, follow the same exponential curve of growth. Various fields

[8] These curves are a composite of many years' work and are generally accepted in principle by students of the subject. Some foremost contributors to their development include: Messrs. P. F. Verhulst (*c.* 1838), Lowell J. Reed and Raymond Pear (*c.* 1920), Edward R. Dewey and Edwin F. Dakin (*c.* 1947).

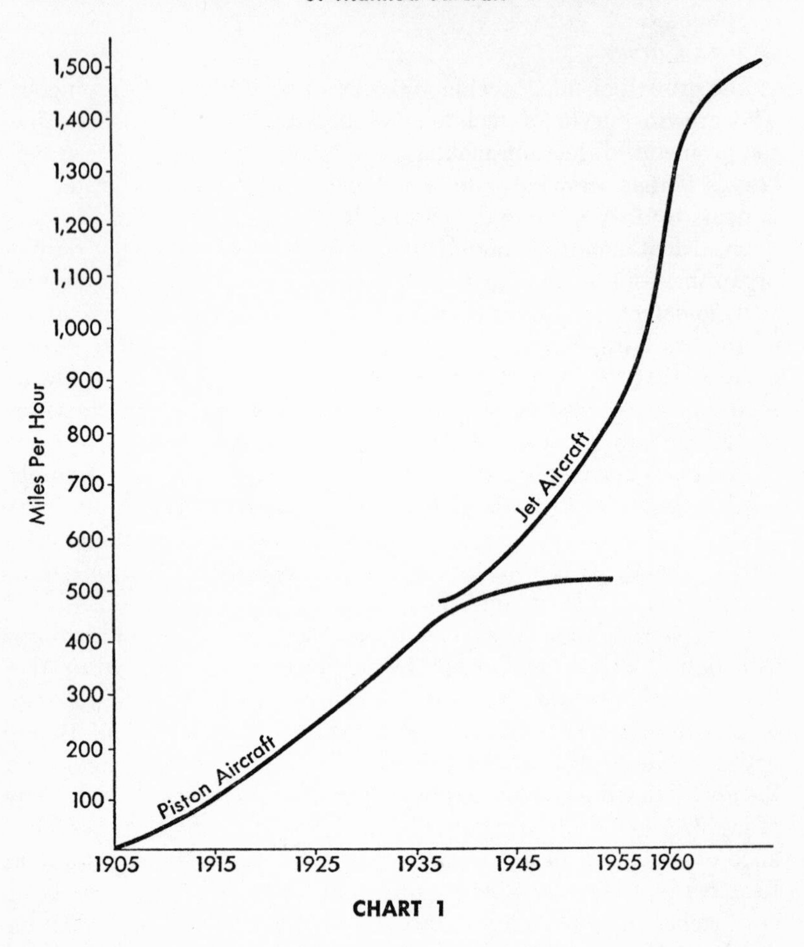

CHART 1

of science and technology develop at different rates in any given period. As touched upon elsewhere, the physical sciences have progressed more rapidly than either the psychological or social sciences. Within the broad purview of the physical sciences, missilery has advanced at a swifter pace than, say, weather control. But, *knowledge as a whole* develops according to an exponential rate-of-growth curve, derived from many discrete but integral growth

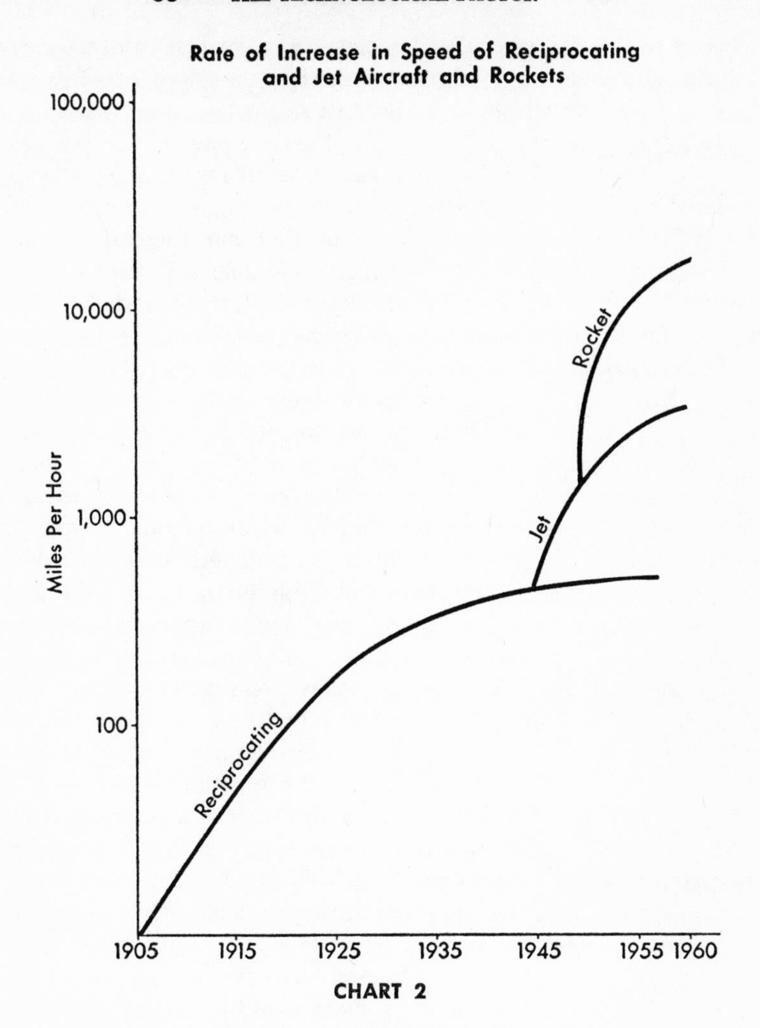

CHART 2

phenomena, each with its own rate and direction.

In much the same way that scientific and technical knowledge multiply exponentially,[9] the number of technological choices available proliferates in geometric progression. A concomitant of the exponential growth process is a rise in the complexity of the vast

[9] Ellis A. Johnson, "Crisis in Science and Technology," *Operations Research* (Journal of ORSA), January-February, 1958, Vol. 6, No. 1.

majority of technological developments. As a general rule, the more complex the methods, tools and products, the more expensive in material resources and human talent. It seems fair to ask where this is leading us. Can the full potential of atomic energy, for example, be realized until further testing takes place? Do our concepts of the human body stand up against what radioisotope tracers may tell us? Will these radioisotopes teach us that our theorizing about photosynthesis is incorrect? The more scientific and technological knowledge we gain, and the more it is tested, the greater becomes the probability of finding errors in existing knowledge and the possibility of making new discoveries. It is the disorderly behavior of this process that may well swamp us unless we become its masters.

The geometric speed-up in the rate of obsolescence is a fundamental characteristic of modern technology. New problems of maintenance, modification, repair and logistics lend themselves to analysis by the use of growth curves of technological development. Obsolescence is one of the greatest headaches of all technologies and an overriding challenge to the makers of modern strategy. In the military field, for instance, no sooner do new weapons roll off the production line than they are likely to be inferior to advanced models in development. If we produce too many items of a particular type of equipment, we may be saddled in a few years with an obsolete inventory and wasted resources which we could more profitably have applied to perfecting a new weapon. If we produce too few, we become vulnerable during the period before the new weapon becomes operational. This is one of the fundamental dilemmas underlying the so-called "missile gap."

Obsolescence of a product is not always unrelated to obsolescence of the means of production. Technology can provide quantum changes in both the demand for and the capability of improving plant methodology, machine tools, stock control and the like.

An overriding factor of growth is lead-time. The problem of lead-time has plagued U.S. military planners for years, and not the least reason for their discomfiture is a lack of understanding by the decision-makers. The United States pursues product design and production planning more or less sequentially. The Soviets, on the other hand, are reported to carry out design and production planning simultaneously, shortening the R. & D.[10] cycle while increasing costs,

[10] Research and development.

financial and human. Soviet scientists and engineers apparently can afford this kind of "waste," for the state provides abundant resources for high-priority projects.

Lead-time is a complex aspect of the entire R. & D. production process. It is a function of time and cost, of decision and priority. Suffice it to generalize here that in recent years the average lead-time for production of major items of U.S. military "hardware" often has been approximately twice that required by the Soviet Union. When a sense of urgency spurred effort, American lead-time has been drastically cut on specific projects, like the Atlas missile. But better management and allocation of resources remain major requirements for the optimum use of American technology.

Another characteristic of the technological process is the continuously increasing shift from "luxury" to "necessity." At first a technological innovation is valued as desirable, but not indispensable; the old technology still serves, if not so well. For example, the private automobile initially gave the city dweller the option of independent mobility; yet he could still travel by public transportation. When society started to build transit systems and living patterns around the new technology, it discovered that it was becoming dependent upon motor cars. The private automobile triggered the phenomenal rise in post-World War II suburbs; today, the automobile is almost a necessity of the suburbanite.

Likewise, a nuclear weapons system is not just a "better way" to attack the opponent's base of power, but it is at present the only effective way. The "luxury" nuclear weapon has become the necessary weapon. This example points up the complexity of technological decision-making in strategy. The Soviets' decision to move into production of ICBM's and IRBM's more rapidly than the U.S. made long-range strategic missiles a "necessity" for both sides, just as the U.S. decision to develop nuclear bombs compelled the U.S.S.R. to acquire nuclear military power.

Discoveries and inventions originally conceived for peaceful purposes frequently acquire military uses. The telegraph began as a business venture but became a chief means of military communication during the Civil War. The internal combustion engine, designed to propel automobiles and ships, moved tanks, warplanes and submarines. The pioneer experimenters in atomic science—the Curies and Einstein—had no idea that their brainchild someday would kill 75,000 people at Hiroshima and revolutionize international relations from that day onward.

Military technology has been a primary stimulant to human development. In recent years, military-oriented research and development has made major and incomparable contributions to the over-all technological progress and competence of the United States in nearly every measurable field of endeavor. It is absurd to write off, as "wasted," all expenditures of human talent and material resources for military purposes. These costs, at the very least, should be included in the essential national overhead.

The Managerial Aspects

The discussion has centered thus far upon the significance of technology in the world struggle. Implicit in such considerations is the question, "What do we need to do that we are not already doing?"

Technology would confront us with new categories of thought and action whether or not we had to reckon with communist hostility and power. We should take care not to limit our national endeavors to "winning" the technological race with the Soviet Union in military hardware. In a sense, the pursuit of the bio-sciences may one day prove to be as important to the advancement and survival of our culture as is now the testing of nuclear warheads.

No other sector of management is so diverse and intrinsically unmanageable as technology. Yet its strategic importance demands a certain degree of efficient and purposeful direction. Unhappily, in the United States at the start of the 1960's a *laissez-faire* method of handling technological matters is reflected in the fragmented management of technology within the federal government.

Managerial considerations are inherent in the technological activities of industry, private foundations and research organizations, the universities, utilities systems and the trade unions. The management of the public sector cannot but take into account the private sector, for only thus can be exercised the strategic direction of our technological resources. Actually, a clear delineation between a public and a private sector is somewhat artificial since many of the so-called private institutions and industries are vitally dependent on federal financial aid and services. Under the American form of government, the relationships between public and private activity in technology will be always fluid and open-ended.

Nevertheless, while there may never be an over-all "system," the federal government is responsible for giving broad direction to the utilization of our technological resources for the "common defense" and the "general welfare." It acquits itself of this responsibility partly on its own authority and partly in concert with the private sector. Most surely, there will be conflict of judgment in the exercise of this function; but general technological management today is as much a federal responsibility as is the management of national defense or the postal service.

Three major considerations should guide the direction of technology for the national good:

First, an enormous job of education needs to be done in both the public and the private sectors, not only in scientific pursuits per se, but also in the impact of technology on human values and on the affairs of state and of the individual alike.

Second, the tools needed for sound technological decision-making need to be sharpened and wielded more purposefully by those who influence the crucial contribution of technology to grand strategy.

Third, a thorough evaluation of technological resources, capabilities and limitations is an essential basis for optimum technological management at all levels.

At first glance, it might seem that these are self-evident requirements. Self-evident or not, they are not being met with vigor and comprehensiveness.

It is a philosophic as well as a practical question whether or not the "decision-makers" can learn enough about technology to take decisions that will make the cause of free men prevail. In any event, the scientist, the politician—all those with strategic responsibilities—must gain a better insight into problems outside their own métier.

What kind of man qualifies as the trustee of technology as a tool of strategy? How much of a physical science background should he have? How deeply steeped should he be in the social sciences? While he may actually possess any number of qualifications, he must have one main attribute—the ability to apply common sense to complex relationships. Today, there are few individuals ideally equipped to cope with our technological environment. We need to train a whole generation of "integrators." For this task, our schools, industries and government are unprepared. Since we cannot call a halt while improved training corrects deficiencies, we must meanwhile do the best we can with competent, well-rounded men—of whom there is a fair abundance—who can give central purpose and direction to our technological effort.

The President's Special Assistant on Science and Technology dealt with part of the problem when he said:

> . . . we, as scientists, may well have an important role to play in the future of the policy-making process. . . . it will demand a new breed of public servant, although I am at a loss to find the appropriate name for him. . . . this new breed of citizen-scientists must be continually aware that the scientific community must accept its appropriate share of the responsibility for the intelligent and successful resolution of the challenges facing the world.
>
> Another kind of individual must be recruited, too . . . with training in science in addition to the usual discipline of the foreign service . . . . Advice from practicing scientists on an ad hoc basis as needed . . . does not fill today's requirements . . . we must also provide a better scientific background for non-scientists in the international affairs field, and this, perhaps, is the most important measure of all.[11]

In the recent past, alarming things have been said about the state of general education for technology and science. The United States, we are told, has neglected the preparation of its people for the pursuit of careers in scientific and technological fields. Compared to the emphasis on, and recent output of, qualified scientists and technologists in the U.S.S.R., the American position does seem to be less than satisfactory. Education lies at the heart of an intelligent appraisal of the technological environment. Trained, competent and high-principled men alone can safeguard the effective application of technology to grand strategy.[12] Once the meaning of the technological race

[11] Speech by Dr. George B. Kistiakowsky, January 29, 1959, New York.

[12] "The march of science and technology is of growing importance to every American as a citizen. Congress regularly appropriates huge sums for scientific research and even larger ones for engineering and development; yet a majority of the voters have little grasp of what this is all about. Do we, for example, seek to make shots at the moon, or send vehicles to Mars, in order to extend scientific knowledge alone—and, if so, how much is that effort worth? . . . The shocks provided by achievement elsewhere may not be an adequate guide to our progress or our efforts. A national effort is required to strengthen our scientific and technological efforts in all fields, aimed at the advance of knowledge and the enhancement of the general welfare. In a democracy such an effort can succeed only if it has widespread public understanding and support." Statement by the President's Scientific Advisory Committee, May 24, 1959.

has entered into public consciousness, certain principles, derived from the conduct of the vast research and development programs initiated during World War II and their successors in the postwar period, should guide our quest for technological advantage:

Risk and payoff are intimately involved in technological decisions. A new technology often is fraught with high initial costs. A high payoff may call for high initial costs.

Modern technology must allow for a reasonable degree of *competition.* The paradox that competition in the private domain is considered admirable but in the public domain deplorable needs to be resolved.

There are inherent *limits* to the extent of effective exploitation of a given technology, regardless of the resources and effort applied.

Broadly speaking, our *lead-time* problem is not of a technological nature. It is *not* derived from the slowness of invention, experimentation and scientific evaluation, but from the unnecessarily lengthy processes of political, military and financial administration.

Understanding of the relation between *obsolescence and modernization* is of overriding importance. We must always strike a balance between what the old technologies will place "on the shelf" and what the new can promise "around the corner."

The *cost and costing of technology* is a fundamental problem in the management of resources.

In seeking ways to determine what needs to be managed, experienced analysts of R. & D. management appear to agree on the following guidelines: First, centralize only decisions that must be made at the top, while insuring that over-all direction will maintain the momentum of research and development and allow for flexibility to experiment with alternative solutions. Second, give free scope to alternative approaches during the less costly basic research and the early development stage, and concentrate effort in the later, more expensive, initial production stage. Third, allocate more resources to technologies needed immediately and slow the pace of those which might remedy less urgent problems, while doing neither of these two things at the expense of long-range advantage.

Operations analysis and research is a new and important instrumentality and one that technology has made both possible and imperative. This relatively new art of applying scientific methods cannot supplant the social and political sciences. It can, however, enable other disciplines to make more effective use of existing knowledge. Through the machine-processing of data, knowledge can be collected, aggregated and rationally applied as a tool to assist in solving problems that face decision-makers in many fields. Though computing machines can improve the use of knowledge and can give unprecedented insight into probalistic problems, they do not relieve us from the exercise of our judgment.

Utilization of Technological Resources

Out of the great mass of published literature and public statements on technology, there is available no authoritative and comprehensive analysis of the resources available for strategic purposes and methods for their use.[13]

Although there are numerous agencies engaged in investigations of particular technological efforts, no one agency has a purview over the complete range of national technological performance. No one government agency seems able to make an over-all evaluation of our posture. The nearest thing to a focal point is the person of the President's Special Assistant on Science and Technology (interdepartmental) who is also the Chairman of the President's Science Advisory Committee (nongovernmental). This arrangement is useful and necessary if the President's Special Assistant is to be, in fact, the fountainhead of technological direction and counsel, and if he is to exercise his influence as an observer at meetings of the National Security Council.

When the President, upon the Soviets' launching of the Sputniks, established this position, it appeared that one authority—a "czar"—would manage technological problems. Unfortunately, this appearance was belied by the modest scope of the newly created office. Both of the committees under the Special Assistant's chairmanship are meant to co-ordinate, consult, prepare studies and advise. Neither committee nor the Office of the Special Assistant

[13] The preparations for this book included a thorough survey of the public domain and official sources. Nowhere was there found a body of data or a system of analyses of "where we stand" technologically. No system of progress reports on over-all technological programs appears to be in effect. Inquiries into the matter made of such diverse agencies as the National Science Foundation, the Smithsonian Institution, the Brookings Institution, R. & D. agencies of the Department of Defense, independent and industrial research organizations, and the Office of the President's Special Assistant on Science and Technology revealed that the United States simply does not have a comprehensive system of keeping track of its vast technology.

has launched an over-all appraisal of resources and performance, neither body has operational or decision-making responsibilities. Nor have the National Science Foundation, the National Academy of Science, the private foundations and research institutions, or any other known agency. The Soviets' knowledge about their own scientific-technological position is generally assumed to be comprehensive. We can only guess at what they know about ours.

In brief, the United States has not made an objective and comprehensive evaluation of its technological resources. Hence, the decision-makers are not entirely sure what is going on in the field of technology as a whole. They have at hand a vast fund of data and knowledge, but no inventory has been taken to provide an over-all view of our technological position. This condition is reflected in the improvised *ad hoc* management of the technological factor at the highest policy- and decision-making levels of the government.

Inside established agencies of the federal government, the level of activity and awareness is uneven. A survey of the activities of agencies in the Executive Branch concerned with technological matters would fill volumes. Congress' interest in the matter would require at least a volume of its own. Technology is not suffering from lack of attention, but it seems to be ailing from the kind it gets. The Department of Defense and its affiliates have "catalyzed" the main incentives and energies for American technological progress. The Defense Department, as a matter of course, is most vitally interested in, and has the greatest responsibility for, technology in the country. The various civilian agencies are not sufficiently aware of military requirements, while military decision-makers are often unfamiliar with technological progress.

The National Aeronautics and Space Agency, the Director of Defense Research and Engineering, the National Science Foundation, the Office of the Science Adviser of the State Department, the Bureau of Standards, the President's Committee on Scientists and Engineers—these and many less well-known agencies concern themselves intensively and effectively with various aspects of the problem. Both Houses of Congress have established committees to "look at technology" in general and to stay abreast of specific developments. But nowhere is the entire range of interest encompassed adequately enough to determine what needs to be done in the aggregate and how to go about this task. In sum, the situation can be described as one where no one has really taken charge.

Outside the specific purview of government, even greater disorder reigns. U.S. industry is the vital, if not the senior, partner in the over-all technological endeavor. While industrial firms and private institutions spend hundreds of millions of dollars on R. & D., most of them look to short-term results from their efforts. Our universities and research institutes generally pursue scientific knowledge without that comprehensive view which would guide their investigations toward national objectives. In an open society, the process of identifying the private with the public interest in technology is difficult indeed. It is not impossible.

To be sure, the technological challenge cannot be met by trying to solve substantive problems, as we are wont to do, by adding ever more *ad hoc* structures to the organizational *status quo*—a quaint procedure that goes by the name "reorganization." This particular manifestation of Parkinson's Law usually succeeds only in consolidating confusion.

The organization of Soviet science and technology gives us a comparative basis for judging our own organization. The Soviet Government, including the Politburo since the days of Lenin, has been acutely aware of the importance of science and technology. The Soviet Academy of Science which began as a co-ordinating body, has been providing central direction and planning for the over-all research effort of the Soviet Union since the 1930's. The Soviets have established a network of scientific institutions under a policy euphemistically called "scientific decentralization." Each Soviet republic boasts of an Academy of Science which possesses expertise in a particular field. The Academy of the Republic of Azerbaijan specializes in petroleum research; in Armenia, the Academy concentrates on stellar astronomy; in the Soviet Republic of Georgia, the Academy emphasizes elasticity and other mechanical fields. In addition, the scientific academies are intimately related to local industries. Their mission is, of course, to assure the best use of new technologies in production.

There is, to be sure, a running argument over the efficacy of some aspects of Soviet technological management, especially in agriculture and the production of consumer goods. From the standpoint of strategic technology, however, one cannot but be impressed by specific features of the Soviet approach, such as methods of handling a functional military area through a complex of specialized research institutions, and their apparent success in imparting technical education in depth.

It seems certain that the system serves Soviet military power reasonably well. There is no reason to doubt Soviet success in reducing lead-time, multiplying production and training technologists. While the Soviet technological system may be better than ours in some respects and inferior in others, the Soviets' management of technology merits certainly our open-minded examination. The United States should not cavil at learning from an adversary, especially since much of his know-how came from the Free World.

The U. S. would be well advised to establish a technological college modeled somewhat on the Industrial College of the Armed Forces for the mid-career training of executives and managers employed by the Defense Department, other government agencies and the private sector. The purpose of the college would be: (a) to familiarize the students with technological trends and (b) to educate them in the management of technological programs and the art of decision-making. The college would not be devoted to the furtherance of technology as such.

A comprehensive system of academies for the sciences and technologies should be considered as a means of invigorating the national effort. An academy system should have government backing and private participation. The lack of such a system constitutes a distinct deficiency in the national research effort. This proposal is cited as one of many that would give vigor and coherence to our technology as a bulwark of national strength and a positive tool of grand strategy.

The United States and its allies possess sufficient technological resources to meet the challenge of the communist bloc and the systemic revolution. No nation, society or culture can lay claim to technological pre-eminence as a God-given right. Technology is a key factor in the struggle between communism and the Free World. The power we derive from, and exert through, technology is mainly a matter of the choices we make. So far, our record has been less than impressive. We have lost much of our previous lead. We must move quickly and intelligently if we are to make the proper choices and to realize the potentialities of technology in time.

"Solutions" are of an importance secondary to understanding, insight and foresight. There is no lack of useful ideas on how to raise our technological efforts. Another listing of particulars would serve little purpose. The particulars will be of slight consequence if they are not fused into an overarching purpose.

If we let the dynamics of science and technology lead us away from our basic values, then we may well become the slave instead of the master of technology. If we fail to take fuller advantage of what is ours to command, then we shall lose more than "technological advantage."

CHAPTER 5 MILITARY STRATEGY, POWER AND POLICY

In the 1960's, force will remain the decisive factor of international politics. The communists conduct their affairs with a growing truculence that stems from real achievement: Their military power is rapidly closing the gap which once restricted its geographical and technological reach; their organization for waging psychopolitical warfare remains as efficient as ever, and enables them to exert more effectively the leverage of growing military power.

The most important new element in the world strategic balance is the likelihood that under any conditions of war, almost surely by 1962, possibly even today, the Soviet Union could wreak unacceptable nuclear damage upon the Continental U.S. It is this contingency which calls more urgently than any other likely international development for a thorough reappraisal of U. S. national security policy.

It is our contention that American policy relies upon a margin of military superiority vis-à-vis the communist bloc which is dangerously narrow by the measure of American global commitments.

During the past few years, the debate over American defense policy has centered on two closely related questions: What is the nature of the Sino-Soviet military threat? Is the United States military posture equal to the task of meeting it? This chapter seeks answers to these crucial questions. Many studies of national security problems have found their way into the public domain. Others have been kept out of the public's view for reasons of security or policy. The authors of this volume believe that on the basis of publicly available evidence, a further analysis of our national security policy need not necessarily carry coal to Newcastle. The topic has attracted some of the keenest minds in our country. We will not attempt to traverse well-covered ground. We will seek with the published material in hand to examine the broad alternatives of American military strategy.

War is an organic whole. The preparations for limited war and general war are not mutually exclusive. A great many current studies addressed to the military challenge of communism quite rightly stress the need for a greater American and allied capability for fighting "limited war." We do not quarrel with this thesis. Not all of these investigations, however, are enlivened by awareness of the intimate interrelationship between total war, quasi peace and intermediate ranges of conflict. All too often, for example, discussions of a hypothetical land war in the NATO area slight its obvious relationship to the size and quality of our strategic nuclear retaliatory force. Yet comprehension of the basic interrelationships of limited war and general war must form the core of strategic planning in the nuclear age.

For several years, the United States held the monopoly of atomic striking power. This monopoly argued conclusively against a major communist aggression, for the Soviet Union offered an open target to our strategic retaliation. When we lost our monopoly, we comforted ourselves with the idea that the prospect of mutual destruction would suffice to deter the potential aggressor.

Indeed, both sides abstained from waging nuclear war. Yet "peace" has not been an unmixed blessing. The communists have gained and continue to gain in power. They have made heavy inroads upon the Free World without resorting to the ultimate weapons. The power balance is changing: American strategic thought is changing with it.

It appears now that ratiocination nudged by necessity has brought forth a strategic doctrine that contains some patent internal contradictions. It reads as follows:

1. A thermonuclear exchange will spell mutual annihilation. Thus it is unlikely to occur. If it does occur, our preponderance of force must be such as to absorb a Soviet first strike and leave us strong enough to retaliate swiftly and conclusively.

2. Limited wars may have to be fought. The protective umbrella of our thermonuclear "deterrent" will provide the principal prerequisite of any limited war strategy.

3. Relatively minor attention need be paid to preparations for warfare on the lower side of the threshold of "limited war" and "thermonuclear exchange."

If this is our strategic doctrine—and the available evidence appears to indicate that, indeed, it is—then its rationale is little more than wishful expectation. This is not to say that it is not valid in part. But it seems that the realities of communist strategy do not fit quite so neatly into the bag of our assumptions.

Certainly, we would *like* to think that our atomic capabilities have deterred communist aggression. "Deterrence" is a psychological concept. We expect the communist rulers to react in a certain way to our strategic posture. In other words, we presume that we can telegraph our hypothetical punches and that the communists will read our signals correctly. Yet, the communists have not been deterred from committing aggressive acts on three or four continents.

Could it be that we have been spared a "big war" because the Sino-Soviet rulers were not *ready* to wage it? Or could it be that their forbearance springs from the healthy desire to consolidate the gains of piecemeal aggression and from their conviction that the revolutionary forces in this world are moving their way and render superfluous risky military adventures? As a matter of fact, there is no conclusive proof for the claim that *we* have held them in check. Despite our military posture, it appears that the communists have had considerable freedom of choice. So far, time seems to have been on their side.

These observations are not expected to strike dumb the many highly competent and articulate observers who have watched the evolution of U.S. strategy over the past decade. They do reduce the obvious to order. The making of a detailed balance sheet of American strategic performance lies beyond the scope of this book. Suffice it to say that, over the past decade, American policy has been less than successful in maintaining what once had been an impregnable position of strength.

It is a Chinese saying that philosophy is the clarification of terms. For purposes of this discussion, "General War" is defined as a conflict in which the forces of the United States and the U.S.S.R. are directly involved and in which atomic weapons presumably will be used from the outset on the homelands of the two superpowers. On the other hand, "Limited War" can be defined as a conflict short of general war in which American forces will or will not use atomic weapons to achieve national objectives. These definitions are ade-

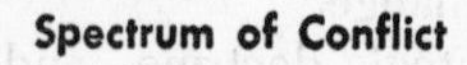

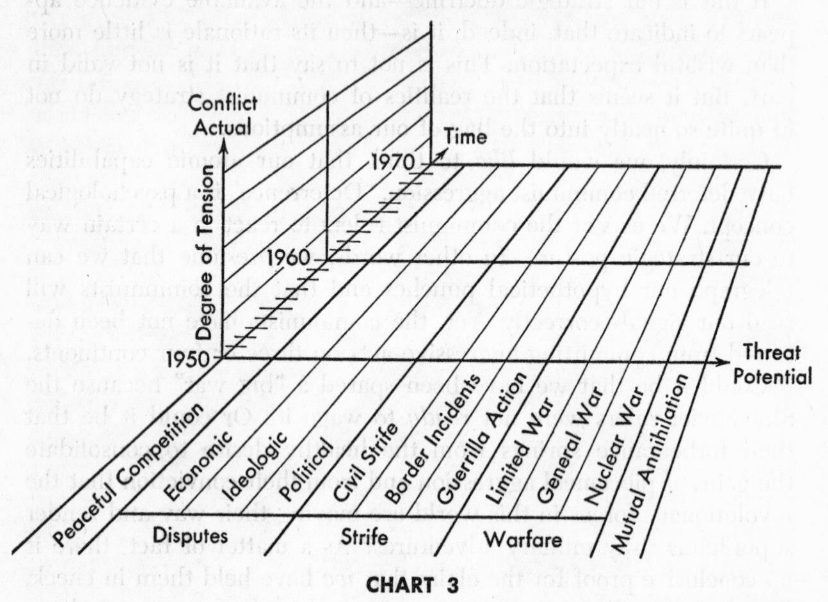

CHART 3

quate—provided we do not let them lead us into the trap of misplaced abstraction. The realities of strategy are multidimensional.

The conflict between the Free World and the communists embraces the full range of force and persuasion from peaceful competition and negotiation at one end to nuclear wars of annihilation on the other. This conflict is being waged over an extended period of time. The intensity of the conflict may vary from sector to sector as well as from year to year. The opposing chart, Spectrum of Conflict, graphically portrays the relationship between modern weapons systems with respect to each other and to time.[1]

[1] "The Spectrum of Conflict," the Stanford Research Institute *Journal*, Fourth Quarter, 1959.

Wars, including general nuclear war, are fought to achieve objectives that lie beyond war. We must presume that the strategic dialogue between the U.S. and the U.S.S.R. is governed by rationality. If it were not, strategy would be a child's tale told by an idiot. Hence we have little choice but to preface our strategic planning with an act of faith. The U.S. and the U.S.S.R. leaders will seek to preserve the value of their respective societies and will strive to limit war to conditions under which both sides can not only survive, but also attain those objectives that lie beyond war. There is, however, an area of doubt: Do the United States and the Soviet Union place the same value on human life? We do not know the degree of damage which the Soviets might accept in order to bring about a conclusive settlement consonant with their objectives. We do know, however, that their current military literature stresses the importance of preparations for a long war and for fighting a nuclear war to a victorious conclusion.[2]

The nature of a nation's commitment to human values will largely determine its selection of a strategy, the composition of its forces for defense and attack, and the way in which it uses its military power. American strategy does and must assign primacy to the contingency of thermonuclear exchange in a general war, the most frightful aspect of a future conflict. Yet war has many faces. To shy away from one is to withdraw into the illusion that war comes in pieces. War is an organic whole. If we must fight a war, its course will be governed by the contingency of thermonuclear exchange, no matter whether nuclear weapons will be used or not. If we do not go to war, nuclear power-in-being will weigh heavily in the scales of peace.

Hence, the capability for waging general nuclear war is the keystone of American defense. To base our strategy on the idea that nuclear war is "unthinkable" is to make such a war more likely. If, however, we cleave to the idea that nuclear war is possible, it will probably never occur. This is the paradoxical "logic of the feedback." To make timely provision for the most distasteful contingency in order to avoid it—this is the basic law of survival in the nuclear age.

[2] See Raymond L. Garthoff, *The Soviet Image of Future War,* New York: Praeger, 1959; and Herbert S. Dinerstein, *War and the Soviet Union,* New York: Praeger, 1959.

All-too-human inhibitions and uncertainties befog the junction point of general nuclear war and other forms of conflict. As the Soviet capability for bringing war to the American continent grows, so grows the West's vulnerability to communist challenges below the threshold of all-out war. Such lesser military challenges range from guerrilla wars and insurrections to wars fought with or without nuclear weapons. In 1953, the United States communicated to the world its decision to place main reliance on nuclear weapons to deal with the full range of military challenges. This decision still stands. The military assistance program was designed to reinforce this strategy by building up allied forces, armed with conventional weapons and "stiffened" by the presence of token U.S. forces. Although incomplete, the core of strategic doctrine is sound—since all national security programs must rest on the bedrock of strategic retaliation. Unfortunately, it leaves largely uncovered the twilight zone between nonmilitary or paramilitary conflict, conventional war and nuclear war. It does so in fact, though not in theory. Presumably, our nuclear power should also check communist moves made in the less violent sectors of the spectrum of conflict. Yet on the record our diplomacy appears to have been inhibited occasionally from blocking these challenges by the reluctance to go too close to the "brink" of nuclear war. Our understandable aversion has been well communicated to friend and foe alike.

The U.S.S.R. still maintains a modern army with ready reserves. Soviet field forces are equipped with both conventional and nuclear weapons. The Chinese Communists keep in the field large and well-equipped armed forces. By comparison, the U.S. and its allies, as we head into the crucial sixties, still lack the weapons, strategies and policies that could cope with fair assurance of success with situations calling for the *measured* use of force, nuclear or otherwise.

Given the communists' comprehensive military posture and a continuation of the Free World's current capabilities, the United States and its allies have five alternative courses of action in the event of further communist politico-military ventures short of all-out war: (1) they can proceed on the assumption that the communists will not commit aggression; (2) they can concede defeat from the outset or run the risk of too little, too late; (3) they can try to handle the threat mainly with tactical nuclear weapons; (4) they can undertake large-scale nuclear retaliation against the communist heartland; (5) they can mobilize to the extent required for the restoration of their power position. None of these choices is particularly attractive from a military point of view—except the last.

The U.S. needs to realign its military strategy to support its overall purpose of safeguarding and extending a Free World society. This strategy should not only guarantee the security of the United States but, in association with America's allies, it ought to protect other areas from the variegated forms of communist aggression, from nuclear blackmail to open warfare in all its permutations and combinations. We cannot afford to lose sight of the fact that Free World strategy, of which the U.S. furnishes the decisive ingredients, must give an acceptable level of security and protection to the entire Free World.

The dynamic influence of technological change since World War II has magnified the confusion about the interrelationships between limited and total war. In particular, nuclear weapons and the systems for delivering them have revolutionized all warfare no matter whether they are ever used in combat again or not. To date, nuclear weapons have never been used against nuclear weapons.

The use to which the United States and her partners will put the military potentials of science and technology may well determine the success of the Forward Strategy. There are other indispensable elements in the matrix of requisite military strength, such as leadership, foresight, morale, training, flexibility, inventiveness, adequate resources and bases; however, although technology offers neither a military panacea nor a substitute for professional competence, the technological choices made in the fluid competition for military superiority will outweigh virtually all other aspects of military activity and posture.

While the spectrum of technology for military purposes offers almost innumerable choices, the selections which actually can be made, when considered from a practical standpoint, are relatively few.

The U.S. is caught inescapably in an "arms race" with the Soviet Union, whether it wishes to recognize this deadly competition or not. Contrary to general belief, such a race need not work against world stability and peace. It could serve as the most effective means to bring the communist rulers to reasonable terms. For *the Free World can far better afford such a competition than the communist bloc.*

The economic resources of the Free World are so much greater than those of the communist bloc that, combined with a masterful exploitation of technology, a strategy based on overwhelming military means is well within our reach.

But because we have not fully joined the race for military-technological supremacy, the decisive advantage in tangible elements of the international power balance has been shifting away from the Free World during the past decade. In the area of military power, the tables have been partly turned. The psychological impact is perhaps the most significant consequence of this shift in power.

A full-blown estimate of the military situation would not be feasible in a book of this nature. Nor is a detailed appraisal of the current politico-military position of the United States vis-à-vis the rest of the world necessary to an understanding of the main elements of the role of the military in national strategic power. The main issues lie in the open. The raw material for intelligent discussion, understanding and action is readily available in the public domain. We hope to bring into sharp relief those factors which must be considered in any intelligent assessment of the world power balance, and let the reader judge for himself.

In the wake of World War II, it was widely held that the United States' possession of atomic weapons gave her the undisputed power advantage in world politics. If raw military force were the sole determining factor, then the U.S. ought to have been able to check communist expansion with relative ease, at least until around 1952, when the U.S.S.R. first exploded a thermonuclear device. But notwithstanding American superiority in nuclear weapons, the communists exploited other forms of military power with great effect during the post-Hiroshima period: They subdued Eastern Europe, stirred strife in Greece, threatened Iran and Turkey, blockaded Berlin, conquered China and half of Korea. After consolidating their position in North Korea, they sought to unite all of Korea by force and partitioned Indochina. In sum, they brandished their strength in a manner which kept the U.S. on the defensive—and all this while the U.S. had an atomic monopoly or preponderance. In subsequent years, the U.S.S.R., thanks to unexpectedly early successes in nuclear technology, developed its own capabilities for nuclear warfare. The result was a bipolar balance of power. The great difference between this kind of "balance" and that of earlier times was the extent to which nuclear weapons weighed in the scales. Never before have nations whose aims and philosophy are so basically incompatible been in possession of such awesome military power.

It is fallacious to assume that any power equation remains constant. The pace of change—military, economic, technological, political and psychological—makes it impossible to assume an absolute power advantage at any given time on the part of either the communist bloc or the Free World. To the simple question, "Who is militarily the stronger, we or the Soviets?" no categoric answer can be given. Missiles, nuclear weapons, submarines and army divisions are typical of some of the tangibles that enter into such a consideration. While measuring the known elements of the power balance as rationally and intelligently as we can, we must bear in mind that the nuclear age has introduced a unique uncertainty into the calculus of relative power. It is necessary to assess the strategic outlook with an open and fairly flexible mind because the unforeseen is almost certain to occur. The art of strategy is to deal with the unknown as well as the known. *The real measure of power advantage in the nuclear age is the degree to which physical power is adequate to sustain the confidence that one will prevail if war should come.* If this degree of power is provided, and this is not easy, then supremacy in the protracted conflict will be determined as much by the purposefulness and the quality of strategic thought as by military "hardware."

The ability to gauge the constantly shifting vectors of power and to react correctly and expeditiously to the changes, while standing firm on fundamental values at issue, will determine the outcome of the present struggle. The task imposed by the systemic world revolution, the protracted conflict and the threat of nuclear holocaust is for the United States to provide intelligently for an effective "mix" of all the elements of power, military and otherwise.

Obviously, not everything is wrong with the national strategy. In many aspects it has been commendably effective and forward-looking. The condition and magnitude of the U.S. military establishment, standing alone, speaks for itself. The United States military profession has been in a constant state of *en garde* in a world seething with tension for some twenty years; it has weathered two major wars and several smaller military conflicts; it has adjusted itself at least in some measure to the technological revolution and unprecedented political commitments. It has developed a unique concept of mutual security; and it has spread itself, albeit thinly, to all corners of the globe in an effort to meet the demands imposed upon it by the communist threat. The armed forces have achieved much. All this bespeaks the general awareness of the American people that liberty is neither cheap nor easy. But the questions raised in these pages are whether that awareness is hard and clear enough and whether the make-up of the U.S. military posture is strong enough to deal with emerging world realities.

Novel as are the problems of the nuclear age, the moral equation of national security remains the same it has been throughout history. Washington in his fifth annual address to the Congress of the United States in Philadelphia, December 3, 1793, said:

> There is a rank due to the United States among nations, which will be withheld, if not absolutely lost, by the reputation of weakness. If we desire to avoid insult, we must be able to repel it; if we desire to secure peace, one of the most powerful instruments of our rising prosperity, it must be known that we are at all times ready for war.

Communist Concepts of War

Until the death of Stalin, classic communist strategy was largely limited and indirect. It was dictated by necessity, for the Soviet Union was relatively weak vis-à-vis the more technologically advanced Western powers. But since the death of Stalin, Soviet strategic thinking has undergone a revision, particularly as regards the view of Soviet military thinkers on the question of the importance of surprise attack. This is not to say that the pre-emptive strike now represents the sole or even primary instrument of Soviet policy and strategy. The Soviets, despite the increased emphasis on all types of surprise attack, still value highly the substrategies and conflict techniques of limited risks. They might well resort to conflict techniques which leave them free to halt short of total war. Communist doctrine is conditioned by Soviet and Chinese historical experience, as well as by the new weapons. The communists, in keeping with the traditional strategy of revolutionary movements, will undoubtedly seek to avoid a direct military encounter with an adversary possessing retaliatory power capable of inflicting unacceptable damage upon themselves. Hence, the communist proclivity for using proxies, "volunteers" and the other devices of ambiguous aggression. Communist military philosophy, however, is as subject to revision as is communist ideology. It will accommodate itself to changes in the objective historical situation.

As far as can be determined, Soviet military doctrine now seems to rest on the following considerations:[3]

Nuclear firepower has become *the decisive* element of strategy. This is not intended to suggest that the Soviets are planning to strike us with a "bolt from the blue," but it does mean that the nuclear weapon will become the prime mover of other, lesser conflict techniques. Ballistic missiles are relatively cheap, carry great firepower and can strike at great range. While ICBM's lend themselves particularly to surprise attack, the Soviets maintain other capabilities of strategic delivery. The Soviets, just like the U.S., will rely on manned aircraft for attack on mobile target systems and on submarines for striking, at relatively short range, at targets on the high seas and on land. Military space vehicles, most likely, are also under development. Nuclear delivery forces are being supported by active and passive defense systems, which will in the future include antimissile missiles.

Nuclear-missile systems support both regular and irregular forces operating deep in the rear of the opponent. Surface forces, in addition to discharging their obligations for defense and internal security, seize and control peoples and territories in the wake of the damage caused by the nuclear exchange. An alternate mission of Soviet surface forces is to fight limited wars should such wars be deemed desirable.

While preparing for a wide variety of warfare, the communists still appear to believe that there is a good chance of avoiding the general nuclear war while leaving their adversaries no other choice but appeasement or surrender. Soviet military doctrine thus comprises a very adroit mixture of the less violent forms of protracted conflict with general nuclear war. In fact, both types of conflict have been raised in importance. Khrushchev's rocket brandishing has simply confirmed the obvious, i.e., nuclear firepower has become the key element in Soviet strategy. But, precisely because this is so, the potentialities of the less violent forms of protracted conflict,

[3] Premier Khrushchev's important policy speech of January 14, 1960 summarized the trends which have now become apparent in Soviet military doctrine.

too, have gained importance in Soviet strategy.

The communist strategic doctrine, thus, holds that growing nuclear power will serve as a deterrent against "imperialist" attempts to interfere with local revolutions, guerrilla operations and proxy wars. Wherever military vacuums develop, increasing military capabilities may enable the communists to manipulate political developments thousands of miles from the bases of their power. In the past, this military support of communist political operations could extend only so far as the shadow cast by the Red armies. Today, and even more so tomorrow, communist nuclear delivery systems can underwrite "leap-frog" operations into the very back yard of the United States. The penetration of Cuba may have been but a prelude to a bolder communist offensive throughout Latin America and, for that matter, most other underdeveloped regions.

During the past few years, progressive communist professional military journals have emphasized the value of military initiative in the nuclear age. The communists, although they favor revolution by political warfare, place their trust on military force as the ultimate means to political ends. The communists contend that their state and highly disciplined party could absorb a nuclear blow better than our loose, more highly diversified political and economic system.

The views of two Soviet marshals on the nature of future war illuminate Soviet policy on military preparedness, and particularly on the role of surface forces. They contain the routine charges against the "western warmongers" and professions of the Soviet Union's attachment to peace. More important is the reference to the Soviets' intention to fight on after an all-out exchange of thermonuclear weapons and to equip their land armies with up-to-date weapons.

Marshal of the Soviet Union Vasili Chirkov wrote as follows:

> We military people in particular have a good idea of what modern warfare looks like with the use of nuclear weapons, rockets and other means of mass destruction. Therefore, we must be among the foremost advocates of peace and the prevention of a new war. . . . There is no fatal inevitability of war, at present . . . the steps taken by our government to further reduce the Armed Forces rest on the granite foundation for the invincible might of our Soviet state and its defense capacity. [Namely, atomic and other modern weapons.][4]

[4] U.S.S.R. Embassy in the U.S., Press Department, Release No. 98 (February 23, 1960).

Rodion Y. Malinovsky, U.S.S.R. Minister of Defense, adds the following observations:

Rocket weapons with nuclear warheads are indeed terrible weapons both as *regards their striking might and their uninterceptibility*.[5] Whereas, considering modern means of warfare, it is not so difficult to sink a ship at sea, or shoot down aircraft or flying bombs in the air, it is still impossible to destroy a launched ballistic rocket on the wing—it is bound to reach its target. In a modern war—that is, if the imperialists dare to let one loose—massed nuclear blows both at objectives deep in in the rear and at troop groupings in the theaters of hostilities will be of prime importance. We are taking all this into consideration, and since we have powerful modern means of bombardment in the shape of rockets with nuclear warheads, we find it quite possible to reduce the Soviet Armed Forces considerably without impairing our defenses. The reduction of their strength by 1.2 million men is quite a reasonable and timely undertaking.

The rocket troops of our Armed Forces are unquestionably the main arm, but we understand that all the tasks of a war cannot be accomplished by one arm of the service alone. For that reason, and proceeding from the premise that in a modern war as well, combat can be successful only if we have the coordinated application of all means of warfare and the combined effort of all the arms of the service, we shall keep at a definite strength and in the appropriate rational proportions all the arms of our services, which, if called on to fight, will have a pattern of organization and methods of warfare, but little resembling those of the past war. . .

In shaping the policy for the further development of our Armed Forces, in view of the reduction of their strength, we proceed from the point that a future war—if let loose by the aggressors—will be fought by using nuclear weapons *en masse*. We are emphasizing this because very much is now being said and written in the West about a "limited nuclear war," the "tactical use of nuclear weapons," "dosed strategy," the "strategy of intimidation," and so on, and so forth. All these "theories" and "strategies," if one may take the liberty of calling them that, show how much the imperialists fear the inevitable retaliation that will be their lot if they attack the countries of the socialist camp.[6]

It is clear from Malinovsky's statement that the Soviets expect a long-drawn-out conflict. This assumption is supported further by Malinovsky's reference to the need for other arms of the service.

[5] Emphasis added.

[6] U.S.S.R. Embassy in the U.S., Press Department, Release No. 37 (January 25, 1960).

More important still, Soviet military doctrine and the size and composition of the Soviet forces illustrate convincingly the Marshal's arguments. The Soviets are fully aware that we are likely to retain residual nuclear capabilities even if they get in the first blow. Their chances of keeping our residual capabilities to a minimum will decrease as we, in the late sixties, attain a higher degree of invulnerability for our striking forces. The probability of this development, which would dim the Soviet prospects for victory, underscores the critical importance in Soviet calculations of the first years of this decade.

Now let us summarize the main lines of current Soviet strategic thought:

1. The Soviets do not accept the finality of mutual thermonuclear deterrence. They do not believe that one weapon by itself will bring victory in total war. Within a delicate, if temporary, equilibrium, they see the possibility that they can launch their creeping aggressions, consolidate their gains and strive for supremacy in military power.

2. The Soviets do not rule out a surprise thermonuclear exchange if the strategic situation seems to warrant it. They appear to believe that both sides could survive it and that in the end they, the Soviets, will not only survive, but also conquer. In any case, they maintain a military posture consistent with this assumption.

3. The current Soviet propaganda that limited wars can no longer be fought seeks to discourage Free World efforts, feeble as they may be, to fight them. Obviously, the communists, who are fully aware of the intimate relationship between limited and general war, would like to dissuade us from preparing for either.

4. The Soviets are also fully aware that a thermonuclear attack on their homeland will bring heavy damage to the "rear" and to the offensive fighting forces as well.

Both sides must appraise and reappraise what might be the outcome of an all-out thermonuclear exchange against their respective homelands. No matter who or what might start it, the aftermath of such an exchange would be fraught with appalling consequences—but would afford great strategic opportunities. In Soviet doctrine the thermonuclear exchange is merely the most violent but not necessarily the conclusive phase of the conflict. After the thermonuclear phase, the survivors still must slug it out.

It follows that the communists reserve a major role to land armies armed with modern weapons, including tactical nuclear arms. Their land forces are assigned the mission to exploit the thermonuclear chaos and press on to final victory.

Their current military posture bears out their belief that, regardless of casualties from nuclear weapons, they expect the conflict to be consummated by the occupation of hostile territory, by a combination of political and military means. To underscore this point in their literature they have emphasized that since nuclear warfare will mean more casualties, it will be necessary to hold sizable manpower in reserve. No matter how else one might rationalize the communists' intentions, it is difficult to shrug off their preparations for a bitter-end fight with the United States.

Alternate Strategies

U.S. military power should reflect a reasonable degree of readiness to employ armed force to support national policy in a variety of situations. The United States has no excuse for being only partly prepared or for being caught by surprise. We and our allies should be prepared to fight any kind of war that may confront us. This we know. But much controversy centers on the question: What kind of war will we have to fight?

The understandable reluctance of peace-loving men to accept with equanimity the possible consequences of nuclear war has led to a widespread belief that a total war would lead to mutual annihilation of the adversaries, if not of the entire civilized world.

Although all parties to the protracted conflict have dutifully expressed the view that war, especially nuclear war, is "unthinkable," the cold facts are that the U.S. and the U.S.S.R. have both provided themselves with considerable ability to engage in just such a nuclear war. Certainly, it cannot be argued logically that mutual possession of nuclear weapons automatically nullifies nuclear war or even that it assures a durable stalemate. It stands to reason that, if we want to preserve the right to work out our own way of life and we intend to advance the cause of freedom, we must be willing and able, *in extremis,* to apply the most powerful weaponry that we have at our command. We cannot prevail against an opponent who is willing to employ weapons which we refrain from using—even when our basic values are in jeopardy. If we should elect to abstain from nuclear warfare under all circumstances, the most rational course would appear to be not to fight at all, but surrender on the most advantageous terms.[7]

But if we choose to stand, our agenda will include at least the following items:

1. Security of the North American base and the survival of its peoples.
2. Maintenance of Free World positions in the regions along the periphery of the Sino-Soviet bloc.
3. Control of the seaways, the airways and outer space.

These are our minimum objectives. We must seek to attain them, even at the risk of general nuclear war. Such a war *is* "thinkable." Let us, therefore, not succumb to popular misconceptions about the nuclear holocaust. Two among these are the most misleading: According to the first, or "short war" concept, the initial nuclear exchange will result in the capitulation of one side or the other, and the unopposed occupation of the defeated nation's territory by the power which "wins." According to the second, the nuclear holocaust is militarily impractical and will never happen. Implicit in both these notions is a resigned acceptance that any plans to survive the nuclear exchange and fight on are futile. Both these extreme views are counsels of despair. The first is not based on the calculus of probability, and the second, in addition to being self-defeating, is nonsensical.

A thermonuclear war can occur in any of several ways. If it does, it may give rise to the ascendancy of one power. This predominance would not, however, be established indisputably by the massive nuclear exchange; it could be wrung from a long and bitter struggle which would call forth the utmost effort of both sides. In this awesome contest all forms of military power, including surviving strategic nuclear forces, conventional forces and unconventional forces would battle for the ultimate decision. Quite conceivably, the final victory might actually fall to a nonbelligerent simply because in the aftermath of nuclear conflict a nonbelligerent might attain superiority as a result of the mutual attrition of the superpowers.

How erroneous is the notion that war has become "unthinkable"

[7] See Bertrand Russell, *Common Sense and Nuclear Warfare,* New York: Simon & Schuster, 1959. The author's arguments are impeccable—provided we accept his explicit (and implicit) premises.

can be shown by a simple arithmetic exercise.

1. Let us assume a war in the style of World War II, but in which ten-kiloton weapons are used. Suppose this war lasts a thousand days, and suppose every day ten such weapons, or a hundred kilotons, are being employed. As a result there would be exploded by both sides, during the course of the entire war, ten thousand atomic weapons at ten kilotons each, or one hundred megatons. These weapons could conceivably be employed so that this amount of nuclear fission would not necessarily cause staggering losses among the civilian population. Losses from fallout would be minimized, hence casualties would not necessarily be much greater than the losses sustained in some of the wars of modern times.

2. Let us assume a war of heavy nuclear exchanges. Suppose two belligerents fight a "strategic" air war and both have five thousand megatons to spend. Side A strikes first at the homeland of Side B with all its weapons, but is unable to conceal the launching preparations. Consequently, Side B is alerted and launches all its weapons before its bases are hit. Under the circumstances, neither belligerent can destroy any delivery vehicles on the bases, and the delivery vehicles pass each other en route. Each side launches and receives five thousand megatons and a total of ten thousand megatons has been expended within a relatively short time. Assuming that the population on both sides is more or less unprepared; that air defenses are equally ineffective; that the time is 1961-1963; and that size of territory, likely target locations, population densities, and other geographic factors resemble those of the United States and the Soviet Union, respectively, then within sixty days each belligerent will lose anywhere from 45 to 80 per cent of its population. Moreover, other countries will be affected in varying degrees by fallout. Such a war might indeed be considered "unthinkable" if only because the attacker would derive no advantage at all from striking.

3. The situation becomes quite different, however, if the basic assumptions are modified in one particular detail: namely, that A, the attacker, is able to conceal his preparations, and that the defender B receives no warning but is struck unexpectedly. Assume that A can knock out all of B's delivery bases so that B is unable to retaliate. The net result would be that B loses about one-third to three-quarters of his population and his main nuclear force while A

receives not the slightest damage. A war of this type might be not only "thinkable," but even attractive to A since it could gain him a decisive victory without risk of serious loss. If the defender lacks both warning and all other forms of defense, such an outcome is not inconceivable.

This oversimplified case rapidly becomes more complex when factors of warning and defense are added. Warning is a key factor in the calculus of nuclear warfare. If warning is given, however, to a military force which has a slow "reaction time" and which is protected by neither air defense, mobility, concealment nor hardening, advance notice would not save a country unprepared for nuclear war.

4. Let us consider now the case in which B maintains an airborne alert and has hardened some of his missile sites, so that despite the punishment of an initial attack without warning, he still has about five hundred megatons for retaliation. The following typical possibilities exist:

a. A delivers four thousand megatons. He causes a population loss of 40 per cent and uses his residual one thousand megatons as a deterrent (a blackmail threat) by telling the defender B that if he delivers his five hundred megatons, a second volley will be launched. It is possible that under such a threat, B will desist even though A's threatened volley might not do too much additional damage. Yet, by giving up now, B might be able to save some of his cities and perhaps 10 per cent of his remaining population.

b. B is not deterred by the second strike threat, but launches his residual five hundred megatons. If B's attack falls on A's urban centers, B achieves a casualty rate in A's country somewhere between 5 and 10 per cent, assuming that A has already taken comprehensive defense measures. Thus, A would lose up to 10 per cent versus 50 per cent for B and would evidently win the war. Such a war would be by no means "unthinkable," provided losses approximating 10 per cent are acceptable to A.

c. As a further variation, let us assume that in addition to the airborne alert which guarantees his five hundred megatons, B receives sufficient warning to launch an additional five hundred megatons. A retaliatory blow of one thousand megatons on A's population would reach the 30 per cent casualty level. It follows that the greater the airborne alert, the faster the reaction time, the stronger the mobile systems, and the more effective the warning, the higher is the megatonnage which a retaliating B can send against A's territory.

Applying these calculations, we can develop a crude, though handy formula for giving A a credible superiority expressed both in megatons and in the number of basic delivery vehicles. First, A could allocate a multiple of the megatons which make up B's fixed systems to destroy B's retaliatory power on the ground. Second, A could keep in reserve a megaton supply which would be a multiple of the maximum retaliatory strike which B could throw against A and which, in addition, would be large enough so that it would inflict, were it directed against undefended population targets, losses at about, let us say, the 80 per cent level. Third, A could maintain defensive weapons systems of sufficient strength so that a large portion of the retaliatory force of B could be intercepted or otherwise militarily neutralized. Fourth, A could maintain an additional reserve for the completion of world conquest. The purpose intended by this simple model of how to calculate "superiority" is not to figure how much stronger an attacker's force must be, but rather to illustrate the decisive role of superiority in the conceivable outcome of a nuclear war.

There is, of course, a great deal the defender can do in order to avoid being entrapped in a hopeless strategic situation. Besides obvious steps, such as technologically improved defense systems and protection of the population, the problem boils down to maintaining numerical superiority in terms of megatons and protected delivery vehicles of such magnitude that even if the attacker expended his entire stockpile, a strong residual force would be left for retaliatory purposes. On this basis, the defender in the hypothetical case above should contrive, by a variety of means, to preserve a retaliatory force of about five thousand megatons and make it known that the attacker must anticipate that, even in case of initial success, the defender's delivery systems can overwhelm him. This rationale furnishes a sound though rudimentary basis for determining the second-strike requirements that circumstances have placed upon the United States for the early 1960's.

The inherent potentialities of surprise attack with nuclear weapons are far greater than the offensive capabilities of any previous weapons system. Nonetheless, the strategic capabilities of the defensive, too, have increased. The defender can develop a posture that is convincing enough to deter the would-be attacker from deciding upon aggression as a rational course of action.

Certainly, the problem is far more complex and its solutions more sophisticated than can be inferred from our generalized models. Yet the basic point made here seems valid. The possible outcomes of "strategic" nuclear conflict cannot be computed strictly in statistical values of megatonnage and percentages of population destroyed. There are many other factors, including the man who shrinks from pressing the button of all-out nuclear war, no matter how favorable the mathematical chances of success may be. Individual idiosyncrasies notwithstanding, the omnipresence of nuclear weapons has *not* eliminated completely either armed conflict, in general, or all-out nuclear war, in particular, as instruments of national policy by either the U.S. or the U.S.S.R., nor can they ever do so.

The prospects of a general nuclear war are so tremendous that the United States has made the deterrence of such a conflict a primary goal of its policy. Deterrence, if it exists at all, is the result of moral, political, economic and military dispositions designed to discourage a potential opponent from initiating war or committing other acts inimical to one's own interests. Deterrence[8] at any given moment is not an absolute condition, but the current state of mind of an adversary. This (intended) state of mind hinges on an estimate of opposing potential strength. Deterrence requires credibility and communicability. Moreover, both sides must arrive at an identical calculus of strategic devices. Deterrence, for all its merits, is too speculative and too negative a concept to make up the whole of United States military policy.

We do not *know* whether the communists will launch a concerted politico-military drive against the Free World or will be deterred by our strategic posture. We do know what they have

[8] See Herman Kahn's useful definition of deterrence in "The Nature and Feasibility of War and Deterrence," *American Strategy for the Nuclear Age*, W. F. Hahn and John C. Neff, editors; New York: Doubleday, Anchor, 1960, pp. 219-238. Kahn distinguishes three types of deterrence. The first of these, *Type 1*, is deterrence against direct attack; *Type 2* is defined as using strategic threats to deter an enemy from engaging in very provocative attacks other than a direct attack on the United States itself; *Type 3* refers to those acts that are deterrents because the potential aggressor is afraid that the defender or others will take limited military or nonmilitary actions that will make the aggression unprofitable.

done, what they have not done, and what they appear capable of doing.

Our strategic retaliatory capacity may or may not have been instrumental in deterring all-out war, yet it has not blocked the communists from committing indirect aggression. Deterrence is credible so long as the communists are convinced that a surprise nuclear attack will not be decisive at the strategic level and that we can successfully deal with lesser conflict situations without the employment of disproportionate force. Furthermore, the communists must be convinced that politico-military adventures beyond major thresholds court the danger of the U. S. resorting to general nuclear war. Such an American aggregate capability must be real—so real that the communists cannot labor under any misapprehension about it. Such a capability cannot be purchased cheaply.

Strategies of deterrence of nuclear war are in reality strategies for waging general nuclear war. It is only by devising *operationally* effective forces that we will have at hand at the crucial moment adequate deterrent forces. Thus, we must test our strategies to insure that we have not left a gap that invites attack.

Strategy must be an integral part of policy; hence strategy for general war also determines the strategy for lesser wars if only by derivation. In 1960, five strategies for war were being debated by the experts.[9] A sixth strategy may be around the corner—a strategy for arms control. Perhaps one of the greatest gaps in our present posture and thinking is the lack of a coherent strategy for arms control or mutual arms stabilization (cf. "Security Through Arms Control?," Chapter 9). Disarmament requires a mutual trust which does not exist; arms control requires a mutual fear of unwanted wars of annihilation. If the Soviet Union really fears an accidental war, or a war by miscalculation, the Kremlin may be ready to seek agreement on how to limit or control armaments. The United States has declared its willingness to reach such an agreement provided it is meshed with a foolproof inspection system. It is doubtful that the

[9] This section is a highly condensed version of selected research memoranda by Richard B. Foster of Stanford Research Institute. Mr. Foster's analysis of the actual strategies being debated in and among the various services is reflected in the work of the RAND Corporation strategists, particularly Herman Kahn's *Nature and Feasibility of War and Deterrence.* (Princeton University Press, 1960), and Harry Rowen's Study Number 18 for the Joint Economic Committee, 1960.

TABLE I
Strategies for War
1960-1970

Strategy and Objectives	Offense	Defense	Other Forces
1. Finite (No Win)	2nd Strike Only* Counter Value	Little Defense	Add Limited War Forces
2. Balanced (Survival)	Same as #1 + Some Counterforce†	Add Defense Including Fallout	Same as #1, but Adds More Limited War Forces
3. Counterforce Pre-emptive ("Crippled" Win 1st Strike)	Same as #2 + 1st Strike CF	Same as #2 Add More Defense	Subtract Some Limited War Forces From #2
4. Counterforce Preventive ("Central War" Win 1st Strike)	Same as #3 + "Splendid" 1st Strike CF	Same as #3	Same as #3, but Subtract Virtually All Limited War Forces
5. Counterforce (Win 2nd Strike)	Same as #4 + "Splendid" 2nd Strike CF	Same as #3 + "Splendid" Defense	Same as #2, but Adds Forces to Exploit Win on 2nd Strike (e.g. Occupation Forces)

*Counter Value = attack against cities
†Counterforce = attack against strike forces

NOTE: #1–#4 assume no-win (or survival at best) following SU first strike. #5 requires a win following SU first strike.

Soviets would concur, for military secrecy in a closed society still endows them with a significant advantage over the U.S.

Five Strategies

Table I lists the five strategies which the United States might adopt in the pursuit of national security.

The first, the strategy of the "finite deterrent," envisages a "no-win" situation. In effect, it is a mutual suicide pact. Its tool is an invulnerable second-strike force that can smash the attacker's cities. It is weighted on the side of offense. It is good only for the defense of the homeland since it renounces the use of intercontinental thermonuclear weapons as instruments of foreign policy. It may have the same effect as nuclear disarmament, because no longer can we use the threat of taking the initiative in general nuclear war for the defense of freedom. It assigns to forces other than general nuclear war forces the task of supporting diplomacy; it is the opposite of "massive retaliation." This strategy underrates the complexities of "limited war"; it underestimates the strength of the nuclear "lid" needed to keep limited wars limited; it makes no provision for the employment of NATO forces. It provides almost no defense of the continental United States.

Furthermore, a "mutual suicide pact" requires two signatories. If both parties were agreed, they could preserve the *status quo.* Both sides now lack adequate defense against nuclear attack. Can we be sure that—pact or no pact—one side or the other will not upset the *status quo*? The Soviet Union might develop an effective system of military and civil defense against nuclear attack. One of the uncertainties in the next decade is the possibility that the balance of power will be upset by growth of defensive power, e.g., anti-missile missiles. Defense includes both active and passive defense measures for civil population, industry, military targets, command centers and control centers. We have some evidence that the Soviets have initiated a workable civil defense program for the protection of their people, especially against fallout. They are almost certainly working on antimissile systems. All single defense systems are imperfect, but their aggregate may be formidable enough to upset the balance of power. This is the fatal weakness of a strategy based upon a "mutual suicide pact" especially when neither of the signatories to the pact trusts the other.

The objective of the next strategy, the "balanced deterrent," is minimum national survival following a first Soviet blow. This strategy is based upon the assumption that we will accept the first strike and, just as in the case of the finite deterrent, be able to level unacceptable damage on the Soviet Union. Proponents of this strategy rely, as do those of the first strategy, upon limited-war forces as principal instruments of policy. But contrary to the finite deterrent strategists, they stress continental defense and the maintenance of an offense-defense balance, including civil defense against fallout. When we retaliate, we do so not only against cities (countervalue) but also against military forces (counterforce), as, for example, against Soviet armies approaching Western Europe. This strategy, too, begs the question of keeping limited wars within bounds.

The third strategy, the "pre-emptive counterforce deterrent," extends the deterrent to defend our major allies. Under this concept, in a state of extreme tension—for example, a major Soviet attack on a NATO ally—we would strike first, and disarm the Soviet Union. We would threaten to strike Soviet cities, but we would spare them, holding them in hostage instead. Simultaneously, we would defend our military force, our cities and our population against the Soviet second strike. As in the balanced deterrent, the emphasis rests on an offense-defense balance. Defense includes fallout shelters as well as active intercept systems.

The requirements of this strategy are more demanding than those of the second, not to speak of the first. Our intercontinental strike force must be considerably larger than the Soviets'. Only then will we be able to destroy the enemy's retaliatory system. Because of problems such as reliability and accuracy, it would take probably *at least* two of our missiles to knock out one of theirs—depending on how accurate and reliable was our missile, and how "hard" or invulnerable their sites were. But even with two missiles for one, we could not destroy all of the adversary's missiles. We must expect the adversary would fire some at us. Therefore, we require defense. A first U.S. strike possibility would not be credible to a Soviet planner, to our Western European allies, or to ourselves if the Soviets could return our attack with several hundred ICBM's and wipe out perhaps fifty American cities. This is the strategy of a "hard" country, one that has the intestinal fortitude to move right to the brink of nuclear war and to leap in order to make good its nuclear threat. Given such a will, that country could chance reduction of its limited-war forces below the requirements of the second strategy.

The fourth strategy—the strategy of "preventive war"—has lost most of its supporters. The United States has abjured it as a policy because it cannot be reconciled with traditional American ethics, its utility from the standpoint of pure deterrence notwithstanding. The capability to strike the Soviets by surprise at any time and to disarm them would relieve us, at least theoretically, from the pain of maintaining limited-war forces. The distinction must be made between a capability to wage preventive war and a policy decision to launch a disarming strike. We are opposed rightly to the willful strike but not to the possession of the capability to punish aggression. The plenitude of power required for waging preventive war would counsel the Soviets against any type of provocation or probing action. The United States could thus pursue a blocking strategy if it possessed the capability of initiating a surprise nuclear attack.

A policy of preventive war, however, is anathema to our sense of values. Moreover, a preventive war must be launched by surprise; preparations for it must be made in secret. The open societies of the West practically rule out such a policy choice. The question can be raised, however, whether it is wise to advertise our reluctance to strike first regardless of circumstances. The open rejection of this option limits the versatility of our political action and hands the initiative to the adversary.

A clear distinction should be made between the terms "preventive war" and "pre-emptive war." The first signifies that war is sooner or later inevitable and that the enemy should be taken by surprise after all preparations have been made. The second assumes that the enemy will be prevented from launching an attack at the moment he is about to strike.

Whether or not the United States will decide against waging pre-emptive war will depend only *in part* on a decision made many years in advance. It will *also* depend on whether or not the pressure of events forces a deliberate or, more likely, an improvised revision of this decision. It is extremely doubtful that a government, once it deems war inevitable, will stick stolidly to a decision made in more secure periods to desist from preventive war. It is even more unlikely that public opinion, aroused to the inevitability of war, will insist that for the sake of consistency, the enemy should be allowed to strike first.

The fifth strategy—the strategy of "win strike second"—is our current official position: We make our bid to win after we have absorbed the Soviet Union's first strike. Thus, we must strike back with counterforce; hold communist bloc cities in hostage; mobilize what is left of our nation; free our allies and the satellites; and seize and occupy the Soviet Union and Red China.

This is the American ideal strategy. It is sound morally—and it may be sound militarily as we approach the late sixties and a higher degree of invulnerability in strategic retaliatory force. What is our concept of the war we would have to fight if this strategy were executed? What is required to carry it out in numbers of ICBM's of all kinds, high-speed supersonic aircraft, defense organization, command of the sea and deployed forces for the defense of forward areas? As of now, we do not have the means adequate for this concept, but can we ever have them? As the missile age comes along, we need active defense not only against aircraft, but also against ballistic missiles.

Strategies two through five include a military requirement for civil defense, particularly fallout shelters. It is well nigh impossible to see how this country can stand up to Soviet nuclear blackmail unless the people of the United States are protected. What is rather contemptuously called "civil defense" is an indispensable element in military strategy.

Areas of Agreement Among Strategists

While it is known that discord on strategy has been rife among the Army, the Navy and the Air Force, we should explore the areas of agreement among them. First, all agree that we must maintain a stable deterrent posture and a mix of military forces which will hold down to an infinitesimal minimum the chance of war by accident or miscalculation. Second, all agree that we must maintain a second-strike force which is invulnerable and capable of inflicting unacceptable damage on the Soviet Union. Third, all agree that the design of this force cannot center upon a single weapon but must embrace mixed forces, offensive and defensive, and a balanced strategic doctrine. They are in agreement that no one weapon by itself will solve the problem of deterrence, for every single weapon has its own unique deficiency that might be exploited by an enemy.

Perhaps the most important proposition on which concurrence has been reached is that, in the nuclear ballistic missile era, a strategy of "Fortress America" is no longer realistic, if it ever was.

All agree that there is an absolute requirement not only for defending the main base of the Free World but also of defending forward areas and approach routes. They agree that our alliances must be kept together and strengthened and widened wherever possible. None can abide the thought of a world in which the Russians have forcibly occupied Western Europe and placed its economy in the service of the Kremlin's power apparatus. The combined economic power of the U.S.S.R., Eastern Europe and Western Europe would constitute an industrial, scientific and manpower base greater than our own. If the Soviets were to conquer Western Europe, then the rest of the world would almost certainly fall under Soviet hegemony. In the nuclear age, it would be impossible to defend the United States, the last major bastion of freedom, in a hostile world.

Finally, nearly all agree that we must continue working hard on the problem of Continental defense. Even the "finite deterrent" advocates are not entirely in agreement among themselves on the wisdom of a "no-defense" posture. Many of the leading "finite deterrent" strategists consider it a military necessity that strategy be supported by an informed public opinion. To support our military strategy in times of crisis, our people must know that they are in danger and that they must prepare to defend themselves against the effect of nuclear weapons.

Despite some discussion of the above alternative strategies, we as a nation, in fact, have in recent years adopted a "mutual suicide pact" posture by default. We lack the forces needed to replace the so-called "massive retaliation" policy. What are the policy implications of this mutual suicide posture? Adoption of this strategy has profound effect upon the diplomatic, political, psychological and economic policies of the nation. Let us demonstrate this by tracing postwar trends in the balance of power.

In the early postwar years after 1945, we had a monopoly of atomic weapons and means of delivering them; we were in the posture of strategy number five, or "win strike second." The Soviets did not have anything with which to strike us first, and we could strike them and win. As the Soviets acquired a few atomic weapons, we gradually went to a pre-emptive war posture (strategy number three), but we still had a great many more deliverable weapons and a great military superiority for general nuclear war, between about 1950 and 1955. Between about 1956 and 1960, we passed through the balanced deterrent posture (strategy number two) to the point where many U. S. students of strategy recommend the adoption of the finite deterrent, or the "mutual suicide pact." In other words we have essentially gone, in only fifteen years, from a position of dominant strength to a position of, at best, nuclear parity based on the threat of mutual annihilation. This history of the change in our strategic posture from 1945 to 1960 is astounding. Never before in history has a balance of power shifted so rapidly.

It is entirely possible that the Soviets are moving in the opposite direction, that is, they may adopt the posture of strategy two, balanced deterrent, having as their objective assured survival of the communist base. More likely than not, they are striving for the posture of strategy three—to win by being prepared to strike first. None of the possibilities can be summarily ruled out. Morality—a decent respect for the opinions of mankind—has never dissuaded the Soviets from venturing upon aggression when aggression did not risk effective retaliation.

We appear to be adopting, without a real national debate on its implications, a single strategy, that of "finite deterrence"—an essentially "no defense" posture based on the assumption that any nuclear war will result in mutual suicide. In the early 1960's, it will provide us with a slim but decreasing margin of safety. There is a widening breach between our announced policies and our low-cost strategic posture. In the long run, we must strive toward strategy five, working as rapidly as possible away from strategy one—a nihilistic strategy at best. The cost would be great—but if we desire security, we must be prepared to pay a higher price.

The capability to counterblock decisively in a general nuclear war is synonymous with the capability to absorb the first blow. If it is possible to devise an effective strategy and forces which allow us to concede the initiative to the adversary, then that strategy patently guarantees our safety and the best interests of the Free World.

Such a military strategy provides the base for grand policy four discussed in Chapter 2. It provides a mix of offense/defense forces for general nuclear war and a balance of *general* and *limited* war forces, and provides the flexibility required to take the diplomatic initiative. It is not a "cheap" military posture. But, in the long run, it is less costly than the costs of retreat and defeat in the protracted conflict, not to speak of the cost of all-out war. The future remains uncertain whatever we do. Hence, wars of different types, including total war, remain an ever-present possibility, and we must learn to live with and provide against persistent, extreme danger.

General Nuclear War Ingredients

Our inquiry now turns to the requirements of a strategy which will insure our survival in a general war.

In the next decade the balance between offense and defense will be determined by the interaction of several basic factors. These include the various elements of the offensive striking forces; the effectiveness of the measures employed to protect the offensive forces of each side; the measures designed to protect civilian populations; active defense against enemy missiles, aircraft and various other launching vehicles (e.g., submarines); and, finally, the effectiveness of combined warning and command control systems designed to co-ordinate both defensive and offensive capabilities.

The interaction of these factors will change as new weapons and new defensive devices are introduced into the arsenals of each side. It is doubtful whether either we or the communists have thought through the complex relationships of these factors. On the strength of available evidence, it is possible to conclude that the offense is not likely to retain indefinitely its present overwhelming superiority. It is, however, even less likely that the United States could *win,* let alone survive, a nuclear war unless it developed a comprehensive defense scheme. Even if we were to adopt a "first-strike" strategy, we could never be certain of destroying all of the enemy's retaliatory force. Thus, even were we to strike first, we could expect to receive a severe retaliatory blow. In short, we cannot possibly defend Continental America by relying solely on a massive offensive delivery system. Furthermore, a first-class defensive capability shields America and her allies against nuclear blackmail. A Communist China, armed with several dozens of submarines capable of launching nuclear missiles or, let us say, with one hundred ICBM's, might hold a large segment of our population as hostage if we continue to ignore the problem of defense. Only a comprehensive defense system will deter a hostile nuclear power from taking advantage of our deep-rooted desire to preserve life at all costs.

A strong defense posture will provide the necessary base for a flexible political strategy. Last, but not least, an anti-nuclear defense "shield" will enhance greatly the credibility of our retaliatory strategy. Since any nuclear war is likely to involve a two-sided exchange, military planners must be concerned with maximizing the level of damage done to the enemy and minimizing the level of damage done to their own country. Effective defense eases greatly the problem of *when* and *how* to attack. Thus, one side might decide to launch its attack upon enemy targets at night when defense is most difficult, and then be prepared to receive the enemy's counter-blows during daytime when defense systems are more effective.

Is an effective defense possible in the nuclear age? Before the advent of the atomic bomb the history of war was the history of clashing offensive and defensive weapons systems. For example, during World War I the defense achieved superiority over offense with the machine gun. The result was a stalemate that lasted three years and cost millions of casualties on the Western Front. The development of new weapons combined with new tactics, i.e., the tank and airplane, contributed to restoring, in 1918, the superiority of the offense. The offense achieved still further gains in World War II, as air power came into its own. The immense increase in firepower brought about by the advent of air-nuclear delivery capabilities in 1945 seemed to usher in a period of unquestioned superiority of the offense. But the superiority of this "ultimate weapon" is now being challenged by nuclear antiaircraft missiles. The belief that aircraft capable of delivering nuclear explosives could always be able to penetrate to targets died hard. Moreover, after fifteen years of research and development it is now clear that highly effective missile defense systems against manned aircraft are well within the realm of the possible. Ground-to-ground missiles, such as ICBM's, pose a far more difficult defense problem than manned aircraft. But this should not be taken to mean that, in the long run, defense against missiles is impossible.

In order to design an effective capability for waging war, we must take steps along the following lines:

First, we need a basic deterrent posture, i.e., invulnerable offensive forces for second-strike attack on the U.S.S.R. Invulnerability implies that we decide what kind of residual capability we need to implement our strategy and then make certain that at least this percentage of our retaliatory force will be safe even after we have absorbed the first blow. Essential to this posture are: (1) liquid- and solid-propelled missiles of global range; (2) jet bombers and, subsequently, supersonic jets; (3) nuclear submarines; (4) unmanned aircraft; (5) nuclear propelled aircraft; and (6) space systems for reconnaissance, warning, communication and possibly defense. For the sake of rendering the U. S. striking force invulnerable, and thus commensurately strengthening the deterrent, our intercontinental missiles should be either highly mobile or protected by structures able to withstand extremely high pressures (over several hundred pounds per square inch).

Secondly, we need an active defense system with two key components. The first, defense against aircraft, must be highly invulnerable to neutralization by ballistic missile attack. If we fail to develop such a system, high-speed enemy bombers with multiple bombs will be able to penetrate the air space over our territory at will. The second component is active defense against enemy missiles. For the decade of the 1960's, the fairest promise of a defense of this type is that offered by Nike-Zeus, a so-called terminal defense system which shoots ground-to-air missiles armed with nuclear warheads up the trajectory of the incoming missile. Interception of the enemy's missile is achieved well above the earth's surface. Yet we should not place all of our hopes in one system, as good as it may be. Research and development on other anti-missile systems should be pushed.

Thirdly, we need to be able to defend vital areas overseas, particularly Western Europe. This requirement involves our ability to command the seas and possess effective local surface and air forces.[10]

[10] Since the United States is a continental island in the geopolitical sense, we cannot afford to take command of the seas for granted. Conventional naval forces continue to be a key instrument of U.S. policy in the protracted conflict, especially in confrontations where a precise lower level of military pressure is needed on the continental rimlands. The role of these forces, the versatility with which they can be used in cold and limited war situations, and the extent of their "reach" when coupled with tactical air forces, have often been underestimated by military analysts. Naval forces must be modernized and maintained at a level which will insure rapid transportation of ground forces and equipment, open lines of communications, and continuing logistics support to our forces overseas and our allies, as well as a sharpened capability for limited confrontations in the rimland areas.

Fourth, we must be able to provide secure communications in case of attack to assure the continuity of governmental operations, the control of our military forces and the co-ordination of our civil defense effort. A dependable and invulnerable multiloop communications and control system should include strategic and tactical warning nets.

Fifth, we need to develop extensive defense measures for the protection of our population against fallout. Such measures will involve the relocation of our offensive striking forces, i.e., removing them as far as possible from the principal centers of population density. They will require the building of shelters properly equipped and stockpiled with food, medical supplies and other necessities, a monitoring service for the purpose of identifying areas of high radioactive contamination, and equipment for the rapid decontamination of such areas.

Sixth, we urgently need a stockpiling program appropriate to the needs of nuclear war. Such a program will assure us the requisite mobilization capability for postattack recovery. The United States has not even begun to think seriously about the necessity for providing an adequate postattack mobilization base. Apparently, the public at large harbors the illusion that the outcome of a nuclear war will be *decided* in the first few hours of general nuclear exchanges. The communists, as we have seen, do not appear to subscribe to the short war theory.

Short-Term Requirements

At least until the middle sixties, most of the Free World's nuclear punch will be carried by aircraft. Missile development is ahead of forecasts; but even a heavy increase in budgets will not replace, for some time to come, aircraft with missiles. The Soviet Union seems to have advanced faster toward the substitution of missile systems for aircraft, but even there the capability of aircraft delivery is likely to remain substantial for the next few years. The megatons deliverable by Soviet Bison and Bear aircraft may still exceed those deliverable by ICBM's. The race for missile superiority holds public attention. Both sides, however, will experience a recurring, indeed a permanent, need for aircraft delivery in order to strike at *mobile* launching systems and other mobile targets, and, last but not least, to deal with unforeseeable circumstances. To put it differently, the more the United States relies on the mobile Polaris and Minuteman, the more necessary it is for the Soviet Union to retain effective bomber forces as part of its own striking power. Both sides will have to rely on aircraft for poststrike reconnaissance missions to determine the damage done to targets, for air surveillance may be a vital factor in determining the residual capabilities of the enemy following a strategic nuclear exchange. Such craft will have to pit themselves against increasingly sophisticated and effective defense systems.

The immediate requirements for stopgap measures which will block the communist bid for a clear military superiority call for expenditures of several billions of dollars over and above the defense budget of 1961. Specific short-term programs include an airborne alert; improved U. S. air defense; accelerated development of antimissile systems, and production of Nike-Zeus; stepped-up ICBM development, production and deployment; the construction of fallout shelters by federal and state governments; intensified antisubmarine programs; strengthening and hardening of U. S. and overseas bases; modernization of surface-battle weapon systems; establishment of a rational "mobilization" base capable of functioning after a nuclear strike; development and production of supersonic aircraft like the B-70; accelerated research and development for nuclear-propelled aircraft, nuclear ram-jet engines, and short-range space systems; a genuine sharing of nuclear weapons with our allies; and the incorporation of some chemical weapons into the military arsenal for tactical purposes.

Only immediate action will tide the U. S. over the incipient period of extreme danger in the early sixties. Half-measures will not solve all the military problems of an effective Forward Strategy; but they will redress at least the power balance and rescue the U. S. from its present predicament. Such measures will also help to change the psychological mood of the Free World. The belief that the world military balance is tipping against the U. S. is at the root of many of our external problems.

In exploiting his nuclear missile systems, the attacker possesses one advantage of overwhelming importance—he is the master of his timing. He can choose at what time he wishes to strike, while the defender must be ready to fight back at any and all times, which presumably would not be of his own choosing. Strategic timing is a matter of years. For example, the aggressor may decide to attack sometime in 1968. Tactical timing is concerned with scheduling the attack itself: the most vital targets may be struck at 4:00 A.M. Then again, an attack might be launched at that time of the day when an infrared satellite warning system gives the least reliable warning; or on a Sunday; or when bad weather diminishes visibility; or when radio communications are disturbed by sunspot activity. The instantaneous characteristics of solid-fueled missiles, to cite a specific factor, would render such timing decisions increasingly practicable for the attacker.

The measures to counter this advantage of the attacker would include—in addition to superior warning, intelligence and counterintelligence—the dispersal and hardening of bases; concealment and mobility; electronic countermeasures; and interference with enemy delivery systems. The fixed, hardened and dispersed ICBM and other projected land-, sea- or air-based delivery systems and space systems all stress different characteristics that would make up a mix to counteract enemy timing and increase the security of our strategic strike forces. No single weapon can do it alone.

Right now, however, the United States is still in the throes of the revolution in warfare. The question "who is ahead?" in the arms race is not particularly relevant. The answer may be whoever strikes first. This rejoinder is not comforting, since it is unlikely, as we have said, that the U. S. would launch a preventive strike. Even worse, a "soft" retaliatory system combined with an unprotected urban population may tempt the enemy in the midst of a crisis situation to destroy both (e.g., a "soft" system might be provocative because the Soviets would know that we had to use it quickly for fear we would be preempted). While the alarming vulnerability of our "soft" system has duly impressed some of our political and military leaders, not nearly enough has been done to make our second-strike retaliatory system secure.

Hardening of dispersed ICBM bases might prove effective against what might be called near-misses; but a close hit on a "hardened" site could throw out of kilter the none too rugged guidance system of the ICBM. But since the attacker must strike a hardened site with several missiles more or less simultaneously and accurately, the price of aggression is boosted by hardening. Furthermore, a "hardened" land-based missile offers the additional advantages of larger warheads and more reliable command control than do the Polaris or mobile ICBM or IRBM's. Unquestionably, a degree of hardening is worth the cost—but the cost is now high and bound to increase. ICBM's and IRBM's which can be concealed during the preparation for attack and fired rapidly are ideal weapons for strategic surprise assaults. However, large as these advantages of the ballistic missile may be, they are far from conclusive. In the first place, the attacker might not succeed in firing in one volley the necessary number of missiles within the critical few minutes. A tardy missile keeps one enemy target operational for the time of this delay. Consequently, the longer the delay of the first strike, the more devastating might be the retaliation. It is more difficult to achieve volley —or "time on target"—capabilities with missiles using liquid fuels than with solid propellants.

Secondly, even if the thrust of the missile is strong—in which case it is more unwieldy, very expensive, and requires liquid fuels —the yield of the ICBM warhead, other things being equal, tends to be smaller than the yield of an aircraft-launched bomb. But, on the other hand, it is much more difficult to intercept the ICBM. Without further nuclear testing, this very basic weakness probably cannot be overcome. Soviet ICBM's possess stronger thrusts than their U. S. counterparts; hence missile for missile they should have a larger yield. Thus, superior thrust would benefit a Soviet surprise attack. More thrust is tantamount to larger warheads.

ICBM's cannot be recalled: once on their way, the war is on. Furthermore, they are not so effective against mobile targets, unless they are coupled with a rapid target-locating system, which may be impossible to develop for some targets. Therefore, they are not ideal weapons to use against cruising submarines, mobile missile sites and troops on the move. If they hit close enough, however, they can ruin the instrumentation of a mobile missile or cause heavy troop casualties. Then, too, since current models of ICBM's fly along a ballistic curve and cannot take evasive action, they may prove sooner or later to be considerably more vulnerable to active defenses than they are at present.

In brief, hardened ICBM systems, although indispensable weapons in any strategic arsenal, may serve best a state intent upon striking the first blow. A nation that prefers to strike second will have to build them in greater quantity. It could, of course, enlarge its mobile land- or water-based missile systems; but the presently existing and working ones do not carry enough megatonnage to deliver in all cases the requisite retaliatory punch unless we have them in abundance. Lack of punch is not their only weakness. Another one is lesser accuracy, and then there is the problem of strategic control. Shore-to-ship communications, for example, might fail at the zero hour.

The submarine IRBM weapons system, incorporating nuclear propulsion with a solid fueled missile, holds great promise. Its advantages include mobility, concealment, remoteness from population and industry, and a fairly high degree of invulnerability that can be increased by using Arctic ice floes as hiding places. In time, this system will be able to reach all major targets anywhere in the world. The submarine itself presently can claim exceptional security because of poorly developed detection techniques; but this advantage may not last indefinitely. From the point of view of dispersion and concealment, the U.S. Polaris system is excellent. Yet the Polaris missile is shorter in range and travels at less speed than the ICBM, and hence might be more vulnerable to antimissile defense, particularly since the system is not capable of firing volleys. The Polaris warhead is not so large as those which can be carried by larger missiles and may remain less accurate. Also, the communications problem of the Polaris system is a formidable one. Thus, the Polaris yield-accuracy "mix" is not adequate for counterforce purposes, especially if the opponent's force is "hardened."

Depending upon deployment on D-Day, submarines and other seagoing weapon carriers might be delayed before going into action against strategic targets. For most practical purposes, Polaris is a countercity and counterindustry weapon. The seaborne Polaris system, however, might well spell, in certain situations, the difference between victory and defeat. Any nuclear exchange between the United States and Russia is likely to be prolonged. Neither side will want to stake its existence on one volley. Neither side will be reluctant to "shoot the works" and see the other emerge victorious because it possesses residual capabilities. It will be necessary, therefore, to have a sure residual capability while we are assessing damages to our opponent. The Polaris sea-based system will provide an excellent force for such purposes. Hence, there is no question that a submarine-based missile force is an indispensable element of any retaliatory capability. The existence of a Polaris submarine fleet would give us a delayed second-strike capability which could be the ace-in-the-hole of an all-out conflict.

There is another system on the horizon which, while so far it has not been developed, offers great promise. Just as the ICBM is the ideal weapon for the would-be aggressor, the nuclear-propelled aircraft which combines rapid mobility over all *land* and *sea* areas with a powerful punch is ideally suited for a second-strike strategy. Nuclear-propelled aircraft can be kept on more effective "permanent" airborne alert than chemically propelled aircraft, and committed to retaliatory missions, could deliver multiple strikes with short-range guided missiles.

The nuclear-propelled aircraft is not free from weaknesses. Since it will be very large, it will be vulnerable. This weakness can be partly offset by a proper choice of altitude; by the plane's wide freedom in selecting tactics and approach routes; and by its cargo carrying capacity, which makes it possible to take along equipment to defend against enemy interception.

It should be added that nuclear propelled aircraft are not the only vehicles that could be powered with nuclear propulsion. The United States has set in motion programs for nuclear-propelled rockets and ramjets. Although nuclear propulsion of all types is a key to the problem of powered flight in space and of carrying big payloads, systems of this kind can be incorporated into various novel types of second-strike capabilities.

Even if such complex second-strike retaliatory systems should be built, the attacker still has a chance to neutralize them, at least partially. The means open to him are to maintain his own second-strike capability which would furnish a counterdeterrent; effective air and missile defenses; and effective civil defense, including rapid evacuation and suitable shelters.

Technological moves and countermoves will continue through many successive cycles: each advance will be followed, or accompanied by, a neutralizing advance that will provoke a countermove. The U.S. position, at any one time, in defense and offense, is not an absolute, for the dynamics of military technology and strategy force us to jockey continuously for position.

In this technological war-of-maneuver, the exploration of space probably presents an enormous challenge to American security. The ability to exploit space through various kinds of satellite vehicles rapidly is becoming an indispensable element of missile warfare.

Space vehicles will provide fast and dependable warning and reconnaissance systems. Furthermore, space vehicles will probably play an important role in future antimissile defense and, as we have already suggested, could carry nuclear warheads. Thus, second-strike forces may be located in cislunar space—and, obviously, many more possibilities of using space for military purposes will become apparent in time, particularly when man achieves powered flights in space. Among these might be the establishment of bases on the moon and the exploration of translunar space. Whether or not these developments will have military signficance cannot be determined at this time.

Space vehicles could pierce the Iron Curtain—there are no walls in outer space—and play the role of detectives in an arms control system. Above all, space vehicles may prove to be the technical means for opening closed societies. It follows that our security will depend on the development of such space systems—and possibly other systems for defending them and counteracting Soviet developments in this area.

If the United States is to come out ahead in a contest which ranges from the bottom of the sea to the dark side of the moon, we must continue effective "counters" and initiatives that keep the opponent off balance, and develop the requisite systems faster, and better, than he. Next to brains and will power, the decisive factor will be our over-all technical and industrial capacity. It would be a travesty of history should the U.S. and the Free World be caught short on wit, will and ware.

The United States, having publicly foregone the option of striking the enemy first, must develop a secure capability to strike second. Strategic defenses, both active and passive, invest a second strike with credibility. This is the first and fundamental requirement which should govern all other considerations in such a strategy.

The outcome of a first strike against a defenseless nation can be calculated with a relatively high degree of accuracy. Respectable defenses introduce important uncertainties in the enemy's calculations. His safety factors must be increased; hence his force requirements mount. This is far more important than the question of how many interceptions a given defense system can achieve.

Formidable defenses are significant for yet another reason that is often overlooked. While it is true that we have been in a military cycle in which defenses have lagged behind offensive capabilities, both the United States and, more aggressively, the Soviet Union are seeking a "breakthrough" in the techniques of strategic defense. The prevailing pessimism—or rather, indifference—that now seems to dog a vigorous approach to the development of an effective U.S. air defense plays into the hands of the enemy. If the latter's defense were to prove effective, and ours not, the resulting imbalance might well spell our defeat. This imbalance, largely dictated by fiscal and *not* technical restraints, could break the back of our national security.

Perhaps the element of strategic defense which can most readily be improved is warning. Development of high-reliability forward and space warning systems, capable of detecting the sorties of ballistic missiles and aircraft, would degrade the effectiveness of a Soviet first strike. The world-wide dispersal of our retaliatory system coupled with a global warning net would place formidable tactical obstacles in the way of a decisive surprise attack.

One purpose of Khrushchev's coexistence strategy is to undermine America's military power by nonmilitary means, particularly by rolling up our base structure overseas. Overseas bases are presently the greatest single advantage which the U.S. has vis-à-vis Soviet Russia in limited conflicts and they are likely to play an important part in our general war posture as well.[11] Limited war requires rapid reaction by sea, air and naval power. Overseas bases make quick reaction possible. Widely scattered, they present the potential enemy with a global war problem of co-ordination difficult to resolve. The diversity of weapons deployed on the overseas bases makes the enemy's defensive problem, like his offensive problem, far more difficult.

The chief danger currently to our overseas bases is—in most cases—danger not of complete elimination by military attack, but of political neutralization. Some we may have to give up, others we may be able to hold. Some of the countries which play host to American bases or military forces fear that they attract Soviet nuclear

[11] For an excellent treatment of the United States base problem see Hanson W. Baldwin, "Kremlin Cloud Over Our Bases," *New York Times Magazine*, October 9, 1960.

strikes. This is offset in some areas, such as Western Europe and Korea, by the morale-building presence of American troops. Developing technology is affecting our base problem: the advent of the ICBM has reduced the offensive importance of overseas bases. Yet technological developments for defending the United States must take advantage of the warning time which distant bases can provide. Politically and psychologically, we can capitalize on the bases we retain. Defensively and psychologically, United States overseas bases are more important than ever in the past. Psychologically, they connote American "presence"—a common sharing of common dangers, a certainty that attack upon one means an attack upon all. Bases are an important part of our strategic retaliatory "mix," and the fact that the Soviets are always leveling broadsides at our base system indicates a healthy respect for their military value.

Civil Defense

A key element in an effective grand strategy in the nuclear age is the nonmilitary defense program. An extensive, well-planned and co-ordinated civil defense program is the most forthright and convincing counter to nuclear blackmail.

The capacity to deliver a second strike embraces both the ability to inflict great damage on the enemy and to ward off heavy damage to one's home. For the foreseeable future, a wide and dangerous gap cleaves our military and nonmilitary preparedness.

Shelters located within metropolitan areas offer the best solution for a large part of our population. It is possible to design shelters which guard against fallout and, within reasonable limits, the immediate effects of nuclear weapons, such as fire and blast. Adequate shelters can reduce exposure to radioactivity by a factor of one thousand. Once built, shelters do not become obsolete; they require, however, perpetual maintenance. The United States has the means and skills to save the bulk of its population in the event of a nuclear war. Such a program would be costly. Yet, of two belligerents armed more or less equally, the one without shelters is the more likely to lose the conflict. Noteworthy is the fact that the Soviet Union has initiated a comprehensive civil defense program.

The attacker, if he is to escape a heavy retaliatory blow, has no choice but to attack the aircraft and missile bases of the defender. This being the case, the defender should, in prudence, place his retaliatory forces at remote distances from urban industrial and population centers, even though the major portion of that force remains based on the home country. At this writing many U.S. installations of great importance are placed in areas of easy access to population and logistical support. We may presume that most of the attacker's weapons will fall within a few miles of our launch pads and the runways, and upon such subsidiary targets as weapons storage and guidance facilities. There is little to be said for U.S. dispositions that offer targets where a large civilian population lives within, say, five to ten miles of the likely ground zeros. For a long time to come large countries like the United States and Canada, whose population densities are relatively low, will be able to disperse effectively their military forces.

Old concepts of strategic bombing, i.e., a preference for industrial targets, are less than helpful in planning for missile war. At present, it is the forces-in-being rather than potentials and industrial capacity that must be the principal targets of both the attack and the defense; this holds certainly for the initial phase of an all-out conflict. This is not to say that the enemy would not, for psychological purposes, strike at industrial complexes and capital cities or that population centers could not be struck by random missiles, nor does it rule out the possibility that begaton and gigaton weapons, once developed, could make hostile populations the prime target of warfare.

The dangers of fallout, because of their psychological ramifications, call for plausible safety measures. Even with little warning, a large portion of the population should be able to take to fallout shelters—if these have been built. The fallout problem will become more manageable for those parts of the population who live at a distance of ten miles or more from the impact areas. For people living twenty to thirty miles distant from the impact area there should be ample time to go into shelters, and in many instances even to improvise additional protection. Fallout is not evenly distributed. Detection instruments, properly located, should allow the population to move to places of lesser contamination. A strategic program that gives realistic regard to civil defense would go a long way toward removing the genocidal implications of nuclear warfare.

No amount of defense will save the entire population. Nevertheless, a large percentage of the people can be given an appreciable measure of protection. The problems of traffic control, public order, public health, food and communication are almost beyond the imagination; but failure to prepare for them would open even more unimaginable and terrible vistas. The task of civilian defense is so important that it must be given greater emphasis and entrusted to hands more capable and better equipped than those to which it has been assigned thus far in the United States. A major responsibility for this task should be assigned to the armed forces. U.S. Army Reserve and National Guard formations could be readily adapted to missions of this type. There hardly seems a more basic or legitimate function of a military establishment than to attend to the distress of its own people in time of disaster. The United Kingdom and Canada have already taken this step.

The development of credible systems which increase the chance of survival and recovery of the U.S. and other members of the Free World might well force the Soviets into so costly an offensive effort as to shelve the idea of a premeditated nuclear attack against the Continental United States.

Recapitulation. In the preceding discussion of general nuclear war, we have attempted to spell out what needs to be done rather than to commend what is commendable in the *status quo*.

It is not a foregone conclusion that massive nuclear attacks would destroy the ability of either side or both sides to go on with the prolonged war. Certainly, they will suffer crippling damage; but life would remain and the issue of survival would still have to be settled. The side which has a stronger mobilization base capable of both resistance and recovery, and which has the firmer resolve —this is the side which will press on to an acceptable outcome.

The outcome of a general nuclear war could be determined by the actions of opposing forces in the battle for Western Europe. So long as the Allies can defend and counterattack in Europe, they should be able to deny the communist rulers their interim objective, the establishment of an Eurasian empire. Consequently, the U.S. and its European allies must, at all cost, achieve the capability—manpower, weapons, organization, tactics and morale—to hold the European bastion even under the most terrible conditions of thermonuclear war.

If our Western Allies do not arm themselves for the defense of free Europe, they are likely to succumb to the adroit and baffling stratagems of nuclear blackmail. Appeasement feeds on weakness. In the last resort, it will be the combined forces of the Free World, capable of fighting in every sphere, as well as the strength and resilience of the great American base, that will determine whether the United States and its allies will prevail in the aftermath of a thermonuclear holocaust.

Short of General War

The atomic bomb dropped on Hiroshima opened a new era in warfare. No one can gainsay this fact. It does not follow, however, that "atomic war" and war are synonymous. Yet public opinion appeared to have drawn the conclusion that henceforth the god of war would stride forth armed only with one, the absolute, weapon. This contagious supposition deleted other forms of war from the popular lexicon and the policy-maker's list of assumptions. While the military professionals groped for the meaning of the new weapons, the structure of classical strategy fell apart almost before the mushroom clouds had dissolved over Japan. The new weapons were so powerful that the older instruments of military power appeared to have lost their place in the making of foreign policy or military strategy. In the aftermath of a costly war this wholesale liquidation seemed appealing.

Events since then have taught us otherwise. They have discredited the notion that all the weapons of the pre-atomic age are outmoded. Yet even now it is a trying task to unravel the distinctive types of war that may confront us. General war could well start with a surprise attack and issue into long and bitter struggles, encompassing many of the less violent types of conflict. Conversely, a "brush fire" war might set off the dreaded contest of mutual nuclear annihilation. Between these extreme alternatives, there is ample room for other contingencies that could arise.

Until now we have focused on the general or central war problem, but the United States needs a military policy and strategy which will be capable of meeting the full range of communist challenges and still be consistent with our over-all foreign policy objectives. History abounds with examples of nations which were defeated because they failed to tailor their defense establishment to their political objectives, and vice versa. For example, the French Army in the period between the two world wars was an extremely powerful force. It was committed to a defensive rather than an offensive strategy, despite the principal strategic objective of the Third Republic: to prevent the rise of Germany to a position where it could again attack France. When the Germans invaded Poland, the French military establishment should have struck immediately against Germany on the Western Front, thus forcing Germany to fight a two-front war. This was the historic doctrine of French strategy. Hence, in 1939, France should have been armed with highly mobile ground forces, supported by tactical air forces. Instead, France opted for a stationary defensive strategy. France was defeated and occupied by Germany.

A nation should steer clear of political objectives which it cannot achieve with appropriate military means. For example, the "liberation" policy vis-à-vis Eastern Europe was never an "operational" policy because the United States, while it may have possessed the hardware, had fashioned a military establishment which was not tailored to its psychological traits. This partially explains our failure to exploit the opportunity presented by the East Berlin uprising in June, 1953, although this event occurred at the height of a major communist internal crisis. Had we mustered the necessary conventional forces-in-being or had we brought our nuclear superiority to bear, East Germany might be free now.

Similarly, the NATO countries could not take advantage of the Soviet predicament during the Hungarian rising in 1956. We were afraid that any move to exploit the Soviet dilemma in Hungary would lead to war with the Soviet Union—a war which, since our policy placed primary reliance on nuclear weapons, could only have been a nuclear one. In short, if we ever wish to exploit one of the most vulnerable communist positions—Eastern Europe—we must build a military establishment which is flexible enough to allow us to exploit, if not create, situations of calculated risk.

Despite the change wrought in the balance of power by the growing Soviet nuclear missile arsenal, the United States and its allies need, for political and psychological reasons, the ability to respond to any given communist aggression at a high level of violence, *without* automatic resort to nuclear weapons.

As we approach the mid-sixties, the willingness of the U.S. to take action which courts the danger of general war will hinge increasingly on American estimates of the resiliency of its own retaliatory force and civilian casualty estimates in the event of a nuclear showdown and, perhaps more importantly, on its ability to meet the communists below the threshold of general war.

Inhibitions and uncertainties about general nuclear war affect directly the rest of the conflict spectrum. Although the Soviets might recoil from a direct strike against the Continental United States, the West still could fall prey to an emboldened Soviet strategy of lesser challenges. Countering this threat may be as difficult as attaining a relatively invulnerable deterrent, for a variety of potential military options are open to the Soviets at the lower end of the conflict spectrum, ranging from psychological-political warfare to limited military conflict.

Soviet capabilities to inflict an unacceptably high level of damage on the Continental United States will reinforce the communist strategy of attrition. In this situation, the Soviets' margin of superiority for waging limited conflict will give Soviet planners greater freedom of action. Indeed, the Soviets have already exploited this superiority in their manipulation of the Berlin crisis. At the root of much of the West's troubles in Berlin is the inadequacy of Western power on the ground. A strategy of main reliance on nuclear weapons for meeting the full range of communist military challenges leaves Western diplomacy an uncomfortably narrow leeway for maneuver under the menace of the Soviet ultimatum on Berlin.

Since the adoption in 1953 of the "New Look" doctrine, the United States defense policy has placed main but not exclusive reliance on nuclear weapons to deal with *all* communist military challenges.

In the past several years there has grown up a dichotomy between the strategy of massive retaliation and the military requirements of mutual security. This was not readily apparent so long as the U.S. enjoyed a significant nuclear-delivery superiority.

United States strategy is inseparable from the concept of alliance systems. The residual wartime alliance—purged of its communist bedfellows—was never really dissolved. The Marshall Plan, and the military and foreign assistance programs that have grown out of it, are vital elements of American strength and Free World security. NATO and the other alliances which link the U.S. in a globe-girdling coalition are uniquely important to the survival of freedom. Alliance systems are indispensable to any sound American strategy. Our task is to design military forces to back our alliances and eschew concepts that tend to divide them.

U.S. military forces must therefore satisfy the demands of an integrated strategy which, beyond deterring and winning general war, insures our allies against attack, defeat and occupation. This requirement spells the need for a convincing capability for local warfare, particularly defense on the ground.

The numerous conflicts after World War II in the era of American nuclear superiority have all been fought with "conventional" arms. In many of these conflicts, the communists were directly engaged. The communists appear to have proceeded on the assumption that limited conflicts, especially conflicts initiated under ambiguous circumstances, are "safe wars"—conflicts that will not trigger all-out nuclear war. The communist instruments of indirect aggression, such as "volunteers," proxies and subversion, have proved highly successful to date. It seems likely they will be used again.

As the contest between the United States and U.S.S.R. for superiority in long-range delivery systems continues, the side which proves itself more resourceful in waging protracted conflict at levels below that of all-out war inevitably will gain considerable and possibly decisive advantages. We are entering an extended period during which American retaliatory power will probably prove far too unwieldy an instrument for deterring limited or local conflicts. In brief, although our strategic nuclear force will be of overriding importance in deterring a direct nuclear attack against the Continental United States and even for forcing the communists to exercise caution in waging limited or local aggression, it is not by itself sufficient to meet challenges which fall below the "threshold" where American survival is at stake.

While much of the criticism of United States military policy has been aimed at its niggardly provisions for fighting "limited war," a more sophisticated controversy centers upon the practicality of fighting *any* level of land warfare with atomic weapons.

Many critics of American defense strategy question the psychological resolve of the United States to meet a nonnuclear attack with nuclear weapons. It has been widely argued that the U. S. should maintain conventional forces strong enough to fight a limited engagement with nonnuclear weapons and thus force the aggressor to consider a return to the conference table rather than continue a conflict which will lead, sooner or later, to all-out nuclear war. Nuclear weapons certainly are massive weapons that cannot be easily restricted to the battlefield—especially when the battlefield lies in close vicinity to dense population centers. Even if tactical nuclear arms should be refined and controlled to the point where they could be used against military targets without heavy damage to surrounding populations, political and psychological inhibitions will continue to weigh heavily in any decision to use them.

These inhibitions against the use of nuclear weapons add to the communists' ability to deal from a position of military-psychological strength. They hold large forces in readiness for potential operations on the Eurasian land mass. Soviet ground forces are equipped to wage either nuclear or nonnuclear war. Consequently the United States and its principal allies must be able to meet a variety of conflict situations without automatic resort to nuclear weapons.

It follows that the United States and its allies require "multi-capability" forces for land operations. Yet, nuclear weapons must be part of this arsenal.

We cannot expose our forces to the danger of annihilating nuclear attacks while denying them the right to defend themselves in kind. The incorporation of tactical nuclear weapons into our "multi-capability" surface forces injects uncertainties into communist military calculations. The knowledge that our forces possess nuclear weapons may inhibit the communists from launching a limited attack or from opening an attack with nuclear weapons, or from concentrating their superior manpower reserves for a massed land assault. The fact that under the threat of nuclear attack neither side can mass its forces is the crux of modern strategy, for it is very difficult for either side to attack without concentrating its effectives. The problem of massing forces in the face of nuclear weapons enters here. To the extent that either side concentrates forces, the other side may be tempted to resort to nuclear weapons. Moreover, either side will be under pressure to opt for nuclear weapons when the "limits" of nonatomic war are pierced by intolerable enemy action. The Soviets are as well aware of this as we. The presence of nuclear weapons changes drastically the character of the land battle. Land forces based on traditional concepts of organization are not adequate to cope with the kind of combat situations which are likely to arise in the nuclear age.

Let us reiterate: We cannot afford to deprive ourselves of the capability of employing whatever weapons are available to a potential foe. Even though it is often stated that nuclear weapons have been around long enough to be classified in some respects as "conventional," the decision to use them poses difficult problems, especially in limited war.

It seems likely that some political penalty will be attached to the first use of nuclear weapons. But the penalty would be less if the U.S. were to use them against unequivocal aggression. Asia's opinion would certainly be less sensitive to their use in Europe than in Asia. There is a widespread fear that once any "A-bomb" enters the fray, a war would spiral inexorably into an all-out nuclear affair. The public at large has never drawn any distinctions between low and high yield weapons and, therefore, is inclined to dismiss the possibility of "limiting" nuclear war as unrealistic.

No one can conclude with certainty that nuclear war can or cannot be kept limited. Nor can anyone say definitely that the development of operational capabilities for the use of tactical nuclear weapons on both sides will either strengthen the deterrence of all-out war or weaken it. Once a small nuclear war has broken out, it may quickly "escalate" into general war. In any event, our reliance on tactical nuclear weapons should go hand in hand with a high degree of strategic invulnerability to reduce the risks of a tactical nuclear war spiraling into a general exchange. It might be prudent, therefore, either to spend much more money on our strategic retaliatory insurance or to pay the bill for maintaining a higher level of multi-capable forces and thus reduce the risk of an unwanted general nuclear war.

The United States cannot renounce the first use of atomic weapons. Such a self-imposed restriction could be disastrous. The United States will have to use nuclear weapons if engaged by the communists at a level of violence in excess of its conventional capabilities. But it stands to reason that it would be desirable on political, psychological and military grounds to shift the onus for initiating the use of nuclear weapons to the communists. By maintaining a sizable nonnuclear military capability we can force the Soviets to use *their* nuclear weapons *first* if they choose to fight to achieve their objectives. It has been suggested that some measure of tactical stalemate may obtain because high casualty rates might make the use of atomic firepower unprofitable for both sides. Some predict that all advances on an atomic battlefield would grind to a halt. Predictions of this type have gone astray in the past.

In military affairs nothing is absolute in the scientific sense; nothing is unthinkable or impossible in war. If the outcome of all wars were predictable many of them would never have been fought. A war or a battle is not decided on the basis of any one factor, not even such an important one as predicted atomic casualties. Nuclear weapons, barring an agreement to outlaw them, are here to stay. Their actual use may indeed be limited, as most weapons are for one reason or another, but the possibility of using atomic weapons will hang over any future battlefield.

Consequently, the Free World's defenses need to be strengthened not only by raising additional ready land forces, but also by increasing their tactical superiority through the intelligent and vigorous integration of all new technologies, among which tactical nuclear weapons are most significant.

Even considering world opinion, the United States must calculate the disastrous harm to its international prestige if it were defeated in a limited war with the communists because it feared to resort to nuclear weapons. Although we hope that the onus for initiating nuclear war will fall upon the Kremlin, the communist strategists must be under no misapprehension that we will not use, if necessary, nuclear arms.

We need surface forces that can fight wars, large or small, with either nuclear or nonnuclear weapons. Our armed forces will need large supplies of munitions other than nuclear, including high explosives, incendiary, and biological-chemical munitions.[12]

[12] Chemical warfare is effective in almost all areas of the temperate zone and also in the tropics, with the exception of desert spaces. Caves, bunkers, etc., which are indispensable to protect troops against nuclear blasts, render these troops susceptible, not only to older agents like mustard, which is very persistent, but also to the newer agents like the V and G agents, including the "psychochemicals." Nearly all populated regions of the earth are also susceptible to enemy action with biological warfare agents. These potentials have not been given the attention they deserve. It makes little sense to handicap ourselves by refraining from the use of weapons that can achieve the political ends of military operations better than others. C/B, like nuclear weapons, should be included in the Free World's military inventory. To do so will not only improve our own capability—and quite economically—but will also complicate the offense and the defense for any enemy whom we confront. For there lie the critical resources for improving the U.S. military position—the relatively un-

Land forces must defend themselves against atomic weapons by dispersal on a wide front and in great depth. They should be formed in small units which will not offer remunerative targets; be comparatively self-contained; possess firepower and supplies for semi-independent operations: and enjoy a high order of mobility for concentrating and dispersing swiftly. As we might expect, the atomic battlefield of tomorrow poses many dilemmas. How best to strike a balance between protection versus mobility and lightness—armor plate versus lightness of a vehicle; how to match the extended range of weapons with the communications necessary to take advantage of their capabilities; how to locate and determine suitable targets for a wide variety of new weapons; and how to prepare for the logistical support of land operations that might run the gamut from light guerrilla fighting to sustained combat between formations armed with low- and medium-yield atomic weapons?

The search for answers to these questions has preoccupied the communist military planners and our own alike. Such matters as the greatly increased requirements for engineer and medical troops; the utilization of chemical and biological weapons and of unclean and clean nuclear weapons as well as "conventional" firepower; alternate means of communication; air and missile defense of field forces; control of close-support atomic fire; and fuel for land and air transport within the battle area—these are the problems to which solutions must be found.

The conflicting demands of organization, equipment, weapons, command, control and tactical doctrine defy straightforward answers. The best we can hope for are reasonable compromises which combine the experience and judgment of American and allied professionals.

The substitution for tried and true methods of new and unknown "hardware" and tactics is bound to be contentious. The U.S. and its principal allies face challenging opportunities in incorporating technological advances in tactical organization, mobility, versatility, weapons, and control and general operational effectiveness for possible nuclear warfare. The optimum "mix" of weapons, transport and supporting systems is yet to be attained.

---

tapped potential of chemical and biological, the so-called C/B, agents. Surely, chemical and biological agents are not less "humane" than the nuclear weaponry to which both sides have so irrevocably committed themselves.

The growing nuclear maturity of the Soviet Union is presenting communist leadership with ever more tempting options, which should spur the land forces of the United States and its allies to keep abreast of the changing military arts. For our greatest needs are military forces designed and equipped to restore greater flexibility of action to Western diplomacy.

The Forward Areas

American strength—and that of the Free World—rests upon defensive arrangements in the North Atlantic area. No one has argued the case for NATO's over-all importance to the United States more eloquently than former Secretary of State Dean Acheson, one of its principal architects:

> One does not become stronger by becoming weaker—a principle which seems to have been embraced by the advocates of disengagement (i.e., the demilitarization of Central Europe). Under present circumstances, there can be no effective unity between Western Europe and North America if the very pillar of this relationship, namely NATO's forward position in Europe, is removed. Therefore, if [West] Germany should be neutralized, disarmed and wrested from the Western Alliance, then the dissolution of the alliance is only a question of time, leaving us no place to make our stand except in the United States. And we cannot solve the problems of the world from Fortress America. If the Atlantic nations were truly united, then many of the problems of the day would become less intricate.[13]

NATO, despite its growing importance in the nonmilitary affairs of the North Atlantic Community, cannot survive unless it meets the test of providing Europe with military security. Nothing makes this clearer than the continuing crisis over Berlin. The Soviet threat to Berlin appears to be part of a larger strategy designed to paralyze NATO. By challenging the Western Alliance in Berlin—perhaps the West's most vulnerable forward position—Moscow seeks to demonstrate to Western Europe, and, indeed, to the world, that America's strategic nuclear capabilities are held at bay by Soviet missile progress and that, therefore, American military power can no longer be counted on to defend the Free World. Should the Soviets succeed in ousting the West from Berlin it could set in motion forces that might prove fatal to NATO.

[13] Dean G. Acheson, "The Premises of American Policy," *Orbis*, Vol. III, No. 3, Fall, 1959, p. 273.

Soviet forces are tailored to compound the predicaments which confront NATO. Soviet forces in Europe are multipurpose: They are armed generously with nuclear, conventional and possibly chemical weapons. So long as the Soviets are deterred from launching a direct attack against the U.S. or its NATO allies, only one course appears open to them: to paralyze and fragmentize NATO by challenges that fall below the "threshold" of American survival. For example, they apparently intend to give their East German satellite a free hand to stir up trouble around Berlin as long as their own power and prestige are not put on the block. The higher that "threshold," the wider the Soviet freedom of maneuver. To raise it is the purpose of nuclear blackmail. This purpose is being achieved when a move which was held yesterday to have been a *casus belli atomici* will not be considered an issue of survival tomorrow.

As we have suggested above, the aim of Soviet strategy in Europe is to neutralize U.S. strategic nuclear power as a key factor in Western European defense. A report to Congress summed up this prospect as follows:

> With the strategic nuclear weapons neutralized Soviet superiority in other forms of military power becomes of greater significance, both militarily and politically. . . . This superiority of military power in the various categories would mean, not necessarily that the Soviet leadership would choose to attack, but that it could bring about political changes in one part of the world or another without having to attack. As the Kremlin seems to see it, what remains is for the Western nations to be "realistic" about adjusting their positions abroad to a weaker power relationship.[14]

The Soviet rulers believe that public opinion in Western Europe will one day come to view the limited American presence on the Continent (bases and troops) as a source of danger rather than of protection. The stage will then be set for the disengagement of Western Europe from NATO, i.e., for splitting Europe from the United States. The Soviets will offer neutrality as an attractive alternative to the nuclear holocaust which the continued presence of American forces will render "inevitable." They will guarantee a

[14] *United States Foreign Policy, USSR and Eastern Europe,* prepared under the direction of the Committee on Foreign Relations, United States Senate, by a Columbia-Harvard Research Group, Columbia University, Washington: United States Government Printing Office, 1960, p. 1092.

"European Security System" and might even ostensibly agree to dissolve one or another West European communist party.

Moscow undoubtedly realizes that such a process cannot be set in motion by propaganda paced by alternating diplomatic threats and cajolery. The simplest method of forcing our allies into neutrality is to expose the unreliability of American strategic nuclear power as a deterrent to Soviet attack. This appears to be the purpose of the perennial Berlin crisis. The Berlin ultimatum is likely to be pushed to a showdown when, in the calculation of the Soviet leadership, Soviet nuclear striking power will have reduced to practically nil the probability of American strategic nuclear retaliation.

Soviet conflict strategy resembles that which, between 1936 and 1939, Hitler found so rewarding. Hitler, by occupying the Rhineland in 1936, demonstrated that France and Britain were no longer dependable allies. Hitler succeeded in bringing about the gradual "disengagement" of Eastern Europe from the French alliance. The process culminated, at the outbreak of World War II, in the dissolution of France's European security system.

If ever the *foreign policy* phase of Soviet strategy is completed—when the major Western European countries have been neutralized and American power has been driven from the Continent—the second, subversive phase of Soviet strategy will begin: the establishment of "popular fronts," followed by full-fledged communist regimes.

Doubt is growing in Western Europe as to whether American strategic nuclear power can defend it against minor aggression. One way to put this doubt to rest is to provide our NATO allies with an independent strategic nuclear deterrent under the strict control of the NATO command. This the United States can do. Its atomic arsenal is well stocked, even though legislative restrictions pose vexing obstacles. In order to derive from nuclear weapons systems the maximum deterrent effect, the potential aggressor must be persuaded that they will be used whenever and wherever required to avoid defeat. His conviction on this score will be a function of his appreciation of the scale, diversification and deployment of our weapons systems.

Soviet belief in Western determination to use nuclear weapons, if necessary, may be strengthened by the wider sharing of atomic weapons. The knowledge that the national forces in any given country possess nuclear delivery systems for their own defense will certainly provide the Soviets with food for thought. Even though most of our allies could never hope to match Soviet offensive capabilities, their possession of nuclear weapons might present the Soviets with risks disproportionate to the worth of territory conquered.

The organizational framework under which we share atomic weapons with our NATO allies will differ with various types of nuclear weapons and with plans for their employment. For example: Atomic land mines (which would explode in the invaded country) could be given outright to friendly forces and the decision to use them in the event of an invasion would be made at the national level. Most types of tactical atomic weapons for land forces would likewise fall under this category. Nuclear-armed antiaircraft or antimissile rockets would presumably come under the control of an international command since an effective air-defense system would require close collaboration between several countries. Some retaliatory weapons could conceivably be incorporated into the existing SHAPE forces, under the control of the Supreme Allied Commander for NATO in Europe, while some might be handled on a national basis.

For example, even a country so small as Denmark, armed with several Polaris submarines, could deliver a level of damage on the Soviet Union which would far exceed the gains which the latter could derive from the occupation of Denmark. Furthermore, a wider distribution of nuclear weapons among NATO members would complicate considerably Soviet strategy by raising NATO's residual force capabilities following an initial exchange with the United States. How much of their force the Soviets will expend on the first strategic blow may depend very largely on their estimate of their position relative to the rest of the world *after* the initial exchange has taken place. In any event, the Soviets could not risk leaving our allies with substantial residual force capabilities whether they had succeeded in knocking us out or not. More important still, the idea that Europe could remain neutral while the two giants would slug it out appears more fatuous than ever.

During the nineteenth century, a multiple balance of power preserved the peace of Europe. Then, the psychological basis of security was the uncertainty of risk which the would-be aggressor had to incur. He could not foresee the alignment of the powers. This multiple balance has been transformed in our generation into a bipolar balance. Because power is polarized, so is the defense. Soviet strategists, contemplating the chances of conquest in Europe, need to be concerned only with skirting the risk of a determined American response. If some semblance of the multiple balance could be restored in the shape of independent nuclear power centers, a new dimension of risk would enter into Soviet calculations. The Soviets, in planning their gambits, might be forced to calculate, with considerable accuracy, the threshold of survival not only of the U.S., but of the countries immediately involved.

The possession of nuclear weapons by individual NATO nations would strengthen considerably the position of all of Western Europe absolutely and in relation to the contiguous communist satellite countries. The United States would derive far greater military and political benefits from sharing nuclear weapons with its allies than would the Soviets from sharing their nuclear weapons with Czechoslovakia, Rumania and Bulgaria, not to speak of Hungary, Poland and East Germany. The reasons are these: The Soviets can now at will station nuclear weapons in any satellite country. They do not need the consent of satellite peoples or governments. Hence, we must assume that they have placed these weapons wherever they deem strategy requires their deployment. The Soviets, although they may have assisted Communist China to develop nuclear weapons, would gain nothing militarily or politically that would warrant the risks involved in sharing nuclear weapons with their satellites. The NATO alliance operates by consent. Our unwillingness to share nuclear weapons with France has weakened our military and political position in Western Europe. This is the problem posed by President de Gaulle. A policy of sharing nuclear weapons with our allies is likely to strengthen NATO politically, for it would affirm our trust in the loyalty and sagacity of our fellow members. We can trust our allies. The Soviets cannot place equal trust in the reliability of their "allies."

The confrontation of nuclear-armed Western European nations and "nonnuclear" East European satellites would impale the Soviets on the horns of a dilemma. It would drastically reduce the chances for success of a Soviet proxy action against Western Europe. It has been argued that this is a dangerous policy precisely because it would be difficult for the Soviets to resist the demands of their satraps for "nuclear parity" with their West European neighbors. The anxiety to head off such a crisis in the internal relationships of the Soviet bloc undoubtedly looms large in Soviet-sponsored proposals for the creation of a nuclear-free zone in Europe. The implications of the Soviet dilemma would transcend Europe: Difficulties over nuclear weapons could arise in the relations between Moscow and Peking. Despite their dilemma, it is doubtful that the Soviets would hand over any nuclear weapons to their Chinese ally. Moreover, the Chinese are likely to have a "nuisance" nuclear capability by 1965; any action we take is unlikely to affect this development.

In addition to the psychological arguments favoring the sharing of nuclear weapons with our European allies, such a policy is consistent with the military purpose of achieving a "multicapability" of the most effective weaponry that technology has to offer. Our decision to share nuclear weapons might also serve as a polite *quid pro quo,* but not a substitute, for a decision by our allies to achieve additional and truly up-to-date capabilities.

The very possibility of an atomic war of uncertain outcome in Europe suggests to many minds that safety lies in not fighting at all. The proponents of a forthright tactical atomic capability argue that the level of the conflict, not the weapons used, will govern its scale and intensity. We are asked to assume that the enemy will agree tacitly to certain nuclear ground rules; that he knows peradventure that the Free World will not start a war that could spiral into thermonuclear war; that he himself is reluctant to start an all-out engagement; and that he will surmise, therefore, that a nuclear weapon dropped by us on him is not intended to start all-out war. This is asking for a perceptiveness, an equanimity and a sangfroid which communist leaders have not managed to display at their best moments. We, ourselves, were we in their boots, might stumble at a turn of this tortuous mental process. A protagonist may very well in the heat of battle mistake the other's intentions and refuse to abide by such vaguely adumbrated rules of nuclear war.

On the other hand, the unmistakable capability of the NATO forces—and this would apply generally to any forces of which the U.S. furnishes a part—would declare unmistakably NATO's intent to deter. NATO does possess by virtue of its present land force composition a measure of deterrent power. The communist rulers, because they have, at present, the edge on NATO, might reason that they can effect a smash-grab of weakly defended areas and thus confront the United States with a *fait accompli* which it would be reluctant to reverse at the risk of initiating general nuclear war. The ability of the United States and its NATO allies to meet a Soviet probe speedily, with effective and versatile military force, would enhance rather than diminish the deterrent to general war.

Yet the plausible limits of limited war in Europe may not obtain very long if put to a test. NATO, therefore, may not profit from a massive conventional establishment capable of sustaining a limited conflict of some duration. But NATO does need strength in depth, sizable enough to contain a Soviet thrust before it reaches the main defense line, *without automatic resort to nuclear weapons.* Since the possibility of nuclear war will always exist, NATO forces must be designed and equipped primarily for such conflict. This implies a major overhaul of NATO forces and, particularly, of logistical systems. It is no secret that today NATO does not possess forces sufficient in strength or composition to be genuinely capable of containing a Soviet thrust, let alone of fighting a nuclear conflict.

The defense of Western Europe requires the creation by the NATO countries of a military posture which will convince the Soviets that they cannot achieve victory, in Europe or elsewhere, at acceptable cost and that they do risk nuclear war. The strengthening of NATO's military power requires a number of steps, including the augmentation of the military efforts of our allies, mutual adjustments in military legislation such as draft laws, and joint military programs. The military weakness of NATO results, in part, from the fact that our allies, like ourselves, have not taken all of the measures required to make the alliance effective. Consequently, our objective must be to bring about an increase in the NATO contribution of our allies in men and arms. To achieve this end, the support of various European parliaments and governments must be secured. To be sure, this is more easily said than done.

The United States does not encourage European support of NATO when it disowns, as it sometimes does, its fellow NATO members in their affairs in other parts of the globe. An alliance, if it is to be effective, requires also psychological, social, ideological and cultural underpinnings. Admittedly, there is need for greater unity within the North Atlantic area. It could be kindled by inspired leadership—the kind of leadership, for example, that "sold" a far more ambiguous (and less workable) international organization, the United Nations, to the Western public.

Strategic circumstances and requirements in Asia differ substantially from those in Europe. For one, reliance on nuclear weapons might be more credible in Asia than in Europe. Our principal adversary in Asia, Communist China, is not yet a nuclear power. Even were the Soviet Union to share some of her nuclear weapons and delivery systems with her Asian ally, or were the Chinese to develop their own nuclear weapons, the latter would not be able for the next decade to join the club of major nuclear powers as a full-fledged member. Therefore, it is less likely that the use of American tactical nuclear weapons to punish Red Chinese aggression would spiral into total war. In short, one of the principal conditions which argues for a fairly large multicapable force in Europe—the potential spiraling effect of nuclear weapons—is not present in Asia.

Second, the controversy between Communist China and Russia on conflict techniques to be employed at this particular stage in history has operational significance for our military and political strategies in Asia. It is clear that the Soviets do not want to be dragged into war—a war in which the Soviet homeland would bear the brunt of the nuclear exchange—by their less powerful Chinese partners. Soviet fears of Chinese temerity in the face of American nuclear strategy in Asia appear to be at the bottom of the doctrinal dispute over the "inevitability" of war with the "imperialists." Therefore, a tactical nuclear strategy endows our diplomacy with greater flexibility in Asia than in Europe. Nevertheless, a situation may arise in which the Soviets may wish to honor their commitment to their Chinese ally. Consequently, in Asia, our freedom of action will depend on a U.S. military posture which will render Soviet support for Communist China least likely.

Third, the Free World nations in Asia cannot possibly muster the forces capable of containing a concerted Communist Chinese offensive. The requirements in Asia are, therefore, not for large forces-in-being at all exposed points, but rather for rapid U.S. and allied action until American "staying power" can arrive on the scene. Under the circumstances, nuclear weapons could be useful in blocking some Chinese communist expansionist adventures.

This is not to imply that such weapons must necessarily be used. Yet, the very fact that they can be used with less risk than their employment would entail in Europe ought to serve as a potent and credible deterrent to Chinese communist aggression for some time to come.

Undoubtedly, a declaratory policy of primary reliance on nuclear weapons in Asia would have adverse effects on Asian public opinion. We can safely assume, however, that such effects would be less injurious than a U.S. retreat in the face of Chinese communist aggression, not to mention communist paramilitary successes, or an American military defeat in a limited conflict with Peking's forces.

Communist China will continue to maintain pressure along the periphery of Asia and threaten to cross deep water. As of 1960, Peking seems to be tactically out of step with Moscow. The Soviet position, in line with its advocacy of "peaceful coexistence," has been that any nuclear war could be disastrous even for the victors; consequently, the Soviets hope to reap the fruits of war, if possible, without war. The Chinese line is much harder: War against the "imperialists" is not only possible, but even probable in spite of nuclear weapons.

In October, 1960, Communist China's veteran top military leader, Marshal Lin Piao, told a meeting of high-ranking officers of the Red Chinese Army about a hypothetical conflict:

> After all the atom bombings and shellings were over, men would still have to face the enemy with courage, consciousness, and the spirit of self-sacrifice from a distance of several dozen meters.
>
> Victory came only with the occupation of the enemy positions in attack, and the enemy could be smashed only in resisting his attack, when on the defensive. This was the key question in deciding victory.

Lin, underscoring Chinese confidence that any atomic attack would still leave his nation with enough troops to fight, said: "We handle both weapons and men, but attach greater importance to man's role."[15]

This confident talk reflects real beliefs, in Chinese minds, that manpower remains the decisive factor. Nonetheless, the communist marshals of China want atomic weapons, and China is doing every-

[15] Akio Konoshima, United Press International, London, October 11, 1960.

thing it can to obtain them. Even when the Chinese communists possess nuclear armaments they will be still far behind in sophisticated weapons systems for delivery, just as the French are today. China will incur mounting difficulties in developing such costly systems while, at the same time, seeking to raise her over-all industrial productivity. In doing so, she will be forced to alter military concepts, as the Soviets have, but this decision is not yet at hand. The intensity of China's pressure on Asia will vary according to the extent of Soviet support and the rate at which she acquires full-fledged military capabilities of her own. In any event, Chinese communist incursions in the Far East and Southeast Asia may pose an even greater threat than they have in the past.

Communist Chinese strategy is composed of one part attraction-coexistence, and one part aggression-pressure. The elements of this formula are periodically and expediently altered, with emphasis placed first on one and then on the other; but both strategic elements are always present.

"The carrot and the stick" are built-in features of communist strategy, and this combination has been successful in practice. It is quite likely, almost inevitable, that alternating Chinese communist policies of attraction and pressure will be continued throughout the 1960's. The alternating use, or combination, of these tactics meanwhile serves to keep China's neighbors too addled to respond promptly and vigorously to the Chinese menace.

The best answer to the many-sided Chinese communist threat is the maintenance of adequate American military forces ready to act in concert with our allies. Since the end of the Korean War, the U.S. has substantially reduced its forces in Asia. Local forces have been strengthened in some respects. More needs to be done; obsolescent weapons must be replaced by modern ones and the forces of our allies must be trained in the skills of modern war. But the backbone of Asian defense remains what it has been for the past fifteen years: American military power.

Should the Chinese communists, in the near future, detect signs of American indecision when it comes to defending their weak neighbors to the South and East, they might be emboldened to launch another round of overt aggression in the style of Korea in 1950, or more ambiguous sorties of the type of Vietnam in 1953-1954, and Laos in 1959-1960.

A revival of the Korean War might place the United States in a grave psychological dilemma. The Korean War was not the most popular of American wars; a second installment is unlikely to kindle the enthusiasm of the American public. On the other hand, if the U.S. were to respond sluggishly to another challenge in Korea, its position in Asia would suffer serious psychological and strategic damage.

None of the free countries in Asia can be strengthened to the point where they could defend themselves against Communist China. The major purpose of American military assistance has been to strengthen the internal security of Asian states. Yet countries situated along the border of the communist bloc cannot afford to concentrate their efforts solely on *internal* security; they must be prepared to resist initial communist *external* aggression as well. This will, of course, require programs of military readiness far beyond their means. Thus, the key factor in the defense of Asian countries against a communist attack is the ability of the U.S. to come to their aid.

American military assistance and training has helped several recipient countries in Southeast Asia to contain internal communist activities. The Philippine government, fortified with U.S. equipment, succeeded in wiping out the Communist HUK guerrillas. Military assistance has enabled the South Vietnam government at least to contain communist guerrilla forces and restore a semblance of order after years of war. Certainly, Laos—uncertain as its future orientation remains—would have collapsed long ago without American military aid. British and other Free World military aid to Burma and Malaya has been essential to the maintenance of order in these areas.

Increasing the strength of indigenous forces would raise the "price of entry" for the Chinese communists. The mission of both is to gain time. However, in the last analysis the defense of Asia will depend on the willingness and ability of the U.S. to bring speedy assistance to local forces.

Unconventional War

Whatever ideological and tactical disagreements may divide the communist camp, they do not extend to the inevitability of certain kinds of war. A Chinese communist publication supplied an instructive list.[16]

"Inevitable" are: (a) wars of independence in the colonial or semicolonial areas, such as the Castro seizure of power in Cuba; (b) civil wars aimed at the overthrow of "reactionary" regimes in independent countries, as, for example, the Iraq *coup d'état,* in 1957; and (c) wars between the imperialist countries themselves (which, of late, have been kept in abeyance).

Of all these "inevitable" wars, the wars of national liberation appear to stand highest on the agenda of communist strategy. Ever since the Russian Revolution, the communists have labored to bring to a boil those "contradictions" which plague colonial rule and to foment revolutionary "wars of national liberation" against Europe's colonial powers.

Guerrilla or revolutionary war has become the principal communist military technique for the reduction, by installments so to speak, of Western influence in the underdeveloped regions of the world. Ideally, the operation consists of two phases: the establishment of a national government and then, after liberation has been won, the subversion of the national government by a communist or communist-controlled faction.

The United States and its allies, if they propose to check this particular communist gambit, have little choice but to maintain forces equipped for scotching civil or regional "liberation warfare movements." This is especially true of Southeast Asia, the Middle East, Africa and Latin America. The Cuban developments are particularly ominous because they open prospects of the establishment of a communist guerrilla base in close proximity to the U.S. This same danger was inherent in the Guatemala crisis of 1954. Cuba might well become the base for the extension of the "Yenan Way" south of the thirtieth parallel. We are beholden to Major "Che" Guevara, who fought with Fidel Castro from Oriente to Havana, for an explicit analogy.

[16] See *Red Flag,* April 15, 1960. It should be noted that reports of an ideological controversy, which is said to trouble Moscow-Peking relations while this book goes to press, revolve presumably around the "inevitability" of *general* or large-scale limited war. They apparently do *not* always agree on direct limited *military* conflict. But, they do not disagree on national liberation warfare carried out by *ad hoc* proxies, i.e., Castro, Pathet Lao, East Germany, etc.

The China of Mao began with an uprising of workers' groups in the South, which were defeated and almost annihilated. Progress was made only after the great Yenan march when the movement was established in rural regions and based on demands for agrarian reform. The struggle of Ho-Chi-Minh in Indo-China was based on the oppressed rice growers under the French colonial yoke, and was carried on with their support until the defeat of the colonialist forces.

Castro likewise came to power only after he had established a rural base in Cuba's Oriente Province. It is worth noting that Guevara is not a Cuban but an Argentinean. He thus stands in the straight line of descent of the communist professional revolutionists who, during the last forty years, moved from country to country to establish a base for revolution in other countries. Until the U.S. and its allies acquire genuine capabilities for handling this kind of conflict technique effectively, a proliferation of communist "leap-frog" beachheads is likely, including some uncomfortably close to our shores.

The technique of screening a communist takeover by national guerrilla movements may well be put to the test in Latin-American countries in addition to Cuba. The techniques employed by Fidel Castro's team were practically identical with those used by the Soviets and Chinese communists in other parts of the world. The leaders of world communism have given the world to understand that they have a considerable stake in the Castro regime. True enough, the problems of Latin America and, indeed, of most other underdeveloped lands are political, ideological and economic. Yet, there is a grave danger that economic problems will be metamorphosed into political-military challenges. No doubt, the first priority of American policy in Latin America and Africa should be to render economic aid to the needy. The poverty and discontent of underdeveloped peoples provide the fertile soil for "national liberation" warfare. However, if we wish to deal with economic issues on the basis of economics, we must restore respect for American military power and our capability to handle the guerrilla warfare.

The United States has created an excellent cadre of special warfare troops for the purpose of assisting in the organization and training of indigenous forces, skilled in guerrilla and counterguerrilla operations. But more than cadre forces are needed to hold the potential areas of guerrilla conflict.

The one tried and true method of handling a crisis such as the one that burst out in Cuba is to head it off before it develops. The disease, once it has eaten to the bone, resists a simple remedy. Faced with the prospect of either intervention or inaction, the United States is bound to lose either prestige or respect. Both American armed intervention and nonintervention would play the tune of the communist propaganda campaign. The communists would have a merry time portraying a war with Cuba as one between "the people" and "Western imperialism." The United States won a victory of sorts when the Arbenz regime in Guatemala fell. Yet the United States suffered a political setback in its hemispheric relations, for its alleged intervention aroused resentment throughout Central and South America.

During the coming decade, similar dilemmas may face the United States elsewhere: to abstain from intervention and thus lose military ground to communist guerrillas, or to intervene and suffer ideological embarrassment in the Cold War. Unfortunately, circumstances appear to push us along a one-way street. If the communists succeed in fomenting insurrections in various parts of the Free World, they are bound to gain whether we intervene or not. Heads, they win; tails, we lose. The escape route from this undignified and potentially disastrous situation is kept open by American power. Once the communists learn that their every foray by force of arms, no matter what its form may be, is blocked by American power, one chapter of Cold War history—the sorry chapter of national liberation subverted by communism—will have been closed. In short, it must be our objective to *deter* the communists at all levels of conflict; but in order to do so we must be able to *fight* them effectively at *every* level of violence.

Ideally, the "unconventional," regular or "organized" armed forces should be ready to engage in general as well as in limited war. Similarly, these forces should be trained and equipped for several missions. The term "unconventional" embraces political warfare and paramilitary, insurrectionist, revolutionary, subversive and guerrilla activities. In its wide variety of phases, unconventional warfare will be, for years to come, an indispensable instrument of American strategy. It is an ideal means for limiting war and for waging limited war. Currently held beliefs to the contrary, "unconventional" forces could use nuclear weapons more opportunely than regulars.

Unconventional warfare has been the stepchild of U.S. military planning. It is true that there is no more reason why we should wage paramilitary warfare on the communist pattern than why we should fire our artillery according to the doctrine of the Red Army. We are not free, however, to choose the weapons and battlegrounds to our liking. In particular, the U.S. Army and Marines must recognize the offensive and defensive potentialities of paramilitary warfare.

Just as purely military operations hinge on the closest co-ordination with regular forces, psychological warfare activities and partisan forces, political conviction provides the basic motivation for the formation of partisan groups.

The armed forces and other interested and competent agencies of the government should step up the training of selected officers in the arts of unconventional warfare. A hurried course of instruction is unlikely to produce experts. Judgment in the proper use of nonmilitary forces and in the reciprocal consequences of the employment of conventional military forces can only be acquired through long study.

The increased eminence of paramilitary warfare does not diminish the crucial importance of regular, organized combat forces. For example, an army lacking well-trained, well-led, seasoned troops can make little headway against irregular forces. But a force that knows how to fight the propaganda war and to fight at the side of partisans, as well as to fight with atomics, tanks, planes, chemicals, machine guns and flame throwers, is a force that indeed brackets the full range of politico-military power.

Such forces should be strong and nimble enough to take on the following tasks:

a. Provide the demonstrable, on-the-spot token of U.S. intent to help defend a country however remote or small; and thereby strengthen Free World solidarity and local power of resistance to communist moves.

b. As a part of our over-all strategy of making open aggression or guerrilla adventures unattractive to the communists, provide a show of mobile force. The very appearance of immobility is an open invitation to the communists to experiment in aggression below the level of all-out war. Hence we must provide indigenous security forces with more mobility. For example, helicopters have proven quite useful in dealing with guerrillas. We need arms and equipment suitable for guerrilla warfare operations and air and sea lift to get forces quickly into action.

c. Engage in police actions against paramilitary risings beyond the control of local security forces.

d. Campaign against hostile organized military forces seeking to gain limited objectives.

e. Seize and hold key strategic areas.

f. Conduct both guerrilla and antiguerrilla missions, if need be in the same area and at the same time.

Asia, the Middle East, Latin America and Africa will continue to be targets for creeping communist aggression for a good many years to come. The basic program for communist expansion appears to envision the progressive isolation and subversion of individual countries utilizing established "base areas" in the U.S.S.R., China, North Korea, North Vietnam and, perhaps, Cuba and West Africa. While allowing for flexibility in tactics, including resort to such now classic devices as the "united front" and "peasant support," communist strategy will not recoil from the use of force of one kind or another against the government of an independent country whenever calculated risk warrants such action.

We must be strong enough—and demonstrably strong enough—to force the communists to show their hand in such a way that the world cannot mistake their aggressive intent, and to concentrate their forces in such a way that they offer military targets for our weapons, atomic and nonatomic.

Leaders of the "Gray Area" countries must be confident that American-Allied power, in combination with their own forces, offers insurance against direct communist military action and subversion alike.

Conclusions

We believe the foregoing analysis of the various military-strategic factors confronting the United States fairly represents a consensus among professional military and other experts on the nature of the military problems confronting the Western Alliance. After fifteen years of study and controversy, students of warfare are beginning to understand the revolution in warfare introduced by nuclear weapons. We have tried to suggest a general approach to our problems without purporting to furnish operational guidance for the United States during the decade of the sixties.

If the United States is to subscribe to an active Forward Strategy during the sixties, it must possess those fundamental military components which are essential for its support. Prime among these will be the establishment and maintenance by the United States and its more advanced allies of military-technological superiority over the communist bloc. Working in close co-operation and pooling their resources, the Atlantic partners must develop an evident capability to absorb and recover from a communist first strike and to retain sufficient power to bring the U.S.S.R. to its knees. Current Soviet military writing makes it abundantly clear that the U.S.S.R. is mobilizing for an extended war and protracted conflict. The only effective military posture for deterring general nuclear war is an up-to-date operational capacity to wage such a war for the purpose of winning it should it be thrust upon us.

The basic way to prevent war is to make certain, by maintaining strong quantitative superiority, that the would-be aggressor has no chance of winning. A one-to-one ratio of equality cannot deter or prevent war, and could never prevail if put to the test of war. *Only a comfortable ratio of quantitative superiority can safeguard freedom.* We must reject any strategy which puts the security coefficient close to one, or even lower. This is a worse choice than either full surrender or resistance by nonviolence since it would be both costly and useless.

Weapons systems are vitally important; but hardware alone is not enough. We urgently need a unified strategic doctrine. A unified strategic doctrine, if it is to be adequate to the challenge of protracted conflict, must: (a) keep pace with advancing weapons technologies; (b) furnish a theoretical framework for the use of a balanced mix of military forces to support our international political commitments; (c) be integrated with our economic, psychological, diplomatic and other strategies.

Such a military doctrine will enable us to plan for future developments with a greater degree of organizational flexibility and a faster rate of equipment modernization, and to introduce tactical innovations. It will stake out the likely tasks which may someday devolve upon the armed forces of the United States. One of these will be to prepare themselves for the quick restoration, following a surprise attack, of the American economy, and thus assure the production base needed for prosecuting the war to a successful conclusion.

The actual choice of weapons systems, the calculation of force levels, the optimum pattern of their deployment, and the phasing of development programs—all these highly complex factors are the responsibility of our professional military men. In discharging their duty, they will have to take into account a number of problems, such as Continental defense; our system of defense alliances; the threats of communist irregular conflict; the relation of our military strategy to the entire spectrum of external policy choices; the intimate relationship between weapons choices and the opportunities for arms security arrangements.

It should be clear from all that we have said in this chapter that no cheap and facile solution of our military problems exists. The versatile forces required to implement the Forward Strategy we advocate will cost substantially more than our present military establishment. More likely than not, any other strategy that seeks to maintain even the *status quo* will be increasingly costly. In the face of the Soviet effort, we have to run very fast in order to stand still.

Taking the steps needed to maximize the nuclear deterrent, to pursue a vigorous program of technological R. & D., to maintain an adequate military assistance program, and to improve our capabilities in the areas of conventional forces, irregular forces and civil defense may very well cost us somewhere in the neighborhood of $55 to $65 billion annually in the early years of the sixties. We will be seized again by such vexing questions as inflation, deficit spending and tax revision. As we will show in Chapter 10 ("Strategy of Ways and Means"), military budgets of this size need not strain unbearably the economic potential of the United States. Proposals for raising military expenditures should be scrutinized to hold waste and inefficiency down to an absolute minimum. It would be desirable if we could correct deficiencies in the defense setup quickly; but in the short run we may have to pay a steep price to get out of the hole. But if our strategic analysts are agreed that higher budgetary levels are essential for the support of programs vital to U.S. and Free World security, the contention that we cannot afford to do any more than we are now doing to survive will have to be proved erroneous—or we will have to throw in the sponge.

The allocation of economic resources to the military account of a Forward Strategy will, during the next few years, be the major task facing the U.S. leadership, the Presidency, the Congress, the Treasury Department and the Defense Department. Our modest hope is that the conceptual framework which we have offered will provide a rough but comprehensive yardstick by which our civilian officials can gauge whether a specific military program is essential to our national security, or whether it can be safely rejected without endangering the United States.

CHAPTER 6 ECONOMIC FRAMEWORK OF STRATEGY

The exercise of economic power as an arm of strategy is as well-established a practice of statecraft as the employment of military force, psychological techniques and politico-diplomatic maneuvers. The United States has more than once harnessed its prodigious economic strength to national security. But never before has the United States confronted the necessity of applying, in a methodical and continuing manner, economic power as an integral part of a comprehensive national strategy.

Americans are beginning to appreciate the concept of "economic strategy" in its widest dimensions and in the context of the contemporary world situation. Economic, like military, strategy is chiefly concerned with the efficient allocation of available resources for the accomplishment of desired goals. A major shortcoming in present U.S. planning, policy-making and strategic programming is the failure of our strategic analysis to come fully to grips with all the relevant economic factors of modern world society.

The logical starting point would be a consensus on the nature of the changes which have transformed the international economic order since the nineteenth century. Historically, the Western free market system has operated as though there were only *one* economic world. This assumption was quite valid in the tranquil era of the gold standard, when the principle of comparative advantage was the best guarantee of the economic well-being of all nations. In fact, the growth of productivity in Germany, Japan and the United States in the latter part of the nineteenth century did redound to the benefit of all countries, including the industrially more advanced Great Britain.

The First World War, however, brought about serious dislocations which led to the disintegration of the single world economy. The period of the great depression witnessed the rise of a number of nationalist-capitalist systems, each bent on insulating its domestic economy against the disturbing effects of forces outside its control. During the 1930's, Germany and Japan posed serious challenges to the international economic *status quo*. But neither country was able, prior to the outbreak of World War II, to complete the execution of its plan for a new regional system—the "New Order" in Europe and the "Co-prosperity Sphere" in Asia. The most significant achievement of the Axis powers was to help set the stage for the appearance of a third and more formidable challenge to the Western economic system.

After World War II, the Soviets sought to cap their territorial conquests with the organization of an international socialist bloc economy which, Stalin declared, would gradually overtake and ultimately stifle the capitalist order. While the free industrial states of the West and the rest of the world have been making moderate progress toward restoring the liberal conditions—free convertibility of currency and the easy movement of goods and persons—which had once characterized the international market, the communist "parallel world market" has been growing apace. Looked at from the standpoint of pure economics, the economic growth of the Soviet Union and the entire communist bloc should benefit a world whose economic needs and desires are multiplying at a fantastic rate. But Soviet economic growth cannot be judged merely from the economic point of view. It is fraught with ominous portents for the fortunes of the free peoples, for the communists regard the productive potential of their empire as an instrument of global power accumulation, not as a means of satisfying human wants. Contrary to the axiom of Marxist ideology that economics are the determinant of politics, communist leaders have usually managed, without doing undue violence to their doctrinal convictions, to subordinate economic policy decisions to power political objectives. The Soviet state allows little room for "purely economic" decisions in the Western sense. The purpose of all productive effort is to strengthen and expand the communist power base for the successful waging of conflict.

The communist leaders certainly do not envision the role of the bloc as one of genuine partnership with nonsocialist industrial states in the development of a stable world market. Whatever the meaning of "peaceful coexistence," it does not tally with our idea of international economic co-operation for the purpose of increasing the purchasing power and hence the well-being of all peoples. To the contrary, the communists are fashioning a separate economic system outside and independent of the world market and radically hostile to it. They seek: (1) to insulate the socialist system against all forms of capitalist interference; (2) to attain complete socialist self-sufficiency, i.e., eliminate the dependence of the bloc upon Western technology; (3) to employ the resources of a state trading monopoly to carry out economic transactions with nonbloc nations on favorable terms; (4) to employ political conflict methods to retard Western economic programs which might serve to strengthen free nations; (5) to carry on the "forced march" of socialist industrial development, beginning with the inner core—i.e., the U.S.S.R.—and working outward through the other members of the bloc, whose individual economic interests are made subsidiary to those of the U.S.S.R.; (6) to integrate the bloc economy and assign specialized tasks according to a central communist blueprint; and (7) to depress forcibly consumption levels through the centralized pricing system, concentrating the maximum proportion of total resources on programs which promote Soviet strategic power.

Since the arrival of Khrushchev upon the Soviet scene, the attention of the West has been drawn to two aspects of Soviet economic policy: the planned rate of domestic growth and the so-called communist "economic offensive" into the underdeveloped areas. In keeping with the standard communist practice of inflating the significance of all bloc achievements, both of these developments have been exaggerated. Every effort to evaluate the U.S.S.R.'s performance encounters a basic analytical difficulty: the ambiguity of published Soviet statistics, emanating solely from a government-party statistical monopoly with an almost obsessive fixation to impress the outside world.

One cannot but suspect that in recent years the Soviet emphasis upon claims of sensational economic and technological gains stems in part from a desire to convince the Free World that the struggle is shifting from the military plane to one of peaceful productivity. While the Soviets rush development of ICBM's and the "fantastic new weapons" of which Premier Khrushchev has boasted, they would like to convince us that the laurel wreath will finally go to the side which can offer the world the higher standard of living. Actually, communist leadership is interested in the standard of living within the bloc countries in much the way an efficient prison warden concerns himself about the diet of his hard labor force.

The communist leaders themselves can hardly take seriously the "standard of living" race. Judging from prevailing patterns of resource allocation (i.e., the ratio of military and capital formation expenditures to consumer expenditures) since the Stalinist era, several decades will be required to equal the Western nations' *present* average consumer levels. In recent years, the communists have been talking like people in a hurry to go places. But they cannot possibly win the race in a hurry if it is a question of outproducing the West in wheat, canned goods, frozen foods, houses, cars, refrigerators, television sets, washers and other appliances. Hence we are forced to conclude that, when Khrushchev promises to bury us, he must be thinking of doing the job with means other than an avalanche of consumer goods.

Let us restate the assumption underlying this study: The communists mean what they say. They assert confidently that their system will grow stronger relative to ours and will ultimately overtake and surpass ours. The annihilation of the West as a viable, free, cultural-economic region, with all its distinctive institutions, processes and values, is their goal. And economics, as the underpinning of strategic power, will be of decisive significance in the struggle. Their expanding productive capacity now supports increasingly policies designed to promote disturbances in the free economic system and to carry on the political penetration and reorientation of the "in-between" regions, thereby diminishing the zone of American and Western political influence, strategic availability and economic transactions.

A comparison of United States and Soviet economic growth appears in Chapter 10, "Strategy of Ways and Means." Here it is sufficient to note that the Soviet economy seems to be expanding at a faster rate than ours and unquestionably is devoting a larger share of its productivity to armaments and capital investment.[1] In brief, the rationale that informs the growth of the Soviet economy is radically different from our own.

For our purposes a comparison of American and Soviet general rate-of-growth projections is meaningless. Estimates of economic parity after four or five decades falsely imply that the danger is equally remote. With each passing year, communist propagandists addressing the so-called uncommitted peoples can make it appear that their system is expanding more dynamically than the West. The communists beat statistical projections of future productive capabilities into psychological weapons. But if the consumer sector of the Soviet economy is still a Potemkin village, Soviet heavy industry is impressively real. If the Soviets' "strategic output" keeps pace with the expansion of their economic base, they may pull well ahead of us not four decades from now but even before 1970.

Free World vis-à-vis the Communist Bloc

The global struggle pits all Western countries against the Sino-Soviet bloc. It is, therefore, unfortunate that nearly all of the detailed comparative studies have been limited to the economics of the U.S.S.R. and the United States. Only too often, the economic significance of Western Europe and other free industrial nations, of Eastern Europe and China, is dragged into the discussion merely as an afterthought. Yet all three regions are economically important; all are intimately linked in one way or another to the principal contestants. The economic role of Eastern Europe, for example, has been rather consistently undervalued in Western efforts to assess bloc strategy. There can be little doubt now that the ambitious industrialization program which the communists have pursued in Eastern Europe has significantly advanced Soviet strategic purposes. It has (1) enhanced the Soviets' over-all capabilities in the areas of both military and nonmilitary technology; (2) contributed substantially to the economic development of China; and (3) raised the communist bloc's capabilities for carrying on the economic and political penetration of the underdeveloped areas.

Similarly Western Europe seems to be a "forgotten region" in

[1] For full discussions of this question, cf. *Comparisons of the United States and Soviet Economies*, papers submitted by panelists appearing before the Subcommittee on Economic Statistics, Joint Economic Committee, Congress of the United States, Parts I, II and III, Washington: G.P.O., 1959.

American economic strategy. Yet the six members of the European Common Market alone have a population nearly equal to ours and a total product approximating that of the U.S.S.R. During the last decade, this fastest-growing region of the Free World outproduced the Soviet Union in crude steel and manufactured ten times as many passenger automobiles as the entire Sino-Soviet bloc. Their projected rates of heavy industrial growth[2] fall somewhere between those of the Soviet Union and the United States during the 1960's. When we include Great Britain, Scandinavia and other members of the OEEC in the designation "Western Europe," the economic capacities of that region dwarf those of Eastern Europe in terms of both total and per capita product. But, again, the crucial question is whether the free industrial nations will integrate their economic efforts and for what purposes they will put their massive productive power to work.

Before attempting to answer this question, a word must be said about the impact of China's entry into the communist bloc upon the world economic balance. Resource-wise the accession of China enhances the bloc's capabilities for waging conflict. Let us not forget that China, then still in a chaotic state, though armed with Soviet weapons, frustrated a powerful United States expeditionary force for three years in Korea. In the "economics" of conflict, a nation with an astute strategic doctrine—one which exploits the caution or pusillanimity of an opponent—may go far with meager resources. Consideration of per capita production and "standard of living" economics, however, suggests the incorporation of China resulted in a heavy drain on the resources of the communist bloc. China's expanding population, now approaching 700,000,000, necessitates rapid industrialization, which requires aid from the bloc's industrial members. While the "build China" policy causes resentments in Eastern Europe,[3] it would be erroneous to think of China as a net

[2] On August 21, 1960, the Executive Commission of the Common Market in Brussels officially estimated that, after a somewhat sluggish 1959, industrial production of the Six would grow at about 11 per cent in 1960, and 6 per cent in 1961. *New York Times,* August 22, 1960.

[3] East Europe's exports to China and her two Asian satellites (North Korea and North Vietnam) have invariably exceeded imports from those countries both in volume and in usefulness. Such imports from the Far East as corn, tobacco, peanuts, pig iron, silks and handicraft products do not satisfy Eastern Europe's real economic wants. But the East Europeans have little choice in the matter. The only alternative to accepting goods of marginal utility is to

liability to the communist bloc. During the past decade, China has contributed major political assets to the communist cause. During the next decade, she will offer increasing economic competition to Japan and India in Southeast Asia.

In the meantime, China's development needs strain the productive resources of other bloc members. But meeting that demand could actually spur the bloc's internal economic consolidation. Admittedly, China is not so fully integrated into the bloc economy as the Soviet-exploited colonies of Eastern Europe. Peking's rugged independence precludes such subservience, but most authorities agree that it is still to China's economic and strategic interest to maintain close ties with the U.S.S.R. and the East European communist states.[4] Internally China's communes program illustrates the ruthlessness with which her productive base is being reorganized. Her radical approach to the tasks of growth seems almost to embarrass a post-Stalin Kremlin. Its psychological and economic impact is presently impossible to calculate. In the long run, however, the communist management and exploitation of the Chinese economy will probably strengthen the bloc's power base for the waging of world conflict.

The communist economic threat, like its other forms, must be understood before it can be thwarted. The Free World must soundly assess, for example, the bloc's so-called "economic offensive," a subject of divergent comments in recent years. Communist foreign trade policies are viewed calmly by those who note that the bloc's transactions with the Free World comprise less than 5 per cent of the international trade total. The real menace arises, however, from the mischief a flexible state trading monopoly can wreak, dealing with individual firms and even unwary governments in free countries.

Concentrating their resources upon promising targets, the So-

---

watch the credit balances in China rise dangerously high while waiting several years until the capital equipment delivered to China could be paid for from its productive earnings. Cf. Jan Wszelaki, *Communist Economic Strategy: The Role of East Central Europe,* Washington, National Planning Association, 1959, pp. 86-88.

[4] During the summer of 1960, a reported "mass departure" of Soviet technical assistance experts from China had no noticeable effect upon China's general trading position within the bloc. The Mutual Economic Assistance Council (*Comecon*) meeting in Budapest in July, 1960, announced that the U.S.S.R. and the East European communist countries had decided on long-term co-ordination of their economic plans for a twenty-five-year period.

viets can wage economic warfare in selected commodities and in selected markets. Divisive effects of Soviet trade with Europe have already assumed serious proportions, notably in oil. Within five years the U.S.S.R. will control a quarter of the Free World's export trade in oil.[5] Soviet-Commonwealth trade, though still relatively small in amount, has been on the increase. Soviet pricing permits the United Kingdom to improve its terms of trade while the U.S.S.R. builds up sterling surpluses to cover trade deficits with other Commonwealth countries. British policy thus contributes to what could become a disturbing situation: The Commonwealth countries, increasingly dependent upon a Soviet market, might find Soviet purchasing power a political club over their heads.

Given their present levels of trade, the Soviets can undersell Western producers whenever they wish to practice "dumping." State-administered prices need not reflect real costs. The state trading apparatus can intensify its offensive against a specific target country simply by manipulating the proper line of goods. It can purchase a free country's export surpluses and later dump them in another market (e.g., Egypt's cotton, Burma's rice, Indonesia's rubber and tin), either to acquire desired currencies or disrupt local market economics. Barter can become a weapon to reduce the earnings of Western countries—e.g., Soviet oil bartered for Brazilian coffee cuts Brazilian purchases of oil in hard-currency areas. The

[5] The Soviets' current Seven-Year Plan calls for doubling crude oil output by 1965 (tripling by 1972). Between 1955 and 1960 Soviet oil exports more than tripled while the number of countries receiving it increased from twenty to thirty. They now include: Italy, Egypt, Finland, Sweden, West Germany, India, Brazil, Uruguay, Lebanon, Ghana, Guinea, Tunisia and, of course, Cuba. During 1950, Soviet negotiators sought agreements to sell oil to Canada, Ethiopia and Ceylon. Exports for 1959 were 25,372,000 metric tons, compared with 18,138,000 in 1958. Attractive to underdeveloped countries is Russian willingness to enter into barter deals or to accept local currency in payment, irrespective of its convertibility. Free World oil companies can meet Russian competition when it comes to price, quality or delivery reliability, but their normal commercial operations cannot match Soviet payment terms in many exchange-poor countries. The one disadvantage at which the U.S.S.R. now finds itself is in transportation. Until now, most Russian oil moved to ports by rail or barge, but pipelines to the Baltic and Black Seas are under construction. Russia lacks sufficient tanker tonnage to carry all of her oil exports, but has usually been bailed out of this difficulty by Free World shipping companies. Expanding Russian tanker construction will reduce this dependence. Even more ominous, increasing Soviet oil production could trigger a dumping campaign, at depreciated prices, to disrupt the oil-based economy of Middle East nations.

long list of techniques includes pre-emptive buying, "conspicuous buying" (to rescue foundering economies distressed by large unmarketable surpluses), the extension of low-interest loans, and the manipulation of foreign exchange and stock market values (frequently through the use of "disguised accounts").

This is not to suggest, of course, that all of the bloc's foreign transactions are primarily motivated by political rather than economic considerations. Most transactions undoubtedly are calculated to satisfy real economic needs. But the important point is that *all* foreign transactions are weighed in the strategic balance by a high command interested in a number of interrelated objectives—strengthening the bloc's power base, penetrating the underdeveloped areas, and loosening and dislodging Western positions in Asia, Africa and South America.

In executing their strategy, the communists have effectively integrated economics and politics. In underdeveloped areas, they support and encourage nationalist policies which jeopardize either the earnings or the resource supplies of Western nations. Granted that the bloc's exportable surpluses are still relatively meager compared to those of the free industrial nations, the communists hope to reorient selected, underdeveloped national economies toward the bloc, and thus to encroach upon Western markets and supply sources. Until now their major export item has been military hardware; but the Soviets and their East European satellites are developing an export capability in light and heavy industrial equipment. In fact, emphasis on industrialization programs, combined with an agricultural policy which seems to fail almost deliberately, enables communist planners to equate "foreign aid" with "mutually beneficial foreign trade." Some Western states, saddled with large agricultural surpluses, find themselves unable to do business with new Afro-Asian nations dependent upon exporting one or two agricultural commodities. By carefully directing their low-interest industrial credits, the Soviets undoubtedly seek economic footholds in the early phase of their general political offensive. Between 1955 and 1960, the bloc made significant efforts to penetrate Afghanistan, Finland, Burma, Egypt, Syria, Iceland, India, Ceylon, Iran, Cuba, Indonesia and Guinea. In accenting capital formation and military technology, the communists seem to be building for a day when the bloc will become a massive industrial processing system for the raw material exports of many underdeveloped countries—a new and greater Britain, wielding the economic power to set world prices on its own terms.

The Soviets always have bought, and are buying now, from the West whatever seems expedient for the success of their development plans. Imports of heavy machinery from Europe and the United States contributed much to the First Five-Year Plan, especially in the period 1929-1931. In recent years, Soviet planners have been anxious to purchase (usually on long-term credit) whole chemical plants, machinery for the production of synthetic fibers and plastics, wood-processing machinery, equipment for rolling nonferrous metals as well as for manufacturing pipe and gas lines, and textile machinery.

There are still not a few industrialists in the Free World who, for the sake of immediate gains, are willing to sell capital equipment to an adversary who has blandly promised to bury them. The Soviet Union is not a mass producer in all sectors of industry. Geared primarily to the output of military weapons, it has sadly neglected the development of many important industries. The Soviets, decades behind the United States in some technological areas, want desperately to catch up the easy way—by technological and financial borrowing. When Western businessmen succumb to the lure of communist bloc trade, they help to open the planners' bottlenecks, thereby alleviating popular dissatisfaction with the performance of communist regimes. At the same time, they help the communists to lay the foundations for future export capacities which will someday be harnessed to the conduct of economic warfare against the West.

The spectacle of capitalist producers importuning their governments for wider latitude in trading with the bloc reinforces the self-confidence of the communists, who regard it as prima facie evidence of mounting difficulties within the capitalist market system. Western businessmen, the communists assert, are beginning to feel the pinch of contracting markets as the "parallel socialist world market" grows stronger. Communist trade delegations, bent on buying desired capital items, dangle before Western exporters the prospect of greatly increased bloc imports of consumer goods, even including the vision of the "limitless" China market. But after the trade fair enthusiasm subsides, orders for consumer goods usually dissolve in thin air. Western industrialists are left with definite requests only for specialized capital shipments—technologically our most advanced wares. At the beginning of 1960, West European firms had commitments to export from $200 to $300 million worth of the most sophisticated machine tools, including, e.g., a sixty-foot vertical boring machine that could be used for machining missile engine shells. Some of the items on order are more advanced than any comparable ones now in operation in the United States.

Economic expansion of the West is likely to produce further industrial surpluses which, in the absence of concerted protective measures, will further enhance the drawing power of the bloc. Great Britain—her erstwhile colonial markets dwindling while her Continental competitors expand—is peculiarly vulnerable. While British exports to both the U.S. and Western Europe showed substantial increases in 1959 over 1958, those to the U.S.S.R. rose a startling 30 per cent. Moreover, for five years the British have constantly and successfully urged the relaxation of Co-ordinating Committee (COCOM) restrictions on trade with China. The British Board of Trade has approved for export to China such items as machine tools, electric motors and generators, motor vehicles and tractors, railway locomotives and other railway equipment, combustion engines, scientific instruments, rubber tires and chemical products—goods vital to China's development plans. Meanwhile, Franco-Soviet and West German-East German trade is also on the upswing. Until now, most American businessmen have regarded the potentialities of Soviet bloc trade with either self-restraint or indifference. But it is inevitable that, as other members of the Free World alliance break ranks to increase trade links with the bloc, U.S. businessmen will begin to feel that they are losing commercial advantages to their less squeamish competitors.

Western Trade Policy Reassessed

In a protracted economic conflict the term "strategic goods" encompasses more than direct contributions to military-industrial potential. The facile distinction between war potential and peaceful industrial potential as the criterion of East-West trade falls wide of the mark. According to communist concepts of power, any trade which facilitates industrial development is strategically important. Trade with the West supplies the bloc with equipment which improves its technological levels, satisfies popular desires, expands the industrial power base, and increases its future capacity to export and thereby disrupt free markets. For a system which has abundantly proved its ability to harness economic capacity to purposes of global power accumulation, such trade is undeniably strategic.[6]

In order to appreciate fully the significance for the Soviets of trade with the West, we need to understand better the limitations and internal problems of their system. They are by no means ten feet tall, and we need not gull ourselves by overestimating their current economic capabilities. Soviet planners are faced with a number of difficulties, some temporary, others of a more enduring character. Underfulfillment of planned goals in the agricultural sector poses chronic problems and will continue to do so. Opening virgin lands in the Soviet East requires large numbers of new tractors at a time when replacement of old equipment everywhere is a pressing need. Furthermore, the Soviet chemical and electronics industries, except in a few strategically important sectors, lag far behind their counterparts in the Western industrial countries. Moscow's achievements in the production of rocket fuels, Sputniks and Luniks have served to distract our attention from a wide area of techno-industrial backwardness. Spectacular space achievements have undoubtedly paid off strategically and politically. But they are less significant as tokens of practical economic progress than is commonly supposed. They tell us what Soviet scientists are capable of doing when the regime concentrates resources upon projects for the purpose of building military power and impressing the outside world, but they do not tell us the story of what the regime has left undone for the benefit of Soviet citizens in the smaller cities and villages.[7] Nearly every visitor to the U.S.S.R. who has strayed from

[6] For example: In 1959, the Soviets tried to purchase large-size pipe in the United States but the deal was vetoed by the Department of Commerce. The Soviets then placed orders with two West German firms for 165,000 tons of large pipe (up to forty inches), valued at about $40 million. At first glance, pipe may appear to be a nonstrategic item. But it is generally believed that the Soviets want the pipe to carry natural gas from recently exploited sources behind the Urals to the East European satellites. The sale of such pipe by the West facilitates the process of intrabloc economic integration and this, decidedly, is a strategic development.

[7] The situation can perhaps best be illustrated from a cartoon that appeared in the Soviet humor magazine, *Crocodil*. An inventor who had designed a new button-sewing machine went to the planning offices to request an allocation of resources for its development. The bureaucrat looked at the inventor incredulously. "Button-sewing machine!" he exclaimed. "In the age of Sputniks, who needs buttons!"

the Moscow-Leningrad-Kiev circuit has found it hard to imagine that a nation most of whose people live under conditions which a Westerner would have deemed primitive in 1900 could ever have gained a lead in space technology.

Within recent years, the problem of depreciation, too, has reared its ugly head. During the Stalin era relatively little attention was paid to maintenance of plant. The general rule was simply to operate all productive machinery at full speed and as long as it would run. Service and repair were regarded as nuisances to be tolerated only when absolutely necessary, and allocation of resources for purposes of replacing a piece of equipment before it finally collapsed from wear was deemed wasteful. Consequently, one of the chief characteristics of the Soviet economy is a widespread obsolescence which has resulted in an appalling underemployment of resources.[8] Actually, the question of depreciation did not appear acute when the bulk of the productive machinery in the U.S.S.R. was still fairly new. Indeed it cannot be called "acute" even now, but the Khrushchev regime apparently realizes that the time has come to adopt a more sensible approach, and a great part of the Seven-Year Plan is devoted to modernization. Within the next few years, much old equipment will have to be replaced. For machinery originally purchased from the West, the Soviets will probably find replacement from abroad cheaper than undertaking the retooling effort themselves.

They have already manifested a desire to modernize their textile industry in this manner. This industry is a real burden upon the economy, with its antiquated machinery, its inordinate waste of manpower, and its inability to turn out a product which can be sold in quantity in foreign markets (apart from the unsophisticated rural areas of the satellite countries). Hence their wish to buy "turnkey"[9] textile factories from the West. Once an up-to-date plant

[8] Over 100,000 small electric power plants, e.g., which produce only 10 per cent of the total output employ more than 800,000 workers and produce one KWH at one to two rubles, while 90 per cent of the output is produced by large power stations employing less than 200,000 workers at a cost of about eight kopeks (i.e., .08 ruble) per KWH.

[9] A "turnkey" factory (a term employed by the Soviets themselves) is one in which the outside supplier designs it, builds it, installs all the equipment and trains Soviet citizens to operate it. When the entire process has been completed, he turns over the key to the Soviet managers.

has been installed, the retooling to replace other dilapidated factories can begin. The Soviets are clever technological imitators. This does not mean that they themselves could not design a modern textile factory if they put their minds to the task. They do not propose, however, to assign their best technical brains to such an economically costly but strategically menial effort. If they can procure the model from the West, mediocre technicians can be entrusted with the job of copying it. Meanwhile, their best engineers need not be diverted from more important work.

Problems confronting Soviet planners[10] are compounded by a critical manpower shortage, the significance of which was not diminished by recent reports of "technological unemployment" in the U.S.S.R. The marked dip in the population growth as a result of severe wartime losses is now making itself felt in the scarcity of young men who are available for military service and the labor force. This situation has compelled a revision of educational policy (e.g., by transferring academically less promising students from the universities to the labor force, by lengthening the school day in the lower grades, thus releasing women from home duties) and the widely advertised reduction of conventional military forces.

There is, of course, a huge pool of labor in the agricultural sector, where manpower is grossly wasted.[11] Transferring labor from the agricultural to the industrial-urban sector raises serious problems of rural reorganization, farm output, technical training and housing. The average worker's productivity in the industrial sector of the economy approximates one-third of that of the U.S. worker. But,

[10] It is not possible here to review all of the internal economic problems facing the U.S.S.R. But there is no doubt that the Soviets today find themselves under pressure along many economic fronts. The opening up of new regions will place an added burden on an already overloaded transportation system. The current Soviet plan calls for higher outlays in transportation, but it seems highly improbable that the enormous backlog will be filled. The Soviets are also beginning to realize that within the next decade they must start to reconcile the location of their industry with the location of future energy resources or else face the costly prospect of an overextended, inefficient productive system. While the Soviets plan a large increase in power generation, they are still not providing for adequate increases in distribution nets. Meanwhile, the Soviet worker is clamoring for improved living conditions in that least productive of areas requiring heavy outlays—housing.

[11] The average output ratio per Soviet and American farm worker is about one to eight. If the comparison were to be drawn between Soviet agriculture and the two million commercial farms in the U.S., the ratio would be closer to one to twenty-five. See Chapter 10, "Strategy of Ways and Means."

significantly, this disparity is greatest in consumer goods and least in strategic industries. The key, however, to raising total industrial output is to increase worker productivity through technological improvements. In the long run, the manpower shortage may prove to be a blessing for Soviet industry.

Western imports of sophisticated items will abet the Soviets' technological progress since Soviet propensity for imitation (with nary a thought of patent rights) can turn a few hundred million dollars' worth of machinery into important Soviet bloc capabilities over the course of one or two decades.

In this light, determined efforts should be made to remove the lure of trade which now draws our private entrepreneurs to the communist bloc market—especially trade on terms set by the Soviet trading monopoly. The United States and its industrial allies should monitor whatever trade does take place and channel it into areas that yield an adequate economic as well as political return. Western exporters (their eyes on the company's next annual statement) are no match for Soviet central planners (whose vision extends into the strategic future).

The real need is for a Free World trade organization to supervise exchanges with the bloc. Such an organization would protect free economies against individual pressures and the disruptive tactics of Soviet economic strategists. Specifically, its task would be to induce free nations to close ranks for purposes of long-range self-protection and to obtain the member nations' agreement to: (a) sell to bloc countries only in exchange for convertible currencies without extending credit; (b) limit sales primarily to raw materials and finished consumer goods; (c) minimize the sale of capital goods, since these relieve Soviet planning bottlenecks and manpower shortages; (d) co-operate to rescue economically weak nations from dependence upon Soviet trade; (e) prohibit Soviet "dumping" within their borders and retaliate against other disruptive tactics by "dumping" in established Soviet foreign markets on which Moscow depends for the acquisition of desirable currencies; and (f) deny the benefits of trade liberalization to any bloc nation which refuses to abide by GATT rules, regardless of any existing "most favored nation" agreements. Moreover, as George F. Kennan has suggested, trade should be made to "bring with it the normal incidental advantages of economic contact—extensive reciprocal travel and residence of businessmen in the other country, the establishment of close personal contacts and associations, the intermingling, in short, not only of the economic life but also of the people of the two countries."[12] We should exact for the trade privileges which we grant to the Soviets widened loopholes in the Iron Curtain.

Minimizing the lure of Soviet trade is much easier said than done. The task requires a great deal more than passing NATO resolutions. A purely negative approach will not satisfy the dynamic entrepreneurial spirit which is a basic Free World strength. Requisite to our needs is a vigorously articulated economic philosophy to furnish the frame for the policy programs which the free industrial nations see fit to adopt.

The total productive capacity of the free nations of the world, according to the most conservative estimates, is more than three times that of the entire Sino-Soviet bloc. Together these nations can create a self-sufficient and expanding community, able to maintain a decisive margin of economic superiority over the communist bloc for an indefinitely long period and to fulfill the economic aspirations of all its members, producers as well as consumers. Achievement of this objective, which should rank high in our economic strategy, will require greater co-operation, co-ordination and integration than most of the free nations have hitherto been willing to accept. As the world's leading economic power, the United States should lead by example, not words, in developing a genuine working partnership. The ultimate responsibility is ours. Regional economic integration should be pursued along trade-creating rather than trade-diverting channels. The aim must be to develop a liberal international economic order instead of sowing the seeds of division within the Free World.

In this effort, the cultivation of proper psychological attitudes will be of the utmost importance. We know that the long-range political and economic interests of the free nations promise abundant opportunities for multilateral growth and well-being. But if our outlook remains narrowly nationalist and protectionist, we compound the insoluble dilemmas and conflicts of interest amongst ourselves. It would be extremely unfortunate if the economic strength of the Free World were vitiated by hostile trading blocs within its ranks, or

[12] "Peaceful Coexistence: A Western View," *Foreign Affairs*, Vol. 38, January, 1960, p. 185.

by fears that the expansion of other free national economies, singly or in groups, represents a more dangerous form of economic rivalry than does the Sino-Soviet bloc. In essence, the question is whether the Free World will contribute to the fulfillment of Stalin's "last thesis," that "capitalist" nations will succumb to narrow selfishness and thereby render themselves susceptible to being picked off one by one.

Certainly one of the major tasks confronting a new Atlantic-wide economic organization[13] will be to bring about rapidly closer co-operation and eventually a union between the Common Market and the other European trading nations. Reconciliation between the six and their neighbors is essential to the continued *élan* of the NATO partnership.

U.S. Economic Position

We need not look far to find evidence of that fear which often eats at the solidarity of the free nations. Within recent years, many Americans have come to dread what they regard as a deterioration in the international competitive position of the United States. The American entrepreneur, it is said, is being "priced out of the world market." The main cause of these misgivings seems to be competition not so much between the U.S. and the Soviets as between the U. S. and its allies—Great Britain, the countries of Western Europe and Japan—which allegedly improve their position in world trade at the expense of the United States.

The criterion most commonly employed to measure the relative American decline has been the balance of payments.[14] During most of the 1950's, our annual payments deficit averaged just a little more than one billion dollars. No one worried too much about this moderate drain on our own reserves, for it represented largely the cost of a foreign economic policy which contributed substantially

[13] While this book was being prepared for publication, a preparatory committee in Paris was writing a charter for a twenty-nation Organization for Economic Co-operation and Development (OECD), to consist of the eighteen OEEC members plus Canada and the United States. This economic counterpart to NATO is expected to have the threefold function of facilitating economic growth, promoting aid to the underdeveloped countries and working out solutions to trade problems, both within the Free World and vis-à-vis the Soviet bloc.

[14] A considerable body of literature dealing with this problem has appeared since 1959. A few representative titles will be found in the Bibliography.

to strengthening our allies. But the two-year period 1958-1959 showed a total deficit of more than seven billion dollars. At this point, not a few vocal and influential quarters pressed for reduction of our overseas economic and military commitments as the means of righting our trade balances.

The viewers-with-alarm failed to distinguish between temporary imbalance and long-term structural changes in America's international economic position. Our balance of payments is always subject to adverse influence from temporary factors, such as cyclical business fluctuations, a strike in a critical industry, the sudden collapse of certain export markets (due perhaps to currency shortages abroad), a sudden jump in our imports to fill transitory domestic shortages, or changes in the trade pattern caused by technological innovation (e.g., a drop in foreign orders for U.S. planes pending a changeover from conventional to jet models). These recurrent dislocations are usually canceled out over a period of two or three years.

Apart from these short-term disturbances, the international economic position of the United States during the last decade has undergone some fundamental changes. Not all of them were adverse. Sizable increases in American tourism, private investment abroad,[15] the rising demand for foreign manufactures, and foreign military and economic assistance—all these outlays represent debit entries on the international accounting ledger, but they also post potential credits in international stability, security, economic and social development, good will, increased purchasing power abroad and income from overseas investments.

Perhaps what has caused most concern is the fact that certain sectors of American industry, e.g., steel and machine tools, having become high-cost producers, are losing foreign markets to European and Japanese competitors. From a few specific instances, however, we should not leap to the conclusion that the American producer is becoming less efficient across the board. In an age of rapid technological progress, occasional transfers of leadership in given productive fields are to be expected. Elements of European and Japanese industry, due to postwar reconstruction and modernization accom-

[15] Accumulated U.S. *private* investment abroad in the postwar period totals approximately forty billion dollars.

plished with U.S. aid, are actually more efficient than their American competitors.

As the Europeans and the Japanese recover their economic vigor, some American firms are encountering difficulties in foreign markets where they were unopposed in the late 1940's. Between 1952 and 1958, Germany's share of the world's exports of manufactures went up from 12 to 18.6 per cent, and Japan's from 3.8 to 6 per cent, while the U.S. share dropped from 26.2 to 23.2 per cent. But these adjustments may indicate a normalization of long-range trade relationship more than they do an unhealthy decline in the American competitive position. The relative improvement in the economic capabilities of our allies, striking testimonial to the success of our foreign economic policies since 1947, should certainly not be viewed as a calamity. The situation does, however, warrant a pondered reassessment of the relative efficiency of the American economic performance.

Many closely interrelated factors affect a country's comparative advantage as an international trader: cost of raw materials; access to cheap transport routes; productivity of labor; degree of plant modernization; managerial and technical skills; marketing procedure; labor union and corporation policies; and national policies regarding taxation, interest rates, social welfare and foreign assistance programs. Their importance varies in different countries. Historically, the United States has found its decisive advantage in the capital goods sector. It is precisely in this sector that a decline in our competitive position has occurred. There cannot be a doubt that when the U.S. decides to apply its energy and resourcefulness to a production problem, it can outperform any other nation. But to maintain capital goods preponderance, or regain it in areas where it is being lost, a more efficient monetary policy and fiscal system is required. Certainly this is one of the high levels of thought and policy upon which economics and strategy must meet.

The United States, because of its key position within the Free World, has a special obligation to keep a watchful eye on all factors which affect its world economic position, and to correct any serious imbalances which may appear. But in the process of correction we should emphasize improvement of domestic productive efficiency and formulate imaginative, liberal trade solutions. We would be ill-advised to stint our international commitments or resort to outmoded protectionist measures. During the decade ahead, the U.S. should seek to strike a rising balance between its global responsibilities and its economic capabilities. Both should grow in proportion to each other.

We can expect a steady upward swing in our international obligations and hence in our outbound payments in the future. Our economic strength can sustain substantial deficits for a few years, but we cannot base our long-range economic strategy on the principle of international deficit financing. If we attempt to do so, sooner or later other free countries will lose confidence in the soundness of the dollar as the Free World's major reserve currency. This is just another way of saying that they will lose confidence in the U.S. as the world's premier economic power. Instead of regarding with equanimity the prospect of a steady drain on our gold reserves and an unlimited increase in the foreign holdings of dollar balances, we must plan over the long haul to finance our international military, economic and other programs through a surplus on current account —i.e., primarily through our exports. Economically speaking, this is the healthiest way and—on an indefinitely continuing basis—the only sound way for the United States to transfer capital and other forms of assistance to our needy friends abroad. If we carry large internal deficits even for a few years, we might find ourselves under mounting domestic pressure to return to isolationism, dismantle our global security system, and fall back upon the concept of "Fortress America."

The U.S. balance of payments problem must be tackled on both a short-term and a long-term basis, with appropriate modifications of both internal and external policy. We should resist temptation to save money by reducing overseas commitments which are justified on political and military grounds.[16] We should not turn our backs upon the policy of gradual trade liberalization by imposing artificial restrictions on imports or on foreign purchases made by countries receiving U.S. economic aid. Such measures as the "Buy American" decision made by the Development Loan Fund in the fall of 1959

[16] Some savings can be made by bringing home the dependents of American military personnel in Europe. This action might undermine the morale of our fighting forces and perhaps reduce European confidence in American economic strength. It might induce the Europeans, however, to share more of the economic burden of collective security.

often convey abroad the very impression of economic weakness which we should seek by every means to avoid.

There are better ways of dealing with the problem. We can, for example, improve credit facilities for U.S. exporters and encourage those American producers who now concentrate almost exclusively on the domestic market to become competitive abroad.[17] We can work through diplomatic channels to persuade our European allies and Japan to continue their policies, launched during the last year, of reducing discrimination against dollar imports. We can take forthright steps to induce our industrial allies to bear a fuller share of the Free World's economic and military aid burdens (measured in terms of the ratio of their expenditures in these areas to their GNP). This will require a more efficient co-ordination of our international trade, investment and development policies, plus a willingness on our part to share with them in the realm of defense and military technology. Offshore Procurement, a Korean War practice, was based largely on the premise that the strengthening of our allies' economies was essential to our own security. Now we should impress upon our economically stronger allies the virtue of full partnership in the common defense and the mutual advantages of "specialization at least costs." Our stockpiling programs and assistance to industries indispensable to security should be reviewed in terms of our broader alliance potentialities for both raw material resources and productive capacities. Here lies the economic testing ground of our alliance-mindedness.

Parallel with these external adjustments should proceed an internal transformation of the American economy. It is imperative that the various elements of our socioeconomic structure—industry, labor, agriculture, advertising and banking, to name only a few of the more important ones—co-operate closely with government policies to promote a national understanding of the communist challenge and to create conditions favorable to rapid capital formation within the United States. As a nation, we must agree to work harder, consume a lower proportion of our total GNP as its absolute volume

[17] A step in this direction has already been taken by the Department of Commerce. Noting that foreign merchants were more skilled than Americans at competing for world trade and also that they have heretofore received more assistance from their governments, Mr. Philip A. Ray, Undersecretary of Commerce, went before the Senate Appropriations Committee in August, 1960, and requested that the Congress vote $1.8 million to finance a drive for the expansion of the U.S. export trade.

expands, and allot more of that product to strategic programs. (The bearing of economic policies on this task will be discussed in Chapter 10, "The Strategy of Ways and Means").

Seeking a Broad Perspective

An expanding free international economy can provide abundant markets for all producers. The idea of a static international economy is outdated. Progress and growth can be contagious, just as stagnation and contraction were during the great depression. The United States, until now every bit as jealous of sovereign prerogatives in economic matters as any of its allies, will be expected to lead in the gradual removal of import quotas and the downward revision of tariff barriers, and to move toward the highest possible degree of currency convertibility. American businessmen will generally agree that an international environment of free trade benefits the country, but will protest bitterly specific rulings that pinch their profits. The answer does not lie in preaching to businessmen devotion to the nation at the expense of their private interests, but rather in furnishing them with the proper incentives for adjusting themselves to a changing world. A rehabilitation fund to minimize the individual sense of insecurity usually attending industrial conversion or relocation would constitute one means of facilitating adjustment.

Creating rational trade patterns requires a broad time perspective. Many adjustments which could not possibly be made within the space of a year can be carried out over the course of a decade without causing undue hardship. We can make haste slowly once we have a clear idea of the goal. Every country has its own set of special economic problems. Allies should be sensitive to each other's economic aspirations and needs. Whenever restrictive economic measures seem unavoidable, the nation adopting them should explain them in advance to its allies and seek means of cushioning their adverse impact upon other countries. The flow of information which leads to understanding needs constantly to be improved, for the essence of a thriving community of free nations is communication. Our statesmen can do much to stimulate both mutual trade and investment by removing such obstacles as currency and capital transfer problems as well as risks of double taxation.

United States policy should be geared to enable the free industrial countries to build mutually an expanded economic base which can sustain increasingly complex programs of military and peaceful technology, social well-being within the industrial nations and economic development of the emergent nations of the world. Wherever it is feasible, regional economic integration ought to be fostered. During the last decade, we have encouraged the integration of Europe for the purposes of increasing productivity, promoting political unity and enhancing Western security. As far as we can judge, our labor in the service of a stronger Europe has turned out to be one of our most noteworthy postwar policy accomplishments.

There are, however, two caveats which must be attached to a policy of support for broader integration in Western Europe. The first is economic. The United States cannot be indifferent to the amount of discrimination which might in the future accompany the development of the Common Market. The level of the common tariff which is to be erected around the Common Market should be lowered gradually. Eventually, as the common tariff serves its purpose of encouraging economies-of-scale among the Six, a general movement toward liberalization of trade with other regions of the Free World will be in order. It will be very important that the underdeveloped areas have expanding opportunities to earn European currencies. The tariff on most raw material imports, of course, will remain relatively low. But it should be made as low as possible for selected manufactured items which represent the bulk of the exports on which some of the hardest-pressed underdeveloped countries depend for the solution of their exchange difficulties. The United States will be in a better position to ask its allies to lower some tariffs and keep others low if it shows that it is, itself, willing to lower duties on imports from the underdeveloped countries.

The second caveat is political. It will be unfortunate if the creation of the Common Market and the subsequent grouping of the Outer Seven should lead to permanent economic rivalry or to the loosening of political ties between Great Britain and the Continent. The Common Market is undoubtedly a positive achievement if for no other reason than that it is symptomatic of a real Franco-German rapprochement. The United States, however, while favoring integration among the Six, should seek to minimize any tendencies toward European regional isolation or preferential arrangements which are prejudicial to the solidarity of the entire Atlantic Community. Should the Common Market become a high-tariff club, it might push Great

Britain and other members of the Outer Seven into closer trade ties with the Sino-Soviet bloc.

The industrial nations of the Free World are likely to become increasingly attractive targets for communist economic warfare as time goes on. The anticipated expansion of their industries is bound to generate manufactured surpluses which might make it hard to resist the attraction of Soviet offers. The Western Allies can maintain a disciplined front in the face of a heightened communist challenge only by shunning every divisive tendency and moving toward greater unity, economic as well as political and military. In summary, regional integration should be encouraged to the extent that it promotes the economic strength of the Free World. But it is imperative that the process of integration be organically linked to a wider sphere of trade liberalization as an essential concomitant of the Free World's unity of political purpose.

Regional economic integration is even more urgently needed in other Free World areas where particularism is now much stronger than it is in Europe. A "common market" for Latin America would make a good deal of sense as part of a hemispheric development program. In the Middle East, too, especially where the Arab states are delineated by artificial boundaries of relatively recent origin, real growth cannot be expected to take place until the frustrating effects of economic truncation have been overcome. United States policy in both regions ought to encourage the removal of man-made barriers to the freedom of economic transactions and rational planning.

The Underdeveloped Areas

Our attitude toward the underdeveloped areas is essentially ambiguous for a number of reasons. Most of the countries of Asia and Africa differ culturally or politically from those of the North Atlantic Community. Occasionally, their nationalistic policies conflict with our interests. We desire political friendship, economic cooperation and socio-cultural exchange with these nations, but many of them do not interpret the message of past and contemporary history as we do. Hence obstacles to mutual understanding are formidable. Yet the hostility they sometimes display toward us need not alarm us unduly as long as they remain free.

We should not insist that the so-called "uncommitted" countries declare themselves anticommunist. Strategically it is quite sufficient that they should stay free to work out their own destinies. As we see it, their real choice is to retain their own identities and loyalty to their own values or to submit to alien domination and have communist values imposed upon them. We cannot properly object when they disagree with us on serious matters so long as they generate their *own* policies rather than act as dummies of the communist ventriloquist. We must, however, make them see that we shall always stand closer to those whose values we share and, specifically, to those who embrace the ideals which we seek to preserve in the world. There are degrees of friendship, and the degree is a function of values shared and communicated.

This does not necessarily mean that in every conflict of interest between our Western Allies and the emergent countries of the world we shall invariably support the former. But generally speaking, our ties of friendship with the Western Allies will always be stronger than those with the non-Western, nonaligned areas. It is idle to cavil at the unalterable facts of contemporary international relations. Many underdeveloped countries are unwilling to draw too close to us and to unite their deepest national purposes with ours. Certainly we cannot force them into the pattern of international friendship which we and our allies have freely woven. Some of the nascent states, of course, have already seen fit to move closer than others to the Western Alliance. Closeness necessarily involves a reciprocal relationship: If a state chooses to move closer to us politically, we cannot avoid moving closer to it. While we should strive constantly to devise economic policies which will redound to the benefit of all free states, it is inevitable that in the long run the convergence of foreign policy aims between ourselves and certain states will be reflected in a consolidation of special economic bonds.

Whatever economic and technological progress the underdeveloped countries have already achieved—and this has been remarkable when we consider their status fifty years ago—can be traced almost entirely to their links with the industrial West. Since World War II, the total of "official" economic aid (exclusive of military assistance) from the free industrial nations to the underdeveloped countries has amounted by the end of 1960 to upwards of $37 billion and is now running about $4 billion annually.

Since 1954, when the communists began to offer foreign assistance, the Sino-Soviet bloc has extended less than two billion dollars in the form of credits.[18] The Soviet program reached its peak in the period 1956-1958 and has since fallen off somewhat, while Western aid programs have been on the increase in recent years. Our European Allies are now beginning to bear a larger share of the international aid and development burden. The flow of aid from the West, as its over-all economic capabilities grow, will undoubtedly continue at an expanded rate in the decades to come.

Government-to-government aid is not the sole prerequisite to development. While most underdeveloped areas labor under foreign exchange shortages and seek to lay the capital foundations of a modern economic order, the role of governments is a leading one. Over the long range, however, economic development should proceed via expanding mutually beneficial foreign trade and private investment rather than dependence upon unrequited loans. The genuine interest of the underdeveloped countries will be served by strengthened ties with the free industrial countries' economies, notably the importation of private capital on mutually advantageous terms.

Western Europe, Great Britain, the United States, Canada, Japan and other free industrial countries hold an important place in the foreign trade of the underdeveloped nations. The former import from the latter at least twenty-five times as much as does the Sino-Soviet bloc. Within the last few years, the leaders of several states in Asia, Africa and Latin America have begun to see the benefits which will accrue to their peoples from hitching their wagon to the West's expanding market economy. Many Western businessmen, too, are coming to realize that the economic development of the underdeveloped nations will ultimately lead to an expansion rather than a contraction of trade.

Even if there were no communist threat, industrially advanced nations would still have a responsibility to the peoples of the newly

[18] As shown before, the communists try to get maximum mileage from their aid by concentrating upon selected countries. Since 1954, they have given more economic aid than the U.S. to the following countries: Egypt, Syria, Ethiopia, Guinea, Yemen and Afghanistan. In Burma, Ceylon and Indonesia their promised aid approaches the aid delivered by the U.S. Cf. *Significant Issues in Economic Aid*, Staff Paper of the International Industrial Development Center, Stanford Research Institute, 1960.

independent states and the nonautonomous territories. We would still have to help them to overcome the harmful effects of rapid population growth which annuls any noticeable gains in living standards; free themselves from an excessive dependence upon a few primary exports; reduce their chronic foreign exchange shortages and import the capital for building the "infrastructure" on which natural economic growth can be grafted. If on no other grounds than enlightened self-interest, it would still be incumbent upon both governments and private enterprise in the industrial states to recognize their vital stake in fostering social stability and economic progress within the regions which contain the greater part of the world's population. There would still be no choice but to heed, as Charles de Gaulle has expressed it, the call upon "those who lack nothing to help those who lack all."

However, the communist menace does indeed exist. If its hot breath on our necks stirs us to embrace our international responsibilities more fervently, then the humanist West may yet succeed in turning the inhuman Bolshevik experiment to the benefit of mankind.

In our approach to the underdeveloped areas we must beware of a mischievous fixation. Forty years of communist propaganda fostered the West's guilt complex about the sins of its colonial past which would prevent it from reconciling ethics and strategy. A massive international economic job waits to be done. There is no reason to feel sheepish about conceiving our economic programs within the framework of a strategy calculated to defend the world against a system which stands for the annihilation of humanist values.

Proposals for increased aid by Western governments encounter two antagonistic attitudes among the public, especially the American public. The first is popular disenchantment with assistance programs on the grounds that we alone have borne the burden of the "global giveaway," that our generous efforts were wasted because the recipient lands are a bottomless pit. The second is the fear that we, the greatest free enterprise society on earth, are straining our economy to engage in a type of international development planning which merely strengthens the socialist tendencies abroad in the world.

It is not surprising that our foreign assistance efforts should be misunderstood and opposed in many quarters and for many different reasons. Like most worth-while programs, they have either not been presented to the public with sufficient force or else have been oversold in a simplified form which insults the intelligence of the American citizen (e.g.: "We must meet the communist challenge on the battleground of the underdeveloped areas"—"Raise the standard of living and defeat communism"). One of our very serious difficulties arises from the fact that by pitching our discussion to the Madison Avenue chimera—the twelve-year-old intelligence—we often end up conditioning our opinion-molding elites to think like twelve-year-olds.

By dint of an intelligently conceived process of public education, we can present the American people with the sophisticated economic facts of life in an era of protracted conflict. The American people are quite capable of understanding why the United States had to bear the major share of the aid burden since World War II, why it gave priority to European recovery and how the Europeans can now make common cause with us as we turn to meet a greater challenge than that which evoked the Marshall Plan.

Technical obstacles exist to be sure: limitations set by capital availability and "economic absorptive capacity," not to mention the frustrations encountered in importing technology and science into preindustrial social structures. We must take into account the drag of illiteracy and lassitude, cultural behavior patterns[19] and time lags, administrative-fiscal inefficiency and corruption. We have to anticipate a rising propensity to consume and import, triggered by the input of development capital, which compounds the recipient country's foreign exchange problems. These problems are complicated further by basic institutional deficiencies, and fundamental differences in the value systems that motivate "them and us." We need to know more about all these intricate phenomena and how they are interrelated.

It is true that many of our aid programs in the underdeveloped world have addressed the necessary task of creating social overhead capital, notably in those types of economic projects which, because

[19] One major obstacle to development in Africa is the psychological orientation of many potential workers to a leisure-centered rather than a production-centered existence. Part-time employment—in the towns and the mining industry and on the plantations—is a widespread phenomenon in many areas south of the Sahara.

they offer no prospect of profit, do not attract private capital. Hence, it seems reasonable to conclude that our official programs *have* strengthened the socialist bias of the leadership groups of societies in transition. Relatively little has been done in the last decade to promote the growth of nongovernmental incentive—that indispensable ingredient of free societies. But the picture changes. More and more "development economists" recognize private investment as an integral part of international development. More and more businessmen realize that foreign aid programs can help to establish conditions favorable to the export of private capital to emergent nations and thereby counter the "drift toward socialism."

The full potential of private development capital, however, cannot possibly be realized unless the constant threat of expropriation is removed from the foreign investment scene. The specter of Iran, Indonesia, Egypt, Cuba and other countries which have sought "liberation through nationalization" has had a very deleterious impact upon the flow of private capital to nearly all the underdeveloped countries. If the United States expects its entrepreneurs to invest abroad, it must assure them that their economic risks will not be compounded by political risks. It must be prepared to guarantee them against confiscation by demonstrating that it has a carefully planned policy to deter any breach of international economic contracts.

Until now, the United States and its industrial allies have handled the task of international development in Asia, Africa and Latin America on a haphazard basis, neglecting to combine their scientific intelligence, vast resources and organizational ability in a coherent approach. During the last decade, the U.S. has carried a disproportionately large share of the burdens. Allied countries have occasionally engaged in economic practices which raised mutual suspicions and animosities. Aid projects have often been evaluated in terms of local political factors rather than broader, regional economic considerations. Some have been vitiated by needless misunderstandings between donor and recipient. Western governments have shown a tendency to channel assistance to those countries which prove most proficient in the use of lobbying techniques. Finally, there has been an amazing proliferation of development programs and institutions: the Export-Import Bank, Mutual Security Program (including Defense Support, Technical Co-operation, Special Assistance and the

Development Loan Fund), Public Law 480 Programs (Agricultural Trade Development and Assistance Act), United Nations Technical Assistance Programs, the Colombo Plan, the International Bank for Reconstruction and Development, the International Finance Corporation, the International Monetary Fund, and the Overseas Countries and Territories Development Fund of the European Common Market.

The mere listing rouses suspicion that some at least owe their life to contradictory economic assumptions and may be working at cross purposes. Clearly the time has come for co-ordinated efforts toward a consistent, efficient pattern of international development policies.

As the free industrial nations undertake concerted development policies, they need a hopeful and realistic vision of their goals—hopeful to those who yearn for decent living conditions, realistic in terms of our capabilities. When we consider the vast expanse of Asia, Africa and Latin America and the wants of their billion desperate people, we must concede the impossibility of closing, within the next quarter of a century, the gap which has opened over two centuries between their standard of living and ours. There is danger in whetting popular appetites with glowing yet futile promises of parity.

Despite a quarter of a century of domestic federal assistance programs, we still have a long way to go toward the goal of closing the gap in economically stagnant regions of our own country. On the other hand, there is no reason to chill the spirits of the underprivileged billion with words like these: "According to our best economists, the gap, far from narrowing, is bound to widen. So far as we can see, it is unlikely that there will be any substantial improvement in your per capita income during the life of the generation now being born. The very best you can hope for is to hold the line." In the long run it will probably be better for the underdeveloped countries if we moderately overestimate the size of the development challenge. Still, if we couch our vision in terms as bleak as these, we shall unnecessarily dismay many of our friends.

Most of the pessimistic estimates are based on per capita income projections, but benefits accruing from economic-technological progress may well surpass purely statistical forecasts that are based solely on past performance. These analyses usually minimize or ignore the cumulative effect of local social change and world-wide economic growth on underdeveloped areas. Factories and dams are going up; roads, railroads, ports and airports are being built; more and more people are being drawn away from barter to market economies; foreign commerce is increasing; health and education are improving; consumption is growing and new technologies are being imported.

If during the decade of the sixties the free industrial nations in concert increase their "official" aid, their trade and their overseas investment, noticeable improvements *can* be made in the absolute standard of living of most underdeveloped peoples—improvements substantial enough to register on the consciousness of the underprivileged masses and give them some reason to face the future with hope. Only the free industrial nations possess the gigantic productive potential needed to give underdeveloped peoples the push toward the better world which the communists, unfortunately, have often proved more eloquent than we in describing.

Economic versus Military Aid

In developing its economic strategy, the United States and its allies would be unwise to assume that the security of the underdeveloped areas against the threat of communism can be procured with economic aid alone. True, the problem of military security against direct communist aggression is much less acute in Africa and Latin America than along the borderlands of the Sino-Soviet bloc. In areas insulated against direct attack, a long-range program of economic development combined with adequate internal security measures may achieve relative stability. But in more vulnerable regions, the effort to furnish security with economic aid alone would be much more costly and less effective than an effort based upon a program of military assistance *with* economic aid.

First priority in threatened areas must for economic as well as strategic reasons be given to strategic-military necessity. A healthy economy cannot develop in an environment beset by military insecurity. Military weakness sooner or later invites conflict that would prove far more wasteful economically than a soundly conceived military program.

We would be ill-advised to sponsor idealistic programs that pare military assistance to the bone in favor of purely economic aid. Our military assistance program should not be regarded as a hindrance to economic development in recipient countries. The dichotomy between "economic aid" and "military aid"—posed as though the two forms were mutually exclusive—is misleading. A given amount of economic aid need not be more conducive to real growth than its equivalent in military funds. The manner in which the aid is managed and fed into the economy may be just as significant as the heading under which the aid is given.

Opponents of military assistance frequently contend that economic and military growth stand in an inverse relationship; the larger the military force, the lower the rate of growth in an underdeveloped country. Actually, no such simplistic correlation can be drawn. Economic growth is affected by psychological and political factors that are every bit as important as the level of either military or economic aid expenditures.

There is no absolute yardstick for measuring the adequacy of our current levels of spending for military assistance. Possibly closer attention to the task of making this reassessment for each recipient is now overdue. Twin perils beset such evaluations. National pride begets requests for sophisticated weapons and equipment, regardless of indigenous technical skills to operate and maintain them. Visible evidence of military strength (more infantry battalions and artillery) is valued higher than the "infrastructure" to make it effective (all-weather roads to enhance mobility and logistic organization to ensure staying power).

Accomplishments of the military in underdeveloped countries (Pakistan and Burma, especially) point to the officer corps as a source of competent, honest public servants for economic and political tasks. Indeed, Chinese communist practices of assigning construction and agricultural responsibilities to the military are being emulated in not a few free lands. Another instance where a military program can contribute to civilian needs is the development of indigenous airlines: economic benefits in peace, and swift, efficient means of deploying troops to dissident areas in emergency. Farm-to-market roads can be laid out to enhance military security (the Romans set one example two thousand years ago).

While military assistance must be conceived primarily as a political instrument of potential military value, its long-term success requires organizational, sociological, economic and political progress in recipient countries. Military assistance can yield valuable economic and social by-products. The United States should encourage the use of indigenous armed forces as a "transmission belt" of socioeconomic reform and development.

"Defense supports" can serve, in addition to their stated objectives, to foster the development of social overhead capital—such as roads, railroads, airfields, ports, communications systems, and power, water and sanitation projects. Greater emphasis upon the development and training of medical, signal, engineer and transport aviation units can contribute to local economic growth, consistent with the requirements of their security mission.

Military forces can be helped by our Military Advisory Assistance Groups to become effective instruments of social change: (1) using their procurement practices to raise local production and improve standards; (2) helping to raise the nation's literacy level and stimulating the desire for higher education; (3) imparting to soldiers basic technical skills useful upon return to civilian life; (4) fostering the spread of English as the major secondary language of the underdeveloped world; (5) breaking down archaic tribalism; (6) inculcating potential leaders with a heightened sense of public responsibility; and (7) advancing local capabilities in management administration, organization, logistics, finance and maintenance through training programs.

Policy for the Underdeveloped World

The free industrialized countries will have to do more than heretofore to help underdeveloped countries resist Soviet bloc trade-and-aid blandishments. The international flow of aid should be increased to countries selected, by reason of size, strategic location and political-psychological influence on the world scene, as key arenas of the protracted conflict.[20] An economically feasible and politically desirable goal, to be achieved by 1970, would be to

[20] Since economic assistance programs cannot be unlimited in size, the United States has no choice but to select those countries which, in both economic and sociopolitical terms, seem prepared to utilize outside aid to the best advantage. In Asia, for example, Pakistan, Taiwan and India apparently offer the best opportunities for sustained industrial growth. Pakistan, under the leadership of Ayub Khan, has achieved a degree of political stability which permits her to start serious planning for economic development. Taiwan has already achieved a surprisingly high rate of growth during the last five years. India, of course, labors under the most gigantic burdens. But compared with other countries in Asia, India appears to be ready to make modest progress. She has a capable civil service as well as honest intelligent leaders. She is not

double the amount of "official" economic aid annually, over the present level of about four billions per year. Aid should be made available on a consistent, long-term basis to assure continuity and facilitate development plans. The increased aid would be channeled for the most part through existing institutions, once their relative performance has been evaluated by the proposed international economic organization of the industrialized allies.

Simultaneously, intensified efforts should be made to siphon private capital into underdeveloped areas, preferably on a "mixed" ownership basis whenever local conditions favor such an arrangement.[21] To take the lead in encouraging such investment the U.S. Congress might permit tax deferral on companies' profits reinvested in underdeveloped countries. Although resulting in an estimated annual revenue loss of thirty to forty million dollars, this policy would help to raise American investments in underdeveloped areas from the present annual rate of half a billion to a rate of one and a half or two billion dollars a year.

Nations willing to create an environment conducive to private investment and enterprise deserve preference in aid allocation. The United States would also do well to lend continued support to the World Bank's policy of making its financial aid contingent upon the acceptance of sound fiscal policies. In the absence of overriding political considerations, the economic recommendations of the International Monetary Fund should not be undercut by U.S. government agencies making substitute loans to nations which reject IMF recommendations for fiscal improvement. Granted that the need for "soft loan" institutions (such as the Development Loan Fund) will grow, nevertheless some system of economic rewards should be retained for a nation which puts its house in order.

There need be no dispute over government aid versus private investment overseas. The industrial allies can co-ordinate their

---

handicapped by xenophobia or ultranationalism. Furthermore, she permits private investment, both domestic and foreign, to participate in at least certain areas of economic development. If the political stability which has been achieved in the Nehru era can be preserved, India may approach what W. W. Rostow calls the "take-off point." Given her political importance on the world scene, India will merit our special consideration among the neutralist states.

[21] In some areas, especially in Africa, the concept of ownership hardly exists. The formulation of rules for the definition and protection of property is an important prerequisite to the construction of a modern, free economy.

development efforts to make for true complementarity of both. Governmental assistance should continue to be concentrated primarily upon the task of sharpening local skills and helping to build the infrastructure of a modern economy, while private capital lays the foundation for a nongovernmental industrial and trade capacity.[22] Economic and technical aid can foster a climate favorable to the growth of pluralist enterprise if it encourages the formation of business firms and voluntary organizations in the recipient countries. Person-to-person contacts are extremely important for the success of such efforts. Our scientists, educators, investors, engineers, businessmen, labor union representatives and governmental mission personnel can do a great deal to promote the rise of free associations within the transitional societies of Latin America, Asia and Africa.[23] This kind of development aid is no less important than the shipping of technical equipment.

The need for exercising greater selectivity in the type of economic aid projects has long been recognized. The problem is often made to appear as if a sharp line could be drawn between impact projects and genuine development projects. Aid should be channeled into developments which will help to satisfy the real wants and aspirations of native peoples. Aid filtering down tangibly to the people of the recipient countries has a deeper political effect than government-to-government capital transfers, which, however essential they may be to relieve balance of payments difficulties, usually remain "invisible" so far as the public is concerned.

At the same time, we should help the underdeveloped countries to chose wisely those economic projects that make most sense because they benefit most. A country's capital, labor and managerial skills should not be wasted on projects that are likely to prove inefficient and to require permanently government subsidies or tariff protection. Industrial projects should be designed, in the words of the 1950 Act for International Development, to "contribute to

[22] This is not a hard and fast rule. Occasionally, it may be politically necessary for the United States to support publicly owned industrial monopolies (e.g., in some of the Latin-American states).

[23] Contacts between U.S. unions and noncommunist labor organizations in Latin America are especially to be encouraged, and American companies operating in Latin America should be urged to adopt labor and public relations programs which will foster higher local purchasing power and help to project a more favorable image of the United States.

raising standards of living, creating new sources of wealth, increasing productivity and expanding purchasing power."

Nearly all the underdeveloped countries want heavy industry in a hurry, irrespective of whether this is a sensible objective from the standpoint of international or even indigenous economics. Ill-conceived industrial projects may lead only to waste of resources. Determination of types of industry most suitable for a given country should emerge from co-operative study among local and foreign government agencies, intergovernmental agencies, private individuals and firms in the developing country, and private investors, professional consultants and banking organizations abroad.

The underdeveloped countries look to the West for technical aid in undertaking the extensive studies and resource surveys needed before realistic development plans can be drafted. If the West lags in conducting oil explorations, for example, even countries linked to the West by treaty will be tempted to turn to the Soviets for assistance, as Pakistan did in the spring of 1960. One of the most obvious ways in which the West could help the underdeveloped countries to arrive at a better understanding of their own economic problems would be to promote periodic regional conferences with leading Western and local economic analysts in attendance.

Intellectuals of the underdeveloped areas sometimes fail to see that some of their favorite objectives, vaguely humanitarian though they may be, do not always make economic sense. The much-admired goal of creating welfare states on a socialist pattern, for example, can stifle economic initiatives in countries where per capita income is extremely low. Heavy taxes upon foreign companies eat up profits and discourage the further investment essential to sustained growth. Labor legislation and other social reforms which have been realized in Western industrial societies must be fitted to the economic capabilities of Latin-American, Asian and African states. They should not be pushed to the point where the incentive to private investment, both local and foreign, is destroyed. Educational programs must make it crystal-clear that the most substantial advances in the condition of working people are made by increasing productivity, not by merely redistributing existing GNP.

The United States will be wise to stimulate direct contact between potential leaders within the underdeveloped areas and Americans in all walks of life. Opportunities for education and business training within the United States should be broadened. It has been suggested that private industrial corporations co-operate with U.S. government agencies in working out programs whereby Latin-American, Asian and African graduates of American universities, technical institutes and business schools could spend a period of internship with an American company before returning home.

The United States should take a vigorous lead within NATO toward establishing centers for the training of civil servants, industrial managers, accountants and other personnel from the underdeveloped countries. Some regional training centers might be established within the underdeveloped countries themselves or in countries (such as Turkey and Argentina) which have reached an intermediate level of economic development but are still keenly aware of the problems of "getting started." Such programs of technical training will be strengthened if, instead of being purely technical, they include the humanities in their curricula to demonstrate the worth of such ideals as political tolerance, cultural freedom, equality of social opportunity, and government limited in power and responsive to the will of the people.

So far as the all-important question of trade is concerned, the United States and its allies should undertake, on an experimental basis, a number of measures designed to alleviate the price and exchange difficulties now besetting the underdeveloped regions. They should take steps to: (a) minimize those harmful fluctuations in world demand patterns which are due to swings in the business cycle; (b) prevent excessive fluctuations of basic commodity and raw material prices by establishing international commodity agreements; (c) institute Free World stockpiling programs or commodity exchange unions in specified lines, which would enable underdeveloped countries to obtain needed development materials on a barter basis; (d) devise triangular trade agreements when these will break through the exchange bottlenecks of some countries and stimulate international trade;[24] (e) move toward the creation of a

[24] The United States might, for example, furnish raw cotton to Japan to be processed into cloth which could then be shipped to countries in Southeast Asia. The latter in turn would send rice and other foodstuffs to Japan to cover the manufacturing costs. Thus the original U.S. foreign aid outlay, viz., the cost of the raw cotton, would have a "multiplier effect" on Free World international trade, provide an economic benefit to two friendly parties, and help to cement regional trade ties that are desirable on political grounds.

limited-liability Free World Payments Union, similar in concept to the former European Payments Union, to serve as a payments clearinghouse and allow member nations to use their trade surpluses with some members to cancel out their trade deficits with others; (f) try, in the meantime, to promote the diversification of the underdeveloped countries' production patterns so that they will be less dependent upon the export of a few primary products.[25]

One problem urgently demands attention: the agricultural dilemma that plagues the Free World. It has often been called the "paradox of the billions." A billion people go badly undernourished while a billion dollars' worth of surplus food rots in American warehouses. Even though the world demand for food far exceeds the supply, an institutional blockage has virtually rendered us powerless to prevent an appalling wastage of part of the supply. This is but one surface phase of the problem. Its roots are deeper. While the underdeveloped areas have just barely begun to rationalize their agricultural techniques, many of the industrialized countries have already accomplished wonders of agricultural productivity. Yet they have not even begun to revise the "farm policies" which they inherited from an age of depression.

In the 1960's, the practice of according agriculture tariff protection and price props which were enacted before World War II is outmoded. It represents a major obstacle to regional economic integration and the improvement of the diet for millions in the underdeveloped areas. The question of agricultural preferences has been one of the main stumbling blocks to an understanding between Britain and the Common Market, and has caused headaches even among the Six. The question of how best to dispose of agricultural surpluses has proved equally nettlesome in the relations between the U.S. and its allies. The dilemmas are compounded and the issues further confused by those in the industrialized West who fear that the improvement of agricultural production in the underdeveloped

[25] Although the desire of the underdeveloped countries to overcome an excessive dependence upon exports is understandable, it cannot be gainsaid that primary products will continue to be a vital source of foreign exchange for many new states. It is essential that mono-product or bi-product economies diversify and that underemployed labor be retrained for work in other productive lines. Nevertheless, care must be taken that the development of new industries not be brought about at the expense of primary product industries which are important both to the local and to the world economy.

areas may lead only to disturbances in international commodity markets or to faster rates of population growth in the congested areas.

The Free World needs an optimum pattern of food production, distribution and storage along with the appropriate institutions to sustain it. The industrial nations, acting through an effective organization for economic co-operation, should formulate policies which will enable them to: (a) use the West's agricultural surpluses to establish international food reserves which will contribute to the security of the Free World; (b) help to raise food production in the undernourished lands by modernizing their agricultural methods; (c) increase the distribution of surplus foods to the hungry people of the world through the United Nations; (d) put our agricultural surpluses to more effective use as instruments of economic growth in selected countries. The immediate question confronting the United States is whether it can expand its P.L. 480 program without arousing the resentment of allies worried about their export markets (especially the Canadians, French, Australians and Argentineans).

From a longer-range point of view, concerted efforts will be required to bring about a better balance between declining world prices of agricultural products and rising world prices of manufactured goods. These efforts are doomed to failure if GATT does not acknowledge the need for a wholesome "discrimination" on behalf of the underdeveloped countries. Whereas the principle of strict trade equality often profits the "haves" at the expense of the "have-nots," paradoxically, the principle of trade "discrimination," intelligently applied, can become a significant instrument of equity.

There are several forms which this healthy "discrimination" might take. Only two possibilities need be mentioned here: (1) On stipulated manufactured exports to the underdeveloped countries, governments of the advanced industrial nations might be allowed to grant export subsidies to shippers who sell at lower-than-domestic prices in order to reduce the exchange difficulties of the underdeveloped countries. In this way, aid funds could be used to promote international development through trade, and funds spent for "foreign aid" could be shown to contribute directly to the stimulation of the domestic economy. Such preferential treatment could be based either on a sliding scale or on a category designation of the underdeveloped countries, depending upon their foreign exchange situation and per capita GNP. (2) GATT should be modified to permit another desirable form of "discrimination." The advanced industrial nations should agree to admit certain products of the underdeveloped countries on a quota-free and tariff-preferential basis. Such a trade policy could be geared to encourage the production of export articles suited to the growth stage of individual countries (e.g., labor-intensive manufactures in the early stages).

These are but a few out of many possible suggestions whereby the process of international development can be organically integrated with the process of expanding trade ties between the nations of the Free World. At this time, spelling out all the precise details of likely and desirable programs is not so important as establishing an interallied organizational mechanism which will accommodate continuous consultation, investigation of alternatives and evolution of practical policies.

Here a postscript may be in order. There is a pressing need for a more dynamic approach to "atoms for peace." Granted that atomic industrial power may still be a long way from commercial practicability in the United States, its potentialities ought to be exploited more vigorously both for our own prestige purposes and for sound international economic reasons. The long-range energy needs of an industrializing world and the special problems of underdeveloped countries suggest the timely planning of certain types of nuclear projects, such as earth-moving and hydrological projects (which use atomic isotopes to chart the courses of underground rivers).[26] Large industrial power reactors can be placed in regions where the lack of conventional energy resources and the difficulties of bulk transportation are serious hindrances to economic progress.[27]

[26] Hydrological projects would be especially attractive in the Middle East, where programs of exploiting underground water resources might give a substantial impetus to the entire process of socioeconomic development. The technological recources and skills for carrying out such programs are already available within the Atlantic Community. For a general discussion of the possible peaceful applications of atomic energy, cf. *Plowshare Series Reports* published by the Livermore Radiation Laboratory of the University of California since 1958; Thomas E. Murray, *Nuclear Policy for War and Peace,* New York: World Publishing Co., 1960, Chapter 6; the Semiannual Reports of the Atomic Energy Commission; the International Atomic Energy Agency *Bulletins;* Ralph Sanders, "Nuclear Dynamite: A New Dimension in Foreign Policy," *Orbis IV* (Fall, 1960), pp. 307-322.

[27] Cheap power alone will not revolutionize the economies of the underdeveloped countries. The demand for energy increases as swiftly as industrializa-

The Direction of Our Economic Offensive

An "economic offensive" confined solely to the underdeveloped areas is, in the nature of things, a limited offensive. However vital the countries of Asia, Africa and Latin America may be for the international power balance, two considerations argue against restricting our drive to them. First, it is axiomatic that an offensive must be directed against the foe, not against a neutral party. Second, a genuine offensive seeks to gain ground, not merely to hold it.

Although we might lose the protracted conflict in the underdeveloped areas, we cannot win it there. Our economic aid may slow down the rate of communist incursions into some of the emergent nations; but we cannot put pressure on the communist system by engaging it in this sector *alone*. In short, although the communists can undertake an economic offensive into the uncommitted regions, the best that the Free World can do is to conduct a defensive, preventive strategy. No matter how much assistance we give to the underdeveloped peoples, the communists will still be standing in the wings, scoring us for not doing more—not nearly so much as they expect to do someday, after they have done us in. Our aid already has been depicted as proof of our sinister motives. The international conditioning machine of the communists paints us blacker than those swashbuckling captains who plundered the coasts of Asia and Africa in the seventeenth century.

We shall blunder gravely if we insist on linking the outcome of our struggle with the Sino-Soviet bloc to the outcome of the systemic revolution in Asia, Africa and Latin America. There are some economic problems in the world which the free industrial nations by themselves can solve on a satisfactory basis. There are others which the Sino-Soviet bloc and the Free World together might solve—if they could ever compose their differences. And, looking ahead

tion progresses. The United States, which first exploited the secrets of the atom, cannot afford to allow itself to be outdone by any nation in the realm of peacetime nuclear technology. To maintain undisputed leadership in this field, the U.S. must carry out a vigorous program of research and experimentation in the reactors of the future. This means building and operating large-scale power reactors of several different designs which have not yet been put to the test. Such a program will involve co-operative efforts between government and private industry in order to resolve the issue of "private versus public power." This controversy has caused the U.S. progress in reactor technology to falter during the past decade.

for the next quarter-century, we can readily surmise that *some* economic problems in that time span will prove insoluble. The free allies will be in a bad way, if, by dint of Soviet propaganda, they come to believe that they alone must solve *all* of the world's problems or else forfeit the game to the communists.

The economic offensive has to be directed, by definition, against the Sino-Soviet bloc itself. Its objectives should be: (1) to weaken the bloc as a monolithic power structure; (2) to put pressure on the Soviet Union to compound the decision-making difficulties which face communism's leaders; (3) to reduce the bloc's capabilities for promoting international conflict; (4) to deprive the communist leaders of the initiative and put them on the defensive; and (5) to convince them that their goal of global hegemony is no longer realistic and must be abandoned. In the nuclear-missile age, economic strategy furnishes one of the most likely avenues by which we can penetrate the bloc and apply punitive pressure.

Such a strategy choice presupposes that we wish to apply pressure of some sort on the communist empire. If we are reluctant to mount an *economic* offensive, then friends, neutrals and foes may presume that we lack the will and the means to assume the initiative in any dimension.

The difficulty of developing a cohesive economic strategy against communism is not to be gainsaid. We presently encounter the bloc on a modest scale in the underdeveloped areas, where we should link economic development efforts with a quarantine on any trade which profits the U.S.S.R. (If this be "political strings attached," then let us make the most of it.) Even this will not be easy. But it may be possible, with careful planning and over the course of a decade, to choke off a substantial portion of the bloc's trade with underdeveloped areas.

At present, it seems that our economic policies will hardly suffice to exert heavy pressure on the Soviet Union. There is much that we can do to alleviate the problems of the communist planners, but not too much to compound them. We do not yet know exactly how the various economic elements of the Soviet system fit together. Take the case of Eastern Europe, for example. To be sure, the Soviets exploit the Eastern European satellites. There is, however, a degree of interdependence which cannot be conjured away, and both sides now see the mutual economic advantages of their liaison.

For the sake of consolidating bloc strength, the Soviets have been willing to modify their own goal of national self-sufficiency. They depend upon Eastern Europe for certain types of industrial equipment, raw materials, and various fuels, foodstuffs and consumer goods. The satellites in turn receive Soviet grain, ores and metals (especially coal, coke, petroleum and iron ore) and industrial equipment. Most of the satellite economies, and not only the older Czechoslovak industrial complex, have become competitive vis-à-vis the Western industrial nations. Hence even if the Soviets do thin out their military occupation forces, the countries of Eastern Europe would still have good reason to maintain bloc cohesion. Disengagement schemes conceived in an economic vacuum probably would not advance substantially the prospects for greater political independence in Eastern Europe. Eastern Europe could not reorient its trade to the West as rapidly as it shifted it away during the postwar decade, except at the risk of serious dislocations.[28]

The West need not be doomed to gaze impotently toward Eastern Europe. If our economic strategy were properly geared to sound political and military strategy, it might be possible to effect a gradual easing of the situation of the Eastern European peoples—or at least to help them attain a quasi-neutral status. But first of all, we have to make up our minds about our policy toward the satellite countries. Is our ultimate objective to wean them away from the U.S.S.R.? If so, unilateral aid shipments, however humanitarian, are a poor strategy for accomplishing the goal. Their net effect reduces the Soviets' problems of retaining untroubled political control.

We shall also require a careful study of intrabloc production, trade and foreign commerce, and the relation of these patterns to the Soviet central plan. Continuous surveillance of the bloc's changing economic activities is essential to a Free World planning group charged with an economic warfare strategy. Such a group, weighing covert as well as open sources of economic data, should investigate on both a theoretical and experimental basis various courses of action open to the West. Perhaps West European countries could

[28] With each passing year economic factors pose greater obstacles to German reunification. Many Western analysts continue to discuss the possibilities of political reunification while ignoring the implications of East Germany's industrial integration into the bloc and West Germany's movement into the Common Market. Khrushchev was right when he said that the two economies will not mix easily.

make attractive offers to contract for Polish shipping at times when such a diversion of transport would cause bottlenecks in the program for the industrial development of China. Perhaps under certain circumstances it would be desirable for Western Europe to purchase Diesels or specialized electrical equipment from the satellites if these items are simultaneously in demand by the Soviets. Such deals would have to be accompanied by diplomatic arrangements as well as with understandings that the Western currencies thus earned could be spent only for approved purposes—e.g., for the importation of consumer and light industrial goods into the satellites.[29] Perhaps it would be useful on occasion for the West to make ostentatious low-price offers of surplus commodities to Eastern Europe, e.g., on corn, tobacco, rice, cotton, peanuts, soybeans and canned foodstuffs. These are the principal items upon which Red China relies to maintain a faint semblance of a trade balance in her East European trade.

The foregoing suggestions illustrate the many opportunities which beckon us once we decide to shift from a passive to an active strategy. It is presumptuous now to say precisely what ought to be done. But it is clear that the Free World ought to establish a mechanism which will enable it to approach the problem on a continuing, systematic basis.

Once the necessary preparations have been made, policies which seem overambitious today can be applied confidently tomorrow. A Free World planning group for economic co-operation could seek to extend Western economic influence into the captive nations. Its purpose would be not to hurt the *peoples* of the satellite countries, whose cultural and spiritual values make them allies of the Free World at heart, but rather to confront their regimes with new pressures—and new opportunities.

Admittedly difficult, Western strategy during the first experimental years will doubtless appear ambiguous, at times inconsistent. We

[29] It may be objected that communist regimes will never agree to enter trade deals, however attractive, which would be on balance detrimental to Soviet interest. If this is true, then the hope of "weaning them away" is groundless. When the satellite regimes seem willing to do business, the deal could be kept relatively quiet. When they are not willing, a public announcement of an attractive Western offer which the communists spurn can help to arouse popular discontent in the satellite country concerned. Whichever way we look at it, this is real *economic* warfare, at least on a modest scale.

may find ourselves simultaneously offering blandishments to one regime and putting the squeeze on another.[30] Reactions to various economic techniques will have to be assayed, and policies modified accordingly, either toward loosening the bonds between the satellite capitals and Moscow or toward making the position of the satellite leaders as uncomfortable as possible. Certain lines of satellite trade with underdeveloped countries friendly to the West might be fostered as a reward for good political behavior, or cut off as a punishment for bad. In every case our actions should be directed toward setting the immediate economic self-interest of the satellite countries against Soviet long-range power interests. The goal should always be to diminish bloc cohesiveness, reduce Eastern Europe's dependence upon the U.S.S.R. and complicate the Kremlin's efforts to maintain absolute bloc control.

Economic warfare on the trade front will be worth all the effort that the Free World can put into it.[31] It will not be decisive in the contest between the two systems, since the bloc and the Free World are largely self-sufficient and trade warfare, sometimes more than other forms of conflict, is a two-edged sword. But economic warfare is a normal aspect of foreign policy in the epoch of protracted conflict. The Soviets have reaped some signal successes by integrating economic, political and psychological policies and concentrating on a few national targets. There is no valid reason why the free nations, with their superior resources, cannot do the same—except a general lassitude which stifles initiative and masks itself as a pseudo-realistic recognition of "insurmountable obstacles."

Another economic dimension besides trade in which our policy decisions can produce profound repercussions upon the Soviet economy is that of armaments expenditures. Too many Americans erroneously fear adverse repercussions upon our own economy should the Soviets turn the world toward the path of disarmament.

[30] One form of potential squeeze which was generally underrated in the West until the Bonn government applied it against East Germany in the fall of 1960 is the economic blockade.

[31] The possibilities are innumerable. We should, e.g., study the pattern of Soviet foreign markets with a view toward disrupting them as a matter of economic retaliation. Western governments could be encouraged to grant export subsidies when there is a good prospect of underselling the Soviet bloc in an established market on which it is dependent for earning hard currencies or where it is using trade for purposes of political penetration.

We should not labor under the misapprehension, discussed in Chapter 9, that calling off the "arms race" would court our economic ruin. Contrariwise, there are economists who theorize that the U.S. could "break" the U.S.S.R. by vastly increasing military spending.

Our amazing ability to raise huge sums of money rapidly and to expand our productive output massively whenever we really wish to do so is one of our greatest assets in the struggle. We can as a matter of policy render obsolete many expensive items of Soviet military equipment, burdening the U.S.S.R. with the task of maintaining parity with us.

The Soviets cannot afford to let us obtain a decisive edge in defense capabilities. A vigorous American-European defense effort (e.g., improving alert capacity, hardening land-based missile sites, expanding a mobile and globally dispersed missile capability, enlarging the weapons spectrum, perfecting intercept systems and building passive defenses in the shape of population shelters) can, by skillful timing and selectivity, strain communist resources already heavily committed to military spending. The Free World's co-ordinated, implacable efforts can grind the Soviet revolutionary dynamism to a halt and dull the glamour of the Leninist system. Then conditions may favor a genuine *détente*, a settlement mutually welcome to both parties. But time is not necessarily on our side. Our present margin of economic advantage which still affords us this opportunity, narrows perceptibly with each passing year. This is perhaps the major fact with which our economic strategists must grapple during the first half of the sixties.

CHAPTER 7 DIPLOMATIC ARM OF STRATEGY

In the age of protracted conflict, American diplomacy faces two separate sets of problems. Like an amphibious creature, American diplomacy must function in two environments. Conflict diplomacy—the diplomacy of the Cold War—governs our relationships with the Sino-Soviet bloc. At the same time, we employ the methods of traditional diplomacy in our dealings with allied and neutral nations of the Free World.

Our diplomatic struggle with the communist bloc has been waged with indifferent success. Behind our defeats and embarrassments at the conference table lies the fundamental failure to see the totality of the conflict. We have attributed to diplomacy a meaning which derives from a more stable historic era in which the quest for legitimacy and the preservation of the existing state system and social order were the mainsprings of diplomatic conduct.

Our diplomacy thus remains keyed to a conception which views peace as the normal condition of the world and conflict as an aberration among peoples who share the same basic values. As a result, we look upon diplomacy as the antithesis of conflict: We cling to the belief that guns will remain silent and we can go about our peaceful business so long as statesmen confer. The experiences of the last fifteen years, if not of the last half-century of disorder and violence, should have cured us of our illusions. For the communist revolutionaries diplomacy is a continuation of war by other means, waged not for the purpose of accommodating conflicting interests, but to spearhead an attritional strategy, to whittle down our power, split our ranks, compel us to ratify our losses and lead us to the ultimate surrender.

At the root of our misconceptions are ingrained notions derived from a particular and unique historical experience. Irrepressible optimism sparked the conquest of an uncharted and hostile continent and sustained the great American experiment. Because our efforts, supported mightily by historical circumstances and geography, managed to solve most of the outstanding problems of our society, we tend to project our faith in the happy ending into the international arena. Firm in this belief, we presume that all problems are eventually soluble, be it racial segregation in the American South or be it the division of Germany. American diplomats and policy-makers seem congenitally inclined to shut unpleasant facts and unwelcome possibilities from their operational thinking: "They are disposed to believe that a thing is feasible because it seems just and desirable for the majority of men."[1] Yet some problems, especially the major ones, persistently resist solution. Even more important, others do not share our anxiety to solve them.

Compromise is the leaven of American society. The principle of compromise has been written into the system of our political checks and balances and the code of our business community. It is only natural, therefore, that we consider it the lubricant of politics, domestic and foreign.

Compromise works admirably as an instrument of diplomacy when genuine interests can be harmonized or when mutual benefits beckon at the end of the negotiating trail. When the penchant for compromise is one-sided, however—as it has been consistently during the Cold War—the diplomatic cards are decisively stacked in favor of the single-minded aggressor who will accept no compromise in his ultimate goal of global domination. Either he mistakes his opponent's attitude for weakness and steps up his demands, or he discerns a convenient method for advancing his interests along a broad front simply by creating or fanning issues and then challenging his opponent to "solve" them. This method has been one of the hallmarks of the communist "crisis strategy." The "negotiable issues" placed by the communists on the agendas of diplomatic conferences have had one common denominator—all of them were confined to threats to Western interests and territories. Therefore,

[1] Stephen D. Kertesz, "American and Soviet Negotiating Behavior," *Diplomacy in a Changing World,* ed. by Stephen D. Kertesz and M. A. Fitzsimmons (University of Notre Dame Press, 1959), p. 89.

compromise on these issues rewarded Soviet diplomacy with a net gain. Thus the communists have pressed the diplomatic offensive without, in the majority of cases, committing a single acre of their own territory and, for that matter, a single lever of "internal" control.

Soviet negotiating behavior has understandably jarred the sensitivities of diplomats trained in the traditional niceties of the art. In fact, some deny that Soviet diplomacy is diplomacy at all. Charles W. Thayer terms it "Byzantine diplomacy," tracing it to the chicanery and deception which were the standard stocks-in-trade of the court of Constantinople.[2] Certainly, communist diplomatic conduct is devoid of any trace of that concept of fair play which, however ill-defined, has guided traditionally the diplomatic interplay of Western society. If Soviet diplomacy subscribes to any code of conduct at all, it is the "morality" defined succinctly by Radio Moscow in a broadcast on August 20, 1950:

> Morals or ethics is the body of norms and rules for the conduct of Soviet peoples. At the root of Communist morality, said Lenin, lies the struggle for the consolidation and the completion of Communism. Therefore, from the point of view of Communist morality, only those acts are moral which contribute to the building of a new Communist society.[3]

Whatever may account for Soviet diplomatic behavior—whether it is the legacy of a historic tradition, a revolutionary philosophy, or a combination of the two—one fact stands out: The Soviets have gauged more accurately than we the revolutionary temper of our times and taken the bearings of the radically changed environment in which diplomacy must operate. As defined by Soviet authorities:

> Soviet diplomacy in its general purpose as well as in its methods differs categorically from the diplomacy of the feudal epoch and the epoch of bourgeois domination. The principal aim of Soviet diplomacy was and will be concentrated on the study of factors of social importance. For this purpose, Soviet Diplomacy has at its disposal unsurpassed Marxist-Leninist methods of perception of world conditions and to a certain degree also of conditions—in the full meaning of that word—connected with the economic, political, historical class and other problems of the countries with which it deals. It is necessary always to remember J. V. Stalin's words ". . . in order to avoid mistakes in politics

[2] Charles W. Thayer, *Diplomat* (New York: Harper & Brothers, 1959), Chapter IV.

[3] Broadcast of August 20, 1950, cited in Kertesz, *op. cit.*, p. 145.

and not to fall into the circle of idle dreamers, the Party of the Proletariat must proceed in its activity not from the abstract 'principles of human intelligence' but from the concrete conditions of material life of the society as the decisive power of the social developments." Marxist-Leninist theory "gives the Party the possibility of orienting itself in the situation, to understand the internal connections of surrounding occurrences, to foresee the course of events and to recognize not only how and where the events will develop at the present time but also how and where they should develop in the future." Here in this foresight and recognition of present and future events, and not in deceit and intrigues, consists the strength of Soviet Diplomacy, which so brilliantly justified itself during the whole history of its activity.[4]

America's power position has shrunk in the diplomatic as well as in other strategic categories because, unlike her opponent, she has failed to discern fully the relationship between diplomacy and the economic, technological, military and psychological arms of an integrated strategy. We have tended to consider diplomacy in isolation, vastly overrating its importance and power. We have clung to the belief that it is the principal task of diplomacy to preserve peace, that war signifies diplomatic failure, and that, in sum, diplomacy is synonymous with peace.

We tend to forget that diplomacy is but *one* of the many instruments of strategy discussed throughout this book. As such, it can indeed be used to head off the clash of arms. By the same token, however, diplomacy can serve to prepare for armed conflict, to insure victory or, conversely, to stave off defeat. If diplomats are to prevent war, they must achieve, in their own right, those objectives which would otherwise be pursued by contending armies on the battlefield; they must *not* be content simply with avoiding conflict.

We have failed to grasp these truths largely because our understanding of diplomacy remains conditioned by its role in an earlier era of history—the halcyon period of the nineteenth century, when diplomacy was largely a matter of communication and negotiation.

That century was a period of general stability—a stability which resulted not so much from a quest for peace as from a generally accepted legitimacy. There existed among the great powers of the nineteenth century a tacit consensus regarding the limits of foreign

[4] A. J. Vyshinsky and S. A. Lozosky, *Diplomaticheskii Slovar,* Vol. I (Moscow, 1948), pp. 591-92, cited in Kertesz, *op. cit.,* pp. 140-41.

policy and the permissible methods by which policy could be pursued—an acceptance of the existing framework of international order. This framework, to be sure, did not preclude conflict. But the statesmen of Europe, haunted by the memories of the French Revolution and its Napoleonic aftermath, were loath to tamper with a structure of values which alone could safeguard their survival against the incipient revolutionary currents of the nineteenth century. Their adherence to a common set of standards made it possible for diplomacy to operate in its "classic" sense—namely, the adjustment of differences through negotiations.

If we accept this definition, then diplomacy no longer functions in the "classic sense." And if there is no longer any consensus regarding acceptable policies and permissible methods, then the side which continues to adhere inflexibly to the traditional ground rules of the game is at a disadvantage vis-à-vis a revolutionary force which cynically disregards them.

Diplomacy has been revolutionized by another development, the agglomeration of power. In the nineteenth century, a distributive balance of power preserved peace in Europe and, through Europe, over the globe. There were shifts within this over-all balance, but no nation could consider its temporary advantages great enough to embark upon a policy of deliberately upsetting the equilibrium. A key element in this balance was the role of Great Britain, which shifted her weight first to one side of the Continent and then to the other—in Dean Acheson's simile, "much as a gyroscope gives balance to a moving craft."[5]

In this environment, diplomats played their game on a chessboard on which the success or failure of a given gambit was not necessarily a measure of the player's objective power position. The diplomats of the past century enjoyed an ample margin for maneuver and bluff. Thus, for example, the wily Talleyrand was able, after the Napoleonic wars, to redeem France from the ignominy of defeat and gain for her a respected place in the new concert of Europe. But Talleyrand turned this trick not because of France's power, but because he could cast the weight of his country onto the scales between the two camps of bickering victors—Great Britain on the one hand, and Austria, Prussia and Russia on the other.

[5] Dean Acheson, *Power and Diplomacy* (Cambridge: Harvard University Press, 1958), p. 4.

The margin for maneuverability has largely disappeared. Power, in the mid-twentieth century, has become polarized, and the play of diplomacy, as an expression of that power, has been restricted to an ever-shrinking range of alternatives. Diplomats today may be as brilliant and resourceful as Castlereagh and Talleyrand, but they can no longer impose their formulas upon intractable realities as plausibly as their luckier predecessors. Diplomacy, at the present stage of history, can maximize and ratify gains in the relative power position of the two opposing sides. It can sharpen the psychopolitical impact of these gains. *But diplomacy by itself cannot contrive arrangements that do not conform closely to concrete power relationships.*

"The test of a statesman," as Henry A. Kissinger puts it, "is his ability to recognize the real relationship of forces and to make this knowledge serve his ends."[6] The communists have measured up to his test because they are graduates of a school which teaches that power is what counts when great historic issues are at stake. American statecraft has yielded ground to communist strategy for two fundamental reasons, namely, because: First, as a people, we find distasteful the crude play of power politics; secondly, too few of our diplomats have been able to relate their individual roles to the grand strategy—to the waging of the conflict as an organic whole. The steady deterioration in the past years of American diplomatic positions can thus be traced to the relative decline in America's substantive power in the military, technological, economic and psychological sectors as well as to the failure to link diplomacy to all the elements of power.

This failure helps to explain why so often in the past decade we have failed to stand up to challenges, to enforce our interests and to maintain our prestige. By giving an impression of sweet reasonableness and striving to be liked rather than respected, we have been subject to extortion and blackmail, not to mention ridicule and contempt. We have yet to realize that any effort to conduct diplomacy with anything but a mature consciousness of power and a firm willingness to stand up for our convictions as well as our material and strategic interests is doomed to failure.

Not fully understanding the conflict, we have sought to escape

[6] Henry A. Kissinger, *A World Restored* (Boston: Houghton Mifflin, 1957), p. 324.

its irritations by conducting "business as usual" in both our domestic and foreign relations. Finding this escape blocked by the intractable facts of the global collision, we have sought refuge in the comforting notion that "time is on our side." Indeed, the tacit objective guiding our post-Sputnik diplomacy has been to buy time, to put off the fateful decisions in the hope that some *deus ex machina* will relieve us of the painful burden of conflict or that our opponents will be metamorphosed magically into staid members of the international community.

Time, however, is neutral: it belongs to him who learns to master it. When challenged in the past, we have conquered time through eleventh-hour resolution and economic and technological preponderance. But our preponderance is waning. And time is not always an ally, let alone a reliable one. As a parameter of conflict, it is being compressed rapidly into the seconds of the countdown.

We are approaching swiftly what may prove to be the decisive phase in the protracted conflict—the phase in which the opponent may make a bold and unambiguous bid for global hegemony. Once he believes he has broken the physical and psychological barrier of American nuclear supremacy, his approach will become more direct and his demands more arrogant and unyielding. The first signs of this change in attitude already are discernible.

We can pass through the dangerous narrows of crisis only by taking the following actions:

1. *Build up U.S. power.* Specific recommendations for increasing American power in the military, technological, economic and psychological realms are discussed in other chapters of this book. In this context, let us note that military power is the muscle and sinew of diplomacy. Our primary objective in the coming years must be to boost that military power to the level of the challenge confronting the United States. The first priority is to close those gaps in the range of military capabilities through which the communists have launched their diplomatic sorties with increasing impunity.

2. *Link U.S. diplomacy more meaningfully to U.S. power positions.* Military power alone is not enough. Political purpose meshes the military and diplomatic strands of strategy into a coherent fabric. The bewildering diffusion of our past diplomatic effort has been due as much to chronic indecision of our policy-makers as to defects of our institutional machinery.

In charting our diplomatic strategies, we have never taken the inventory of the economic and ideological bargaining assets in our military storeroom. For example, throughout the Cold War, we have made a number of changes in our military establishment. Thus, our force levels in Europe have been cut and several of our overseas SAC bases are in the process of being dismantled. Leaving aside the strategic merit of these changes, it should be obvious that by gearing strategic decisions to diplomatic operations we can reap considerable political advantages. Whenever a weapons system is nearing obsolescence, a foreign base is to be abandoned or force levels are to be altered, such plans should be presented as negotiable issues rather than as unilateral concessions.

Our fumbling with the problem of sharing nuclear weapons with our allies is an example in point. The United States has been under increasing pressure from its NATO allies, particularly France, to amend the MacMahon Act, which bars our friends from access to America's store of nuclear hardware and skills. For a number of reasons—including perhaps their reluctance to share their own nuclear arsenal with their "allies"—the Soviets seem to be apprehensive lest we give NATO the combination to our nuclear safe. This fear is echoed by various propaganda broadsides and campaigns for denuclearized zones in Europe. Yet, as if to assuage these fears, President Eisenhower, in a letter made public on March 19, 1960, assured the Soviet Premier that the United States did not contemplate sharing her nuclear knowledge and weapons with her Western partners in the foreseeable future.

Without arguing the pros and cons of "nuclearizing" NATO, it seems logical to assume that the very *threat* to do so would have given us an additional bargaining leverage in our dealings with the Soviets. Thus, President Eisenhower relinquished a high card before meeting the Soviets across the table. Whatever may have been our ultimate intentions, silence or even ambiguity would have served a better purpose than a categorical announcement.

These gaps between our diplomacy and the other arms of U.S. strategy reflect in part defects in our national security machinery. These shortcomings and proposed remedies will be discussed in a later chapter. Suffice it here to say that the governmental bias for piecemeal interdepartmental planning has opened disastrous gaps and given rise to contrariness and duplication in our political, economic, psychological and military programs.

While the men charged with the formulation and execution of U.S. military, economic and technological strategies often tend to slight the diplomatic implications of their activities, the converse holds true for many of our diplomats. They frequently lack the training to view their mission in the matrix of grand strategy.

Certainly, the growing range and complexity of international issues places tremendous demands upon the negotiator. The diplomat cannot hope to master all the skills of the specialist in the military, economic, psychological and technological sectors of strategy. He, too, is a specialist. But he *can* acquire a fair general knowledge of the other strategic elements and so put his work into better perspective. He can gain this acquaintance through as intensive a training in the *functional* areas of strategy as he now receives in area studies and foreign language schools.

Underlying all of these measures must be the realization that diplomacy—and, for that matter, foreign policy as a whole—is but a technique subordinate to the exigencies of an over-all strategy. We have tended to raise diplomacy to the apex of foreign policy-making, trailed by over-all strategy as a somewhat irritating afterthought. Yet strategy is diplomacy's elder brother. Once that normal relationship has been established, diplomacy will serve as one of the most effective tools—even the indispensable tool—of Forward Strategy.

Diplomacy and Psychological Warfare

Probably the greatest advantage which the Iron Curtain gives to communist diplomacy is the ability to co-ordinate the diplomatic with the psychological arm of strategy. Diplomacy, conducted as it is today on a floodlighted stage, has been degraded to a weapon of psychopolitical conflict. The perversion of its traditional purposes can be laid in part on our own doorstep. American diplomacy has never fully recovered from the great "moral crusade" during World War I, when Woodrow Wilson introduced the term "open covenants openly arrived at" into the lexicon of international politics.

Whatever its origin, "open diplomacy" serves as an ideal proving ground for the communists' arsenal of psychopolitical weapons. It does so partly because communist policy-makers, by dint of their training and revolutionary doctrine, are seasoned propagandists and agitators, quick to recognize and exploit the psychological implications of diplomatic moves. Even more important, however, is the fact that "open diplomacy" is open to the view only of the non-communist world. Because their own subjects glimpse the events of the day mainly through the distorted prisms of *Pravda* and official announcements, the communists are able to lay their psychopolitical mines with impunity. They need not fear the countermines of the Western powers, whose psychopolitical trumpets are even more uncertain than their military ones.

Communist diplomatic strategy neatly fits into the category of political warfare which Nazi Propaganda Minister Joseph Goebbels termed "total diplomacy." Like traditional diplomacy, it seeks to effect a change in the viewpoint and position of opposing governments. Unlike traditional diplomacy, however, it pursues this objective indirectly—by aiming its thrusts over the heads of government at the great masses of the people. The West's vulnerability to communist psychological thrusts seems irremediable. We cannot close an open society. We cannot convince our campaigning politicians that the "water's edge" of political debate now circumscribes nearly every facet of our national security, nor can we enjoin our free press from printing the full text of Khrushchev's speeches and reporting every detail of a diplomatic conference. We cannot abolish "open diplomacy." What we can do is play the diplomatic game more prudently and shun the conference table when it is clear to us from the outset that a conference will not yield any advantages to ourselves.

The counsel of prudence applies to the staging of the most spectacular of all modern-day diplomatic spectacles, the summit conference. There is nothing novel about "summitry." Ever since the birth of the modern nation-state, heads of government have met occasionally to make peace, to form alliances, and to thrash out the more acute international problems. Its novelty today consists in the extent to which it appears to have become an institutionalized form of diplomacy in the Cold War and in the manner in which it is used by the communists as a vehicle for their conflict strategy.

Summit diplomacy works against the West in general and the United States in particular in a number of ways. It does so, first, by imposing upon the American head of state the combined burden of policy-making and diplomacy.

In theory, politics in the United States, as well as in the Soviet Union, may be an adequate training school for diplomatic proficiency. Yet even if we accept this premise—and career diplomats would quarrel with it vehemently—there are important differences in the credentials of an American President and a Soviet Premier. The President of the United States owes his position as much to the fortuitous interactions of a unique political system as to thorough political schooling. The Soviet Premier, by contrast, has risen to power by the brutal working of a political Darwin's law: At every step of his ascent, he has had to stride, often literally, over the corpses of his political rivals. By very definition, therefore, he is a shrewd and ruthless "politician" who can apply his skills as easily to the power struggle at home as to hard-and-fast bargaining in diplomatic conferences abroad.

It follows that in terms of background and training alone the American head of state invariably is at a stark disadvantage vis-à-vis his communist adversary. He can reduce this handicap somewhat through intensive briefings before a conference and by surrounding himself with a staff of competent advisers. But in the pressure-laden atmosphere of a summit conference, he will find it extremely difficult to refer constantly to facts and advice—especially when there is a loud and insistent public clamor for a settlement.

It is public pressure within the West which constitutes the main Soviet weapon in summit diplomacy. Khrushchev has successfully foisted on many quarters of Western opinion the bizarre notion that the complex problems of the day cannot be solved by diplomatic "hirelings," but only through a "frank exchange" between the two men who "determine the destinies of the world." As a result, summit meetings are surrounded invariably by wistful expectations of a "new era" opening in East-West relations—a climate of optimistic languor which tends to suffocate the kind of national effort which could deliver the bargaining punch toward a real and meaningful settlement.

Paralysis seems to grip Western policy until well after the summit conference itself. A good example was the meeting at Geneva in the summer of 1955. Even as hard a realist as the late Secretary of State John Foster Dulles stated that "for the predictable future we can subject our differences to the patient processes of diplomacy with less fear that war will come. . . ."[7] And Lester B. Pearson, then Canada's Secretary of State of External Affairs, remarked: "The results achieved there [at Geneva] have been rightly hailed throughout the world as marking the beginning of an effort by the leading nations of the two power blocs to adjust by discussion and negotiation their conflicts of national interest and ideological difference which have divided and distressed the world during the last decade."[8]

Geneva, of course, accomplished none of these things. The conference was a sham. At best, it served as a brief lull in the conflict which the communists used to regroup their forces for a new offensive—the thrust into the Middle East. By the time the numbness induced by Geneva had worn off, the West saw itself confronted with a phenomenon unprecedented in modern history, the emergence of Soviet Russia as a Middle East power.

Summitry, in short, has been a cat-and-mouse game in which the West continually has grasped for the same deceptive bait of tensions lessened and issues resolved. It will continue to be a trap for Western diplomacy unless we subject it to the following conditions:

First, agree to meet the Soviets only if negotiations "in the valley" have progressed to the point where there is a tangible hope for solutions at the summit.

Second, insist that the agendas of summit meetings be agreed upon in advance and be adhered to rigidly once the conference has convened.

Finally, insist that those "nonsummit" allied powers whose rights or interests are at stake in the negotiations be allowed to attend the conference as *ad hoc* participants. In general, in negotiating with the Soviets we should guard against giving the impression that our allies may become the objects of bargaining.

Implicit in all the suggestions outlined above is a hardening of the resistance of U.S. leadership to the stresses and strains of "public opinion," at home and abroad. Too often in the course of the Cold War we have invoked this phantom as a convenient alibi for our failure to take the necessary steps in the interests of our survival. We have yet to realize that "world opinion" on a given issue is not a cohesive phenomenon, but a conflicting cross current of opinions,

[7] *New York Times,* July 27, 1955.

[8] "After Geneva: A Greater Task for NATO," *Foreign Affairs,* XXXII (October, 1955), p. 14.

attitudes and preconceptions. We must, by all means, always gauge the psychological impact of specific policies. But we should not, and cannot, permit oversensitivity to ephemeral and transitory public opinion—the popular mood of the moment—to prejudice the rightful advancement of our national interests.

Opening Communist Society

The melancholy lessons which flow from our experiments on the summit might prove to have been salutary. If they taught us nothing else, they did expose the fallacy of equating diplomacy simply with formal negotiation. The tools of diplomacy are, in addition to negotiation, representation and intelligence. The task of the diplomat is to explore and to persuade. The diplomat, in order to achieve his purpose, employs whatever tools fit a particular historic situation.

In our diplomatic dealings with the Soviets we have let ourselves be drawn onto the slippery ground of negotiation and, for that matter, of negotiation in the glare of klieg lights. We have never really come to grips with the question of which issues are negotiable and which ones are not. It is likely that, in the foreseeable future, only minor issues will be negotiable, while the main political problems will not be solved by negotiated settlement.

We have fallen into Soviet traps because we feel compelled constantly to reaffirm our devotion to peace—a compulsion which warps the pattern of our diplomacy toward the Soviet Union. When we do negotiate with the Soviets, we tend to equivocate, to compromise and to spurn proper *quid pro quos*. The blame lies not so much with our professional diplomats, who are the agents of our policymakers. It is the latter, and not diplomats, who alone can decide to negotiate and about what. In any event, the Soviets perceive clearly the weaknesses of our diplomatic stance and do not hesitate to exploit them.

Diplomatic concourse with the Soviet Union cannot center on formal negotiations. If we keep on telling ourselves that we must negotiate on any issue raised by the Soviets, our diplomacy will inevitably be ineffective. Before entering into serious talks, we should make sure that the Soviets are willing to give as well as take. In the absence of such an assurance, our diplomacy with the Soviets has but one basic mission, namely to *converse*—to talk, *not* to negotiate—on political matters, partly for purposes of mutual information and partly to chip away at the Kremlin's ideological preconceptions, which are so largely responsible for world tensions. The stronger our military power and the less our inclination toward compromise, the more persuasive will be our diplomatic arguments and the more likely will it be that the Soviets will abandon at least their more aggressive revolutionary projects.

By entering into negotiations, we are bestowing upon the Soviets, and hence communism, respectability—a cherished prize of any revolutionary movement and hence of communist strategy. By persuading ourselves that meaningful negotiations on major issues are possible, we strengthen the communist strategy of deception instead of exposing it; yet to expose the objectives and methods of communist strategy is the first step toward dissuading neutrals from aligning themselves with Moscow. We should hew forthrightly to the line that negotiations with the Soviets are impractical so long as the communists remain attached to their deceitful code and their global ambitions. If we are too anxious to negotiate now, we will only strengthen the communist belief in the success of their revolutionary strategy. As long as the Soviets are convinced —and with good reason—that they have the ability to outmaneuver us, they will not modify their system and only accelerate the progression toward war. To be sure, *some* issues can be negotiated, provided it is clearly understood that the negotiation is genuine and not a tactical maneuver. Fruitful negotiations on major issues must await the day when a meaningful change *has occurred* in the Soviet system.

It is unlikely, to say the least, that the West can negotiate with the Soviets successfully on the great issues of world politics unless it faces across the conference table men who are responsive to a people no longer insulated from the world at large. The objective of American diplomacy must be, in close concert with a dynamic psychopolitical strategy, to lift the Iron Curtain, shift the diplomatic struggle more onto the communist terrain, reach the minds of the peoples behind Soviet borders, increase the domestic pressures upon the decisions of the Soviet dictatorship and thus lay the basis for realistic negotiations leading toward conclusive settlements.

In an excellent summary of the Berlin Crisis, Hans Speier suggested three general courses of action open to American diplomacy in trying to resolve an international conflict by nonviolent means. First, it can counter Soviet demands with *counterproposals.* Secondly, it can try to *enlarge the issue* raised by the opponent: The West's "package plan" linking Berlin to the problem of Germany during the Geneva Conference of 1955 was an example of this technique. Finally, it can endeavor to *enlarge the arena of conflict.*

The last alternative represents the key to a purposeful diplomatic Forward Strategy for the United States. Throughout the Cold War, American diplomacy has adhered supinely to the implicit "ground rules" imposed by the Soviets upon the conflict. According to these rules, the territory of the Free World represents the "war zone" in which the communist conflict apparatus is free to operate at will and in which all issues fall within the purview of East-West diplomacy. Conversely, the communist empire represents the "peace zone," where any "meddling" by the Western powers, diplomatic or otherwise, is threatened with an immediate and brutal Soviet riposte.

We must endeavor to reverse these "rules" and press a concerted diplomatic offensive into the most vulnerable sector of the communist domain, namely Eastern Europe. We have screened our timidity in the past with the notion that any proposal relating to the freedom of captive nations would be "unrealistic." We have yet to grasp the fact that a given proposal's "realism" is not necessarily a measure of its merit. The Soviets may not accept it today; they may well be driven to accept it under the pressure of future circumstances —for example, another crisis of leadership succession in the Kremlin.

Whether or not the communists accept or reject this or that proposal, however, is relatively unimportant. What is important is that we seize the initiative and subject the Soviet decision-making machinery to maximum pressure. We often overlook the fact that such pressure is generated by the very act of posing a demand and forcing the opponent to formulate a response.

An American diplomatic offensive must capitalize upon the assets of a free and open society. We must convince the world, if not our opponents, that a closed society is an anachronism in an age when the accelerating force of technology is smashing traditional boundaries and gripping the globe in a tightening embrace of knowledge and mutual perception.

Improving America's Alliance Diplomacy

The essential purpose of an alliance diplomacy is to provide the framework wherein the power, resources and efforts of several nations can be harnessed to a common goal. The United States must rely on willing allies, for only with their consent can we check the ubiquitous advance of communism and assist in the creation of open societies. The Soviets, because they control absolutely one empire and are marching in tactical-ideological harmony with one another, need not expend a commensurate diplomatic effort on the care and feeding of alliances. This fact alone saddles the United States with a considerable handicap—a handicap aggravated by the immense diversity of nations which America is called upon to lead.

The very contrasts within the Free World's alliance system point to the chronic tensions straining at common bonds. The system includes colonial powers and their former colonial wards. It holds both allies and enemies of World War II. It brackets democratic states and authoritarian regimes. Finally, it embraces nations whose vulnerability to the communist threat varies in degree and hence tempers their views on their rights and obligations as allies.

On the face of it, the score sheet of our alliance diplomacy is not altogether unfavorable. We have managed to ring the Sino-Soviet empire with a chain of allies spanning four continents. After 1949, with one exception—the loss of North Vietnam—we have blocked a physical expansion of the communist empire. But a close look at the strategic map shows sinister shadings. The chain has been breached at one vital point, the Baghdad Pact, and ominous rumblings in other countries suggest that Iraq may not be the last defector from the ranks of the alliance system. In another important area, Southeast Asia, our SEATO allies lack strength to contain a concerted Chinese communist push to the south. And deep fissures have opened in our hemispheric system of defense, the area covered by the Rio Pact.

The *sine qua non* of a successful diplomatic Forward Strategy against communism is a cohesive Western alliance. We cannot weather the storms of the century ensconced in "Fortress America." The cornerstone of the world we seek is a revitalized Atlantic Community, linked by the spiritual bonds of a common ethical and cultural heritage, the arteries of trade and technology, and the sinews of political institutions.

There has been considerable progress toward an effective functional integration of the West. At the same time, however, dangerous rifts have opened in the political and economic physiognomy of Western Europe. Perhaps this paradox inheres in a voluntary association of separate political units: The very strength which nations seek by combining tends, if not applied to common purpose, to drive them apart.

In 1948, Europe was a weak and disorganized band of nations which contemplated helplessly internal socioeconomic chaos, powerful communist fifth columns, and the ubiquitous Soviet military threat. Today, these nations have made an almost miraculous economic recovery, achieved a certain measure of internal stability, and forged at least the organizational framework for security against attack. As a result, they have become less subservient to U.S. policy and more assertive of their national interests and objectives. The task for U.S. policy in the next decade will thus be fundamentally different from what it was in the period immediately following World War II: No longer is it a question simply of giving goods, treasure and arms to war-ravaged nations, but the problem is to reconcile the diverse and often divergent interests of our principal NATO partners within the framework of a strengthened Atlantic Community.

According to a popular theory, the cohesiveness of an alliance system is almost exclusively a function of external dangers. According to this theory, NATO was born in the communist *coup* in Prague in 1948 and was weaned on the communist assault upon South Korea in 1950. Strains in the alliance, it is argued, can be attributed to whatever dulcet tones of "peaceful coexistence" emanate from the Kremlin.

This interpretation is unconvincing. No doubt, the "cement of fear," as General Alfred N. Gruenther has termed it, is a potent one, but it binds effectively only when balanced by the conviction on the part of individual nations that there is genuine safety in their combination. NATO has been faltering not because the fear of Soviet aggression has waned—on the contrary, despite talk of coexistence, that fear has grown in direct proportion to the Soviet military-technological progress—but because of the deepening suspicion on the part of our allies that the United States will hesitate to live up to its alliance commitments in the event of a nuclear showdown. This fear underlies to a varying extent the self-assertiveness of the de Gaulle government in France, the apparent timidity of British policy, apprehensions of the West German leaders, and the mutual suspicions among these powers. This fear, too, has prompted a growing number of prominent European strategists to propose the establishment of a European strategic retaliatory force which would not be dependent upon a signal from the United States. For example, Alastair Buchan of the Institute of Strategic Studies in London suggests "the great importance of creating in Europe as quickly as possible the least vulnerable nuclear IRBM system to be deployed along the whole periphery of the NATO area from North Cape to Alexandretta, under the direct control of SACEUR or some other special command."[9]

The United States has exacerbated European fears by tending to cater to the sensitivities of one ally, Great Britain, to the neglect and even detriment of others. At the root of one of the most disturbing political developments in Europe today—the Franco-British estrangement—with its ups and downs, is an American policy which, largely for reasons of historical friendship and ethnic affinity, has assigned to Great Britain a pivotal role within the alliance. This bias was understandable in the immediate postwar period: Great Britain was the sole formal West European victor of World War II; France held only symbolic rank among the victorious powers, and Germany and Italy were defeated enemies. Yet, the Continental powers, as they staged their remarkable comeback from defeat and economic prostration, could not but regard with growing resentment the Anglo-American directorate within the alliance. They have suspected Great Britain of attempting to buy from the Soviets security at the price of a demilitarized Continental Europe, and they have blamed the United States for allowing its diplomatic policy to be determined by the vagaries of British opinion rather than by the concrete requirements of Western defense.

The United States, in short, has failed to establish the requisite political soil for its military and diplomatic strategies in Western Europe—a failure which has opened dangerous breaches into which

[9] Alastair Buchan, *NATO in the 1960's* (New York: Praeger, 1960), p. 125.

the Soviets can press their divisive strategy with increasing success. The Soviets have singled out Great Britain as the principal target for nuclear blackmail because Great Britain, one of the most vulnerable countries in Western Europe, holds a commanding position in the councils of the Western Alliance. As a natural consequence of a U.S. policy which—France's atomic progress notwithstanding—allows Great Britain a virtual nuclear monopoly in Western Europe, the Soviets can use the negotiations for a nuclear test ban as a wedge against Atlantic unity: Not so surprisingly, France and Germany oppose any arrangement which would bar them from full membership in the "nuclear club" and thus freeze them in the status of third-class military powers.

Indispensable to a viable Atlantic Community is the spirit of equality among its members. We are, to be sure, the most powerful nation within the alliance and its uncontested leader. But we can make the British concept of Commonwealth leadership our own. Our role should be that of *primus inter pares.* We can and should draw more liberally upon the counsel of our alliance partners not only in our dealings with the common threat but in coping with the manifold problems which confront our policy throughout the globe.

In this context, we should not play favorites in our alliance dealings. Certainly, the importance to us of individual alliance partners varies with their military and economic contribution and their geopolitical location. All of them, however, have a substantial share in the common effort. Indeed, one of the key objectives of the alliance must be to distribute the effort and diversify the common task more equitably.

Our lack of wisdom in intramural alliance diplomacy has been matched by our conduct in another area—our lack of support for our allies in extra-alliance issues.

Admittedly, the task of balancing our Free World interests is a delicate one. We have significant stakes in areas which, while not directly tied to us through any alliance, are prime targets of communist strategy: the oil-rich countries of the Middle East, the raw-materials-producing states of Southeast Asia and Africa south of the Sahara, and the strategically vital nations along the southern rim of the Mediterranean littoral. We must, in good conscience, live up to our standard of international justice and we must be sensitive to that amorphous force called "world opinion." For all of these reasons, we cannot extend a blank check to our allies in their extra-alliance dealings.

While the problem calls for a goodly measure of forbearance on our part, however, we have tended to err on the side of ambivalence. It has been tempting for us to strike a pose of Olympian detachment and to fancy ourselves the arbiters of rival claims. Could this neat trick be turned, we would indeed have the best of both worlds: the loyalty of our allies and the acclaim of the "anticolonialists." But the intractable realities of the globe preclude such a happy and comfortable course. While we must judge each issue on its merits—and the merits of the opposing claims—we have yet to embrace the principle that our allies rate our diplomatic preference. Invariably, our ambivalence has earned us little except the suspicions, if not outright hostility, of both parties to a given dispute. This was true of our role in the Anglo-Egyptian wrangle over the British rights in the Suez Canal in 1953—a dispute which keynoted the massive Western retreat from the Middle East.

Our dealings with our allies are taking place within the deepening shadows of new crises. The abortive summit meeting in Paris in June, 1960, did not herald the end of the Kremlin's emphasis upon the "soft sell" as a divisive wedge against the Free World's alliance system, but it marked the resumption of an accelerated campaign of violent political warfare in the form of missile threats from without and riots, demonstrations and parliamentary obstructionism against elected governments from within.

The shock troops in this campaign will be, as always, the apparatus of international communism. But communist fifth columns cannot hope to achieve the Kremlin's objectives on their own. There will be an intensified effort to penetrate and influence indigenous forces opposed to pro-American policies—to whiplash them with the now standard communist threat that any measure directed against Moscow (such as playing host to American military installations) will court nuclear retribution.

These communist tactics sharpen a dilemma which has confounded American alliance diplomacy throughout the Cold War: Our relations with our allies frequently tend to be limited to the highest levels of governmental interaction. The communists, for their part, maintain or control political parties which influence directly mass opinion and thus counteract, in varying degrees, the pro-American policies of incumbent governments.

The creation of a stable alliance base at levels below that of governmental co-operation admittedly is a long-range task. Meanwhile, we and our allies face the problem of how to bring about a meeting of minds on the evolution of the international situation and the broad outlines of our strategic planning. Thus far, we have failed to solve this problem. We have failed largely because our alliance diplomacy operates on a day-to-day basis and is unsupported by any effective permanent mechanism of interallied diplomacy. We have not progressed appreciably beyond the pre-1939 practices of "mutual consultation," restricting both the timing and the scope of such consultations to acute world crises. Although our diplomacy has, to some extent, managed to co-ordinate allied policies in the realms of defense and trade, it has yet to achieve closer co-operation in such areas as technology and science, not to speak of joint political planning.

Since World War II the peoples of the Atlantic Community have achieved through NATO a limited integration in the military sector. Perhaps more important still in the long run, NATO has developed the rudimentary machinery for Atlantic political consultation and co-operation. Within the Atlantic Community several groups of states have joined in regional organizations for functional co-operation. But the Atlantic Community has only begun to become aware of itself.

If Atlantic integration is to move ahead, then the peoples of the West must achieve a greater responsiveness to each other's needs and ideas. One means of achieving this goal is to implement Article 2 of the NATO Pact. This Article provides for greater co-operation in nonmilitary, political and economic affairs. Unfortunately, the United States has sometimes given the appearance of being more preoccupied with exchanges of people and ideas with the Soviet Union than with the Atlantic countries. Existing transatlantic exchanges in the arts and sciences are inadequate. In any case they do not appear to have diminished significantly the parochialism of political elites.

The effectiveness of the North Atlantic Alliance is dependent on the effectiveness of Western military and political co-operation on a global scale. Since the communists pursue a global strategy, the self-imposed geographical limits of NATO invite communist flanking thrusts across areas that are not specifically covered by the Atlantic Pact. It is difficult to see why the Middle East and North Africa are less vital to the defense of NATO than, let us say, Iceland and Portugal. The recurring divergences of NATO members' policies concerning a wide range of international problems, both within the geographical area of the alliance and in Africa and Asia, plead forcefully and, sometimes, poignantly for closer collaboration among the Atlantic countries. The crises of Berlin, Suez, Lebanon, Cyprus, Algeria, Quemoy and Matsu, and the Congo found the NATO countries at odds with one another concerning problems which affected all members of the alliance. The first and obvious step toward closing this chapter of lamentable episodes is to improve methods of consultation and co-operation among the nations of the North Atlantic area. Frequent and regular meetings of political leaders should be held within the community, similar to those which European leaders now attend in European organizations. The machinery should be adequate to enable the Atlantic Community to deal with incipient crisis situations and other problems arising within or outside the North Atlantic area that affect vitally the interests of the Community as a whole. Within this institutional setting consultations should be broadened to promote agreement on common policies on a world-wide basis, for a good many common problems will remain insoluble so long as co-operation is confined to activities solely within the North Atlantic area itself. It may be useful to create, within the NATO Secretariat, a central intelligence agency, staffed by experts on communist policy and strategy, to act as a "clearinghouse" for the findings of the various national intelligence services.

Measures such as the exchange of civil servants among the governments of the Atlantic Community could create a greater appreciation of the problems confronting member states and the common interests and values shared by Atlantic peoples. One pressing need is the creation of information programs to publicize the defense, economic and political problems of the North Atlantic area. In the past, publicity about NATO has all too often stressed its weaknesses, unfilled quotas and unmet goals. Much less publicity has been given to the alliance's achievements—its substructure of political agreement and military co-operation. NATO itself, member governments and private organizations should develop information programs designed to create a greater public awareness of the nature and importance of the Atlantic Community.

At present, the efforts of private and governmental organizations to cultivate an Atlantic sense of community are largely dissipated by a profusion of endeavors. An Atlantic organization for cultural, scientific and educational co-operation has been conspicuous by its absence. The proposal for an Atlantic Institute, endorsed by numerous private Atlantic conferences and groups, would answer this pressing need. Its creation, long overdue, would provide a forum and clearinghouse for the discussion and study of Atlantic economic, social and cultural problems.

Closer intergovernmental co-operation—as, for example, long-term exchanges between policy-makers at various levels of government below that of foreign secretary—should be reinforced by co-ordination among the legislatures of the alliance members. This could be accomplished by the appointment by each parliament of observers to all other NATO member legislatures. Ultimately, this system could be enlarged to an inter-NATO parliamentary steering committee. The various political parties favoring the further growth of NATO might establish a systematic correspondence on ideas and proposals of common concern.

Some important steps have already been taken. For example, on August 24, 1960, the House of Representatives passed a resolution calling for a NATO Citizens Convention. A substantial majority from both parties supported this resolution. It became law with President Eisenhower's signature on September 7, 1960, and an appropriation was voted before Congress adjourned. A bipartisan commission was created to arrange for and to participate in meetings and conferences with similar citizens' organizations in other NATO countries. The sponsors of the resolution envisage the Atlantic Convention as a first step toward the establishment of permanent Atlantic institutions.

None of these proposals go beyond the spirit and the letter of Article 2 of the Atlantic Pact. Surely, they are not revolutionary. Implicit in the suggested reforms is the assumption that, here and now, the Atlantic nations will not abandon formally their sovereignty over internal matters. Indeed, to encourage the rapid dissolution of traditional structures might weaken the historical loyalties of populations without substituting a loyalty to a new supranational structure. For the foreseeable future, each country will continue to maintain its own parties, hold its own elections and be run by its own government, and the political composition of the various governments will differ at any given time. Rather than strive for a full-fledged central authority in the North Atlantic area, we must start with the more effective co-ordination within the existing national frameworks.

The NATO members, in working for greater Atlantic unity, should seek to avoid the proliferation of international agencies which would duplicate national effort. By creating one institution after another, the West might well create an organizational conglomeration far less effective than the existing national machinery. The Atlantic nations should simplify their own national administrative structures, decision-making processes and legal systems. New organizations for international co-operation should be created only when they will supersede existing agencies and hence simplify the Community structure. Measures designed to simplify tax laws and to standardize social benefits, such as pensions and disability payments, will facilitate further steps toward co-ordination of national policies. These reforms, in order to be effective, should not be improvised, but instead need to be carefully prepared and promulgated by the joint efforts of NATO members.

Since the end of World War II an all-European nationalism, committed more or less openly to neutrality between the United States and the Soviet Union, has gained adherents in many parts of Western Europe. The highest card the United States has to play against this force is its own forthright commitment to the Atlantic Community. Such a policy offers Europe the best solution of her gravest problem: The divisive nationalisms of the European NATO powers can be more readily accommodated and sublimated within a broader Atlantic framework than within a Western European union. Great Britain and other European nations outside the "Little Europe" of the Six would probably find mutual co-operation easier within an Atlantic Community embracing the United States and Canada. A shift in emphasis from European to Atlantic unity could lead to the reduction of divisions within Western Europe, on the one hand, and between Western Europe and the United States, on the other.

Americans have often tended to take for granted the continued friendship and co-operation of Canada in the Atlantic Community. By virtue of its growing strength and strategic location, Canada has an important part in efforts to strengthen the Atlantic Community. Together with the United States, Canada forms an important component of the North American core area of Free World defenses. Moreover, Canada provides a "bridge" between the United States and Western Europe because of its historic political and economic ties with Great Britain and its cultural bonds with both Britain and France. As a result of its Commonwealth membership Canada also has developed unique relationships with newly independent states in Asia and Africa.

Outside NATO, the majority of international organizations are designed to deal with the economic problems either on a global basis or strictly within a European context. Although Canadian commercial ties with Western Europe are of great importance, Canada is by geography excluded from European trade organizations. Canadian fears about European integration might be allayed if Europe's regional problems were resolved within the context of a broader Atlantic-wide framework. A European trading community aiming at greater economic self-sufficiency behind high tariff walls would run counter to the interests of both the Atlantic nations and the underdeveloped world.

U.S. Diplomacy in the Underdeveloped World

The task of U.S. leadership is infinitely more complicated in the broad areas of the Free World lying outside the Atlantic Alliance, where the systemic revolution is battering the last defenses of the old order. The initial thrust of this revolution is directed squarely against the West and the United States as its leader; behind it lie the grievances accumulated in centuries of colonial domination and the envy of the more bountiful life enjoyed by the industrialized nations of the West.

Our policy toward this unorganized, amorphous force must be based on the optimistic assumption that the destructive phase of the social revolution in the underdeveloped areas will spend itself —in time.

Broadly speaking, the primary function of our diplomacy toward the emerging nations is to help them to resist communist penetration, maintain internal and external security, and move ahead economically. A large part of our dealings with the new states of Asia and Africa will center on working out economic programs and such practical matters as aviation rights, research programs and personnel or cultural exchanges. Negotiations in these functional fields should be carried on patiently and tactfully.

In the past, the United States, in its dealings with the emerging nations, has tended to oscillate between two extremes of diplomatic style: high pressure on the one hand and excessive softness on the other. Too frequently we have tolerated effrontery on the part of smaller nations simply because we deem it beneath our dignity to insist upon the preservation of our rights and interests. While American policy-makers seem to subscribe officially to the view that we seek to be respected rather than liked, in practice we often act as though we prefer the opposite. A nation can evoke international respect by a determined policy to protect its own legitimate interests and to help its allies protect theirs, even though the action required may sometimes prove temporarily unpopular. In brief, it might be said that our diplomacy toward the neutral and underdeveloped countries is vulnerable to criticism on grounds of style rather than substance.

In the vast reaches of the underdeveloped world, U.S. policy must be content, in the shorter run, to stage a delaying action. No one policy can adequately bracket the diversity of conditions and problems facing us in immensely different areas of the world. We must essentially play the diplomatic instruments by ear, guiding wherever possible the revolution into constructive channels and countering wherever possible attempts by the communists to exploit the revolution for their own ends. Again, however, there are several broad guidelines which American diplomatic and political strategy can profitably follow:

1. *Show reasonable deference to local sensitivities.* Diplomacy, for many of the newly emergent countries, represents the only available form of self-expression. They have little or no military strength with which to back up their ambitions, nor economic strength to satisfy their desire for quick and lasting results. They look to the United Nations as the only forum in which they can make their existence felt and their voices heard. Without turning the other cheek, we can afford to be tolerant of the attempts by new leaders at self-assertion, meanwhile persuading them, with all available

means, to turn their energies to their real and abiding problems at home.

2. *Recognize the utility of declaratory policies.* We can declare our support, in principle, of the legitimate aspirations of this or that nationalist movement without permitting such declaratory policy to guide our immediate actions. This should not be construed as hypocrisy but simply as the differentiation between long- and short-term goals. In the long run, we stand for the self-determination of nations. In the short run, however, we must temper this aspiration with much more immediate considerations, as, for example, the stability of a given area, our alliance commitments and current strategic demands.

3. *Ease the sociopolitical transition of unstable countries.* Post-war revolutions have left a trail of violence in such countries as Egypt, Syria, Indochina, Iraq, Cuba, South Korea and the Congo. In other places, regimes are perched on the powder keg of social-political upheaval. It is problematic as to whether U.S. policy could have forestalled these convulsions or whether it can do so in the future. Our dilemma is particularly acute in countries where we are committed to existing regimes by the ties of alliance or the dictates of strategic interests. American policy has been scored consistently for identifying itself irrevocably with the *status quo,* for shoring up arrogant and repressive regimes and for alienating permanently the spokesmen of the rising new order.

This criticism is leveled against us on moral, psychological and political grounds. Morally, it is alleged, we forfeit both our heritage and our right to speak for freedom and international justice when we support unpopular regimes. Psychologically, we provide grist for the communist propaganda mill which never tires of depicting us as the leader of a capitalist-feudalist combine dedicated to guarding its vested interests and ill-gotten gains against the forces of social progress. Politically, it is argued, our policy courts disaster by basing itself upon regimes which are bound either to crumble under their own corrupt weight or be obliterated by revolution. The same explosion which shattered the monarchies in Egypt and Iraq and forced the resignation of Syngman Rhee in South Korea and Menderes in Turkey, is building up in Iran, in Jordan and in Saudi Arabia.

Morality in the conduct of international affairs is an elusive and subjective standard. We may well be striving for a world which will reflect on the highest human plane those values which we cherish in our own moral code. Meanwhile, however, we are forced to deal with the world as it is, not as we might like it to be. Dean Acheson wrote:

> Morality in individual life has to do with those restraints upon conduct which are adopted or imposed because there are others upon whom one's conduct impinges with more or less directness of effect. So, too, restraints upon the conduct of a society as a whole may be adopted or imposed because of the effect of one society upon others. But they are not the same restraints. They deal with different situations; and it is best to state principles in terms of their purpose and effect without characterizing them as moral or immoral.[10]

As regards practical action, criticism is infinitely easier than remedy. We are faced, in many of the less mature countries, with situations in which the alternatives are stark: the *status quo* or socioeconomic chaos. No matter how inadequate and even painful may be the former alternative, we cannot, even if we have it in our power, opt blithely for the latter. The only thing we can do is try, within the limits both of propriety and our diplomatic leverage, to bridge the gulf between regimes and peoples.

The task is not a simple one. We cannot interfere blatantly in the internal affairs of countries without risking serious local and international repercussions. We cannot order King Saud to donate a greater share of his oil revenues toward raising the living standard of the people of Saudi Arabia, nor can we force Riza Shah Pahlevi to cultivate a genuine, popularly based opposition party in Iran. But we can, within the range of our diplomatic influence, make every effort to persuade unpopular regimes, in the interests of their own survival, to remove the major obstacles to socioeconomic progress. Apparently, we have made some headway in this respect with our hemispheric neighbor, the Dominican Republic, where Dictator Trujillo is introducing at least some of the trappings of political and social reform.

4. *Do not permit our preconceptions to color policy toward authoritarian and military regimes.* One of the primary goals of American foreign policy is to support the establishment and growth

[10] Dean Acheson, *op. cit.*, p. 108.

of representative government throughout the Free World, especially in the newly emergent nations of Asia and Africa. The realization of this goal is perforce a long-term process. Many of the new countries are ill-equipped to practice democracy as we know it. Most of the newcomers to the international community, when they achieved independence, copied their political institutions from Western models. They have since learned the lesson that democracy cannot be easily transplanted; it must be grafted onto indigenous political systems and requires a period of preparation before it can take effective root in non-Western societies.

During the last decade, the majority of the Afro-Asian nations have been plagued by chronic political instability brought on by economic dislocations, irresponsible politicians, a high rate of illiteracy, bureaucratic bungling and venality and a multitude of other ills common to most underdeveloped countries. By 1960, many countries of the Afro-Asian world appeared to veer away from democracy toward authoritarian, military governments. This trend occurred in different degrees in the Sudan, Pakistan, Thailand and Indonesia. In other countries of North Africa, the Middle East and Asia democracy has either failed to develop (United Arab Republic, Jordan, Iraq, Saudi Arabia) or else has run into serious trouble (Morocco, Tunisia, Lebanon, Iran, Ceylon, Cambodia, Laos, South Vietnam and South Korea).

The development of representative governments, responsive to the governed, is our long-term goal; but many countries have yet to develop those standards of education and public responsibility which support meaningful democratic institutions. The patterns of government which evolve in other societies will in all probability differ markedly from ours. Similarly, the economic systems of other societies cannot be expected necessarily to mirror that of the United States.

In some areas charismatic leadership, authoritarianism and one-party government seem to be inevitable at this stage of political development. Western-type democratic institutions do not always conform to traditional political practices. One-party political systems, kindred to the "democratic centralism" of the communist world rather than to Western political practices, are characteristic of many newly independent states and tend to mirror traditional patterns of political behavior. These authoritarian governments are often the only means of assuring progress toward stability—if for no other reason than that other practical alternatives are not yet in sight. The United States, therefore, cannot do better than to cooperate with those authoritarian (but not totalitarian) governments that provide a degree of stability and an environment favorable to economic growth and the gradual attainment of political maturity.

Some authoritarian leaders see themselves as forced by circumstances beyond their control to travel a circuitous route toward the long-term goal of democracy. Many new authoritarian governments have expressed the intention—and some have already carried it out—to work toward the establishment of representative institutions once political stability has been achieved and their countries have been placed on the road to economic and social progress. The United States should encourage these efforts, keep an open mind and display confidence in the sincerity of professed intentions. In some cases this is the least we can do to bring about what we desire; in other cases, this is the best policy, since there is little else we can do.

In many of the underdeveloped countries, especially in South and Southeast Asia, the officer corps has emerged as a major political force. As the civilian governments, run by self-serving politicians and inefficient bureaucracies, have become discredited, the officer corps has been faced with the choice of either being the passive witness to its country's economic and political disintegration or of displacing civilian authority and assuming political responsibility. Almost without exception these officer corps, by initiating various reforms, have placed their countries on the road to stability and governmental efficiency. Trained and equipped in most cases by British or American armed forces, indigenous officer corps have proven in certain countries to be strong foes of communism and open friends of the West. Wherever democracy seems to require a period of incubation, the United States should continue to provide diplomatic support and military and economic assistance to governments controlled by a coalition of noncommunist civilian and military elites.[11]

[11] See "A Study of United States Military Assistance Programs in Underdeveloped Areas," by the Foreign Policy Research Institute, University of Pennsylvania, Annex D, Vol. II, Supplement to the Composite Report of the President's Committee to Study the United States Military Assistance Program, Washington: U.S. Government Printing Office, 1959, p. 79.

The make-up and behavior of these regimes often may grate upon our preconceptions of how political society should be constituted and how it should operate. But again, we must deal with the world as it is and not as we would like it to be. We must look upon the new authoritarian regimes as a transitional phase between national beginnings and political maturity, and support their quest for the kind of stability on which representative institutions can be based.

5. *Support federative schemes wherever feasible and politically desirable.* The systemic revolution has unleashed forces which are rapidly altering the nation-state system. Structurally, the evolution of international society has tended toward larger groupings of states. The federative spirit is alive in Western Europe, in the Atlantic Community, and also in many areas of the underdeveloped world. The impulse for this drive originates in differing motivations. In some instances it is the recognition that combination offers the sole hope for survival; in others, the ambition of individual national leaders bent upon regional hegemony. Some of the federative trends in Africa conform to the former category; the drive of Nasser to combine the Arab world under his leadership belongs to the latter. The United States should encourage such efforts provided they (1) conform to political and economic needs of peoples directly affected; (2) reflect the voluntary desire by all parties to the union; and (3) do not upset a tenuous politico-military-economic equilibrium in a given area.

Most of the emerging states of Asia and Africa are political synthetics, fashioned not by the forces of ethnic and linguistic cohesion but by the arbitrary administrative boundaries of former colonial systems. They are slated either for new amalgamations or a twilight existence at the mercy of forces far less controllable than the whims of the former colonial rulers. As the following discussion illustrates, there are similar as well as unique problems confronting each of the major regions of the Free World.

In North Africa the federative principle is discernible in many of the proposals advanced for the political evolution and economic development of the Maghreb. Geographic, religious and historic ties, in addition to economic and political necessities, provide the basis for co-operation among the peoples of North Africa. The application of the federative principle in the Maghreb would facilitate the more effective utilization of the resources of the entire region. Admittedly, closer co-operation in the Maghreb cannot be achieved so long as the Algerian conflict continues. With peace in Algeria, the states of the Maghreb could take steps to remove customs barriers, integrate their programs of economic development and co-ordinate their foreign policies. The implementation of the federative principle would permit human skills to be pooled and utilized where needed. In co-operation with each other and with the Atlantic Community, the states of the Maghreb could find the means necessary to tap that region's resources and thus to provide a better life for its peoples.

In the Middle East, national political stability cannot be isolated from the broad politics of the entire area. Federalism, on a regional basis, offers the most likely approach toward achieving national stability as well as economic development. The growth of voluntary regional associations, perhaps first functional and later political, holds out the greatest promise of reducing many of the Middle East's petty antagonisms. Appeals for regionalism form an important element of modern Arab nationalism. At present, however, internecine conflicts hinder the growth of a true Arab community. The regional economic development of the Middle East—especially the exploitation of water and mineral resources and the improvement of transportation—is heavily dependent upon co-operation among the Arab states. Thus, for example, the most pressing problem of the area, namely, the creation of an adequate water supply, can be solved only by a degree of regional planning and collaboration. Virtually all important rivers—the Nile, the Tigris, the Euphrates, the Jordan—are international waterways. The Atlantic Community has many skills to offer for the hydrological problems of the Middle East. Programs to develop water resources could aid immeasurably in creating the infrastructure for economic development in the Middle East. Indeed, the long-range political and economic interests of the Middle Eastern peoples are best served by a close association with the West. The West has no desire to dominate the Middle East politically. On the other hand, Soviet expansionist policies seek to exacerbate the region's problems and to utilize the Middle East as a bridge for the penetration of the Mediterranean littoral and Africa. Yet, again the disunity of the West has managed to becloud these obvious facts and to prevent a common approach to Middle Eastern problems.

Africans, just as the Arab peoples, could benefit from regional arrangements which offer an alternative to the Balkanization of Africa and facilitate the more rational development of her economic potentialities.

Sub-Saharan Africa is engulfed in a series of revolutions which are transforming the old political, economic and social order perhaps more rapidly than in any other part of the world. The political revolution has stirred masses of detribalized Africans to an explosive anticolonial fervor and, in many places, has transferred political power, more or less abruptly, from European authorities to African elite groups. The social revolution has aroused Africans to demand equality with the white man and to challenge the political and economic domination by settlers of European origin. The economic revolution has undermined traditional tribal structures; the growing cities have attracted Africans from the bush to a money economy which places emphasis upon production and consumption.

All African states, from the Negro states to the multiracial territories and states of East and South Africa, lack that underlying and deeply felt unity which distinguishes nations in the Western sense. Nationalism in Africa has been in large measure the ideological contrivance of an educated African minority demanding opportunities and rewards equal to those of the white man. The leaders of newly independent African states face an immense task if they are to weld their peoples into nations and their territories into viable political units. The nation-state experience of the Western world is not easily transferrable to a continent divided by tribal antagonisms and formidable physical barriers. Moreover, the present political boundaries, the product of agreements among the European colonial powers for the administration of African dependencies, often bear little resemblance to the tribal divisions. In some areas tribal units transcend territorial boundaries. Irredentist movements, based upon tribal cleavages, constitute a source of potential conflict.

Most of the new African states are either poorly structured or too small or too poor to afford the considerable expense of national sovereignty. In some areas the ability of central governments to exercise effective control over territory nominally under their suzerainty is doubtful. Admittedly, great obstacles stand in the way of regional federation, not to speak of a "United States of Africa," which is a political slogan rather than a practical answer to the problems of this unhappy continent. African leaders are becoming increasingly aware of the need for co-operative arrangements to meet the problems posed by Africa's many political divisions. The United States should lend its support to the Africans' own efforts to form voluntary associations among their countries. This does not mean, however, that we should necessarily support movements which would seek to submerge smaller political units against their will into a new kind of African empire.

Africa probably contains the largest untapped reserve of human and natural resources remaining in the world. But vast distances between mineral deposits and ports, separated from one another by thick forests, deserts and mountains, together with inadequate facilities for transportation hinder their effective utilization. Still another obstacle is the psychological orientation of many Africans to a leisure-centered, rather than a production-centered existence. The part-time, urban, mining, or plantation worker is a phenomenon characteristic of many areas of Africa. Large turnovers in the labor force diminish African productivity. Moreover, at practically all levels of employment, from technicians and administrators to skilled laborers and agriculturists, most areas of Africa lack the personnel necessary to build modern economies. It follows that American and European scholarships, travel grants and other educational awards should not be confined to highly intellectual pursuits. Africans should be given the opportunity to benefit from training as instructors in technical and skilled fields. To meet the acute shortage of civil servants, the NATO countries might form an international civil service, a pool of trained personnel to be loaned to African governments.

The future economic systems and trade orientation of Africa will be determined by many forces, some indigenous and some international. They are certain not to evolve along lines favorable to the North Atlantic peoples if the latter do not play a more vigorous and constructive role in helping to develop further that economic "infrastructure"—highways, railroads, ports and electric grids—which is indispensable for balanced economic growth. Not all the undertakings which provide the base necessary for economic development are profitable commercially or yield direct returns on capital investment. It is here that foreign governmental aid has its proper scope. Private investment is not and must not be barred from the building of "infrastructure." But, in the nature of things, governmental economic aid will play the major role.

In 1957, the Council of Europe considered the general question of co-ordination of European policies toward development and investment in Africa and recommended the creation of a Consultative Committee, a Bank for African Development, and an African Investment Fund and a Technical Assistance Bureau. The United States should encourage such efforts and should seek to co-ordinate Western governmental aid and private investment in Africa. It is probably in the economic sector that the relationship between independent African states and the West can best be institutionalized within the framework of Atlantic co-operation.

The West enjoys a number of advantages in its relationships with Africa. The Western nations have been on the scene for centuries. Whereas colonialism has created tensions, it has also bred friendships, respect and allegiance. Moreover, the African economies, at the present stage of their development, fit much more logically into the Free World system than into that of the communist trading bloc. These considerations favor the West. The United States and Western Europe should not regard these advantages as justifications for complacency, but should make every effort to capitalize on them in order to forestall serious reversals in the years to come. Continuous race wars and the loss of Western interests in Africa are not foreordained. These calamities are more likely to occur if Western power weakens and Western will and imagination flag.

Like other continents, Asia stands to benefit from regional political and economic arrangements. A variety of historical and contemporary problems still hampers the growth of Asian regionalism. Across the lines of historical antagonisms, some new Asian states have embarked upon varying forms of regional association. Among these, the most successful has been the Colombo Plan. In this association, both Asian and Western countries are teamed in an ambitious, long-range program for the advancement of Asian living standards and international economic exchanges. Likewise the Southeast Asia Treaty Organization (SEATO), organized after the French debacle at Dien Bien Phu to halt communist advances, has made possible not only joint training and planning, exchanges of intelligence, improvements of military base facilities and standardization of weapons and military doctrine among its members, but also political consultation and a measure of regional co-operation in nonmilitary fields.

Were the strength of the West to decline in relation to that of the Soviets and Chinese, the nonaligned states of Asia would face the alternative of submitting to increasing communist pressure or casting their lot with the West. In fact, Asian neutralism is buttressed by Western military strength. It follows that, even in the face of neutralist complaints, the United States should demonstrate its determination to protect the Asian rimlands against communist aggression; maintain or increase its military capabilities in or near the region and strengthen SEATO. While we should be respectful of neutrals' desires and attitudes, the United States should not feel compelled to modify its defense arrangements to placate neutralist opinion. Indeed, it is more than likely that most of the neutral and noncommitted states of Asia are not entirely displeased with an American posture of strength.

In the Western Hemisphere many regional groupings have come into existence to meet the needs of the Latin-American peoples and to link them to the United States in co-operative efforts. Among the Latin-American peoples themselves, historical ties of language, culture and religion provide the basis for regional co-operation. Furthermore, Latin America, in contrast with many other underdeveloped areas, is an integral part of the Western world. Many of the needs of Latin-American countries could be met best by regional co-operation and by joint efforts in collaboration with the United States and Western Europe.

During the coming decade Latin America can play a constructive role in Free World global strategy. But the United States must provide vigorous leadership to assist Latin America in changing herself from a region of comparative poverty and discontent into a more orderly and progressive community. The success of such efforts will rest ultimately upon co-operation between the United States and the Latin-American countries. Although the United States can play an important role in such joint efforts, their success depends primarily upon the Latin-Americans themselves.

One of the major vehicles for Latin-American economic progress is higher education. Measures could be taken by the United States, in co-operation with other North Atlantic nations, to transform the character of Latin-American universities. These include massive translation, publication and subsidized distribution of good textbooks. Exchange of professors and students between the North Atlantic area and Latin America should be increased. Such a program would probably call for United States government subsidies, as well as assistance by other Atlantic nations. Members of the social science faculties of Latin-American universities should be given the opportunity to visit, for one or two semesters, universities in the North Atlantic countries and to travel in the host country. Firsthand observation might yield salutary insights: Latin-American intellectuals might thus awaken to the fact that the economic and social systems of the United States and other North Atlantic countries offer the individual and the great bulk of society higher living standards and greater freedom than do the outmoded Marxian theories that still have currency south of the Rio Grande.

It is probable that Latin-American nations will continue, for the most part, to maintain their ties with the United States in the various schemes of Western Hemisphere co-operation which have evolved in the last generation. As in the past, the United States can properly serve as a link between the Atlantic Community and our Latin-American neighbors. Where possible, however, the United States should seek to team its resources with those of other North Atlantic countries in joint programs of hemispheric development and defense.

The United Nations as a Forum of Diplomacy

In the short space of fifteen years, the politics of the Cold War and the emergence of many new nation-states have altered profoundly the nature of the United Nations. Initially, the UN was envisaged as an international clearinghouse where disputes could be settled in a spirit of compromise and to the mutual satisfaction of most members. But the cynical and disdainful attitude of the Soviet Union toward the principles of the UN has rendered inoperable several of its original purposes. Indeed, through the past decade, the Security Council and the General Assembly have done little to lessen the causes of world tensions, or to harmonize points of fundamental conflict.

It is true that the UN has become a useful center for airing disputes. It is equally true, however, that it has become a major center for the dissemination of Soviet propaganda. Nothing attests to this more vividly than the fact that Premier Khrushchev has reserved his more spectacular proposals for universal disarmament for the rostrum of the General Assembly.

From its outset, the UN was crippled by a serious institutional weakness: Its decision-making body, the Security Council, could be rendered impotent by the veto of any of the five Great Powers; the General Assembly, governed by a veto-free two-thirds vote, was empowered merely to "discuss and recommend." The United States, frustrated by this procedural impasse, induced the General Assembly, in the fall of 1950, to approve the "Uniting for Peace" resolution. Under this resolution, the General Assembly can be called into an emergency session to take up any threat to peace on which action has been blocked by a veto in the Security Council. Thus, in an effort to circumvent flagrant Soviet obstructionism, the General Assembly arrogated to itself an authority far exceeding that provided in the original Charter.

In the decade after World War II, it seemed that we would always command a sufficient majority to safeguard our interests and those of our allies in the UN. In almost all cases in which the Western Allies have stood united, the vote in the General Assembly has been favorable. But the rapid influx of new nations may soon render the outcome of future votes less certain. Thus, for example, one American policy, namely the exclusion of the Peking regime from the United Nations, and specifically from the Security Council, appears to be running into difficulties in the General Assembly. On this issue, the United States has been able to retain, with few exceptions, its following among its friends and allies. With the increase in membership, however, the margin of votes cast on the side of the United States has been growing slimmer. In the fall of 1960, the vote on whether or not to consider the admission of the Peking regime was forty-two to thirty-four, with twenty-two abstentions. For the first time, the abstaining members held the balance. Up until then, the United States could have carried the day even had the abstaining members changed their minds and voted on the side of Red China. Now, a shift in the vote from abstaining to opposing the American motion would have sealed the first major American defeat in the UN.

In brief, the United States is no longer assured, on major issues, a "safe" majority in the United Nations. This uncertainty, however, is not an isolated phenomenon restricted to the United Nations; instead, it reflects the changing nature of the postwar world. It places into sharp focus a dilemma which confronts the United States: Since the United States is no longer assured of majority support on all issues raised before the General Assembly, can its vital interests best be served by close support of the United Nations in the future?

The United Nations is not a world government. Although it has been severely chastised in the past for its failure to resolve serious international conflicts—such as Hungary and the Soviet seizure of Central Europe—the UN, according to its Charter, is ill-equipped to impose its decisions upon any unwilling member. Perhaps, in the past, Americans have expected too much of the United Nations; from time to time throughout the Cold War, we have entrusted to the UN tasks with which we felt unable to deal. Hungary will remain the classic example of the consignment to the UN of an American policy problem. Sometimes it seems as if we had talked ourselves into believing that the UN is capable of accomplishing for the cause of freedom what we are either unable or unwilling to do. Conceivably, our policy can work through the UN. It would be totally unrealistic, however, were we to look to the majority of the UN for the formulation of *our* policy.

Given its past record, it seems doubtful that the United Nations can, at least in the immediate future, deal effectively with such problems as disarmament, Berlin and European security. The UN can, however, play an increasingly important role in preserving the independence and furthering the economic development of the emerging nations of Africa and Asia.

The Congo crisis of 1960 brought into high relief the altered nature of the United Nations. Under the mantle of the UN, troops from the small powers—logistically supported by the United States—sought to restore order; UN technicians moved in to establish an emergency civil administration; and economic assistance was funneled through the United Nations. All these moves were in the West's interests. The UN has initiated a program of political and economic stabilization which would have proved extremely awkward if undertaken by Belgium, even if in concert with her NATO allies.

Yet, the West cannot but view with some misgivings the UN's

role in the Congo, for a precedent has been established for the reinterpretation of two crucial articles of the Charter. Thus, for example, the character of the Secretary General's office has undergone a profound transformation. The Charter empowered the Secretary General "to bring to the attention of the Security Council any matter which in his opinion may threaten the maintenance of international peace and security." Dag Hammarskjöld's broad interpretation of UN resolutions has permitted him considerable personal flexibility as the commander of a substantial military force and as an international diplomat. On his initiative, the article on "domestic jurisdiction," a clause invoked in the past by the French to safeguard their interests in Algeria and by South Africa to shield apartheid against censure, now has been interpreted far beyond the text of the Charter. In 1956, when United Nations Emergency Forces were dispatched to Egypt, the Secretary General acknowledged that their composition was dependent upon Egypt's wishes, and the dismissal of any contingent subject to President Nasser's whim. By 1960, he decided, by improvisation, that the Congo government, having invited UN troops, could not dismiss individual contingents and, more significantly, that the UN could, against the expressed wish of the local government, disarm indigenous troops, seize the radio station, and close all airports.

Certainly some bold precedents have thus been established. The West, if it were to be confronted by an openly hostile, pro-Soviet General Assembly, would be well advised to limit severely the prerogatives of the United Nations. But if we feel confident in the maturity and the genuine desire for independence of a majority of the underdeveloped nations, then we must associate ourselves boldly with the fortunes of an organization grounded in the principles of world order under law. Recently, in the Congo, Western interests were served "by proxy" through the UN; in the future, we might well profit from similar military and economic actions under the UN aegis.

The United Nations still stands as a monument of American and Western diplomacy. It has always been regarded, and rightly so, as a vehicle of the traditional Western concepts of the rule of law, the nonviolent settlement of disputes, and decision by majority after free debate in a representative assembly.

True, the UN cannot be relied upon for a solution to all the problems which confront us in an era of protracted conflict. The UN, in a sense, is the open society writ large. The Soviets would derive lasting pleasure not from its successes but only from its ultimate subversion and failure.

For the United States, the UN is one of the important ideological and diplomatic battlegrounds of the protracted conflict. The organization *can* serve as a useful instrument of American policy in several ways:

1. The UN provides a channel of diplomatic communications with the Soviet Union. The principal task of American diplomacy toward the Soviet Union is to conduct an unofficial dialogue for the purpose of exploration and gradual persuasion. The "corridor diplomacy" in the United Nations not only lends itself to this objective, but occasionally yields some immediate results. Thus, for example, the Soviets lifted their blockade of West Berlin in 1949 as a result of quiet conversations in the United Nations between the chief delegates of the United States and the U.S.S.R.
2. The specialized agencies of the United Nations carry out broad humanitarian projects in the indigent areas of the globe.
3. For the time being, the United Nations and its specialized agencies can serve as a multilateral funnel for American economic and technical assistance to nations whose economic health is vital to our objectives but who, for various reasons, are reluctant to accept aid on a bilateral basis. The U.S. should observe closely the effectiveness of the UN aid programs. In the long run, there may be plausible arguments for assigning this function increasingly to appropriate institutions within the Atlantic Community.
4. The United Nations can provide some measure of peace enforcement in highly charged emotional issues in which neither side can risk a loss of face—or, indeed, in which one side may be unwilling officially to recognize the existence of the other. A good example is the UNEF contingent stationed in Gaza and at Sharm el Sheikh.
5. The United Nations can be useful in averting the total breakdown of order in strife-torn nations. UN intervention in the Congo in the summer of 1960 was the only feasible alternative to complete chaos. Yet the tragic course of events in the Congo may well have been averted had the NATO allies concerted their policies in good time.

The United Nations, in short, still offers a forum in which hope for the promotion of peace—and especially the peaceful evolution of the underdeveloped areas—can be kept alive. But as long as the Soviet Union continues to seek a dictated, universal peace by the ultimate destruction of nations opposed to communism, the survival of Western society depends less upon the UN than upon American determination to match Soviet power by organizing within regional political frameworks the economic, military and moral power of the Free World. Indeed, it is not a question of choosing the UN *or* regional groupings. Healthy development of regional groupings throughout the world can eventually provide the UN with the strong underpinnings which it now lacks, for the United Nations, founded upon the legal artifact of national sovereignty, must keep pace with the federative movement which bids fair to gain further momentum during the latter half of the twentieth century.

Conclusions

Much has been said and written about the shortcomings of our diplomatic service. American diplomats have been criticized for lacking the combative spirit demanded of men "on the first line of our defenses," for failing in the acumen, insight and foresight, and tactical flexibility needed to accomplish their functions. They have been characterized as poor diagnosticians who do not have a prescient feel for the dynamics of a revolutionary situation and thus fail to comprehend the communist strategy of manipulating turmoil and upheaval.

Many of these charges may be true. They fail to take into account, however, that our diplomats, by and large, have been operating in a vacuum of policy. They have lacked the broad guidelines of central strategy to which their analyses, recommendations and individual actions could be meaningfully related. There has been intensive, long-range planning in the military and economic spheres of our strategy. No such long-range projections have guided our diplomatic conduct.

Planning flows from purpose, and purpose issues from a conceptual framework. The burden of this analysis has been not to concoct schematic solutions for the battery of problems facing American diplomacy in the nuclear age, nor to lecture diplomats on the proper techniques of their craft. Our purpose has been to lay the conceptual framework within which long-range strategy can be constructed. This framework can be summarized briefly as follows:

1. We are engaged in a pervasive struggle with the forces of communism—a conflict between two gigantic systems, each armed with massive military power, and both locked in a contest in which even a minor mistake may prove fatal. In this situation, we can find salvation neither in "gimmick" solutions nor in the leaven of compromise. The sources of conflict are not arms races, clashes of interest or the "unresolved issues" along the battle lines of the Cold War. The root causes of conflict are the closed monolithic society and revolutionary doctrine of an implacable adversary bent upon remaking the world in his own image. Not until the closed system of communism is opened and powerful pressures are brought to bear upon the decisions of its leadership can we hope for a genuine surcease from the struggle.

2. We cannot master this task alone. We need the combined material and intellectual resources of the Free World. If the United States, as the leader of the Western world, is to prevent the further shift of power eastward to the communist bloc and to deal successfully with the proliferating problems of awakening continents, then it can do so only in close co-operation with that kindred center of power in the Free World: Western Europe. Our problem is one of priorities. It is not that we consider Europeans superior as peoples to those inhabiting the underdeveloped countries of Asia, Africa and Latin America. It is simply that, if we are to help the newly emerging nations, as we must, we must seek first to organize effectively the primary resources of the Western world—the resources of Western Europe and America.

These are the basic premises from which a purposeful American diplomatic strategy must proceed. Only if our national effort is made to rest upon these premises will diplomacy serve as a more powerful instrument for building the Free World and bringing the communist engine of conflict to a halt. And only then will diplomacy, instead of being buffeted by the exigencies of each passing day, trace the design for a more logical, more harmonious world community.

CHAPTER 8 PSYCHOLOGICAL OPERATIONS

It is by no means easy to measure the weight of the psychological factor in political affairs. Yet we know from the history of our times as well as past centuries that psychological strategy and the systematic use of propaganda influences, and at times influences decisively, international action. Psychological strategy—like any other strategy—can be no more successful than the resolution, the skills and the means that go into the execution of its design. So far, American psychological strategy has met with indifferent success. We did not lack either the means or skills: but somehow our voice has come through muffled and has not elicited, as effective propaganda should, the desired political response abroad.

The history of propaganda begins with recorded history. The Pharaohs were master propagandists; so were the Prophets. The leaders of the American Revolution used successfully the psychological weapon, and the leaders of the French Revolution and Napoleon employed propaganda on a considerable scale and with no mean sophistication. Woodrow Wilson's "Fourteen Points" were, in large measure, a propaganda effort to end World War I by driving a wedge between the governments of the Central Powers and their peoples. Yet, only in recent decades has the propaganda weapon been used on a mass scale as well as against key individuals. During two world wars, the democracies engaged in vast propaganda efforts to rally their peoples against aggression and to demoralize the enemy. In peacetime, the democracies discarded propaganda as an expensive and unnecessary adjunct to foreign policy and diplomacy. In the hands of the totalitarians, however, propaganda has virtually become a substitute for diplomacy; it has become a major technique of "peaceful" conflict and conquest.

The advent of mass communications—the swift transmission of news, of harangues and falsehoods, carried across thousands of miles by radio into millions of homes and public places—extended the reach of totalitarian systems, disinterested in the settlement of differences by diplomacy, into the minds not only of their own peoples but also of peoples everywhere. With this development, the lubricants of diplomacy among civilized states, such as patience and deliberation, trust and confidence, compromise and adjustment, evaporated literally into the ether. Totalitarian states, to whom "peace" is the consummation of conquest, have fashioned by electronics a new tyranny over the mind. No previous despotisms in history have ever gained a comparable power to mesmerize such masses of people and to propagate such evil as have nazism and communism. Hitler once described the desired ends of propaganda as "mental confusion, contradiction of feeling, indecision, panic." The communists—forerunners, mentors and then successors of Hitler—have contrived an imposing engine of psychological warfare and propaganda. It meshes symphonic orchestras and sports teams with military threats, and technological breakthroughs with the propagation of the Marxist-Leninist myth. As a matter of fact, so complete is the amalgam of military strategy, diplomacy, ideological agitation and cultural and scientific activities that no one can say where communist propaganda begins and where it ends.

The Soviets' strongest ally has been our own distaste for psychological warfare in a time of "peace." Soviet propaganda has made serious inroads into free societies, particularly in economically underdeveloped countries. It has persuaded millions of people—the illiterate dwellers of the African jungle, the highly sophisticated denizens of the West's literary and artistic drawing rooms, and the demonstrating students in Havana and Tokyo—to believe myths and lies by their constant repetition.[1] Therefore, an American psychological

[1] "The Soviets understand the secret of the mass conscience. They have learned that the mass, or mob, provides the precise vehicle through which the individual is able to express his hostile feelings and not be held personally responsible for his deeds. . . .

"Communism does more than merely provide an outlet for general hostility. Once it arouses mob passions, it directs these emotions toward a specific common enemy. This is accomplished by establishing what might be called the

strategy, before it can take the offensive, must begin with an effort to regain lost ground. It must seek to recover the truth from the den of falsehood. To set the record straight will require a forthright program of education of the American and all free peoples. The President and other leaders of the United States should be the most effective teachers of this course in the true meaning of the Cold War. The Soviets have so distorted the true nature of this conflict that many peoples, including Americans, can no longer see its real dimensions, it causes and its stakes, and not a few cannot see it at all. The educational program should begin with a thorough exposition of the nature and purpose of Soviet propaganda.

American propaganda is based on the assumption that people tend to act rationally, that truth will ultimately prevail and that a mere presentation of the "facts" will suffice to win over widely differing audiences.[2] The communists are skeptics. In their concept of propaganda, rationality occupies but a modest place.

Soviet psychological warfare seeks to condition. Soviet psychological thrusts are aimed at whole peoples, not solely at heads of governments. Thus, the Soviet campaign of missile-rattling and portraying vividly the horrors of atomic warfare in Europe are designed to frighten the European peoples and to bully their governments into rejecting the American alliance. The communist calculation is simple: Once the European peoples will fear the nuclear holocaust more than the threat to their political liberties, they will pressure their governments into unilateral reduction of armaments, acceptance of arms limitations agreements without adequate inspection and control, and other suicidal concessions. Not so surprisingly, the Soviets make the most of the differences of opinion which luxuriate in all free societies. There is no scheme for ending the Cold War quickly and painlessly, no matter how

---

anticause. It is a known fact that the easiest way to acquire an ally is to first find a common enemy." Bernard J. Flatow, "A Suggestion for Meeting the Communist Threat in Latin America," *Export Trade*, August 8, 1960.

[2] The presentation of facts is, of course, indispensable, but if we hope to persuade our audiences, then these facts must be integrated under some guiding notion. We labor too often under the illusion that "the facts speak for themselves." They do not, particularly when they cannot be seen. Facts must be interpreted, and interpretations require a general conceptual framework.

eccentric, that does not find among us some vocal advocates. The Soviet threats of nuclear destruction and devastating reprisals against Great Britain, Italy, neutral Austria, Greece, Pakistan, Japan and many other nations are an integral part of a deliberate campaign of psychological warfare to instill fear of Soviet military power and spread serious doubts as to the wisdom of accepting American military bases and assistance or following a pro-American policy.

Conditioning is a slow psychological process. Yet, since 1945, the communists have conditioned world opinion to accept certain ground rules for fighting the Cold War. They have marked out noncommunist territory as the "war zone" and have, by and large, succeeded in so befuddling the Free World that the Cold War has been limited indeed to this "war zone." Under these quaint rules the West is to condone communist forays into its territory and abstain from disturbing the communist "peace zone." Almost all the debates in the United Nations from 1948 to the present over "threats to peace," "intervention," "imperialism" and "self-determination" have dealt with problems and tensions arising *within* the noncommunist world. The issues of Soviet imperialism and colonialism, denial of self-determination, intervention and threats to the peace have been raised much less frequently, and with a noticeable lack of fervor, by the majority of the United Nations members. Indeed, the U.S. government itself has often been reluctant to exploit Soviet vulnerabilities in the "peace zone." For example, during Khrushchev's visit to the United States in 1959, the American people were urged not to embarrass him or offend his sensibilities by questioning him on the most blatant and ruthless example of imperialism in the twentieth century—Soviet suppression of the Hungarian Revolution. Apparently, the government did not wish to arouse the ire of the man who had ordered the massacre and execution of the Hungarian freedom fighters.

Communist mass conditioning features a variety of themes, designed to keep the opponent in a constant state of confusion about the real nature and intent of Soviet policies and objectives. Thus, demonstrations of technological and military prowess alternate with proposals to "relax tensions"; threats of war are followed by protestations of peace. A classic example was the Stockholm peace appeal, an international chain letter circulated during the Korean War—a conflict initiated by Moscow. Similarly, an invitation to pay a "peaceful" call on the United States rewarded Premier Khrushchev for keeping the lid on the crisis over Berlin—a crisis provoked by none other than Premier Khrushchev himself.

Communist propaganda is as protean as it is cynical. In an era of mass communications, every act—even a feat of "nonpolitical" scientific research—can be projected onto the immense screen of world opinion and made to carry a poignant political message. Thus, recent Soviet successes on the international scene have been achieved in large measure by putting to use the physical instruments of military and technological power in the waging of psychological warfare.

Each of the major Soviet space achievements was calculated to excite the imagination of peoples everywhere and to reap political and psychological dividends. Many of them were timed carefully to political events: The launching of a space vehicle complete with a dummy was timed close to the 1960 summit meeting in Paris. Soviet technological achievements, skillfully co-ordinated with psychological strategy, have contributed substantially to the public image of the Soviet Union as an imaginative, energetic, technologically advanced society, imbued with that eagerness and daring which world public opinion had associated previously with the United States, and capable now of feats which no other nation can equal.[3] This is but one of the projections of Soviet propaganda imagery.

Another legend which the Soviets seek to spread is that of the "peace-loving" nature of the Soviet Union and its leaders. To foist these images upon the minds of peoples, to seduce and bend them to their purpose—no matter how self-destructive such a surrender of reason might be—this is the task of communist psychological strategy. The accomplishment of this task requires the conditioning of men's minds over a period of time so that they

[3] On the psychological battlefield, the West, until 1960, lagged far behind Soviet achievements—despite its over-all superiority in material resources. The United States had the wherewithal to beat the Soviets in the technological race but the determination to win was lacking. American space ventures were accorded low priority and were hampered by inadequate budgets. Before 1958 our government did not foresee the tremendous impact of Soviet space accomplishments on the imagination of other peoples and on our own national prestige.

will accept as a matter of fact the distorted Soviet version of world politics.

The communists have never been so preoccupied with foreign affairs as to neglect the development of novel means of waging psychological warfare on their own peoples. The Red Chinese are mass-producing the new "commune-man." An even more significant development in the human sciences is now under way in the Soviet Union.

In the mid-1950's, the Soviet rulers, pursuing both their stated goal of world domination and the development of a new Soviet man, launched a program of systematic inquiry into the factors of human behavior. The Party leaders realized that the state of Soviet morale constituted a strategic vulnerability; that a major effort was needed to modernize the human sciences in the U.S.S.R. so that they could serve the Party; and that the regime would have to rely on new techniques of controlling and manipulating the behavior of the masses.

Khrushchev's "manipulative decompression" is the sophisticated and insidious successor to Stalin's method of rule. Stalin ruled by terror. Stalin's "new Soviet man" was a simple and crude being whose behavior reflected simple and crude stimuli. When, in Stalin's times, a Soviet citizen deviated from the official model, Stalin's policemen dealt summarily with the recalcitrant. Stalin did not care to explore either the individual personality or the social environment in order to develop more efficacious techniques of rule. The post-Stalinist leaders adjusted methods of control to the growing sophistication of an urban-industrial society. This is perhaps their strongest claim to office—except the fact that they survived Stalin. Their rediscovery of personality—by our standards, a rediscovery of the obvious—led to a revision in Soviet sociological and psychological thought. The role of man is judged now to be more vital than ever in Soviet strategy. The Seven-Year Plan for Soviet Research, 1959-1965, reveals that the human sciences, particularly the social and biological sciences, have been assigned an important mission in accomplishing Khrushchev's objectives of developing the "new Soviet man."

Along similar lines, scientists of the Soviet Union and the satellite countries are carefully studying national cultures in the Free World to mark out specific strengths and weaknesses which may be exploited in support of Soviet objectives abroad. Studies on Africa in support of African liberation movements are now receiving considerable attention.

The Soviet scheme for building communism in the homeland and promoting its fortunes in the Free World relies no longer on relatively uncontrolled historical processes—the *deus ex machina* of classic Marxist theory. Now the Soviets apply "science" to human affairs. Thus, the development of a "science of man" in the U.S.S.R. has vital strategic implications. All other factors being equal, a struggle for total power may be won by the society whose human resources are best organized. A "social technology," based upon the accomplishments of human science, could serve to achieve such an integrated society in the U.S.S.R.

The Necessity for American Action

The peoples of the Free World, if they do not awaken to the meaning and purpose of Soviet propaganda and its conditioning techniques, will drift into confusion and demoralization. Then they will be unable to rouse themselves when communism, having done with the pretense of "peaceful coexistence," launches the final blow against the fragmented Free World. To date, the United States has only partially blocked the psychological assaults on the Free World—assaults which can be as deadly over the long run as a massive military attack against an unarmed people.

Our failure may well be due, in part, to a misunderstanding: One of the most ill-defined and misinterpreted words in our vocabulary is still the word "propaganda." Public opinion in the democracies continues to associate propaganda with falsehood and evil. This is a misleading, one-sided definition. There is, indeed, a propaganda that propagates big and small lies, and, more insidiously, half-lies and half-truths; there is another propaganda—the propaganda of the true faith and the just cause. The propaganda that serves democracy best is the skillful and persistent dissemination of the truth. The case for freedom stands and falls on its own merits. In the long run, the most successful propaganda is the one that cleaves to high standards of reliability and integrity. It should not, and need not, risk the temporary expedient or token victory at the expense of enduring credibility. We should be truthful in our propaganda; moreover, we can afford to be so.

A free and open society should not be reluctant to engage in propaganda and to conduct a psychological campaign in pursuit of its just goals. But propaganda disseminated by a democratic nation is not a magic instrument for influencing the thinking of peoples according to a desired pattern, irrespective of the factors of national strength and dynamism. Our propaganda cannot supersede reality, as it can and does in a totalitarian system. The content of a democratic psychological strategy is given by the true nature of government, society and power position. It is difficult to create false images of national strength and national purpose where the true state of society is exposed freely to everyone's inspection. Free nations generally appear abroad as they are in fact at home. If they are resolute, purposeful, well led and progressive at home, they will appear to other people as being just that. Democracies cannot afford to preach what they do not practice. A successful American psychological strategy rests on deeds. It is through deeds that we apprehend the vigor and wisdom of our leadership, the strength of our military establishment, the soundness of our economy, the firmness of our determination and the depth of our belief in the future. A true image of the live society must then be projected into the international scene. It is under this sign that we can enter confidently the struggle for the minds of men.

In fact, we have no alternative but to engage the enemy in the psychological arena of the Cold War—provided, of course, that we are serious about preserving our way of life. For, short of the outbreak of the Third World War, the immediate prospect is for a continuation and intensification of the Cold War—the great and protracted psychopolitical conflict. For Moscow, the real alternative to a nuclear showdown is not peace or "peaceful coexistence" as we understand these terms, but the waging of a psychopolitical war that will so weaken, demoralize and divide the Free World that a general nuclear war need not be fought at all or can be waged with impunity against distraught and defenseless peoples.

In many respects, then, the most conspicuous communist threat today is in the waging of political and psychological warfare; it is on this battleground that the communists, backed by military power, have scored their most spectacular advances. No one can now foretell the outcome of the Cold War; not every round has gone to the communists. It would be a gross exaggeration to charge our foreign policy-makers with neglect of the psychopolitical implications of their decisions. The Cold War itself has been a hard school in the psychology of international politics. There is, however, a fairly wide agreement in this country, buttressed by the best available expert opinion, that we have not drawn on the vast pool of talent and technical resources which are ours for the asking. The question is thus not so much whether our psychopolitical effort is inept or fruitless—it is neither—but whether it is adequate. If it is inadequate, then we may give the communists the very opening through which our entire position, diplomatic and military, can be outflanked.

Since we have no real choice other than to take up the communist challenge in the psychological arena, the only remaining question is whether we should meet it in order not merely to check it but to defeat it. Our effort in psychological strategy, because we have been forced into it almost against our will, has been piecemeal, inadequate in scale, and without continuity of action. Moreover, our psychological strategy has not been geared to the conduct of our grand strategy, but rather relegated to an auxiliary role—a loose and slightly embarrassing appendix of our diplomacy.

Before psychopolitical warfare can take its rightful place in the high council of our strategy, we must agree on its purpose. Thus, we are led back inexorably to the question of the goal of our strategy itself—of our national purpose. Indeed, the psychological weapon will remain an expensive and only mildly diverting toy as long as the American people have not decided unequivocally that they must press the fight against communist imperialism to a finish—just as they decided that nazism and fascism had to be fought to the end. This purpose must be communicated to the entire world as boldly and energetically as the Soviets now communicate theirs.

Once the decision has been made to wage the psychological battle on a scale adequate to win it, the issues of this vital campaign become clearer. Among the major tasks of an American psychological strategy are:

1. To clarify the main lines of American foreign policy and, particularly, the alliance policies which support it, so that both domestic and foreign audiences will understand clearly the reasons and the urgency of American conduct.

2. To project the great ideals of freedom, responsible govern-

ment and human welfare to the peoples of newly emerging lands so that they can identify their aspirations with those of other peoples in the Free World.

3. To expose the communist designs upon mankind, to portray the Soviet-initiated Cold War in its true nature, and to unmask communist techniques of direct and indirect aggression, including psychological warfare.

4. To refute the unscientific and outmoded Marxist-Leninist-Stalinist dogma, to dispel the "wave of the future" halo of communism, to pit against the "inevitability" of communism a deepening certainty that the "end of communism is inevitable."

5. To carry across the Iron Curtain the truth about world events and to seek with all the means of propaganda and technology to break down the barriers which so artificially separate the peoples under communist rule from the greater part of mankind.

6. To keep alive throughout the Soviet empire the spirit of resistance and the hope of eventual freedom and independence, and to assure the Kremlin's internal enemies that they have devoted friends and powerful allies beyond their frontiers.

The American information program, with respect to the first three tasks has, on the whole, been successful. The men who staff our information centers abroad have often carried the brunt of the Cold War. They have been seasoned by the fire of communist propaganda barrages. Their imagination and skills make them a major asset in American foreign policy. By the very nature of their trade, they often display a more perceptive understanding of the protracted conflict than do their colleagues in the economic, military and even the diplomatic fields.

Our psychological programs, directed toward opening up the closed societies of communism, have been far less effective. This failure does not reflect on the competence of the men who have attempted to carry our message into the communist heartlands. It derives, in part, from the inadequacies of the means at our disposal for piercing the electronic and censorship barriers erected by the communist rulers around their domains. More importantly, the deficiencies of our psychological operations throughout the Sino-Soviet bloc can be traced to our reluctance to drive home the errors and inadequacies of the communist system and ideology. The belief that such a discussion will only harden the hostility of the communist leaders has come to dominate U.S. psychological policy; it is the basic source of the weakness of our propaganda message to Moscow.

The planning and execution of a dynamic American psychological strategy of major scope is fully within our national capabilities. Psychological warfare requires as much professional competence as planning a military campaign or negotiating around a conference table. The United States has established academies to train men for war and a Foreign Service Institute to train diplomats. No comparable establishment trains Americans in the art of psychological warfare. Yet the need for professional competence in the field of psychopolitical warfare is just as great as that for military and diplomatic skills. It is in the field of revolutionary conflict techniques that the communists hold a decisive margin of superiority over the Western powers. Communist strategy is not an enigma: it is to seize, under the umbrella of nuclear terror, the Afro-Asian lands and other free countries piecemeal by *coups d'état*, subversion, psychopolitical appeals and the proved tactic of the "popular front."

It has been proposed to establish a career service similar to the foreign and military services for those who elect to specialize in the "unconventional" methods of international conflict. Although these methods are studied closely by several agencies of our government, an Academy of Psychopolitical Studies should be entrusted with the training of career specialists.[4] An expanded political-psychological service should have a voice in the highest councils of national security. Until our national leaders recognize the need for a positive psychological strategy to assist and reinforce our military and economic policies and the need for a professional corps of specialists in the operation of the complex and dangerous weapons of the mind, the United States will be armed for all kinds of conceivable conflicts—except the one in which it is already engaged.

Only in wartime has our propaganda effort approximated the scope and unity of the everyday communist psychological offensive. In times of so-called peace we are handicapped by one of the most admirable features of the democratic system—freedom of expres-

[4] A major step in this direction was taken by the United States Senate during the 1960 Special Session of Congress when it passed, with no recorded opposition, the Freedom Academy Bill, S-1689.

sion. This makes inevitable a virtually uninhibited partisan debate over foreign policy and reduces the effectiveness of a psychological strategy.

We are undercut by our own more commendable attributes as well as by naïveté and divided counsel. These handicaps in psychological strategy stem from the very matrix of democratic mores: The "open" mind gives the opponent the benefit of the doubt and another chance; sides with the underdog; and refuses to reach obvious conclusions until "all the evidence is in." And deeply religious impulses are conducive to a sense of guilt for past misdoings, whether real or fancied. In everyday, personal life—among friends and competitors—these are admirable qualities; they have been a source of moral strength for many generations, both in our domestic affairs and in our external relations. When confronting an aggressive, unscrupulous adversary, however, these characteristics and attributes can become handicaps. Soviet propaganda is predicated on a detailed knowledge of our national psychology; if we do not strengthen the "soft spots" in our national psychological make-up, the Soviets will exploit them.

There exists, largely because of sharp divisions in opinion and counsel among leaders and among the public at large, a certain malaise in all Western society. The American public cannot be expected to understand the issues of the day and find sufficient cause for personal sacrifice until American leadership reaches and sets forth its own agreement on the Soviet threat, the challenges posed by vast social upheavals throughout the world, and the policies which it proposes. In a democracy, where public opinion limits foreign policy, it is of the greatest importance that the people be taken into the confidence of their government and receive regular briefings on the basic facts of the international situation. The following are examples of the essential information which the American government should communicate to its own people as well as to other peoples, in order to clarify the issues of the Cold War:

1. The first principle of our foreign policy should be the extension of freedom and thus the security of the nation—the bastion of freedom. All men want to survive; so do all animals. Man seeks to achieve ends beyond survival.

2. The main adversaries of the United States today are the Soviet Union, its Chinese ally and their respective fifth columns, called

"international communism." Our attention must not be diverted from this danger by carping critics, at home and abroad, who point to our shortcomings, e.g., racial discrimination, city slums and crowded highways, and insist that we put our own nation in order *before* we engage the communists.

3. The great issue is not between the United States and the Soviet Union, two superstates dueling for world domination and equally blameworthy for the chaotic state of world affairs, but between the totalitarian Sino-Soviet system of some twenty disenfranchised countries and the free and open societies of the Atlantic Community and their allies.

4. The Soviet propaganda machine has perpetrated successfully the hoax of "peaceful coexistence." Coexistence, in the repertory of communist foreign policy, serves as a diversion for calming the West's suspicions and weakening its determination to provide for its defense.

5. The communist system, as now constituted, will not accede to any just peace with that same Western civilization which it has vowed to destroy.

6. Nuclear weapons have been and will continue to be the guardians of freedom. Consequently, the Western peoples should be given the facts about nuclear warfare, nuclear weapons, test bans and arms control. The truth will steel them against despair and give them the stamina for facing up to the uncertain dangers of the nuclear age. Our failure to explain the measures which can be taken to ward off the nuclear threat has diverted public discussion toward utopian schemes such as total disarmament.

Only by a clear understanding and a forceful presentation of our goals, of communist objectives, and of the irreconcilable conflict between the two ideologies, can American leaders blunt the Soviet psychological offensive, set the record straight, and restore unity of purpose to the West.

The Ideological Struggle

Ideologies about man, society, political and economic systems have been a prime motivating force in all historical epochs. The systemic revolution of the twentieth century is no exception. Today, the leaders and peoples of many nations, especially those of the newly emergent nations, are looking for perfect political systems, sure answers to their innumerable problems and immutable guides for their actions. In brief, they are searching for an ideology, an ideal image of a future society or a blueprint from which a future society ought to be constructed. They are in a hurry and prone to judge summarily the relative merits of alternative ways for organizing society.

The communists offer their ideology as a blueprint for a future society. Democracy has not fully joined the competition. The democratic societies have not yet presented the case for responsible government and human dignity as persuasively as they have presented, for example, the case *against* nazism and fascism. The Free World has carried on haltingly its own dialogue on the pattern and goals of a free and economically progressive society. The resulting vacuum has been filled by the appeals of communism.

The contest between the free, pluralist, democratic society, represented by most of the nations of the Atlantic Community, and the monolithic, totalitarian system of the communist bloc is being waged today primarily in the underdeveloped areas of the Free World. These two methods of organizing society are competing for the allegiance of the Afro-Asian peoples and nations in the throes of neo-nationalism.

Many of the new nations have inherited from their colonial past political institutions patterned on Western models. Confronted by vast socioeconomic problems, Western-style governments will often fall short of achieving the social cohesion and discipline necessary to modernize their turbulent societies. Many educated Asians and Africans associate the economic systems of the West with exploitation, and are thus drawn to the idea of socialism. Communism projects and exploits these preconceptions and holds up the Soviet Union as a model for rapid industrial progress.

This is the plot, then, of the ideological struggle. One theater of conflict lies within the noncommunist or Free World, i.e., the underdeveloped areas over which fly the banners of nationalism, neutralism and racialism. During the next generation, these countries will make their choice: to continue their association with the industrial nations of the West or link themselves to the communist bloc. The other theater is the communist bloc itself.

The stage for the ideological struggle is set, but the real nature and fundamental issues of the struggle remain obscure. The communists have attempted, especially since the advent to power of Khrushchev, to convince the world that the great struggle in the Cold War is the contest between two differing *economic* systems; one a "peaceful socialist" economy operated for and by the people, the other a rapacious and compulsively aggressive capitalist system run for and by Wall Street magnates and military adventurers. The communists have sought to focus the attention of the world's peoples upon this ludicrous contest between dummies for two reasons: to draw attention away from the Soviet totalitarian political system, which seriously compromises the acceptability of communism as an economic system; and to take advantage of a Fabian preference, which is fashionable especially in the underdeveloped world, for socialism and planned economies.

If the Soviets are successful in convincing the bulk of the world's population that the Soviet-American confrontation is primarily a struggle between economic systems—between socialist co-operation and capitalist exploitation—our task in the ideological conflict will be rendered more difficult. For in the underdeveloped areas an acceptance of some measure of socialism and state planning is the rule. By and large, the general concept of a free enterprise society, associated in many parts of the globe with the United States, does not command many adherents in Asia, Africa and much of Latin America (or does not command as many as it might, were it better understood). Hence, the logic of the Soviet campaign to portray us as the blackest of reactionaries who would favor in other countries only the privileged opposed to necessary socioeconomic change.

To be sure, there are major differences between the economic systems of the Soviet bloc and the Free World. Inevitably, the new nations will be concerned with the differences in economic concepts and systems represented by Soviet and Chinese communism and free Western economies, capitalist and socialist. The West certainly need not shrink from this competition in economic ideas. We should emphasize the obvious fact that the Western world is not "capitalist" nor is the communist bloc "socialist." The West is composed no longer of *laissez-faire* capitalist countries but is a family of socialist and free enterprise states whose major economic concern is to assure to everyone a decent standard of living; while the Soviet Union is a fascist and state-monopolistic country whose primary economic concern is to supply the state with the resources for the pursuit of its imperialist policies.

We should indeed emphasize the differences between our economic systems, for, when all the propaganda dies away, our system can stand on its merits whereas that of the communists cannot. It is perfectly true that these various *economic* systems could coexist peacefully. Their differences have not brought on the Cold War. The crucial ideological conflict rages in the realm of the image of man, of political institutions and the organization of society.

Communism is not an *economic system* but a *political weapon,* shaped by Lenin and Stalin for seizing and consolidating political power. Economically, communism is nothing more nor less than economic management designed to maximize the power and resources of the state in its quest for world domination.

The basic conflict between the Soviet bloc and the Western world is between an oppressive totalitarian political structure run by a power elite and a pluralist democratic society founded on respect for the individual and the rule of law. At issue are two rival conceptions of political order and social organization. A dialectic examination of both ideologies is requisite to the successful prosecution of our psychological strategy.

To assume the ideological initiative we need not develop a doctrinaire philosophy to refute Marxism-Leninism. If such a dogmatic ideology were a *sine qua non* of ideological competition, the United States might have to withdraw from the contest. We do violence to the basic traits of American psychology if we seek to contrive a unitary, succinct and dogmatic doctrine which can answer all questions for all men. We are, for better or worse, a pragmatic people: We believe in developing "practical" solutions, "workable" compromises, individual roads to salvation. We are, by our temperament and our history, deeply wedded to the nondogmatic approach. Any militant ideology presupposes a mystical sense of certainty, a fanatical fervor, an inclination to think in absolute terms, and an intolerance which are alien to our national character.

This does not mean that the concept of democracy—of individual freedom and responsive government—is so nebulous as to be undefinable and unpersuasive to peoples unfamiliar with our way of life. A generally accepted body of premises and principles about the individual, government and society are commonplaces in the minds and lives of Americans and the peoples living in most other nations bordering the North Atlantic. They ring with universality. Clearly enunciated, these principles can find widespread support throughout the world, and thus form the foundation for a concerted effort to win the ideological struggle for the kind of world we believe in.

Clearly, one of our sorest deficiencies is the inability of most Americans to articulate their deep beliefs and make them meaningful to peoples unfamiliar with our way of life. We must seek to adapt these principles to the environment and the problems of today's world.

This, then, is the great challenge: to adapt democracy and the Western concept of human dignity to new environments. Democracy is founded upon representative institutions. The communist "people's democracy" is so crude a counterfeit that we need not concern ourselves unduly with its acceptance as hard currency by other peoples. The crucial test is the day-by-day performance of our institutions. Democracy speaks for itself; it is its own publicist. Although the experience of American democracy is highly relevant to all peoples, rich or poor, Western or non-Western, it cannot be compressed into six easy lessons in the theory and practice of democracy under any and all conditions. Let us concede gracefully the truth: Among all forms of government, democracy is the most advanced—and the most precarious. Even advanced nations, after a long period of developing democratic institutions and habits in step with social and economic change, still have not perfected their systems of representative government. Indeed, democracy *is* a daily plebiscite. Its greatest enemies are complacency and sloth. Even in its birthplace, Europe, democracy has suffered grievous defeats. The history of democracy in Italy, Germany and France—countries boasting of high standards of living and literacy compared with the underdeveloped world—tells an ambiguous message. In brief, we cannot in candor tell other peoples that the learning of democracy is easy and anything but slow, that there is just one road to free representative institutions and not many and sometimes circuitous ones.

For the new nations, authoritarian governments, sometimes dominated by the military, may be the only kind of dependable and effective government in the immediate future. To new lands searching for patterns and principles of social organization, the orthodoxy of government may not be the best immediate answer. The alternative is an appeal, through responsible indigenous elites, to the evolutionary concept of reform by due process. Such an appeal will lack the dramatic impact of a revolutionary utopia; but it will have the force of soundness and the ring of historical truth.

Where the prospects for representative government are remote, we need to convince the new states that there is a better method of organizing society and providing for human needs than following blindly after an all-embracing ideology or "ism" such as communism. Militant ideologies promise rapid solutions of problems by radical institutional changes. The fact is that such "solutions" are often far from complete, or are even irrelevant. For example, the fundamental problem of economic betterment is a matter of the use of resources and increased productivity, not simply of institutional change.

We must strive to impress upon new leaders that concepts and solutions must remain open-ended; that solutions to difficult problems cannot be found by repeating slogans and clichés; that there are tried organizational techniques available for the improvement of institutions; and that men must learn to use these techniques, abandoning as useless and dangerous their propensity to talk and act in a fog of unscientific ideologies.

In the vital theater of the uncommitted and new nations, the United States must help create a realistic image of the future, free from the chimeras of utopian states. Utopia presupposes that history terminates and a static society emerges. It should be easy to demolish this foolish concept. In any case, we should not try to compete with the Marxists in creating it. The underlying issue is the nature of change: Must change always be violent and irrational, as it has been in many troubled areas of the world? It is the thesis of democracy, the heart of its credo, that human societies can and—when properly educated and led—will respond rationally to rational objectives.

This is not to say that emotions and prejudices can be purged from politics. Nevertheless, we have the choice of appealing either to the rationality or the irrationality of the human being, be he an individual leader or be he the common man. The communists, with their practiced skill in semantics and sophistry, choose for their own ends to appeal to the irrational—though often in the guise of logic starting from false generalizations. As Americans, we have made a choice for an ethos of truth and reason; it is the task of our psychological strategists to let our ways be known throughout the earth—to undo the work of forty years of relentless propaganda by the enemy.

We should not labor under the illusion that the underdeveloped states will be able to pass rapidly through the present ideological phase of their history. In our approach to their problems, logic and reason must be supported by emotional persuasion, lest the communists defeat us before we get started. Ideas, to be politically effective, must be emotionally charged. If this is true even in advanced democratic societies, how much more will it be true of those we have to reach in the underdeveloped lands?

This does not mean a retreat into the irrational. Our propaganda programs must be founded on truth, experience and the best interests of those to whom they are addressed. Truth itself, in exposing falsehood, is a rallying cry, but only if it is couched in terms that appeal to the heart and its emotions—the pamphlet, the poster, the cartoon—and not just to the intellect.

The Vulnerabilities of the Soviet System

Thus far, the Free World, under the impact of Moscow's Cold War victories and propaganda, has actually paid too much attention to Soviet strengths and not enough to Soviet vulnerabilities. Within the Soviet empire, the real tensions and injustices are incomparably greater than the discontent existing anywhere within the Free World. We have not seized our opportunity to exacerbate the Kremlin's domestic problems. Within the communist bloc a large audience awaits an ideological offensive.

Such an ideological offensive should present to the world a carefully reasoned and historical analysis of communist ideology and practice. It should demonstrate that communism is *not* the "wave of the future," but that it is an aberration from the mainstream of Western political thought, that it is rent by serious inconsistencies, and that it has fallen into fatal error and relies on repressive totalitarian methods to achieve its goals.

The communists would like us to believe that their revolution is the terminus of all revolutions. Yet they themselves fear nothing more than a new revolution.

An orientation theory for revolution and reform must serve as a comprehensive goal for action. Let us illustrate some of the elements of such a theory: (1) a return to individual rights, i.e., free speech, freedom of assembly, the abolition of a one-party monopoly; (2) decentralization of the Soviet economy, i.e., a return to property ownership, either in the form of profit-sharing co-operatives or in some other form; (3) return of the land to the peasants, to be owned individually or by co-operatives; (4) restoration of nationality rights, including the right of secession. These are but some points of a reform program to assist the return to liberty and representative government. Such a program proposes to wrest from the state that "collective ownership" which is the synonym of state capitalism, and to vest ownership, collectively if so desired, in the hands of those who operate the various enterprises. This reform program would give the lie to the often repeated accusation that the West aims at the restoration of the former factory owners and landed gentry who have departed long since.

The proposed reform program can be broken down into more limited objectives which appear to be attainable under the Soviet system itself. These could be as follows: (a) restoration of democracy inside the Communist Party; (b) restoration of the independence of the labor unions by the abolition of Party control, thus restoring to the workers some of the authority they were supposed to exercise under the Soviet system; (c) a return to voluntary participation in Soviet collectives, thus doing away with compulsory servitude to the state, and restoration to the peasants of the status of equal partners which they were supposed to enjoy under Lenin's concept of the Workers' and Peasants' State; (d) abolition of the internal passport system, which limits the right of travel and choice of employment and chains the workers and peasants to their present locations and jobs; and (e) abolition of the political police and its system of forced labor camps.

The major reforms suggested should guide the *strategy* to be pursued in the *abolition of the communist totalitarian state,* while the minor or immediate demands aim to ameliorate its tyranny.

There are many other aspects of communist dogma and practice which are vulnerable to rational analysis and argument. A concentrated offensive against these weak spots can render communism a most implausible system and ideology.

1. *The Transformation of Society.* Marx and Engels, in the *Communist Manifesto,* predicted that, since the defects of industrial

society were integral to the system, it would have to be shattered and replaced by another system. Marx assigned the special mission to accomplish the overthrow of capitalism to the working class. When this upheaval did not come to pass, the communists had to devise other "scientific" foundations for their revolutionary polemic.

Marx and Engels assumed that history is clearly predictable, which it is not. They predicted that capitalism would collapse because of its inner contradictions. This did not happen. The historic record shows that, over time, the capitalist system has become ever more productive while, at the same time, reforming many of its institutions.

Marx also predicted that under a capitalist system "misery" would constantly increase (the theory of "immiseration" of the proletariat). Up to 1900 or so, the Marxists interpreted this to mean that wages would fall constantly, unemployment would rise, and large segments of the population would die of hunger. After 1900, this theory was reinterpreted to mean that poverty would increase relative to wealth so that while the poor would become less "miserable" than in the past, nevertheless the differential between their income and the income of the rich would grow. This, too, has not come to pass. History has shown that under a free enterprise system the differentials of income tend to decrease. Contrary to Marx's prediction that the class struggle would grow more acute, it has abated throughout the Free World. In the collision between reality and the "scientific doctrine" of communism, the latter has fared none too well.

The development of industrial society has given the lie to Marxist prophecies. In place of becoming an executive committee of a shrinking bourgeoisie, as Marx described it, industrial society has become increasingly democratic, subject to the pressure of the labor vote, the farm vote, middle-class vote, and the minorities' vote. Out of the "proletarian" pressure on government, and out of the classless pressure of the whole of society, has come state regulation of economic life, legal limitation of the hours of work, a minimum wage, collective bargaining, the right to organize into labor unions and the sweep of social security legislation.

Our propaganda programs have paid only scant attention to the thoroughgoing transformation of nineteenth-century capitalist society into the modern capitalist economy systems of Western Europe and the United States. A careful and lucid description of these changes and the consequent benefits accruing to peoples living in free societies is an indispensable part of any American effort to explain our way of life and expose the unscientific dogma of communism.

2. *Communism and Nationalism.* The *Communist Manifesto* in 1848 prophesied the end of nationalism. Today, nationalism is the one great cause for which millions in the world are ready to fight and die. It has spread from Europe to Asia and Africa, which in 1848 knew nothing of nationalism or the nation. Communism is the antithesis of nationalism. It exploits nationalism so as to weaken the West, and then subverts and suppresses nationalism when the communists are strong enough to seize power. Thus, we hold a telling psychological weapon, if we have the wit to exploit it. At the present time, however, the issue of nationalism is being turned against the Free World because the Kremlin manages to exploit the very nationalism which the *Communist Manifesto* declared defunct.

The Leninist explanation of imperialism has been the single most effective statement of the grievances of colonial peoples. His "imperialism" has been an extremely appealing explanation of past subjugation and a justification for delays in the rapid improvement of conditions after the achievement of national statehood. Since the economic system of the imperialist powers in the nineteenth and early twentieth centuries happened to be capitalist, and since the benefits accruing to the colonies are rarely mentioned, the communists have given to capitalism the epithets "exploitative" and "oppressive." That imperialism cannot be associated historically with any one economic system; that socialism, communism and nationalism may all be expanionist; and that capitalism may flourish, and today certainly does, without being expansionist—these are lessons which have not yet been learned by those still under the influence of Lenin's interpretation of capitalist imperialism. Thus, Soviet imperialism in Eastern Europe has scarcely raised a nationalist eyebrow in Asia or elsewhere, for the Asians' attention is still glued on the residual Western colonialism in Africa.

Many of the newly independent peoples are entering the second phase of their nationalist revolution, namely that of nation-building. In this new epoch, they may slough off their anti-Western and anticolonialist attitudes and take a more realistic view of communist imperialism. Chinese communist imperialism in Tibet, for instance, has already become an issue of concern in India, which has cultural, religious, historical, geographical and economic links with Tibet. This episode has touched the consciousness of many Asians. Moreover, the threat posed by Communist China to India and other parts of South and Southeast Asia has prompted many Indians and other Asians to brand the Chinese communist regime as imperialist.

Cases of past, present and possibly future aggression can provide our ideological and psychological strategists with the damaging evidence which can destroy the ideological pretension that communism is not imperialist.

Our psychological offensive should clearly point up the unyielding conflict between communism and true nationalism. The clash between communism and nationalism is further intensified by the fact that communism as an international conspiracy has been integrally linked with the interests of the Russian state.

In Eastern Europe, the communist puppet governments are politically and militarily dependent on Soviet support. This dependence has already awakened mounting nationalist resentments and may produce a series of conflicts such as those which, in past history, have plagued declining empires. The Hungarian Revolution has shown that rejection of communism as an ideology is closely related to a nationalist rejection of Russian domination. The local communist rulers are seen both as the standard bearers of an ideology which is almost unanimously rejected and as the puppets of a foreign power. The temporary popularity of Gomulka was due precisely to the fact that he succeeded in becoming for a time a genuine Pole. The desire for national independence, most dramatically asserted by the Hungarians, is thus a basic factor of East European politics. This too is a potent psychological weapon, if we but have the skill and determination to use it against the Soviet empire.

3. *The Role of the Communist Party.* Communist spokesmen are fond of explaining, in defense of communist parties, that communism can be built only if there is "monolithic unity of the laboring class around the Marxist-Leninist movement." They reject the notion that the working class can build communism spontaneously (for they know that the majority of the working class does not yearn for communism), or that the working class itself can wield power through such institutions as the workers' councils (for they

fear that such councils will turn out to be noncommunist and will form the basis for a social democracy rather than a totalitarian communist state). They assert, therefore, that the responsibility for the building of communism must rest with the communist party as the vanguard of the proletariat. In other words, the building of the communist utopia requires the establishment of dictatorship because the ordinary person does not have a true idea of what he wants from life, and should be content to permit the great communist party to do his thinking for him. This affronts a man's self-respect, and a concerted attack on this fundamental concept of the communist dogma could cause the Kremlin substantial ideological embarrassment in the lands they are trying to subvert.

4. *The New Class Structure.* Instead of the classless society which communist theory promises, the Soviet dictators have merely replaced the old upper strata with a new and much more oppressive one. Lenin's promised collective ownership, upon which the abolition of classes was to be based, has been transformed into a state ownership exercised by the new upper class of communists.[5] Thus, in spite of all the double-talk about a new communist society where social and hierarchical distinctions would disappear, present-day communist society contains the same class categories as existed before —the bureaucratic elite, the proletariat and the peasants. Despite the tremendous increase in the Soviet Union's wealth and productive capacity, only the upper class, i.e., the communist elite, has benefited substantially; the proletariat and peasantry have reaped relatively meager economic benefits.

5. *Soviet Promise and Performance.*[6] The communist experiment in Russia is now more than forty years old. During these four decades of total communist power, all of its original promises have turned into their opposites. It promised "land to the peasants." But the Soviets, after they had consolidated their power, took away the land which the peasants had owned under the Czars, and collectivized them into a new state-directed serfdom.

Communism promised "perpetual peace," but has pressed against

[5] See Milovan Djilas, *The New Class: An Analysis of the Communist System,* New York: Praeger, 1957, pp. 37-40.

[6] This section is based on an article by Bertram D. Wolfe, entitled "Communist Vulnerabilities." Reprinted from the *New Leader,* September 7, 1959, in *American Strategy for the Nuclear Age,* Walter F. Hahn and John C. Neff, eds., New York: Doubleday Anchor Original, 1960, pp. 89-102.

the outside world a "protracted conflict" which will not cease until its goal of world domination is reached.

Communism promised "production for use," for the benefit of the consumer. But instead it has set up a productive system controlled by the communist party, which produces for no other purpose but the expansion of the oppressive totalitarian state. Communism throws to the consumer the scraps of marginal production, if any. The revolution promised "plenty" and then, thanks to its inefficient and ruthless economic planning, ruined Russian agriculture and channeled its resources into producing war materials.

It promised that the state would "wither away"; instead it has expanded to totality and even now engages in psychological warfare against its own and the captive peoples, trying to remake them into the "new Soviet man." It promised "freedoms" and has managed to abolish virtually every freedom. It promised "the workers' paradise," but created a regimented labor force.

These are but a few examples of the gap between promise and performance. The revolutionary slogans which Lenin and his successors have used against the peoples, governments and institutions of the noncommunist world can be turned against them in a concerted propaganda offensive.

Though the Free World has its imperfections, the communists are vulnerable on almost every count; but they will be able to camouflage their ideological and psychological vulnerabilities until we have the wit and the understanding to hold them up to the light of day.

The Psychological Fronts

Our ideological offensive can be no more effective than the means which it employs to communicate with the peoples of the Free World and the communist bloc. Physical communication with the peoples of the Free World is not a difficult matter. Mass media already exist within most of the free nations; the major task is to utilize them more fully. Communicating to the peoples behind the Iron Curtain is a vastly more difficult task, but not an insuperable one—provided we are determined to make the required effort.

The most obvious means of getting our message across to other peoples is through the existing domestic and overseas organization of the United States Information Agency, including its Voice of America program. Given the absence of an over-all American psychological strategy and adequate directives, and—until recently—of a career service, and the relatively small sums allocated to these programs, the United States Information Agency has performed creditably. Through its radio broadcasts, informational and cultural exchange programs, distribution of American publications, university, and special educational programs, student and leadership exchange programs and the like, USIA has influenced thousands of young people and influential citizens who make up leadership elites and opinion-forming groups. These programs form a vital part of a psychological strategy, but they represent only a beginning toward the strategy set forth in this chapter. Before USIA can improve upon its performance, the decision must be made at the highest policy-making level that the United States *needs* a modern psychological strategy and that sufficient human and financial resources will be made available to devise and execute it.

It is imperative that we devote additional resources and skill to our psychological strategy; it is equally important to place our total propaganda effort in perspective and determine *where* our greatest efforts should be made. For purposes of a psychological strategy, the world is divided into three separate zones of operation: the North Atlantic area and our allies elsewhere; the largely uncommitted and underdeveloped lands of the world, especially in Afro-Asia; and the communist bloc.

The need for increased understanding and cohesion among the nations in the North Atlantic area can be met by voluntary activities undertaken by local political elements friendly to the United States; by systematic official programs to publicize the achievements and potentialities of the North Atlantic area; by increased cultural exchanges, discussions and books on the meaning and value of the Atlantic Community concept; and, above all, by a greater American effort to provide dynamic leadership to the Atlantic Alliance and to increased political consultation and military and economic co-operation among its members.

Among America's allies outside the North Atlantic area, i.e., primarily those in Latin America and along the periphery of Communist China, our propaganda effort should be geared to showing how the national and practical interests of our friends benefit from their ties with the Free World. American political support and military and economic assistance should underpin the propaganda effort.

In the underdeveloped and uncommitted world, the situation is far more difficult. Given the nature of the systemic revolution in Afro-Asia; the psychology of xenophobic nationalism and anti-colonialism now gripping many Afro-Asian peoples; their misunderstanding of, and often irrational behavior toward, the West; the present vogue of Marxist socialism; and tremendous social and economic problems, the United States will be hard-pressed to do more than conduct a holding operation to prevent these countries from being swallowed up behind the Iron Curtain. In these regions we need to secure emotional attachment to the logic of our message. Only thus can we render them less vulnerable to communist blandishments.

Student and leadership exchange programs are among the most valuable programs in communicating with the African and Asian peoples. They should be greatly increased. Among the firmest friends of the United States and the staunchest supporters of freedom in the new nations are those students and civilian and military leaders who came to the United States for study, training and practical experience. Some of our finest ambassadors of good will and the American way of life have been American students and professors who have spent one or more years studying and teaching in distant lands.

A deeper understanding of the American people, their culture and their aspirations, should be fostered among foreign peoples, particularly in the underdeveloped world. Cultural appreciation is, of course, a two-way street; and a broader and deeper sympathy by Americans toward foreign cultures, peoples and problems should be part of our program. In order to effect stronger cultural interaction between the United States and the new nations, the institutions and means through which such interaction must take place need to be strengthened.

Activities related to cultural exchange in its broadest sense should be centralized in a single government agency and given appropriate emphasis in national policy. Most effective cultural interaction, however, will result chiefly from numerous individuals and groups genuinely seeking better understanding and closer ties with peoples abroad. There is a general shortage of Western literature throughout the underdeveloped world. At the same time, there exists a great demand for English editions of Western classics, texts and other forms of serious literature. While the Russian and Chinese communists supply many of these nations with an abundance of communist literature at nominal prices, many of the Western books most in demand arrive in expensive editions, printed on fine paper and bound in hard covers, and are thus available only to the richer classes. An avalanche of inexpensive paperback editions of standard Western works and serious texts, in English or in translation, must be made available if we are ever to compete with the communist press. Many Western-trained teachers and professors would prefer to use texts with which they are familiar, but very often they are obliged to employ inferior materials because the better ones are not being placed within their financial reach. Once the initial translation and typesetting expenses are incurred, it is relatively inexpensive to mass-produce books in paperback. This is particularly true when the work is performed in the foreign country. The program, already under way, of providing inexpensive paperback editions of standard American literature to the youth and intellectuals of poorer countries should be greatly expanded.

The use of visual mass media in the underdeveloped countries can scarcely be overemphasized. Mobile units equipped with documentary films and large-screen operation should be enlarged so that even larger audiences in Asia and Africa, where masses of people are still barred by illiteracy from the written word, can be reached. As television spreads to the underdeveloped world, there will undoubtedly be some difficulty in filling program schedules. News films, documentaries covering a wide range of typical American life, and cultural and educational series should be made available inexpensively. This medium of information and cultural activity will become vastly more important when, in the not too distant future, intercontinental television becomes a reality.

In recent years, the Kremlin has sought deliberately to divert our efforts to the uncommitted nations, for our preoccupation with the neutrals distracts us from launching a counteroffensive against the communists' weakest point—the communist bloc, especially Eastern Europe. The Soviets seek to keep the psychological battle in the "war zone," where everyone is fair game. However, it is in Eastern Europe and the rest of the "peace zone" that communism, suppressing the aspirations of millions of people, is most vulnerable, for these peoples of Eastern Europe are not only anticommunist, but they also long to renew their strong ties with Western Europe and the United States. If we succeed in dealing a series of successful psychological blows to the enemy on his own ground, then we achieve, though indirectly, immeasurable gains for the Free World. The United States should concentrate its greatest propaganda efforts upon the communist bloc itself. For it is there that it enjoys a clear psychological advantage.

We must, first of all, focus the attention of the entire Free World upon the abiding source of world tension—the nature of the Soviet system. The psychological warriors of communism have hammered persistently at the theme that decadent capitalism is responsible for the world's ills. They have embossed the "war zone-peace zone" concept with the "immutable principle of Leninism": Only capitalism is racked by those "inherent contradictions" which spawn economic crises and "imperialist wars"; communist society, by definition, is a placid sea of harmony on which all "contradictions" have subsided.

The leaders of the West, we trust, have not accepted consciously the bland Leninist view of global conflict. There is little doubt, however, that some of them and a large segment of the intellectual elite suffer from an acute case of guilt feeling about the woes of the world. Admittedly, many of the crises sweeping the globe are the legacy of past Western mistakes and shortcomings. But in our anxious search for solutions to these problems we should not lose sight of the most obvious cause of the global crisis: the irreconcilable conflict between two diametrically opposed social and political systems.

In our information programs and diplomatic pronouncements, we must hew vigorously and persistently to the line that the crucial obstacle to lasting peace and security is a closed system of society which is impervious to the aspirations of mankind. We must stress that so long as this society remains hermetically sealed to the outside world there cannot be any mutual trust or common recognition, let alone acceptance, of those values on which enduring peace and conclusive settlements can be based. So long as the closed society embraces conflict as its mission and its natural way of life, the major problems which confront us across the globe will remain unmanageable—if for no other reason than systematic communist sabotage of peaceful solution.

The minimum objective of "coexistence" is to preserve the communist *status quo*. The communists insist that *their* domination of the satellites is a "reality" which we must accept as final and irreversible. This notion should be rejected. We should turn the table and affirm that the communist world is an area of concern to the outside world and is itself undergoing a process of change giving rise to many contradictions. In particular, the noncommunist states should keep in the foreground the issue of Soviet domination of the captive nations, and should not be deterred by Soviet claims that to keep alive the memory of Soviet iniquity in Eastern Europe is to keep alive the Cold War.

American ingenuity will be called upon to evolve devices and techniques to exploit weaknesses and vulnerabilities in the communist world, to impose upon it problems, embarrassments and crises instead of waiting to counteract crises of the communists' making. We should remind the communist leaders, by all the instruments of communication, that we intend to keep alive in the communist bloc the memory of human dignity, the demand for justice, the hope of liberation and the courage of resistance. In the debates in the United Nations and at diplomatic conferences, no reference to "colonialism" should be permitted to pass without exposing communist imperialism and reiterating our devotion to the principles of self-determination. We should seek to turn the communist world into the principal battlefield of ideological and political conflict. The immunity which the communists have so long enjoyed should be lifted with fanfare and with vigor.

The use of communications and mass media within the communist orbit will continue to be limited by the controls of the closed society. For this very reason, greater efforts should be made to pierce the Iron Curtain. The Voice of America, Radio Free Europe and Radio Liberty should be provided with sufficient modern equipment and adequate finances to beam their broadcasts into the communist nations—over communist jamming. The very fact that the communists spend millions of dollars to jam the Voice of America is sufficient evidence that the voice of truth and freedom is a mighty weapon for breaking down the closed society. We must keep, around the clock, the captive peoples accurately informed of events in the outside world and, to the best of our ability, about events in their own countries and the rest of the communist bloc. The United States should periodically call upon the Soviet Union to permit an exchange of news and other informational radio and television programs and to permit the free circulation of information and ideas by the press services, newspapers, magazines and journals. An effective program could be beamed into the communist bloc and elaborated in books and pamphlets, giving Soviet satellite citizens the very information which their governments are withholding. We should constantly challenge the Soviets to our own form of peaceful competition—in ideas. We might call this program "All Peoples Have the Right to Know."

One of the more effective ways of influencing Soviet domestic evolution leads through the communist-ruled European states. In the past, it was the Slavic peoples in Eastern Europe who transmitted Western ideas, values and styles to Russia. The satellite regimes are probably even more fearful of meaningful cultural exchange programs than their Soviet masters, for it is primarily their traditionally Western-oriented peoples who are starved for the resumption of free exchanges with the Atlantic world.

Efforts might be made to draw the satellite states into the European community through economic and cultural co-operation. Even if the regimes at first denounce such efforts, the economic attraction of Western markets, as well as traditional cultural ties of Eastern Europe to Western Europe, would gradually begin to assert themselves and to exert a centrifugal pull. The U.S. ought to continue to assert with even greater force than it has done thus far that it stands for self-determination within the communist bloc as well as within the Free World.

To encourage political evolution within the Soviet system and the communist bloc and to lift the Iron Curtain, we should promote the most extensive contacts possible with the communist world. Soviet leaders fear broader cultural exchanges, knowing that massive contact with Western ideas and realities might undermine the ideological commitment of their wards.

It ought to be our policy to promote massive exchanges as contrasted to the hand-picked type of exchange desired by the communists.[7] The Soviet Union now emphasizes exchanges of ballets, sports teams and orchestras, which are not likely to result in an exchange of ideas and viewpoints and, on balance, pay the communists handsome propaganda dividends. The U.S. should strive to develop extensive contacts with intellectuals, scientists and managers in the communist orbit not only for the sake of professional exchanges-of-view but also for the systematic purpose of affecting ideological commitment.

These exchanges and contacts between peoples will not serve our purpose unless and until our envoys from student to tourist are ready to debate issues with the communists. The communist traveler abroad is a trained agitator and propagandist. His American counterpart is less likely to understand the nature and purpose of communism. More likely than not, he is intellectually unprepared to advance the merits of democracy and the open society. An exchange program, if it is serve the purpose of gradually opening the Soviet Union to new ideas and ultimately breaking down the closed society, must be carefully planned and promoted by men and women who know the issues at stake.

Even under the most ideal conditions, not too much should be expected from such exchanges in the near future. The cumulative effect is not likely to be felt for several years. Extensive intellectual

[7] "A Soviet citizen cannot decide for himself spontaneously, as can an American, that he will go abroad. This is a matter, which in all cases, and at all times, is decided by the Soviet government, as a matter of policy. . . . When the members of the delegation return to Russia, each is expected to submit an exhaustive report to his own agency. But no tourist would dare to submit to the totalitarian press of the U.S.S.R. a description of the United States contrary to the official propaganda line. . . . It has been observed that a relatively large number (possibly 25 percent) of the Soviet citizens visiting the United States under the exchange program after an initial trip to the United States, return to America on a second mission. . . . These people are apparently trained professional 'tourists,' whose objective is far from mere tourism. It has been further observed that a certain percentage of visitors visiting the United States under the guise of representatives of Soviet culture are actually leading workers of Communist or Communist-front organizations. A vivid example is Nina Popova, candidate member (alternate) of the Central Committee of the Communist Party of the Soviet Union and until February 1958, board chairman of the All-Union Society for Cultural Relations with Foreign Countries (VOKS)." *The United States Through the Eyes of Soviet Tourists*, by the Staff of the Subcommittee to Investigate the Administration of the Internal Security Act and other Internal Security Laws of the Committee on the Judiciary, United States Senate, Eighty-Sixth Congress, Washington: Government Printing Office, 1960, pp. 2, 4.

and political "dialogues" are not adequate by themselves to alter the communist belief in the inevitable victory of communism and the ultimate collapse of our social and economic system. They must be accompanied by an active, unambiguous policy which seeks, through peaceful means, to liberate the peoples now languishing under the yoke of communist imperialism.

The proposals set forth in this chapter for an American psychological strategy are concerned primarily with the content of the message which the United States should carry to foreign audiences, and less with the means and techniques for propagating this message. Once American leaders have embraced a coherent strategy for the psychopolitical conduct of the Cold War, a strengthened propaganda arm of government will devise the means for carrying out this part of the Forward Strategy.

The United States can compete successfully in the market of ideas only *after* our policy-makers have made the decision to develop a long-range strategy for waging the conflict for the minds of men. This decision must be made now, for the communists are devoting many times our resources and efforts to this crucial arena of the Cold War and are reaping rich returns on their investment. Once the decision has been made, we will find not only that we can identify ourselves with the aspirations of mankind but also that the aspirations of mankind are our own.

CHAPTER 9 SECURITY THROUGH ARMS CONTROL?

More likely than not, the issues of disarmament, arms control and arms reduction will, during the next ten years, loom large in the management of the protracted conflict. These issues are fraught with far-reaching political implications and poignant emotions. The prospect of putting a quick end to the arms race with a flick of the pen is one of the principal stalking horses in the communists' propaganda stables. The question of disarmament lends itself admirably to the manipulations of a multidimensional strategy because it is itself such an all-inclusive concept—so much so as to be almost meaningless. Efforts to achieve international and national security through the negotiation of formal arms agreements impinge upon the entire complex of military, diplomatic, economic and technological problems of world politics. It was quite natural that Soviet strategy should have fastened upon this theme.

The United States, within the last five years, has been caught in an uncomfortable trap set by the communists. Today, we fear that our position of international political leadership and prestige will suffer unless we outdo the Soviet Union in contriving disarmament plans which will appeal dramatically to that nebulous phenomenon known as "world opinion." This latter term encompasses the opinions of all kinds of people in all kinds of places. A few people are knowledgeable in this area. A good many have been misguided by communist propaganda or by the anxiety arguments put forth by various organizations and causes, good, bad and neutral. Most people are at best unconversant with the highly complicated technical problems involved in disarmament and arms control discussions.

Precisely because our policy-makers have made such a valiant attempt to placate world opinion on the subject of disarmament, the United States has been slowly drifting into a position which is ambiguous, confusing and fraught with danger for our security and that of our Free World allies. Moreover, we cannot extricate ourselves from this awkward position in the same manner in which we got into it—by a series of subtle diplomatic maneuvers. We cannot disentangle ourselves by modifying in scarcely perceptible degrees now this, now that paragraph of the many proposals which have been placed on the conference table. What we really have to do is to go back to the drawing board and design a new approach to national policy.

The primary task confronting American diplomatic strategists is *not* to devise more ingenious and intricate formulas for inspection and control in any specific sector. Such an approach is now inadequate, for in recent years the problem of disarmament has become entirely too cumbersome—politically and technically. The kind of pragmatic procedures on which we have been relying, characterized by day-to-day shifts and amendments, cannot furnish us with a unified and coherent arms control strategy.

The growing complexity of this policy field can be illustrated by listing the subjects which have been proposed for negotiation since 1955: (a) geographical zones of disengagement (e.g., Central Europe); (b) the establishment of nuclear-free zones (e.g., Central Europe, Antarctica and the Western Pacific); (c) the exercise of self-restraint among the major powers in the shipment of arms to trouble spots (e.g., the Middle East, Africa or the Caribbean); (d) reduction in the size of conventional armed forces among the major powers; (e) special control arrangements for nuclear weapons (e.g., a ban on tests and on the production of fissionable materials for military purposes; the reduction or elimination of existing nuclear weapons stockpiles; a ban on the production of weapons devices or control of the number produced; elimination or control of the means of intercontinental delivery); (f) the elimination of great power bases on foreign territory; (g) control of the passage of military craft on, under or over the oceans of the world; (h) control of outer space (especially a prohibition against orbiting weapons of mass destruction and against the laying of national claims to any extraterrestrial body or area of outer space in order to prevent the erection of spheres of armed influence); (i) prohibiting the testing, production and use of chemical and bacteriological weapons; (j) control of the means of irregular warfare (guerrilla forces, paramilitary organizations and other international subversive agencies); and (k) safeguards against surprise attack, as well as nuclear war by technical accident, human error or political miscalculation (e.g., provocation with unanticipated results, limited war followed by "escalation," or "catalytic war"[1]).

All this is but the beginning of troubles. Turning from the species of disarmament to the procedural difficulties which arise in all attempts to reach arms agreements, we behold a picture that is even more confusing. Immediately we are seized by such questions as these: How do we define the objectives of disarmament or arms control negotiations—as the elimination of armaments or the balancing of arms at a level consistent with both national and international security? Should nations try to disarm all the way down to the minimum needs of preserving domestic social order or must they retain a deterrent against attack? Is it more fruitful to adopt the "package" (i.e., comprehensive) approach or the specific segment approach to disarmament negotiations? Which military components, if any, ought to be completely eliminated and which should merely be reduced, and to what levels? Is it necessary to think of arms control in terms of *raising* certain types of force levels (e.g., conventional or counterguerrilla) while *reducing* others (e.g., nuclear)? What kind of military and technological information has to be exchanged before realistic negotiations can even get under way? Which should have priority—the control of weapons or the control of delivery systems? Does the inspection system accompanying an agreement have to be "foolproof" or can a probability calculus be applied? In the early and intermediate stages of an arms reduction agreement, should inspection be limited to "declared facilities," i.e., to installations which the signatory parties declare abolished, or can the international inspectors go anywhere to check on the levels of forces still in being? What should be the composition, powers and decision-making procedures of the international control commissions created to police the agreements? What contribution can be made toward strengthening the safeguards against violation by instituting such technical procedures as surveillance of govern-

[1] Cf. *infra*, p. 306.

mental budgets, materials accounting, registration of scientific personnel, transfer of selected armaments from national military establishments to international depots, and aerial or satellite reconnaissance? Must all significant arms limitation agreements be universal, at least in the sense that they are ratified by all major powers and potential powers? Finally, what sanctions are to be attached for "nonperformance of covenant," and what has to be "proved" before a power which suspects that it has been duped or offended can withdraw from the agreement and resume its own unilateral armaments program? Boring as this recitation might seem, these are but the more obvious and the thornier procedural questions. A score of others—all of them highly relevant ones at that—could be plausibly added.

If one pushes on to examine the technical aspects of arms control, he encounters additional labyrinthine problems. For the sake of holding this discussion down to manageable proportions, we might select the nuclear test ban negotiations as a fair example to illustrate the sort of roadblocks which obstruct agreement by introducing imponderables into the security equation. As the reader surveys this sketchy list of difficulties, he should remember that each specific segment of the arms control spectrum poses a comparable though unique set of problems.[2]

Since 1958, American-British and Soviet scientific experts and diplomatic negotiators have argued long and hard over the following aspects of the nuclear test ban: (a) the total number of seismic stations needed to police a ban; (b) the number of stations which should be located on the soil of each nuclear power; (c) the number of ship stations required to police the oceanic areas; (d) the relationship of manned to unmanned stations; (e) the question of whether the host nation should have any decisive voice in the location of the control stations; (f) the number and national-

[2] Some idea of the complexity of this area of policy can be gleaned from the following works: Seymour Melman, ed., *Inspection for Disarmament*, New York: Columbia University Press, 1959; Bernard T. Feld and others, *The Technical Problems of Arms Control*, New York: Institute for International Order, 1960; *Control and Reduction of Armaments*, Final Report of the Committee on Foreign Relations, Subcommittee on Disarmament, Report No. 2501, 85th Congress, Washington: G.P.O., October, 1958; and the excellent Special Issue on Arms Control of *Daedalus* (Journal of the American Academy of Arts and Sciences), Fall, 1960.

ity of the staff needed to man a control station; (g) the problem of detecting underground explosions and distinguishing them from earthquakes; (h) the significance of the strength of various seismic signals; (i) the question of establishing an annual quota of "on-site" inspections to investigate seismic signals of a doubtful character; (j) the method whereby "on-site" inspections can be conducted (aerial overflight, ground surveys, and actual drilling operations); (k) the possibilities of decoupling or muffling underground tests by conducting them in large cavities, such as salt domes; (1) the membership of the international control commission and the scope of its powers (e.g., determining aerial inspection routes and budgeting its own operations); (m) the question of renewing the moratorium on tests that fall below the agreed threshold of the detectable range; (n) the procedures for carrying on joint tests aimed at seismic improvement; (o) the question as to whether the effective date of the treaty should be before or after the network of control stations has been completed; (p) the reliability of various methods of detecting outer space tests; (q) the possibility of shielding outer space tests behind the moon; (r) the problems of fixing responsibility for nuclear tests in remote oceanic areas; (s) the question of conducting nuclear explosions for such peaceful purposes as earth-moving projects; (t) the political feasibility of extending the control system to France, China and other would-be nuclear powers who have not been parties to the negotiations. This listing could be increased at random. Each one of its items can be subdivided into numerous, complicated subproblems, on each of which several treatises might be written.

The Illusion of Universal Disarmament

However currently attractive and ultimately desirable it may be, the concept of complete, speedy and universal disarmament is a pure chimera.

Communist propaganda, from Litvinov to Khrushchev, has sought to exploit the Western democracies' yearning for surcease of tension, disarmament and lower taxes. The Anglo-Saxon countries have presented a vulnerable target for this propaganda. Protected against invasion through most of their history by an insular position, English and Americans have generally felt slightly uncomfortable about maintaining a large military establishment in peacetime. Their elite groups have always clutched eagerly the illusion of disarmament, often failing to discern the nexus of armaments and security, of power and peace.

The advocates of disarmament contend that nations, by building up their arsenals, create increasing international tensions until these tensions threaten to burst out in war. At this danger point, so it is argued, there is no better means for smothering tensions than disarmament. But this notion is not based on conclusive historical evidence. When in the past nations have decreased their forces, they have usually done so within the scope of a larger settlement concluded at the end of a major war. Arms reduction has usually come as a consequence, and not a prior cause, of political settlements.

Although there is no doubt that an arms race can heighten international tensions, such a race is, in the first instance, the result of sociological incompatibility or deep-rooted power-political antagonisms. There is no need, however, to assume that armaments competition must always lead inexorably to disaster. If man is the creator of technology rather than its slave, then military power is more the servant than the master of national policies.

True enough, international disarmament negotiations prior to both world wars did collapse. It is not correct to infer, however, that it was this failure which brought on the war. The futility of disarmament efforts was but a symptom of a much more profound malaise—a political inability to resolve the pressing conflict of national interests. In each case, the war was the final consequence of this same failure. Indeed, a good case can be made for the contention that one of the contributing causes of the First World War and perhaps the major cause of the second was a disparity of armaments. One of the two contesting sides, confident of at least a temporary military superiority, cast the die for war.

There is much in logic and history to support the proposition that competition in armaments, when carried on by two seasoned practitioners of international politics who make the magnitudes of their strength relatively open to public view, can lead to a remarkably stable strategic situation. While the specter of modern weapons may cause apprehensiveness in the popular mind, a technical knowledge of their performance characteristics and their deployment, as well as of the various strategies for their use, may give rise among the "pros" to a surprisingly rational assessment of the futility of war. More and more strategic analysts are inclining toward the view that the achievement of a stable arms balance represents a sensible goal, whereas moves to bring about drastic reductions may plunge us into a situation in which the deterrent will break down and large-scale war will once again seem profitable to an aggressor.[3]

We do not think that the cause of arms reduction is doomed to failure under all circumstances. Conceivably, two nations, having achieved a certain military parity and being determined to maintain it regardless of cost, may decide that limiting the arms effort at least for a prescribed period will redound to their mutual advantage. The United States and Great Britain agreed, back in the early twenties, upon such limitation in the Washington Conference on Naval Armaments. But what made the agreement possible and effective was the fact that the British and the Americans were not divided by major political differences. Their foreign policy objectives were basically kindred. A similar harmony did not prevail in the relations between the two Western democratic powers on the one hand and the Japanese on the other. The Japanese viewed the statutory limitations from an altogether different point of view: They took surreptitious advantage of the treaty to promote their own strategic interests in the Far East. An even more striking example of the crucial importance of the political climate to disarmament is furnished by the history of the 1930's. The fundamental conflict of interest between the Western democracies, defenders of the *status quo*, and the dynamic fascist states, bent on the revision of the Versailles settlement, rendered futile all the earnest efforts of the Geneva Disarmament Conference.

The crucial question confronting the Western allies today is whether, in the contemporary climate of world politics, meaningful arms security negotiations between the U.S.S.R. and the Atlantic nations are possible—and desirable. The Soviets' behavior in recent years has not inspired the West with confidence in the sincerity of communist disarmament proposals. Since 1957, the Soviets have rushed the "serial production" of ICBM's. Early in 1960, Khrushchev

[3] Among those who subscribe to this view are Thomas C. Schelling, Oscar Morgenstern, Henry A. Kissinger, Hedley Bull and Robert R. Bowie. The question will be discussed in somewhat greater detail later in the chapter. Cf. pp. 322-324 and the Bibliography.

boasted of "fantastic new weapons" under development. Although the Soviets have engaged in protracted negotiations on the nuclear test ban issue—a false issue, created by communist propaganda—they have steadfastly refused to take any concrete steps which would safeguard the world against war. In the spring and summer of 1960, before and after the abortive summit conference, the Western countries were besieged with threats of rocket warfare at almost weekly intervals. It hardly seems rational to engage in a quest for arms control in some segments of the weapons spectrum while in other segments the quest for developing instruments of mass destruction proceeds at a furious pace.

Many times in history, aggressive regimes have camouflaged intensive armament with demonstrative and irresponsible proposals for rapid total disarmament. We know, from the experience of the 1930's, that international disarmament discussions can serve to nurture that great pacifist illusion which suffocates the political will of the democracies.

Five years of intensive communist disarmament propaganda have persuaded large segments of Western public opinion of the adequacy of military budgets, if not of their downright "wastefulness." The molelike patience of the Soviets is beginning to pay off. They have begun to reap the fruits of the "ban the bomb" campaign which they launched more than a decade ago. The United States now faces the prospect of continuing negotiations on arms control at the very time when its military preponderance has become a matter of doubt. The Soviets, by fully exploiting the potentialities of time as a strategic fourth dimension, have frequently outbargained us in the past—when their over-all strategic posture was decidedly inferior to ours. They can be expected to drive much more ruthless bargains in the future.

A fresh approach to arms security negotiations must start from the frank recognition that the commonly accepted philosophy of disarmament or "arms control" agreements is fallacious. The increasing complexity of modern weapons technology makes comprehensive arms control plans more unwieldy than ever. The single sector approach is patently unsatisfactory, since it invariably renders the proposing nation subject to the suspicion that it is seeking to enhance a military advantage which it already enjoys, or to maneuver its potential opponent out of a relative advantage which he has gained. But the more sectors we try to bring within the scope of the arms control plan, the more complicated the effort becomes from the analytical point of view. The human mind is staggered by the attempt to evaluate the effects upon the international security situation which would result from changes in the levels of ground forces, surface and submarine navies, manned bomber wings and bases, intermediate and intercontinental range missiles with warheads of different capacities, and so on. Even if nations were willing to submit to the dispassionate judgment of the electronic computer (which they are not), the calculations would be constantly upset by novel scientific discoveries and technological applications outside the scope of the agreement. Technology has reached such a stage of development as to render absurd the concept of stable and enduring strategic equations (if, indeed, that concept ever had any validity). Whatever control and inspection systems might be established to police an arms agreement would constantly be outmoded by technological advances—unless we either abolish all technology or bring it under the control of an international policing authority. Control systems will lag inevitably behind the sudden and unpredictable leaps of technology. If either party is determined to violate the agreement it will have plenty of opportunities to do so. In sum, it is impossible to devise a formal disarmament or arms reduction scheme which can guarantee credibly a symmetrical improvement in the security situation of both sides.

The second obstacle is the absence of an adequate basis for a world system of law. No doubt, the ideal of "world peace through world law" is a noble one. But the world is a long way from developing such a lawful order and a common, workable agreement to enforce it. Establishing legal institutions for the peaceful settlement of disputes is not merely a question of solving technical problems. A world system of law must rest on an international consensus. In the West, international law was a product of a single cultural community which was more or less united in its concept of the fundamental norms governing the relation of states. True, the world today is united by technical communications and, to some extent, by fear of thermonuclear war. But its peoples do not yet subscribe to a common set of social and ethical values. Indeed, some useful international procedural agreements have already been drawn, but their significance should not be overestimated. Existing universal-membership organizations have not yet made much headway in the effort to overcome the semantic difficulties which mask profound ideological differences. The United Nations, for example, has not even been able to arrive at agreed definitions covering all forms of international "aggression," much less devise ways of coping with them. Advances in this area are to be encouraged. But for at least the next decade, and probably for much longer, the best hope of inducing nations to divest themselves of their sovereign prerogatives will lie in a force at work outside of the United Nations: regional integration among states which are capable of understanding and trusting one another by reason of cultural and political affinities, as well as common economic and security interests.

The third obstacle to international arms control agreements is the disparity between the capabilities of the Western Alliance and the Sino-Soviet bloc for carrying on the power struggle by nonmilitary means. The Western nations have been compelled to proceed with extreme caution in disarmament negotiations, for, though successful up until now in preventing large-scale military aggression, they have fumbled repeatedly in the arena of lesser conflict. The communists have waged international conflict in many dimensions, some of which the Western peoples have traditionally looked upon as the domains of peace. A reduction of organized military power would leave the West increasingly at the mercy of the psychopolitical, conspiratorial and guerrilla methods and other unlovely techniques of irregular conflict practiced by the communists. Unless the Western nations develop a comparable range of weapons, they cannot, in prudence, dismantle their military deterrent, for to do so would be to invite disaster on the installment plan.

In sum, the problem confronting us is in the first instance a political one, which, in the present historical situation, arises out of the vast difference in the political character of two social systems and their fundamental strategic objectives. An open, liberal society confronts a closed, totalitarian society. The former's philosophy places it in an essentially defensive position; the latter is armed with an ideology and an operational code of global conflict which are basically and avowedly aggressive. A totalitarian power, no matter how conciliatory a pose it may strike at any given time, can conceal its true objectives more easily, reverse its field more swiftly and obstruct an inspection system more readily than can a democracy.

The problems of arms control are *not* the same for the Soviets as they are for ourselves. To be always willing to meet the Soviets halfway on all points of disagreement may seem at first glance to be an eminently fair attitude. But our two societies are not at all similar. Whenever we have talked about the need for effective inspection systems, we have really been talking about problems posed by the character of their society, not of ours. The profundity of the difference was clearly reflected in the two original negotiating positions. Throughout most of the postwar period, the United States has insisted that any arms control agreement must be founded upon a fully effective system of inspection. The Soviets, anxious to maintain their Iron Curtain, have postulated a zero per cent effective inspection system. In fact, they began by demanding a purely fiduciary agreement. After several years of bargaining, they have deigned to concede that at least a minimum of inspection would be a necessary part of any agreement.

Within recent years, many Western experts have toyed with statistical sampling techniques which, combined with the alleged deterrent power of world political opinion, would *probably* serve to discourage any potential violations. But probability calculus is not at all applicable to this problem. There is no guarantee of security in "probable deterrence," especially that variety which relies excessively upon mathematical computation and discards as irrelevant the insights of traditional political wisdom. Let us assume that we and the Soviets finally compromise on a formula that provides a control mechanism substantially less effective than we originally insisted upon. Then the agreement will work to the advantage of Soviet security. The Soviets have easy access to our open society and hence can verify our compliance with the agreement. We have no such access to theirs. No amount of clever punning on this score—"The Soviets want disarmament without controls and the West wants controls without disarmament"—can alter this fact.

The Lessons of the Nuclear Test Ban Negotiations

Since 1958 nuclear test ban negotiations have assumed a disproportionate place in world opinion on disarmament and arms control. At Geneva, the United States reversed its fundamental postwar policy; it no longer insisted on a comprehensive disarmament package. It agreed instead to separate the problem of test control from the general problem of arms control and to place this comparatively minor item at the top of the agenda instead of at its bottom. This retreat occurred under the pressure of a public opinion that was either uninformed or misinformed as to the nature of the issues involved. From October, 1958, onward, American policy, especially the unilateral moratorium on tests, has actually jeopardized national security. The only good purpose which the policy can be said to have served was that it gradually brought into the open many of the fallacious assumptions underlying the American disarmament policies. Among these assumptions were the following:

Fallacy 1. *Since we and the Soviets have arrived at a nuclear "stalemate," we need not push the development of nuclear weapons any farther.*

Not too long ago, this assumption was as widespread as it was naïve. As indicated previously, the notion of stalemate or of freezing the state of any weapons art in an era of fast-changing technology is intrinsically absurd. The United States needs to continue its nuclear research and development programs for several reasons.

First of all, we must increase the efficiency and discrimination of our missile warheads, so that they would not contaminate the atmosphere all over the world in the event of war. We need new multimegaton missile systems to deal with hardened missile sites. For this as well as other purposes the yield-to-weight and yield-to-diameter ratios have to be increased. If we can achieve this, the value of our strategic deterrent would be enhanced, and the cause of world peace would be advanced commensurately. Dr. Edward Teller wrote:

> With continued nuclear testing we could reduce to one-half or one-third the weight of our retaliatory bombs. Lighter bombs can be carried by smaller missiles. Smaller missiles are less expensive. They can be handled by fewer people on smaller and more secure bases. They can be made safer against destruction by shock from an enemy bomb. They can be dispersed and hidden more easily, or better still, they can be made very mobile. If their position can be easily changed every day . . . the aggressor will have a virtually impossible task in finding them. Additional testing will make it certain that a reliable second-strike force can be constructed within our means.[4]

[4] *New York Herald Tribune,* August 17, 1960.

One can readily imagine the effect upon the American public of a decision to halt testing at Cape Canaveral. Such a move would be regarded as the height of irrationality. Nevertheless, the value of all of our experiments in rocketry was partially vitiated after October, 1958, by our self-imposed restraint on developing the nuclear warheads of the future. The United States has never even fired a fully armed ICBM for test purposes and, while the moratorium remains in effect, cannot do so.

Moreover, further nuclear tests are needed for improving our small atomic weapons. The United States cannot spare any of the capabilities that can be developed in any segment of the weapons spectrum. Hans Bethe, the atomic physicist, has attempted to reassure us on this score:

> We have nuclear weapons ranging from twenty kilotons down to a fraction of a kiloton. We have different sizes. . . . We have nuclear weapons which can be shot in short-range rockets, like Honest John; we have nuclear weapons so small that they can be carried by the infantry with relative ease. We have an enormous arsenal of such weapons.[5]

Granted that we may have all these weapons and that they are portable, this does not mean that all our tactical atomic weapons have become reliable and optimal tools of defense. We also need "clean" nuclear weapons for both strategic and tactical use to reduce contamination and fallout to a practical minimum, especially in the battle zone in which our own forces must operate. Furthermore, it is questionable that our tactical atomic weapons have been integrated *operationally* into our military organization. The United States has never been able to carry out a training program which would give field units genuine practical experience in the use of these weapons under combat conditions. Few military commanders relish the prospect of having to commit their forces to tactics which, because of the moratorium, they have not been able to rehearse.[6]

[5] Hans A. Bethe, "The Case for Ending Nuclear Tests," *The Atlantic*, August, 1960, p. 49.

[6] Although the "Davy Crockett," a one-man, bazooka-launched nuclear weapon, is now being produced for the Army, it has not been tested in the field because of the moratorium. Naturally, the Army is reluctant to order it in quantity until it has been thoroughly proved. *Washington Post*, January 31, 1960.

Another reason for carrying on tests is to perfect the technical defense capabilities which are inherent in nuclear technology. In this connection, only two possibilities need be mentioned. (a) We know from the theory of the "Christofolos effect" and from the experimental results obtained in the "Argus" and Johnston Island tests of 1958 that nuclear explosions in outer space can disrupt the operations of weapons systems, communications systems and early warning systems which depend upon electronic components for the transmission of intelligence and guidance. These jamming potentialities may prove to be of substantial significance both for the attacking and the defending side. But additional thermonuclear experiments are necessary before we can fully understand the natural phenomena, let alone their strategic implications. (b) It is also likely that a testing program would lead to the development of sophisticated warheads which could be packed in clusters in the nose of a ballistic missile warhead. In view of the problems of tracking, identifying and destroying targets, such a weapon might have important offensive uses. But it is possible that it might have equally important defensive uses if developed as part of an anti-missile missile. Whether this latter proposition should prove technically feasible or not, it would still be essential for the United States to understand fully the operational characteristics of a "cluster" warhead in order to begin devising some sort of defense against it. Such knowledge can be acquired only by testing.[7]

Finally, the continuation of nuclear testing is necessary for the development of "third generation" nuclear weapons. Americans once thought that the A-bomb was the "ultimate" weapon—until the H-bomb appeared. Indeed, it is always difficult to anticipate further quantum jumps in the realm of weapons technology. Yet such leaps might well become the order of the day. More than a year after the U.S. test moratorium went into effect, Premier Khrushchev boasted publicly that the U.S.S.R. was developing "fantastic new weapons." If Premier Khrushchev's "new weapons" were nuclear or armed with nuclear warheads, we may safely assume that they necessitated nuclear tests—and that such tests

[7] In fact, to strengthen the defensive aspects of our entire military system and thus improve the deterrent, we must test the effects of nuclear weapons on various ground installations, ships, hardened missile sites, weapons and shelters.

were made after the United States stopped testing.

In an address before the Senate on May 12, 1960, Senator Thomas J. Dodd of Connecticut, meditating upon the possibility of developing "fastastic new weapons," said:

> Then there is the matter of the neutron bomb, to which there has already been some reference in the press. Such a bomb can theoretically be produced by tailoring the energy of a fusion explosion so that, instead of heat and blast, its primary product is a burst of neutrons. Such a burst would do negligible physical damage,[8] but it would immediately destroy all life in the target area. It would, in short, operate as a kind of death-ray. I have heard that, in the light of present theoretical knowledge, the neutron bomb is no more questionable than the hydrogen bomb was 6 months before it was demonstrated that one could be built.

In brief, there is no such thing as a military-technological plateau. It is tempting to take comfort in the thought that further research and development of weapons can be carried forward without tests. To some extent, this is a justified assumption. But it is not a safe one under all circumstances. Although our scientists can arrive at certain theoretical formulations and develop some designs on the drawing board and in the laboratory, they are bound to reach a point beyond which they cannot advance unless they test their findings by experiment. Without tests, the range of the technologically possible quickly narrows. Testing is the very foundation of the scientific process. When it is discontinued even theory itself begins to wilt.

In hearings on the technical aspects of a test ban held by the Joint Committee on Atomic Energy in April 1960,[9] scientists disagreed on the military significance of clandestine tests in the low kiloton range. But nearly all the scientists who testified concurred in the opinion that the results of tests at low yields can be extrapolated to higher yields. They also agreed that the nuclear powers could achieve improvements in weapons design through underground tests and then carry out large-scale proof tests in outer space. The primary value of testing does not lie in the possibility

[8] Although the so-called neutron bomb would release considerably more radiation for a given amount of fissionable material, there would still be some blast and thermal effects.

[9] A summary analysis of the hearings has been published under the title, *Technical Aspects of Detection and Inspection Controls of a Nuclear Test Ban,* Joint Committee on Atomic Energy, Washington: G.P.O., May, 1960.

of improving by a few percentage points the efficiency of the weapons which we already possess. It lies rather in the expectation that completely new vistas of scientific investigation will be opened up and will lead to the discovery of hitherto unsuspected phenomena incalculably important for defense.

As a consequence of the unilateral moratorium which the United States put into effect on October 31, 1958, we have lost ground in the technological race. While the Soviets were spinning out the Geneva talks, construction on American testing sites practically came to a halt. For a period of at least eighteen months, no steps were taken to appropriate funds to the AEC for testing purposes. When such steps were finally taken, with the announcement of the Vela Project, they were surrounded by public confusion. A host of questions arose. Would this project involve a unilateral testing program by the U.S. or would its implementation depend upon securing Soviet co-operation in the research? Had the plans for the project been announced merely to "put the heat on" the Geneva negotiations? We could have diminished the harmful effects of the test moratorium by enlarging our computer facilities. Apparently, this was not done. As a result, we exiled ourselves deliberately from the whole realm of scientific discovery in the nuclear field. We recorded the latest experiment in our nuclear journal and then we closed the book. At the same time, we could not be certain that the Soviets had closed theirs. In the meantime, there were rumblings that morale among the teams of top-flight scientists in our nuclear laboratories had dropped.[10]

Fallacy 2. *Our technical detection capabilities had progressed to a point where the policing of an all-inclusive test ban was feasible. Moreover, our unilateral moratorium was perfectly safe from the standpoint of national security because our scientists could certainly tell us whether the Soviets were testing.*

The scientists who advised the President in the spring of 1958 committed a serious blunder. They overestimated our ability to detect underground tests. At the Geneva Conference of Technical Experts, some of our scientists obviously allowed their ardent personal yearning for a test ban to influence their scientific judgment.

[10] This aspect of the moratorium is discussed by former Atomic Energy Commissioner Thomas E. Murray in *Nuclear Policy for War and Peace*, New York: World Publishing Co., 1960, Chapter 5.

They approved as adequate a plan for 170 control stations for detecting underground nuclear tests down to five kilotons. This expert judgment appears now to have been based on insufficient evidence—evidence obtained from only one experiment (the "Ranier" shot), which, moreover, had not been designed for studying seismic effects. Had the scientists evaluated their data more carefully and had they been willing to wait for a few more months until the completion of the impending "Hardtack" series, they would have learned that their initial hypothesis could not be verified. Instead, their zeal led them to ratify a proposal from which the United States later had to retreat.

Subsequently, a special panel of scientists under the chairmanship of Lloyd V. Berkner estimated that the network of 170 stations proposed by the Geneva Conference of Experts (including twenty-one manned stations on Soviet soil) could obtain satisfactory results only down to about twenty kilotons and that hence the possibility of confusing underground tests with earthquakes would be substantially greater than the Geneva experts had thought. Later still, an even more startling discovery was made. Theoretical predictions which were experimentally confirmed in the "Cowboy" series of chemical explosions led to the conclusion that decoupling (or muffling) of underground tests up to a factor of three hundred would be possible if the explosions were detonated in large, deep cavities (such as salt domes).[11] In other words, it now appears possible to disguise a three hundred-kiloton explosion so that it would cause no greater seismic disturbance than a one-kiloton tamped shot. True, it is both costly and time-consuming to excavate a salt dome sizable enough to provide optimum coupling for a nuclear explosion. But some large salt domes already exist in the Soviet Union as well as in the United States, and at least partial decoupling is possible in underground cavities of less than optimum size. In sum, it became painfully obvious during 1959 and 1960 that man's knowledge of methods of disguising tests has been advancing faster than his knowledge of the methods of detecting, identifying and fixing responsibility for violations of a test ban.

Practically all of the public discussion concerning detection capabilities has focused upon what we can detect once the proposed international network of seismic stations has been completed and

[11] Cf. Summary analysis of hearings, *cit. supra*, pp. 8 and 25-29.

put into operation. But that network does not yet exist. Ground has not yet been broken for a single inspection station on Soviet soil, much less in China. We know that the communists are no longer conducting atmospheric tests. But we have no idea of what they may be doing underground in the vast, remote expanse of Soviet and Red Chinese territory.

We never had, and we do not have now, the means for policing so large a territory, and we could not even develop "probably adequate" means for several years after the signing of a formal test ban treaty.[12] More important still, we know very little about the possibility of detecting and fixing responsibility for nuclear tests in remote oceanic areas or in outer space at distances of hundreds of thousands of miles. Outer space tests would be particularly difficult to detect if the testing nation would shield them behind the moon and thus reduce the intensity of telltale X-rays from the explosion.

In the absence of the proposed international network of inspection stations and in view of the various possibilities for decoupling and disguising tests,[13] it is clear that the Soviets may have been conducting nuclear tests of a relatively large size without risking detection. On June 10, 1960, in a hearing on the latest disarmament developments before a subcommittee of the Senate Foreign Relations Committee, Philip Farley, Special Assistant to the Secretary of State for Disarmament and Atomic Energy, and John N. Irwin II, Assistant Secretary of Defense for International Security Affairs, both conceded that we cannot detect Soviet testing. The latter said: "I think that they have gains that they could make from testing. . . . If they decide those gains are such that they are willing to take what

[12] On August 12, 1960, the *New York Times* reported that: "The Soviet Union agreed with the United States today that the projected worldwide control system to ban nuclear tests should be fully operational within six years after a treaty is effective."

[13] Freeman J. Dyson, Professor at the Princeton Institute for Advanced Studies, writes: "My personal opinion is that nuclear explosions in the kiloton range could be concealed very completely. That is to say, I believe it will be feasible to build a building looking externally like a normal industrial structure, within which kiloton explosions can be contained. The cost of such facility may not be exorbitant, and the earth tremors which it produces may be no larger than those produced by ordinary industrial operations. . . . Concealment of this sort could be detected only if the international control authority were empowered to travel everywhere and to open all doors." "The Future Development of Nuclear Weapons," *Foreign Affairs,* Vol. 38, April, 1960, p. 462.

is obviously a very remote risk of being discovered, they may wish to do so."

American scientists have been divided on the significance of further testing. In the face of this division of opinion our policy response after October, 1958, was to discontinue tests. There is no reason to assume that, if Soviet scientists were similarly divided, the Soviet government, too, would discontinue tests. It is much more likely that the Soviets would find out which group was right by going ahead with tests, regardless of cost. The stakes are so high that it would be to their advantage to continue a vigorous research and development program, testing whenever they deemed it necessary.

The American unilateral test moratorium has given the Soviets exactly what they wanted—an unpoliced test ban. For all practical purposes, the United States is just as fully committed to an all-inclusive test ban as if it had signed a treaty two years ago, replete with red ribbon, wax and seal. The only difference is this: If the United States had actually signed the treaty, there would have been a start made on the construction of an inspection system, however inadequate. As it is, the United States has not advanced farther than it started from, namely, at point zero.

The *de facto* moratorium enabled the Soviets to achieve their objective *before* the test ban treaty negotiations even got under way at Geneva, for we had thrown away our bargaining leverage before the U.S. delegation ever arrived on the scene. During two years of treaty negotiations, we were unable to offer the Soviets anything more attractive than the boon we had already conferred upon them—an uncontrolled ban which we seemed willing to prolong indefinitely. At one point in the spring of 1960, when some American political leaders had begun to insist that the moratorium was producing potentially disastrous consequences, and should be discontinued, the Soviets took the wind out of their sails by proposing that it be extended for at least four more years to cover all tests below the detectable range as defined in the treaty. Just as the communists had once employed truce talks as an instrument of warfare to deprive the West of the tactical initiative in Korea,[14] so after October, 1958, they may very well have employed hundreds of

[14] Cf. Strausz-Hupé, *et al., Protracted Conflict,* New York: Harper & Brothers, 1959, Chapter 6.

nuclear test ban conferences for an analogous purpose—this time to steal a march on the United States in nuclear technology.

Fallacy 3. *All nuclear tests contaminate man's physical environment and jeopardize the health of mankind.*

The experts, of course, never fell for this canard, but the uncritical public did, having been subjected for years to a barrage of horror stories.

It is true that thermonuclear tests at atmospheric levels have created, to an unknown degree, a menace to human health in the form of strontium 90. But scientific estimates concerning the gravity and immediacy of the fallout threat have varied widely. According to the latest responsible evaluation, strontium 90 appears to be descending from the stratosphere more rapidly than had earlier been supposed, but its genetic effects now seem to be less serious than formerly anticipated. For the sake of allaying popular fears, whether they be founded in scientific fact or flow from hysteria, we can renounce unclean thermonuclear tests in the megaton range at atmospheric levels. This was the type of test which originally gave rise to world-wide fears of fallout. If the motive of the United States in going to Geneva had really been to calm world fears, then we should have concentrated our attention on these types of tests. Such tests were no longer required by national security considerations. We could have entered forthwith an agreement to stop all tests which cause world-wide fallout hazards; we could have put into effect a foolproof international inspection system, since the basis for such a system was already in existence. We had instruments for measuring and analyzing acoustic and hydroacoustic waves, electromagnetic light and radio waves, and equipment for gathering radioactive debris so sensitive that our scientists were able to reconstruct from the debris collected the design of the bomb detonated. We could have offered our detection network for immediate international use.

The Soviets, however, who had played a prime role in building up the world's fears of fallout through their international propaganda apparatus, were not the least bit interested in putting those fears to rest. Once they had maneuvered us into going to Geneva, they talked only about an all-inclusive ban—one which would prohibit all tests, not only the harmful ones but also those which, with proper safeguards, can be conducted without harm to human beings (e.g., underground tests, tests in outer space, and even certain types of tests of low-yield weapons at atmospheric levels).[15] It had now become their evident purpose to bring the U.S. program of nuclear development to an absolute halt.

Fallacy 4. *A test ban treaty among the "Big Three" nuclear powers would resolve the so-called "Nth Country Problem" by limiting the membership in the "Nuclear Club."*

Within recent years, a great deal of concern has been expressed over the possibility that other nations large and small, either through their own efforts or by purchases and grants, may acquire nuclear weapons. Such a development, it is feared, would increase the possibility of nuclear war by accident (as a result of local mischief-making). This in turn raises the specter of the "catalytic war," i.e., one which breaks out between small nations but finally embroils their great-power patrons. Consequently, a significant amount of effort has gone into studies of the ways in which the inevitable spread of nuclear reactor technology over the face of the globe can be controlled for peaceful purposes. A number of methods have been suggested: strict accountability of all fissionable materials; registration of scientific personnel; design of reactors so that they are most efficient for power production and least efficient for producing weapons-grade material; complete freedom of access to plants by the inspectorate (of either the International Atomic Energy Agency or by the donor nation); and so on.[16]

No one has yet come forth with a politically satisfactory explanation of just how the "Big Three" solution is to be imposed upon all the other nations of the world, especially those like France and Red China who entertain serious nuclear-power ambitions but have not been parties to the Geneva negotiations. Any nation with the necessary industrial resources (e.g., West Germany, Italy, Sweden, Canada, Japan, Belgium or India) can, within the space of a decade or so, develop a significant nuclear weapons technology,

[15] Soviet negotiators have never been willing to talk about "safe" tests for military purposes. They have been extremely reluctant to discuss treaty provisions for tests in which they professed keen interest some years ago—atomic explosions for earth-moving and other peaceful projects. They have dragged their feet on the subject of testing for seismic improvement.

[16] Cf. *The Nth Country Problem and Arms Control,* A Statement by the NPA Special Project Committee on Security through Arms Control and a Technical Report by W. Davidson, M. Kalkstein, and C. Hohenemser, Washington: National Planning Association, January, 1960.

provided that it has the will to allocate sufficient resources to this undertaking. Conceivably, an overwhelming majority of the states of the world would now support a United Nations General Assembly resolution directed against the further proliferation of nuclear powers. But it is very doubtful that either the French or Communist Chinese leadership will be deterred from developing their own nuclear arsenal. A test ban treaty would be fraught with two major political consequences: (1) It would place heavy political strains upon the NATO alliance and might very well prove the first step toward its eventual disintegration. (2) It would necessitate a complete reversal of U.S. policy toward China. Either of these political implications should have been sufficiently important to compel us to take a long, hard look at the notion of a test ban treaty. Both were brushed under the diplomatic carpet.

Fallacy 5. *The nuclear test ban will provide a significant precedent in international arms control administration and will serve to "open up" the Soviets' closed society.*

It would undoubtedly be a healthy development if the Soviets could be induced to overcome their secrecy complex and their xenophobia to the extent of allowing a widespread system of international inspection stations to be established on their soil. It would be an encouraging step forward in East-West relations were the Soviets to accord the personnel staffing the stations the same kind of free-roaming privileges which the United States and Great Britain would be willing to grant them. But an effective inspection system (the only sort which would provide a useful precedent) is farther away today than it was in 1958 when the negotiations first got under way, for today we know a good deal more than we did then about the possibilities of evasion.

Although the Soviets had originally agreed to the stipulation of twenty-one stations on their territory, by August, 1960, they were arguing that fifteen would be enough. To circumvent the Soviets' professed fears of "foreign spies," some Western scientists suggested that the manned posts be supplemented by a network of unmanned seismic stations equipped with automatic recording devices. If these could be made foolproof against tampering, they could serve a useful function from a technical point of view. But their role would always have to be kept subordinate to that of manned posts.

When Prime Minister Macmillan, during his visit to Moscow, suggested a compromise on an annual quota of on-site inspections, the Soviets seized upon this formula to vitiate the notion of the on-site verification. Although John McCone, Chairman of the Atomic Energy Commission, saw a need for as many as 366 inpections per year, and Dr. Hans A. Bethe (who, incidentally, favored the treaty) suggested a formula permitting up to three hundred per year, the Soviets refused to budge beyond "a very small number"—perhaps three per year. Even if this number were doubled or tripled, the detection of a violation would still be reduced from a probability to a mere possibility. When we further consider that the composition of both the control commission and the inspection stations would probably comprise Anglo-American, Soviet and neutral members, and that a two-thirds vote might be required for any positive action (such as an on-site inspection), it becomes clear that it would be extremely difficult to catch the Soviets in a violation.

Setting up a handful of stations in isolated areas of the U.S.S.R. (where conditions of travel by motor vehicle, rail or aircraft would not be available) will contribute little to the "opening up" of six million square miles of totalitarian society. The Soviets obviously have no intention of permitting the international staffs of scientists and technicians to engage in either casual movement or unsupervised contacts. If the cultural exchange programs which involve much large numbers of persons have not succeeded in opening "Western windows" into the U.S.S.R., certainly a test ban treaty cannot.

Toward Arms Security by Consent

The present plight of the United States in the sphere of disarmament negotiations can be traced to a combination of several factors —sentimental idealism concerning the realities of international politics; the desire to be liked more than respected throughout the world; an undue sensitivity to the vagaries of public opinion; and ignorance of the relations which prevail among technology, strategy and psychological methods in the contemporary conduct of international relations. It is these flaws in the character of our own society which have abetted Soviet strategy.

No doubt, mankind's contemporary plight is tragic. Contemplating the destructive potentialities of modern technology, we are assailed by fear, morbidity and remorse. The strategy of the communists exploits all these psychological factors for their own purpose: to defeat us by disarming us first and then to blackmail us into surrender. Hence, if we are to avoid traps, we must move with extreme caution in this area.[17]

There are two sides to the story of thermonuclear weapons. We hear much about the dangers of the technological race and its inevitable culmination in the mutual incineration of the contestants. Seldom are we reminded that the existence of thermonuclear establishments has had the salutary effect of making the leaders of the major powers more cautious in the execution of their foreign policies —more cautious, probably, than statesmen have been for a long time. Since 1954, the major powers have abstained from gestures that might have provoked general war. From time to time, the communists have probed by measured challenges the Middle East, the Far East and Berlin. When the United States has shown its determination to stand firm, the communists did not press on. This is not to suggest that the nuclear-missile race can proceed indefinitely with relative safety for both sides. It might, or might not; no one can predict the outcome with certainty one way or the other. But when we set out to disassemble the overarching structure of thermonuclear power, we must reckon with the danger that its disap-

[17] Not a few Americans are uneasy about the economic implications of arms control. Some believe that our reluctance to disarm stems largely from fear that arms reduction will give rise to adverse repercussions in our economy. Such a fear is unfounded for at least four reasons: (1) If there ever is any practical movement toward arms control, it will necessarily be phased out over many years, and this will provide ample opportunity for whatever economic adjustments must be made. (2) International arms control poses formidable technical problems, the solution of which will involve heavy, sustained expenditures for several decades. The nuclear test ban alone, which represents only one of several arms control steps, would probably cost several billions to put into effect and a billion dollars per year to maintain. (3) If military expenditures were to be cut, there would be an increased demand for federal expenditures in the area of social services, public works and foreign assistance programs. (4) Even a substantial reduction in public expenditures for military purposes need have no adverse effect upon the domestic economy, provided that it is accompanied by, or preferably even led by, an appropriate revision of the tax schedules. We know a great deal today about "cushioning," "phasing," "readjusting" and "relocating." We certainly should not fall prey to the myth that we cannot call off the "arms race" without courting economic ruin.

pearance might usher in a new period of international instability.

We should not, therefore, desist from "constantly throwing up technical obstacles to arms control," as the Soviets frequently accuse us of doing. This is precisely what the concept of arms control demands—adequate controllability. Nothing short of this could possibly satisfy our basic security requirements. But it is clear that the difficulties of formal control increase as the state of technology advances. Nor is it even remotely possible that the world can, in one leap, reach complete and universal disarmament, as the communists claim tongue-in-cheek.

An entirely new approach to the problem of arms security negotiations is required. The gravest threat to the peace and well-being of mankind today is posed less by the mere existence of national military establishments than by the fears and suspicions which inevitably arise when one of two contesting systems places, for military reasons, an excessively high premium on secrecy. It is these psychological factors, rooted in the different political structures of the two systems, which render the deterrent much less stable than it might otherwise be. We would be committing a fatal blunder if, at the present stage of international security negotiations, we proceed more rapidly toward the curtailment of armaments than toward breaking down the barrier of secrecy which now obstructs the international flow of information on armaments.

For the United States, there is promise in an approach which might be called "security by consent." This concept is based on the assumption that the major powers have a common interest in the promotion of their own security and in the avoidance of general nuclear war. By definition, a system of security founded on mutual consent requires genuine communication on the mutual strategic interests of the contracting parties.[18] It cannot be created in the atmosphere of propaganda and "ploymanship" which have characterized disarmament negotiations until now.

Thus far, both sides, although for different reasons, have been playing to world opinion. Ironically enough, the Soviets have made practically all the enduring propaganda gains without even slightly impairing their defense posture. The United States, on the other

[18] We must be careful, however, when speaking of agreements which it would be to the Soviets' interest to observe, not to assume that their concept of "national interest" is the same as ours.

hand, by trying to demonstrate both its sincerity and its realism, has placed itself in an awkward position without ever receiving more than polite applause from the galleries. So long as we persist in talking about disarmament as if it were the main feature of a three-ring circus, the Soviets will prove more adept than we in pleasing the crowd. The Soviets, not so surprisingly, are reluctant to move from a ground which has been decidedly favorable to themselves to a quieter corner of genuine "give and take." But unless they do this, we should break off arms negotiations and disengage our military security from the caprices of grandstand diplomacy.

If Soviet and Western strategists were to enter into a frank, continuing dialogue at regular intervals, carried out privately and informally (without embodying the results in formal treaties) they might be able to arrive at a consensus on the objectives and methods of a security-through-consent arrangement. No doubt, it would be highly desirable were the general movement of history henceforth to lead us to social concord and away from unrestrained violence. Yet in a system of sovereign nations the contingency of war still weighs upon policy. By accepting the possibility of war as an aspect of the human condition and by providing for our normal security needs, we may have the best chance of deterring war and breaking through the vicious circle of fear, insecurity and arms races. Ideally, no state wants to awaken unwarranted suspicions abroad and would, in fact, feel much more secure if other states would not be afraid of it. With fears reduced, armament levels could also go down, not by formal agreement, but by the unilateral decision of each side. Then a sense of mutual security could bridge the chasm of conflicting national interests.

The hard logic which prompted the U-2 flights was generally overlooked in the stormy aftermath of Pilot Powers' descent near Sverdlovsk. Secrecy is nowadays the first and indispensable prerequisite for aggressive acts. To lay the specter of nuclear aggression, more information concerning strategic capabilities must be known to both sides. Americans can be confident that the more knowledge the Soviets acquire about us, the less justified they will be in regarding our posture as anything but a purely defensive one, precisely because we rely on a second-strike strategy. Moreover, it is to our advantage to keep the Soviets from underestimating our deterrent power. Communist propaganda alleges that the Soviet people are afraid of being encircled by a ring of American strategic bases. We can be sure, however, that Soviet strategists understand full well that the U.S. overseas base structure is a defensive-retaliatory instrument and not an offensive–pre-emptive one. They can properly estimate our strategic intentions. They can do so confidently because we are an open society.

The United States, therefore, rightly stressed, from 1955 to 1960, the need for "open skies" and other safeguards against surprise attack.[19] Several analysts have stressed the utility of setting up a system of instantaneous communication between the two nuclear contestants which would permit the swift transmission of nonbelligerent assurances in the event a nuclear accident should occur.[20] This suggestion deserves study. Meanwhile, we have to guard against freezing our concept of the surprise attack problem. True, in the present situation, when nuclear weapons lend themselves particularly to offensive utilization and when ICBM's have not yet been neutralized by antimissile missiles and by the hardening of stationary missile sites and by the improved mobility of other missile launchers on land and sea, the usefulness of a system for diminishing the danger of surprise attack would be very great indeed. We should not, however, arouse unwarranted hopes. By the time any real progress can be made toward establishing a specific

[19] "The original open skies proposal," writes Thomas C. Schelling, "was unorthodox in its idea that arms themselves are not provocative so long as they are clearly held in reserve—so long as their stance is deterrent. That proposal was novel also in its dramatic reminder that, important as it may be to keep secrets from an enemy and in some matters to keep him guessing about our plans, it can be more important to see that the enemy is *not* guessing about our intentions toward initiating surprise attack—if in fact we are not planning any such attack. In the open-skies idea we are interested not only in assuring ourselves with our own eyes that he is not preparing an attack against us; we are interested as well in assuring *him* through *his* own eyes that we are preparing no deliberate attack against *him*." Schelling then goes further and says that a genuine antisurprise-attack scheme should be so designed as to eliminate the advantage of striking first by improving the safety and the invulnerability of the other side's retaliatory weapons. He admits that this approach to the problem of mutual security—i.e., trying to achieve it through mutual deterrence by way of a stable balance of weapons—is probably not compatible with "disarmament," in the literal sense. "Surprise Attack and Disarmament," in the *Bulletin of the Atomic Scientists*, Vol. XV, December, 1959, p. 413.

[20] Cf. *ibid.* and also Henry A. Kissinger, "Arms Control, Inspection and Surprise Attack," *Foreign Affairs*, Vol. 38, July, 1960.

anti-surprise-attack system, the particular military situation for which it was designed will have altered. It will then be apparent that concentrating on what now appears to us to be the most obvious threat of surprise attack was not sufficient. We must also seek to find counters against threats other than bomber or missile attack, especially against the menace, as yet scarcely apprehended by the general public, which may be posed in the future by the various uses of secret armaments (such as bacteriological, chemical and radiological weapons).

Whatever arms security system we adopt must be responsive to technical and political change—incessant, rapid and unpredictable. This change is the bane of all rigidly structured inspection and control agreements, which diplomatically negotiated instruments must inevitably be. When one considers the endless wrangling over the difficulties which have arisen in connection with the test ban negotiations and then tries to imagine what the task of "servicing" multiform agreements through semiannual or annual modifications would be like, he can only come to the conclusion that such a scheme is unworkable. The diplomatic process simply does not admit of completely open-ended agreements which need constantly to undergo "instantaneous" revisions.

In our efforts, then, to arrive at a system of arms security by consent, we should work from a set of premises which may be summarized as follows:

1. It is not feasible to single out specific weapons systems or other isolated factors for special agreements (e.g., disengagement, nuclear-free zones, test bans, agreements on the civilian uses of space, cessation of nuclear production for military purposes, or the outlawing of chemical and biological weapons). A basic deficiency of this approach is that it flaunts the principles of war as an organic whole which cannot be dealt with in piecemeal fashion. The elimination of one particular weapons system or related strategic factor is bound to prove a net benefit to one side or the other and affect the strategic balance.

2. We should quench the flickering hope that the sources of the present international conflict can be removed if only the two main competitors could be separated by a sort of *cordon sanitaire*. This concept may have had a limited applicability in the past under certain circumstances (such as the artificial buffer zones in the Himal-

ayas which serve to separate Russia from India). But in the modern technological environment the Soviet Union and the United States confront each other with weapons of global range. A man-made military vacuum would not only impose very severe handicaps on defenses (probably on both sides). It would also lead to a heightening of tension if one side could fill the vacuum faster than the other. The latter would feel that the former was under constant temptation to do so. Going beyond mere strategic analysis to a consideration of the basic political and human values involved, we must reject disengagement schemes and neutralized zones simply on the grounds that every proposed demilitarized zone contains populations that are entitled to their own proper defenses.

3. It is no longer possible to draw a neat distinction between military weapons and civilian-industrial capabilities. We cannot, for example, eliminate all production of fissionable materials for warlike purposes and keep developing nuclear technology for its peaceful applications. Biological warfare, moreover, could conceivably be waged exclusively by civilian establishments. Each organized society possesses numerous weapons which may range all the way from fists and clubs to civilian aircraft and chemical laboratories. These facts alone vitiate as a workable concept the contemporary facile notion of complete disarmament.

4. Since all inspections systems must of necessity incorporate standardized procedures, foolproof arms control arrangements are out of the question. All the plans now being discussed either implicitly or explicitly call for specific numbers of inspectors and quotas of inspection visits. The freedom of action of the inspectors would be circumscribed by a large number of ground rules which, in due time, would be hardened by repetitive behavior patterns. Even assuming that at the time of the agreement both parties subscribe in good faith to the principle of full disclosure, the crucial challenge to the system will nevertheless arise precisely at the moment when one of the participating governments secretly reverses its policy and decides to arm again for aggression. In this case, the inspection system can very easily be circumvented. Political pressure can be applied to selected members of the control commission; the movement of inspectors can be curtailed or interfered with; deceptive and decoy methods can be employed; detection apparatus can be tampered with; communications can be cut or

falsified; and the corps of inspectors can be infiltrated. Such evasion techniques are unlimited. While some of them may be detected, others might remain hidden. As soon as doubt arises about the reliability of the control mechanism, tensions may be aggravated. In sum, every inspection system has to develop its own bureaucratic routine. For this very reason it is always vulnerable to a skillful group of strategists who set out to circumvent it; better still, who calculate in their plan for aggression the help they might receive from a hoodwinked inspectorate.

5. Arms control systems cannot be policed. The only sanction, once we have discovered a violation by the other side, is to scrap the agreement and resume the arms race. But once a violation has been reported, a Western democratic nation will be reluctant to take the required counteraction—viz., canceling the agreement and seemingly precipitating a grave international crisis. Public opinion would be loath to condone such a move. Had not the inspection system proved a blessing to mankind, and do, therefore, a few "little" violations justify scrapping it? Democracies are prone to assume that conferences will dissolve any and all international unpleasantness. Does it not seem reasonable to convene a summit conference in order to obtain a solemn promise from the other side that it will abstain from further violations of the arms control agreement? Security in a multistate society is best achieved when the individual states retain the unilateral right to make whatever immediate decisions they deem necessary for the maintenance of an adequate defense force without having to cancel international treaties, wreck international co-operation and upset public opinion.

6. The concepts of equity and symmetry cannot be incorporated into any control or inspection systems. The major powers are divided by vast geographical differences, different levels of development in various technological sectors, different security requirements, and hence by different strategies. Since it is futile to expect any formula to be worked out which would compensate for all these asymmetrical factors, we should acknowledge the right of each government to determine according to its own unilateral decision-making processes what security forces it needs and how it wants them deployed and armed. There is no other way in which each government and each people can be made to feel secure. Some may object that, on the face of it, there is nothing novel about such a proposal.

It contains, however, one vitally important additional feature: a system of international intelligence-gathering which will enable governments henceforth to make their decisions in the light of relatively complete and reliable knowledge.

What precisely do we propose? We propose, in the first place, an increasingly liberal policy for the release of information on security-related developments. More pictures and data showing the performance of various types of weapons should be released by both sides, and be presented to the public on both sides in such a sober way as to enhance the sense of mutual deterrence rather than to promote war hysteria. We should publish data on the total nuclear megatonnage in our stockpiles, the total number of multimegaton weapons, and the total number of installations from which they could be fired in retaliation. We should remind the world that they represent essentially a defensive, second-strike capability and impress upon the Soviet strategists the fact that, collectively, these weapons and installations pose a number of variables so great as to render a "first strike with impunity" impossible and irrational. We would, of course, call upon the Soviets to make similar information available to us. We should also work toward the mutual elimination of restrictions on travel and the meeting of foreign nationals, the abolition of forbidden zones and the ease of access to defense plants and military sites. The security of the United States could be substantially improved if we could induce the Soviets to allow us one-half the freedom of movement which they and their friends now enjoy in the United States.

In the second place, we should facilitate the establishment of various technical collections systems. Orbital intelligence vehicles will soon be operational, but much could be done to improve, by true international co-operation, the effectiveness and the reliability of this type of system. It is most unfortunate that the Soviets have seen fit to refuse, during the International Geophysical Year and thereafter, any meaningful exchange of data in a spirit of genuine co-operation. Although most of the intelligence satellites to be orbited in the years ahead will still be under national control, a few might be operated under United Nations auspices and the data obtained thereby could be made public. Observer teams might also be exchanged to take up positions at central rail and air transport points to watch for unusually heavy movements of military personnel and matériel. No single collection system by itself would be reliable, but several in combination could serve through the steady flow of data to enhance a sense of mutual security.

In the third place, we should make a special effort to augment the system of military attachés which has proved useful and workable during the last 150 years. The major powers should admit foreign military observers down to the lower echelons of military forces, beginning with the major commands and gradually extending downward to lower operating levels. The ground rules defining permissible and impermissible actions by these attachés should be drawn liberally.

Pushing the logic of this idea farther, we should try to conclude an international convention on espionage by which all states would adopt the same definitions of espionage and prescribe similar penalties for similar acts, preferably on the lower side of the penal range. The convention should stipulate either that espionage cases be tried before an international tribunal or that national trials be open with a fair defense guaranteed to the accused. The convention, as a matter of international comity, should provide for the periodic exchange of persons who have been convicted of espionage by the respective signatory governments. Even a year or two ago, such a proposal would have seemed extremely farfetched. The U-2 incident, however, has taught a few lessons which need not benefit exclusively the Soviets.

Meanwhile, both the Americans and the Soviets would continue to maintain a sharp lookout, each for their own security. Each side would continue to conduct nuclear tests (with due regard for the health of mankind). Each would continue with its space shots. But all tests and missile launchings ought to be carried out only after the United Nations has been formally notified and foreign observers have been invited to such events. Perhaps the United Nations could be converted gradually from a sounding board for misleading propaganda into a genuine educational forum for the rational discussion of the real problems of arms control. Incalculably happy results might issue from a substitution of facts for myths.

At the heart of our proposal lies the mutual increase of information. Each national government would gather information through its own intelligence services, operating according to specific directives in order to answer specific questions. In brief, freedom of information and freedom of intelligence would become the main pillars of the system which we have called "security-by-consent." This system may not be nearly so glamorous as one embracing an international network of technical inspection stations. But it would work much better—if we take a heightened sense of security as the token of success. A government that has become convinced, on the basis of competent and dependable intelligence information gathered over a period of time, that its potential adversary harbors no aggressive designs may then feel free to start reducing its armaments.

Under present conditions it is impossible to conduct completely open diplomatic negotiations on armaments because either the diplomat does not really know the whole intelligence picture or, if he does, cannot frankly disclose his knowledge in the negotiations. But under the conditions envisioned in the proposal outlined above, it is quite conceivable that governments could communicate their intentions in something like the following manner: "We shall be willing to reduce our air force by three groups if you are willing to eliminate three air defense battalions. If you signify compliance, we shall start taking steps immediately toward this reduction and you can verify it in the usual manner. We shall expect to verify your parallel action within the year." Each nation could make proposals, whenever it saw fit, which would be contingent on counter-offerings by the other party. At the same time, each nation would remain free either to increase or decrease its strength unilaterally. In sum, the philosophy behind our proposal can be stated succinctly: The only secure world is an open world.

Armament and Disarmament

It is often said that prolonged armaments effort does not provide a dependable or stable solution to the problem of United States security, for American ethics rule out the initiation of a preventive war. It has been argued that, in the long run, the maintenance of massive military establishments, armed with all the latest devices which modern technology can produce, will favor the Soviet Union, for Soviet leadership will have no moral compunctions about attempting a surprise attack. Hence, it is only by disarmament that the United States can achieve real and lasting security.

In the light of the dynamic character of modern military technology and the possibilities for "outflanking" all technical control systems, it should be clear that disarmament programs cannot furnish guarantees against aggression. We should, therefore, kiss good-by the hope that our security difficulties will yield themselves to the magic formula of disarmament.

While it is possible to forge swords into plowshares, man has shown himself no less adept at doing exactly the opposite. He has generally found at hand an abundance of technical instruments which, by a more or less ingenious twist, can be turned into weapons. We do cherish the vision of peace without arms. But no longings can transform, as a matter of course, the disarmament plans which are now under discussion into masterpieces of logic, technical competence and statecraft. Within the time span under consideration in this book—1960-1970—the present strategic-ideologic conflict, the existing state system and the current rate of technological progress are likely to endure. It is these factors, if not others, which preclude a sizable reduction of national armaments and the creation of comprehensive control systems.

The Soviets have been able, in part, to maintain the initiative in the negotiations for nuclear arms control because of their acknowledged superiority in the realm of non-nuclear forces. The Western disarmament negotiators are hampered by the reliance of their governments on a strategy in which nuclear weapons hold almost an exclusive place. The adverse ratio of the conventional forces of the West to those of the communist bloc has resulted in a disproportion of negotiable assets. Nuclear parity throws the advantage on the table of negotiation to the Soviets armed with superior non-nuclear capabilities.

We cannot hope to achieve security by outlawing nuclear weapons and falling back upon conventional military establishments. A defective system of nuclear arms control might prove the most deadly military trap of history: A nation which had managed to hide away one hundred or two hundred multimegaton weapons, or just a few of the so-called begaton weapons, would be in a position to dominate the world.

There is no practical method of preventing such concealment. Even if there were, it has now become fairly obvious that the production of the nuclear weapons of the future can be undertaken at relatively modest cost in small and inconspicuous installations. It would be virtually impossible for quota-bound international inspectors to uncover nuclear weapons production which is hidden within huge industrial complexes manufacturing commodities for everyday peaceful use.

Even if it were possible to prevent clandestine nuclear armament, it is impossible to prevent nuclear war. Were a war between denuclearized powers to break out, the conflict could be won by that side which has made the necessary preparations to move more speedily into nuclear production. Let us imagine that toward the end of a conventional war one side would come into possession of nuclear weapons. It could use its nuclear arms with impunity against the opponent's main bases and population centers and thus win a conclusive victory. The potential aggressor need only make sure that he can win the nuclear production race after the war has begun. If he can, the issue is no longer in doubt. The defender can guard against such a contingency only by maintaining "blitzkrieg" conventional forces capable of overwhelming the aggressor quickly enough to forestall the production of nuclear weapons.

The abolition of nuclear weapons is a pipe dream. Is there no possibility, therefore, of reducing armaments or at least relaxing military postures rather than disarming altogether? We are not quite that pessimistic. We are convinced that, in view of certain likely developments during the next decade, some progress toward arms stability can be made.

The technological feasibility of producing begaton or larger weapons will no doubt cause the United States and the Soviet Union to pause and think seriously about where they are heading. With each passing year, the manufacture of weapons with "a bigger bang for a buck" (or "more rubble for a ruble") makes less sense from the military standpoint. It will be increasingly difficult to incorporate such weapons into any rational strategy that contemplates their actual use. (If the Soviets were to gain the jump on us and achieve a monopoly of begaton weapons which would enable them to destroy our second-strike forces, they could not be deterred from doing so except perhaps by their concern over the postattack contamination of the world's atmosphere.) But the nihilistic implications of a weapon furnishes no guarantee that it will not be produced. Undoubtedly the Soviets would put begaton devices that they had launched into orbit to good use as weapons of psychological strategy. A relatively small number of begaton weapons, properly deployed, could enable the Soviets to neutralize our thermonuclear deterrent and thus open the way for another "flow period" of communism. The United States, therefore, might feel that it had no choice but to develop a similar begaton capability to narrow the Soviets' technological margin for blackmail operations.

The United States should ponder carefully the course of action which it will adopt toward the fearsome weapons developments which are now entering the realm of technological feasibility—especially the begatons-in-orbit and the so-called Doomsday Machines upon which strategists are beginning to speculate. We should not blandly assume that, merely because these apocalyptic devices are now theoretically possible, the Soviets will be any more eager than we are to build them. It is not a question of their being held back by humanitarian considerations. But something else in Marxist rationality or in their own biological instincts might make them shun this road to the precipice.

The United States must reckon on the possibility, ironic though it may seem, that if it decides to construct these nihilistic weapons it may find itself alone in the venture. Such a development might well turn out to be history's greatest white elephant—politically, strategically and morally. The very possession of these weapons could cause world-wide political revulsion against the United States. They could not possibly be integrated into any sensible military strategy, nor detonated morally under any circumstances. Because they would pose such terrible dangers of global catastrophe, they might serve to paralyze us more than the communists. We should not forget that when the United States possessed a monopoly on the A-bomb, Americans often seemed more frightened by its specter than other peoples in the world. If the declaratory policy of "massive retaliation" has come to be regarded as obsolete because incredible, what would be the outcome of a policy for which an appropriate code name is GABRIEL?

The United States and the Soviet Union, confronted with these stark prospects, might conceivably agree that the time has come to back away from a competition which could, by a mere miscalculation, lead to their swift, mutual annihilation. But two ideological-social systems which have been locked for many years in mortal combat are not likely to pledge themselves to military-technological abstemiousness. The difficulties of reaching a *détente,* even if both sides should wish it, should not be underestimated. Deep-rooted sociological and power-political tensions do not subside overnight. On both sides, institutions would have to change and concessions would have to be made; but the changes required in Soviet objectives and in Soviet society would be by far the more drastic. No one can say whether the Soviets will ever renounce their aims of global hegemony, their tactics of relentless psychopolitical warfare, and their policy of secrecy. And if they should elect to do so, they would still have the task of communicating this intention to us in a credible manner, demonstrating tangibly that henceforth they will abide by certain international rules. Mutual acceptance of the international *status quo* (i.e., the existing distribution of power relationships and zones of influence) is the *sine qua non* of any arms reduction plan.

Assuming that both sides do desire a genuine accommodation, efforts toward working out a practical balance between communist and Western security needs could be initiated. The first step would be to approach the arms security problem in a professional manner. Soviet and Western strategists, for example, could join in war-gaming exercises to examine the possibilities of increasing mutual security through various alternative postures involving different weapons mixes. Each side would gradually come to see what constitutes the optimum combination of weapons and defense systems (i.e., types of equipment, force levels and deployment) for the maintenance of a relatively invulnerable defense—either nuclear, conventional or irregular. Realization of the optimum mix in the military establishment of each side would strengthen the deterrent and thus symmetrically enhance the two contestants' sense of security.

Even then, one question remains unanswered: Can a balanced security for both sides be achieved best at a high or low level of deterrent forces? It takes little imagination to see that acceptance of a low force level plays into the hands of a potential aggressor. If the latter is forced to attack numerous hardened sites, a reasonably large number of air bases, mobile air and missile systems and submarines, and space and warning systems, he must attack with a very large, complex and technologically advanced force. Such a force cannot be raised clandestinely, and it would be difficult, if not impossible, to conceal it. It cannot be launched without touching off some unequivocal warning. In fact, an aggressor may be unable, for technical-military as well as political-economic reasons, to mobilize such a force at all. If an arms reduction agreement concedes each contracting power a legal quota of twenty ICBM's and one side conceals twenty-five additional missiles, the latter may be tempted to launch a pre-emptive attack. The temptation is strong, for violation courts the risk of detection. It grows even stronger if the violator has acquired fairly complete intelligence as to the exact locations of the opponent's force. But if the legal quota for each side were five hundred to a thousand ICBM's, it would require a supreme if not a prohibitive effort at cheating to upset the balance of firepower and catch the opponent unawares. If the aggressor has to attack only a limited number of targets and target systems, his problems of clandestine preparations are fairly simple. The attack can be launched with a high probability of success. Perhaps most important of all, the penalties for partial failure—the risks incident to retaliation—are light.

In short, a low-level arms control agreement is risky. The objective of all arms security agreements should be greater international stability. It seems clear that a low-level agreement invites violation, breeds suspicions and hence increases the danger of war. It follows that we should seek an agreement, preferably tacit, that provides for the retention of that quantity of nuclear weapons that does not pose the specter of human extinction or the prospect of terrible losses to the two contestants, but at the same time is adequate to impose an insuperable obstacle to any attempt by a would-be aggressor to gain world hegemony through a skillfully planned pre-emptive attack.

It should be emphasized that massive nuclear weapons of the megaton variety are one factor only of what might be called the strategic equation. In addition, considerable amounts of fissile materials are necessary for the conduct of ground warfare and for defense against missiles, aircraft and submarines. The relatively simple strategic equation is further complicated by such matters as the hardening of sites, mobility of missiles and continental defense. Defensive measures of this sort, while expensive, obviously tend to increase the force levels required by the aggressor. A well-balanced offense-defense mix will render it very unlikely that a general nuclear war could be a short war. If each side divides its military resources more or less evenly between offensive and defensive capabilities, neither side can afford to risk its whole long-range striking force in a single attempted blow. A potential aggressor, not knowing what the enemy might still be able to do after the first strike, or how many nuclear exchanges might be involved, or how long the war might last, must keep some of his forces in reserve. The development of an offense-defense balance to replace the current overemphasis on offense would immeasurably compound an aggressor's planning problems, greatly increase the cost of an effort on his part to attain a first-strike capability, and introduce major uncertainties into his computations of victory. This type of "arms control"—if that be the proper term for it—is more likely to lead toward relaxation and stability than is a type of arms control which postulates drastic force reductions.

The greatest hope for progress toward mutual arms security lies in the technological-military competition itself, and in mutual, informal arrangements for the unveiling of military secrets. There is every reason to believe that both of the superpowers will, in the not too distant future, develop highly invulnerable strategic delivery systems. When this development takes place—probably shortly after the mid-1960's—the present unstable order, overshadowed by the ever-present danger of surprise attack, will likely give way to a more stable one. It may then be possible to reach an understanding on arms reduction which will guarantee the invulnerability of the superpowers' strategic forces. Our security and that of mankind lies in the direction of stable arms balance—rationally pursued—not in the direction of utopian schemes of disarmament.

CHAPTER 10 STRATEGY OF WAYS AND MEANS

For the next few years, the fortunes of the Free World will be decided by the relative accomplishments of the United States and the Soviet Union. Growing economic productivity feeds expanding Soviet military, scientific, technological and foreign aid programs. It has significantly raised the standard of living of the Soviet peoples, regardless of how inadequate even the new level may appear by our standards. But this sop to the heavily burdened populace is trivial compared to the influence of the burgeoning Soviet economy as a whole upon the strategic purpose which comprises both cause and goal of the communist empire. Indeed, this is the heart of the matter when we tally our economic achievements against those of the Soviets. The present discussion will center, therefore, on the significant differences in the structure and thrust of the two economic systems. It will then proceed to examine the American economy's great capacity for expansion and those policy trends which must guide the U.S. in parrying Russia's competitive challenge.

Agreement seems general that the United States must "do more than it has been doing" to guarantee, through the decade of the 1960's, its own security and that of its allies. But agreement upon principle only exacerbates "haggling over the price." Exactly what and how much "more" should we do? Accepting the need for greater exertion does not calm widespread fears of possibly dire economic consequences. Increased expenditures for military hardware, foreign aid, research and development, or other strategically significant purposes are regarded by some as pathways to harmful inflation, confiscatory taxes, deficit spending or, in extreme views, bankruptcy itself. Others warn that many Soviet claims of technological achievements and rapid growth rates are calculated, at least in part, to induce us to spend our way into ruin, and that, therefore, keeping our economy on an even budgetary keel should be the prime strategic objective of the United States.

It is the basic thesis of this chapter that substantial augmentation of U.S. strategic efforts within the next few years, efforts well above the Soviet level, would not involve undue sacrifice or unmanageable inflation, much less "economic ruin." We shall contend that America *can* "afford to survive" and *must* make almost herculean efforts to do so within the next few years.

Confidence that the American economy is the world's most remarkable productive establishment and that it could sustain vastly increased output seems more justified than the doubts of the timid, but it does not prescribe the complex economic policies required to deal adequately with the mounting crisis. It is one of the abiding characteristics of fundamental disagreements that they give rise to polar positions, although a practical solution of the controversial problem might well be found somewhere in the middle. Prolonged debate over optimum economic policy has hardened opposing points of view: (1) Do we need a quantitative or a qualitative improvement of the national product? (2) Do we want to produce more goods and services of all types or shift our resources into those productive sectors which weigh heavily on the strategic scale? (3) Which warrants greater emphasis: plant expansion or plant modernization? (4) Can we accomplish our desired goals mainly through the instrumentality of the federal budget or will other monetary and tax reforms be necessary? (5) If it appears necessary to raise the federal budget for military and other strategic expenditures, should we proceed on a "pay-as-you-go" or a deficit basis?

Before we seek to answer these questions, we must understand clearly the nature of the economic challenge confronting us, as well as of the various characteristics and potentialities of the U.S. economy which bear directly upon our efforts to use that economy as a tool of strategy.

The Soviet and U.S. Economies Compared

The usual starting point for a comparison of two national economies is the Gross National Product (GNP)—the total of goods and services produced, lumping steel girders and missile warheads with TV programs, six-packs of beer and clean shirts from the laundry. The size of that total ultimately limits a nation's achievement in programs to enhance its power position. But GNP is an awkward measuring rod with which to compare the United States and U.S.S.R. economies.

To begin with, the concept of Gross National Product cannot be applied in the same way to both a free enterprise and a communist economy. In a capitalist system prices are set by millions of consumers and thousands of entrepreneurs, whereas in the Soviet Union prices are wholly controlled by the government. Since the Soviets allocate all resources according to a central plan rather than according to the workings of a free market, there is little resemblance between the two economic structures. In the United States, where the consumer ostensibly reigns supreme,[1] the major part of our finest technology is devoted to the mass production of consumer goods at low prices. The Soviets, on the other hand, have not yet permitted a genuine mass production economy to develop in consumer goods. Their technology still concentrates on military production and capital formation.

The disparity of the two systems makes it impossible to regard the ruble as money in the Western sense. Ruble/dollar ratios range anywhere from 1/1 up to 50/1, depending upon the Soviet government's attitude[2] toward the product, the vendor and the buyer. In addition to the problem of money, there simply is no way of reconciling Soviet and American statistics—or, more accurately, communist statistics with those of a free and open society. The Soviets are notorious for employing various devices to inflate production statistics when it suits their purposes.[3] At the same time,

[1] Threats to consumer control in a "free" market can develop through industrial monopolies, artificially stimulated obsolescence, government regulation or "interference" in certain industries, etc.

[2] The official currency conversion rate of four rubles to the dollar, often a useful norm of comparison for trade in capital goods, is totally irrelevant as regards consumer goods. Recognizing this, the Soviets peg the rate of exchange for tourists at ten rubles to the dollar. On the black market in 1960, the dollar was traded for as high as forty rubles. For a discussion of the difficulties involved in a comparison of the two countries' GNP's, cf. Francis P. Hoeber, "Soviet Economic Potential and Strategies," *SRI Journal*, Vol. 3, 4th Quarter, 1959, pp. 160-172.

[3] The ambiguity of published Soviet economic statistics is treated in Robert Strausz-Hupé *et al.*, *Protracted Conflict*, pp. 72-74.

they disguise part of their military outlay under the heading of peaceful technological research for outer space. Repair and maintenance charges frequently are accounted as capital formation, rendering futile any attempt to place a proper evaluation on depreciation and net investment rates.

Despite these difficulties, we must make the frustrating attempt to place a percentage tag, however crude, on Soviet production vis-à-vis ours. In the protracted conflict, the whole spectrum of a nation's economic potential affects the strategic balance. Missiles, planes, submarines and tanks may weigh heaviest, but they are not the only things that count. One side may score a political gain or at least make a good psychological impression with cars and trucks, the other with tractors; one with computers, the other with generators; one with TV sets and self-service stores, the other with jet passenger planes and nuclear reactors. However great a degree of unevenness may be built into a nation's GNP figures, nevertheless they comprise an essential index to over-all national strength in a complex economic-technological era. Properly discounted, GNP statistics serve as a useful starting point for analysis.

As of 1960, the Soviet GNP (expressed in dollar valuation of resources) appeared to be between 40 and 45 per cent of that of the United States. The latter estimate was made by Allen Dulles, Director of the Central Intelligence Agency, before the Congressional Joint Economic Committee in November, 1959. Mr. Dulles' calculation probably reflects evaluations based not only on published statistics but also on classified sources. It has been found acceptable by a majority of American students of the Soviet economy.

Probably the most important single fact about the Soviet economy, however, is the fact that the Soviets, operating from an economic base less than half the size of ours, are able to match us, or to outdo us, in the absolute volume of resources poured into military and other strategic programs. In a word, the Soviets allocate their economic resources for strategic purposes far more efficiently than we do. They concentrate on military production and on those sectors of industry which are in close support of military-technological power. So far as we can tell, the U.S.S.R. seems to be devoting from 15 to 20 per cent of its total productive resources, in dollar terms, to military and military-related expenditures, while U.S.

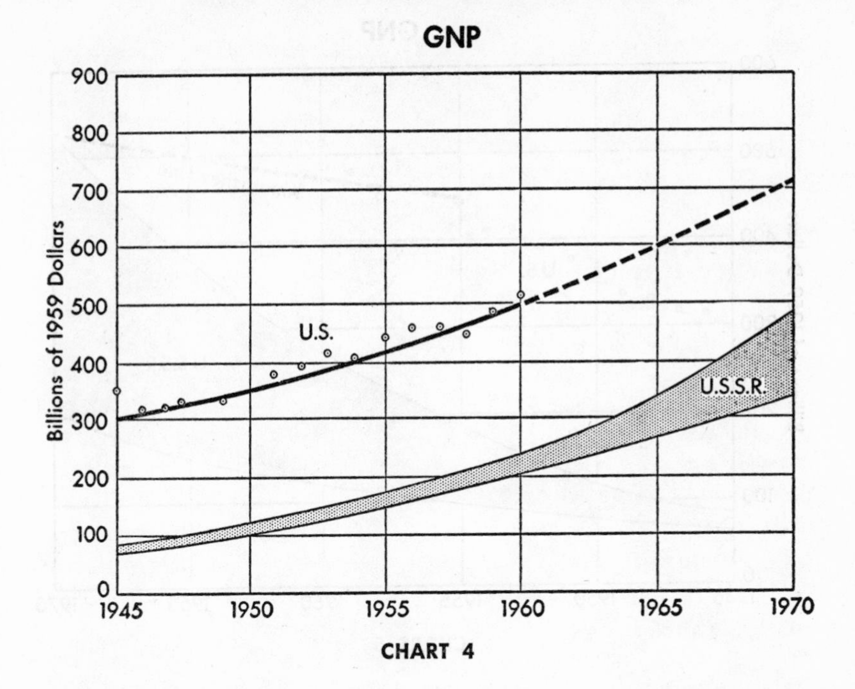

CHART 4

national security expenditures have declined to about 9 per cent of our GNP.

Nor is this the whole story. The Soviets have not merely drawn abreast of us in their military-technological effort. In some respects they lead us qualitatively since they have accelerated production of those capital goods which contribute significantly to critical strategic programs. Most American experts agree that Soviet *industrial* output is growing at the rate of about 8 per cent per year, or double the 4 per cent which the U.S. averages. This estimate is roughly in line with Mr. Dulles' calculations.

About 30 per cent of the Soviet GNP is reinvested, compared to 18 per cent in the United States.[4] In absolute amounts, the Soviet investment total, perhaps only three-fourths of ours, provides a leverage that exceeds ours since more than half of it goes into capital goods formation in industries which support the military

[4] The 18 per cent figure for the United States includes a rough estimate of government investment for comparison with the Soviet figure.

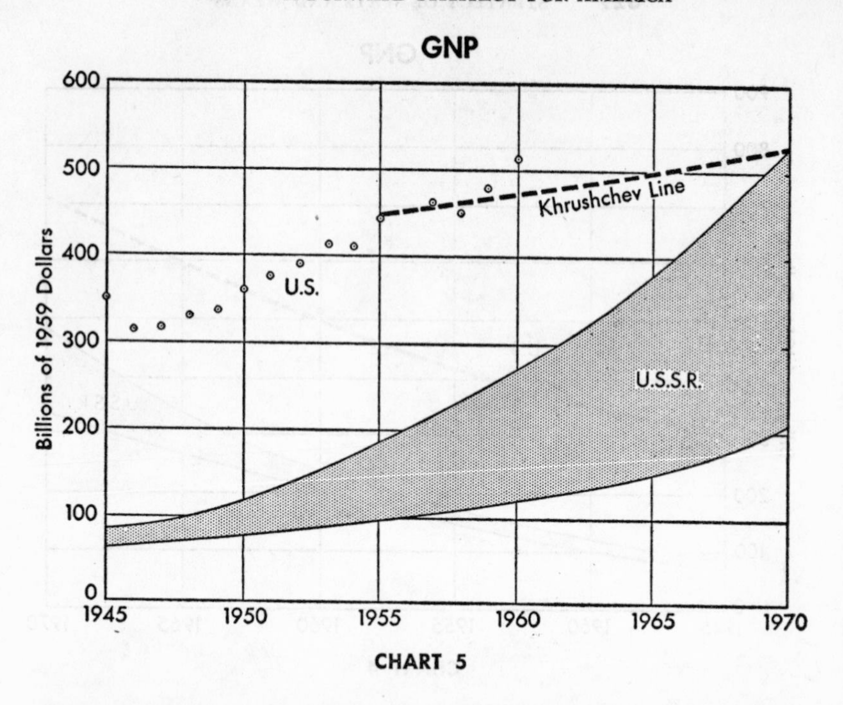

CHART 5

sector. In the American consumer-oriented economy, on the other hand, not much more than a quarter of the investment is directed toward the growth of heavy industry. Another quarter goes into housing, an area given much less attention in the Soviet Union. Most of the remainder of our industrial investment is sunk into promoting consumption—expanding consumer durables production, packaging, and planned obsolescence through frequent model changes, with all the costly retooling which that characteristic American practice involves.

The significance of this difference between the Soviets and ourselves cannot be overstressed. Soviet economic institutions are primarily designed to promote growth that contributes to power; ours are not. This is not to suggest that we should abandon our traditional goal of distributing material benefits as widely as possible throughout our society. But we should clearly recognize the strategic implications and costs of affluence.

The question of producer versus consumer goods does go to the heart of the matter. The Soviet Union pushes the production of producer durables and the expansion of military capabilities. In the United States, by contrast, too little attention has been given to tax, patent and other legislative policies which encourage the expansion of producer durables output.

The machine tool industry provides an excellent case in point. We do practically nothing to improve the replacement process, e.g., keeping the age of machine tools down to a level where replacement is adequate and innovation a matter of annual routine. Our

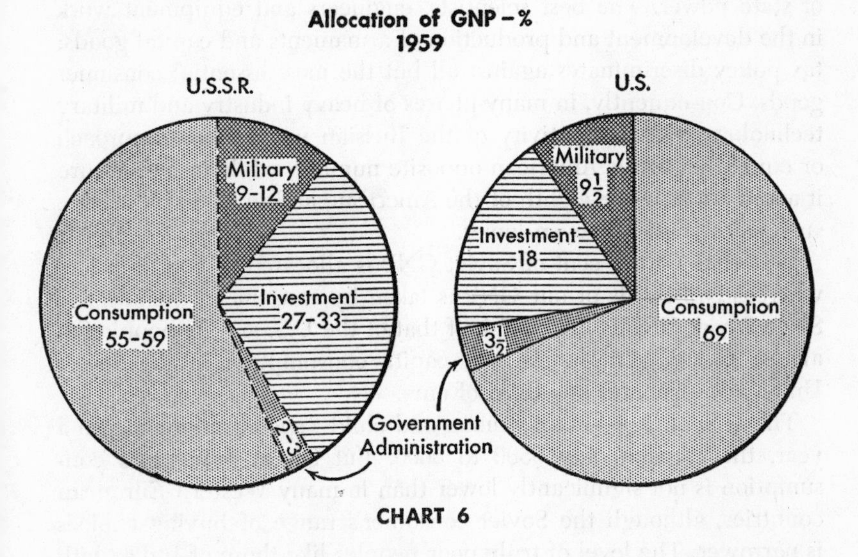

CHART 6

present tax laws prevent amortization at rates which provide adequate incentive to develop, produce and use new types of machinery. The modular system of using machine tools (employment of machine tools with changeable-parts design), widely used in Russia, might measurably reduce production costs. But, under our tax structure, only a few of our industrial giants can afford this type of innovation. Not only can the modular system reduce the cost of final products, but it also makes possible cheaper and more frequent model changes. It could cut lead-times in military production by facilitating the modernization of weapons, from tanks to bombers, without costly retooling.

The Soviet Union has not caught up with the United States as a modern, technological nation. On the average, one American industrial worker produces as much as three Russians. But, again, much of our most efficient industry produces consumer goods. We mass-produce, on a scale unknown to the Soviet Union, automobiles, appliances, clothes and other products for the satisfaction of human wants, at relatively high quality and low prices.

Exaltation of the consumer is appropriate in a society that cherishes man's dignity and his right to the pursuit of happiness. Communism bends its efforts in the opposite direction: the enhancement of state power. The best scientists, engineers and equipment work in the development and production of armaments and capital goods; tax policy discriminates against all but the most essential consumer goods. Consequently, in many phases of heavy industry and military technology, the productivity of the Russian worker may approach or equal that of his American opposite number, while in agriculture it averages only one-eighth of the American, and in some industries, such as textiles, it is even lower.

Less than 60 per cent of Soviet GNP is allocated to consumption, whereas two-thirds of our GNP is taken by consumer expenditures. Since Soviet GNP is less than half that of the U.S. and its population almost 20 per cent larger, per capita consumption in the Soviet Union approximates one-third of ours.

The U.S. citizen—man, woman and child—spends about $1,750 a year, the Russian only $500 to $600. But Soviet per capita consumption is not significantly lower than in many Western European countries, although the Soviet consumer's range of buying choices is narrower. The level of truly poor peoples like those of India, with perhaps forty to fifty dollars to spend per person per year, or China, or other underdeveloped Asian, African and South American countries, is substantially below Soviet standards. Less than twenty nations of the world can be called industrialized societies today.

More important to the international situation, there is room in Soviet allocations for steady improvement in consumption—at a rate probably sufficient to make the worker feel himself a little better off each year. The Seven-Year Plan promises rapid rises in the standard of living: "a shorter working day and a shorter working week; an expansion in the output of consumer goods, and an improvement of public, cultural and other services." The Soviet citizen is told that it will no longer be necessary to hold back consumption, and that "all this will enable us to end taxation of the population in the next few years."[5]

Yet planned increases in consumer goods are still far behind those for military and capital goods. Consumers will not share proportionately in the high growth rate, although their status *will* continue to improve.

And Soviet improvement *is* continuous. It is not interrupted by periodic recessions, in which consumers take one step backward for every three forward. It would seem that the betterment of the average Russian's lot will be sufficiently noticeable and steady enough to insure his loyalty to the regime. But it does not follow that Soviet society, because it becomes more affluent, will become less aggressive. In sum, the Soviets, though still far behind in production and productivity, match our military efforts without curtailing their investment for growth or curtailing the improvement in the lot of their citizens.

There is one other aspect of the Soviet economy which merits our closest attention. The Soviets are now encountering a serious manpower shortage. This scarcity of hands undoubtedly creates bottlenecks in planning which may compel the Soviets to change their hitherto extravagant use of manpower. If so it could prove to be a blessing in disguise. The sixth Five-Year Plan came to grief because it was no longer possible to fulfill goals simply by adding new workers to the productive system. The current Plan, with its unprecedented emphasis upon plant modernization, represents a fundamental turn in Soviet economic history.

During recent years, Soviet planners have shown keen interest in automation techniques. At a time when many American labor unions are becoming concerned over the rate of technological innovation in industry, the Soviets, undeterred by any fear of technological unemployment (which they look upon as only a temporary dislocation) are pressing ahead as quickly as possible toward automation. Successes in this area during the sixties may do more than alleviate their basic manpower problem. They might score against us a

[5] In May, 1960, Khrushchev announced that income taxes would be abolished in 1961. It must be remembered, however, that Soviet income taxes are a minor source of revenue and their elimination does not have the meaning for the wage earner or the government that it would in this country.

quantum jump in the area of industrial productivity, to the detriment of our entire international position.

The United States attitude in the face of the Soviet military-industrial challenge has thus far been a passive one. Since the Korean War, our dollar allocations to national security have remained almost constant, signifying an actual decline in our national level of effort. The cost of technologically advanced weapons systems has risen with weapon complexity, while the dollar is being moderately yet steadily eroded by inflation. This aspect of the problem becomes more serious because of the two- or three-year lead-time between budgeting and end item delivery. As our GNP rises, a fairly constant security budget represents an annually smaller proportion of national resources. We have consented to this relative decrease although our adversary has sustained or raised the proportion of his expanding GNP devoted to military and military-related programs. Our budget-minded national security policy of recent years has been unaccompanied by any dynamic action to increase either the strength of our economy or our industrial base.

There is a question as to whether our growth rate has dropped below the 3.5 per cent average prevailing since World War II. Certainly there has been no acceleration. The United States, in sharp contrast to the Soviet Union, enjoyed a baby boom during the war, creating a manpower situation the obverse of the Soviets'. Unemployment has edged steadily upward. After the 1949 recession, it leveled off at about 3 per cent; after 1954, it was a little above 4 per cent; and since 1958, it has been in the 5 to 6 per cent range. Meanwhile, the average work week has continued its slow decline at roughly 0.5 per cent per year. By 1960 the thirty-five-hour week was being discussed as the next major objective of organized labor.

In our liberal industrial society, the maximization of leisure for the workingman has long been regarded as a criterion of social and economic progress. Technological innovation and the humanization of labor conditions have benefited all or nearly all. The movement toward a thirty-five-hour week could be hailed as a wholesome development if the productive resources of the United States were more fully employed than they are at the present time. Actually, a great slack exists in our economic system. This fact alone justifies the suspicion that the static nature of our national security efforts in recent years has been a matter of political choice, not economic necessity.

The charge cannot be fairly leveled at any one interest group alone. Management, labor, financiers, farmers, professional people could all be accused of "self-pampering," advancing group well-being regardless of the public interest.

Viewed in an economic vacuum, lower tax rates, wider tax loopholes, higher wages, shorter work weeks, a lower price index and a sounder dollar, broader welfare benefits and stouter corporation profits appear desirable, possibly beneficial. Most of us want some or all of them. But if political expedience yields to selfish group interests, the growth rate of heavy American industry assuredly will suffer.

The chances seem remote that Americans will succumb, as foreign critics predict in malice or sorrow, to insatiable urges for comfort, convenience and self-indulgence. Nevertheless, a free market economy can scarcely be growth-conscious in the strategic sense. To be sure, the sum total of individual preferences, given free play in the market system, promotes the growth of GNP. But a great part of that growth develops in consumer goods and services, with relatively little gain in heavy industry. Constituent economic elements of a liberal economic community, by definition, manifest little interest in the *quality of the whole national product.* The nation's over-all economic health, strength and growth remain the concern of statesmen whose leadership must guide free market dynamism without degrading it into the socialist state.

To serve our national purpose best, we should mold our economy to increase our total productive effort both quantitatively and qualitatively. This does not imply setting a precise percentage of annual GNP growth as a national policy goal. Rather, we should view the U.S. economy as a means—a tool for achieving programs which can be defended on their own merits. Annual growth and qualitative improvement are necessary conditions for the conduct of our global strategy, a normal concomitant of our efforts to secure worthy foreign policy objectives—political, economic, technological and military.

It seems that priority tasks outlined in other chapters require action along two general lines: (1) a relatively rapid federal budget expansion during the period 1961-1964 to achieve the additional *quantitative* output adequate to the challenge confronting us; (2)

simultaneously, a long-range program of monetary, tax and other reforms to effect *qualitative* improvement in our productive capacity for a sustained national effort.

The U.S. Potential for Raising the Level of Effort

At this point we are not considering what the United States *should* do in defense, foreign aid or any other field. Nor are we here concerned with what is feasible and desirable as to military, technological or other specific programs. We will confine ourselves to one topic only: What are the economic limits on likely strategies? *If* large new programs—be they military, foreign aid or domestic programs—are developed and adopted, how far and how rapidly can our economy expand?

A review of the United States economic performance in two recent emergencies—the Korean War and World War II—are relevant guidelines. These two conflicts were emergencies of the traditional military type, situations in which the American people traditionally support large governmental expenditures and tighter public controls. The protracted conflict, too, confronts us with a permanent emergency, albeit one that too many Americans have not yet recognized.

A review of the two historical lessons readiest at hand provides perspective for estimating in terms of the available labor force, productivity increases, levels of governmental and private expenditures, the rate at which America's economy can grow. We shall then consider the implications of alternative domestic programs; needs for controls to restrict individual choices; the implications for our standard of living, and optimum procedures for financing expanded strategic programs. In short, how can our economy be used most effectively as an instrument of public policy?

First, the Korean period:[6] From 1950 to 1953, government expenditures for goods and services rose by almost $50 billion,[7] from one-seventh of the GNP to a quarter, almost all in the federal sector. Concurrently, GNP rose by $60 billion—a rate of 5 per cent per year. Personal consumption went up 3 per cent a year, and more than

[6] This analysis of the U.S. mobilization effort in the two wars is elaborated in Appendix A.

[7] Throughout this discussion, the data are given in "1959 dollars" to eliminate the intervening effects of inflation.

1 per cent per capita after allowing for population growth. Private investment grew at a lower rate than it otherwise would have, but it grew nevertheless. Direct economic controls were instituted by the government, but subsequent events proved most of them unnecessary.

Next, the World War II picture: In three years, 1941 to 1944, total government expenditures including federal, rose by some $125 billion[8] but the GNP increase was only $90 billion, representing a 10 per cent annual increase. Private consumption continued to rise, even on a per capita basis, except in 1942. But the prewar rate of private domestic investment was curtailed by 50 per cent. By 1944 the proportion of government expenditure was about half the GNP.

In both World War II and the Korean War, the economy grew primarily by net additions to the labor force. Despite the fact that the one followed a major depression and the other a recession, in each case more new workers were added than the number of unemployed rehired. Housewives, early retired workers and young people normally outside the labor market swelled the workers' ranks. And in each case, increased productivity per worker accounted for two-fifths of the nation's production growth.

Since 1945, our GNP, measured in constant prices, has been increasing at an annual rate of about 3.5 per cent. Rising employment has accounted for 1.1 per cent of this increase with the remainder attributed to greater productivity per worker.

During the 1960's, with an unemployment ratio holding steady at 5 per cent, we can expect employment to rise 1.75 per cent annually and productivity some 2.75 per cent. This conservative estimate of 4.5 per cent growth rate across the entire production board begs the vital question of its apportionment between strategically important capital accumulation and expansion of consumer goods and services.

Government economic programs in this coming decade might be scaled against our selected examples. Those equivalent to the 1950-1953 effort would not invoke direct economic controls; but programs comparable to current Soviet allocations might necessitate temporary controls.

Under the conditions of increased demand postulated in the first

[8] Figures also in 1959 dollars.

case, at least an additional 0.75 per cent employment increase may be anticipated annually as well as 0.5 per cent increase in productivity. This would indicate 5.75 per cent annual growth rate. The stimulus of the second and larger program might expand employment 3 per cent annually (as it did during the Korean War) accompanied by a 4 per cent annual increase in per capita productivity.[9] These factors in combination would result in a 7 per cent growth rate, higher than most estimates of Soviet progress. If we could achieve this rate within the next three or four years, shifting our resources to strategically significant areas, Soviet timetables for overtaking and surpassing the American economy would be drastically upset if not wholly invalidated.

A forecast of funds required for national programming would obviously be extremely useful during the sixties in determining how increased demands could be met and what burdens they would place on our society in 1970.

Unfortunately, no one can say with any degree of certitude what our security expenditures should be in 1970. Exploiting an unexpected technological breakthrough might mean spending twenty or thirty billion dollars in a hurry. In the face of all contingencies, neat and orderly ten-year blueprints are out of the question, as the frequency with which Five- and Seven-Year Plans go awry attests. The economic process does not lend itself to meticulous, extended planning.

Nevertheless, the current critical situation leaves little choice but to project our strategic requirements on a tentative basis. Gearing the national effort to a partial mobilization of our national resources suggests an extraordinary effort during 1961-1964 to raise our national programs by 30-50 per cent. This spurt might then be somewhat relaxed in the period 1965-1970, though still sufficient to keep the budget in step with the increase of our GNP until our output for vital security programs is at least double what it is today. Present spending for all strategic purposes approximates $50 billion.[10] By

[9] Increased demand alone, of course, in the form of an expanded federal budget will not assure such an annual increase in per capita productivity. A steady rate of industrial modernization will require concomitant monetary and tax reforms.

[10] This figure includes not only "National Security" and "International" expenditures, but also some items tucked away in "General Government Operating Expenses," "Agriculture," "Natural Resources" and so on.

1964, it should range between $67 and $75 billion or, perhaps, even higher. By 1970, when our GNP will be approaching $800 billion ($505 billion in 1960), our strategic expenditures might well be at least $100 billion. The total outlay on goods and services, including all our domestic programs, would be in the neighborhood of $175 billion. Staggering as the figures appear, these projections are no more impressive than is our latent productive prowess.

In the absence of a detailed governmental study—and such a study is overdue—one can hazard only the roughest estimates of what will be needed in the period 1961-1964. But it is possible to indicate high-priority areas. The largest increase will undoubtedly have to be in military weapons production and military-technological research and development.[11] These two closely related sectors of the budget are the most crucial. A well-conceived R. & D. program can lead, however, to substantial cuts in procurement costs. We must assume, for the present analysis, that coherent strategic doctrines, a deeper comprehension of modern technological problems, and improved organization will keep pace with increased production. Higher expenditures are called for to maintain a nuclear deterrent second to none; to develop our technological defense capabilities; to improve our military posture (especially our conventional and irregular warfare forces) for dealing with the intermediate range of communist challenges; to develop adequate continental defense, both active and passive; to modernize our foreign military assistance program and keep it up to date during the next decade; to gain and maintain a decisive lead in the technology of outer space.

Our expenditures for international development aid should be doubled (i.e., from $2.2 to at least $4.5 billions), provided that our industrialized allies raise their current aid efforts commensurately. This is a feasible goal, both in terms of our own capabilities and the economic absorptive capacity of the underdeveloped areas. An increase of this magnitude would have a material impact upon our friends abroad. It should be closely linked to increasing private investment and to a further consolidation of trade ties between the underdeveloped areas and the industrial nations of the Free World.

[11] The U.S. government will probably continue to budget research and development programs as expenditures rather than as investments, even though a strong case can be made out for the latter alternative since research and development makes an important contribution to the nation's social overhead capital in the development of knowledge, tooling, technical processes and skills.

In the sphere of psychological-political strategy, the primary requirement is not so much technical equipment as an improved idea-content of our programs and a more adroit political approach to the peoples of the world. Nonetheless, we shall need additional facilities for waging the global ideological battle more effectively (e.g., an expanded network of powerful transmitters abroad). Books, magazines, libraries and information centers, motion pictures, radio and TV programs, student exchanges and international cultural missions of various sorts (such as theatrical and orchestral tours) cost a great deal of money. There is no reason why the United States should ever allow itself to be outdone or even equaled in this field of endeavor.

Military, technological, foreign aid and political-psychological programs—these by no means complete the list of necessary projects. A number of others must be also considered. An expanded program of civil defense alone could be enormously expensive, depending upon the type of civil defense chosen. But before funds could be efficiently spent here scientific investigation of various civil defense possibilities seems mandatory.[12]

Another goal, important for strategic as well as social reasons, is the qualitative improvement of higher education in the United States. While not a direct federal responsibility, loans to students and special internship programs for teachers can do a great deal to encourage needed changes.

It is impossible, at present, to place a price tag on the programs discussed above. Their enumeration, however, should make it clear that a proposal for a 33-50 per cent rise in the strategic sectors of the budget by 1964 is not even a remote kin to schemes for "priming the pump." Every additional dollar spent can be put to good use.

Inflation, varying in intensity, has continuously plagued the U.S. economy for years. Since the Korean War, it has continued despite the gradual decline of the real federal government expenditures and of the share of all government in the total economy. Continued decline in the government share of the economy may restrict the growth of GNP to the 3.5 per cent average of the postwar years

[12] Herman Kahn of the RAND Corporation has suggested, for example, that the U.S. should spend about $200 million over a period of two or three years just on the preliminary phases of a civil defense program—research, development, analysis, planning and design.

at best and, more probably, to the 2½-3 per cent average since the Korean War period.

Without new programs there will be gross under-utilization of our resources, continued growth of unemployment and a real threat of recession.[13] The only countervailing development on the horizon is a drastic reduction in the length of the work week. Such a reduction might occur under the pressure of unemployment, probably accompanied by painful industrial strife. Unemployment and the threat of an actual recession would bring about tax cuts and consequent government deficit spending to "restore economic health." Unfortunately, tax cuts and deficits sufficient to forestall a recession might engender a "depression psychology" which would speed rather than slow the slide downhill. Along this road, there seems to be no escape from our dilemma.

As an alternative let us suppose that larger programs were undertaken in the service of a comprehensive national strategy while government expenditures grew at the 4.5 per cent rate that obtains in the private sector of the economy.[14] If taxes were maintained at current rates,[15] the continued growth of the economy would provide steadily rising government revenues. It is likely that the most rapid phases of the build-up of government expenditures would be accompanied by temporary deficits, for increased expenditures would precede the growth of revenues. Government policy for handling such deficits could control inflationary influences. Government borrowing procedures that minimize the net increase in the nation's stock of money and prevent credit inflation (a possible concomitant of its own spending activities) could restrict inflation to less than that of the post-Korean years. Continued unemployment at the 5 per cent rate assumed in this hypothesis would also operate against inflationary pressures.

The inflation accompanying a 4.5 per cent growth rate under the conditions described above would not be intolerable. National well-being improves as the economy grows in terms of real goods and services. The twenty-year rise in GNP from 1939, for example,

[13] Cf. the second column of Table IV in the Appendix.
[14] Cf. Model A in the Appendix.
[15] *Average* tax rates, without prejudice to the possibility of tax reforms that should be undertaken to strengthen the economy and support our over-all strategic objectives. These will be discussed later.

constituted a two-thirds rise of real income, and only one-third of it was due to inflation.[16]

True enough, all inflation pinches fixed-income groups: the salaried professions, pensioners and government bond holders. But their plight is subject to specific remedies, which are cheaper than policies that slow economic growth and thus work to the long-range disadvantage of all the people.

There is no question but that inflation—a devious debasement of the coinage—is an evil which distributes its burden inequitably as it corrodes the real income of everyone, the government included. It dilutes the value of the dollars budgeted for defense. It can undermine a nation's international trade position if foreign competitors do not suffer from similar trends. Yet the United States is not compelled to live with steady, though moderate inflation as if it were a law unto itself.

It is absurd, however, to sacrifice economic growth on the grounds that it brings inflation automatically. The bulk of our peacetime inflation was not caused by economic growth per se, but rather, as the Joint Economic Committee of the Congress found, by a combination of factors: e.g., increasing steel and machine tools prices, combined with the downward rigidity of all prices.[17] Inflation is not an invincible foe. Ways can be found for preventing it from snowballing while we proceed with the programs to ensure our survival as a free society.

This concept should also be tested against conditions attending a more rapid national growth rate and coincident rise in government expenditure; say, to the Korean period's level of effort, where the government share approaches one-quarter of the total economy.[18] The average level of federal taxation during the Korean War

[16] *The Incidents of Inflation: or Who Gets Hurt,* Study Paper No. 7 prepared for the Joint Economic Committee of the Congress, November, 1959, p. 26.

[17] Downward rigidity is caused by the fact that, when the composition of demand changes, certain prices tend to increase and these increases are transmitted throughout the economy. Even industries confronted by a sagging demand experience rising costs and hence cannot lower prices. It has been estimated that the per cent of change in the wholesale price index caused by the rise in steel prices was 31 per cent in the period 1947-1953 and 52 per cent from 1953-1958. Cf. *Steel and the Postwar Deflation* and *An Analysis of the Inflation in Machinery Prices* (one booklet), Study Papers Nos. 2 and 3 prepared for the Joint Economic Committee of the Congress, November, 1959, p. 12.

[18] Cf. Model B in Appendix A.

was about 10 per cent above that now in effect. A return to the Korean level of effort should be accompanied by taxation slightly higher than prevailed from 1951 to 1953. (This should not be taken as a plea for an increase in the progression rate, for, as we shall show presently, there is a more promising approach to the taxation problem.) Tax increases, if properly timed, can help to check deficits during the build-up period and hold deficits within bounds during an emergency expansion of programs. Tax increases alone can put our national strategy for the long haul on a more or less pay-as-you-go basis. In the art of public finance, timing is of the essence. In a few years, the growth rate will reduce or eliminate the need for further increases in tax rates. Meanwhile, if we can keep the federal deficit within manageable proportions, a minimum set of economic controls will suffice. Whatever controls are instituted should be progressively initiated when they are needed, never imposed in advance of necessity. This does not imply that thorough *planning* for imposing a wide range of controls should be left to last-minute adjudication.

This country would not encounter serious problems until the government sector of the economy approached the proportion of one-third of the GNP.[19] Such a level of government expenditures for goods and services would amount to over $150 billion—an effort level comparable to or perhaps exceeding that now being made by the Soviet Union.[20] To accomplish this degree of federal expansion within the framework of a balanced budget would require federal taxes some 15-20 per cent above those of the Korean period, or 20-30 per cent above those of today, a prospect which makes politicians blanch. Except in wartime, such precipitous tax increases are politically unacceptable. Hence it would be necessary to raise the debt limit and to finance a large part of the increased expenditures

[19] Cf. Model C in Appendix A.

[20] The immediate reaction of many Americans to proposals for a substantial expansion of our defense budget is to argue that military, foreign aid and outer space expenditures are "unproductive" and "wasteful." Yet such expenditures *are* productive if they achieve their purpose of deterring attack and preserving the nation's freedom. Looking at the question purely from a business standpoint, we might compare our whole national economy to a $2,000 billion investment and our security outlays to the annual premiums on a comprehensive insurance policy (fire, catastrophe, accident, liability). If, on top of this, life insurance for the whole American population were added, the figures used in this model seem reasonable indeed.

out of deficits. Stronger inflationary pressures would be generated than in the first two models. Direct price and credit controls, plus government allocation of materials, would be required. Even these could not halt the march of inflation altogether, but they could prevent that *acceleration* of inflation which feeds on itself and obstructs the very programs that invoked it.

Under a national effort of the magnitude postulated in this case, the U.S. would simply have to accept controls that find their warrant in the logic of strategic necessity. People who are determined to preserve values basic to their beliefs do not cavil at temporary restrictions or sacrifices. Not even a $150-billion federal budget by 1964 would entail unbearable hardship or real sacrifice. The private economy would continue to grow in real terms, i.e., GNP gains would not be wholly consumed by inflation and taxes. Americans would still go on buying new cars, color TV's, stereo sets, and all the other things which have made so pleasant the life of abundance with freedom and that provide much of the incentive for individual contributions to the growth we are looking toward.

"National Bankruptcy"

The specter of "national bankruptcy" is more frequently invoked than defined. Loaded with emotional ballast, it conjures up images of economies at a standstill, of governments and currencies collapsing after exhausting wars. There is not the slightest connection between such calamitous situations and that confronting the United States under the conditions discussed above. Never in history has inflation, in periods of full employment and high rates of growth, "run away" so long as it was kept in rein by sensible fiscal and monetary policies.

A nation that fully employs its people and other resources, steadily increases private as well as public consumption of goods and services, and takes prudent measures of direct and indirect economic control to insure the accomplishment of its objectives is not going broke.

In the great depression of the thirties, there was no inflation. On the contrary, deflation was one of the major problems facing the nation. With up to fourteen million unemployed—28 per cent of the labor force—America came perilously close to bankruptcy.

The size of the national debt is often taken as a portent of bankruptcy. In 1932, when the national debt was less than $20 billion, or almost exactly one-third of the GNP, some alarmists told us that we stood on the brink of national bankruptcy. In four years, the debt doubled to over $38 billion, or 47 per cent of the GNP while, concurrently, GNP rose 41 per cent and unemployment declined 44 per cent.[21] Few historians dispute the fact that we were much better off and much farther from bankruptcy in 1936 than in 1932. And today, we find much higher levels of national debt not only tolerable, but compatible with much higher levels of employment and general prosperity.

It should be pointed out that the government debt has steadily declined since the end of World War II (when it stood at 130 per cent of GNP) in proportion to the size of the economy, although private debt has kept pace with, and in some categories has even exceeded, the growth of our economy. Government indebtedness was down to about 100 per cent of GNP by 1948. Today, twelve years later, it amounts to less than 60 per cent. While any increase in this percentage should be weighed carefully, it neither implies unmanageable problems, nor should be viewed with such awe as to prevent us from action when action is necessary. Assuming only a 4.5 per cent rate of growth for our GNP (as in our first model above), it would be possible for us to increase the national debt by as much as five billion dollars a year and still witness a drop during the period 1960-1970 in the ratio of national debt to GNP.

The fear of government debt appears to be based on misconceptions as to its nature. Comparisons of government debt to that of individuals often overlook the fact that an individual's safe debt limit is always evaluated in relation to his income *and assets.* While the U.S. government has tremendous assets, as do the state and local governments, government accounting practices do not maintain a balance sheet. We have available, therefore, only the partial comparison: debt to income, best measured in the national case by gross national product. Moreover, the annual cost of some eight to nine billion dollars for servicing the national debt is less than 2 per cent of GNP.

Nations have paid proportionately greater war debts and reparations in the past and achieved prosperity. But we do not have to

[21] GNP in 1932—$60 billion; in 1936—$85 billion.

pay this charge in external tribute. On the contrary, the interest on the debt is paid to citizens out of taxes collected from citizens—a transfer payment, involving circulation of money among individuals in the country but no net drain on the national goods and services output and consumption.

Should the national debt expand faster than our GNP, our financial stability might be disrupted, burdensome frictions created and the growth of our national economy inhibited. If we commit ourselves to a Korean War level of effort during the sixties—and this most likely will be the necessary level—we could run sizable deficits for a few years without allowing the federal debt to exceed its present 60 per cent ratio to the GNP. On the basis of the 5.8 per cent rate of GNP growth assumed in Model B (Cf. Appendix A), the present debt could, in the first year, be increased by seventeen billion dollars and by larger amounts in succeeding years. Such increases, approximately enough to finance Korean level strategic programs, could not by any stretch of the fiscal imagination be said to bring the United States near the verge of "national bankruptcy."

Pending a thorough revision of our tax structure (discussed later in this chapter), it appears that we shall have to lean more toward the notion of deficit financing than of "pay-as-you-go" for our strategic programs from 1961 to 1964. Increasing the progression rates on taxes could have more harmful consequences for our economy today than a modest rise in the national debt.

Conviction that, in prosperity, the federal government should budget an annual surplus of revenues over expenditures to reduce the public debt is economically sound; but these are not normal times. The gravity of the international situation, combined with the fact that for the past seven years our strategic expenditures have steadily declined in relation to our GNP, now make a partial mobilization of our national resources imperative. This entails an immediate and substantial rise in federal expenditures as it always has in past national emergencies. There are two methods of financing such a rise—increasing taxes or increasing the national debt. At least for the next three-year period, heavier reliance upon the latter is the preferable course.

In order to minimize the inflationary impact of governmental borrowing, it will be necessary to make sure that the government's action does not substantially increase the nation's money or credit supply. Government should limit its borrowing as much as possible to individual savers and firms other than banks. For this purpose, it may be advisable for the government to issue a special tax-credit bond—i.e., a bond with an attractive premium attached for those who will hold it until maturity and then turn it in for tax credits. Whatever funds the government borrows from banks should be money the banks stand ready to lend to individuals and firms. Federal Reserve controls can be utilized to curb credit inflation and restrict the private capital supply. This involves hardships; yet hardships of some kind or another are the price we pay for *any* economic policy.

Loss of Freedoms?

The charge that in mobilizing for economic competition we may win the battle but lose the war—that we may lose in the Cold War the freedom which we would fight to preserve in a hot war—appears to rest on two main arguments.

First, direct controls—materials allocation, price ceilings, credit restrictions—will impose undemocratic restraints on our way of life, which, once imposed, might be very difficult to remove.

Second, and perhaps more basically, the larger the area of government participation in the economy, the more decisions would be made by bureaucrats rather than individual entrepreneurs and consumers.

The problem of direct controls enters significantly only into the construction of our third hypothesis above, which envisages expenditures massive enough to stay ahead of any possible Soviet efforts to outdo us in the military, foreign aid or any other field related to our national security. Such expenditures would strain at the peacetime limits of our resources. Hence during the initial phase of rapid build-up, private demand would have to be restrained and priority given to government programs. Controls would have to dam the inflationary tide in order to protect some of the population against severe hardship. Controls, however, would be temporary, since the government expenditures, once the build-up has been completed, would be expected to level off, or at most increase moderately from year to year, while the private sector could be permitted to grow much more rapidly than the 2.7 per cent shown on Table V (page 417). Increased productivity could easily meet increased private demand.

The ease and speed with which temporary direct controls can be rescinded has been amply demonstrated by the experiences of World War II and the Korean War. This is not to say that controls are proof against abuse. Eternal vigilance is still the price of liberty. If controls prove necessary, we must once again see to it that they do not exceed minimum requirements and that they are administered efficiently and equitably. Materials allocation, rationing and price controls do not imperil democratic institutions so long as they are kept to their fundamental purpose: to insure fair shares to all.

We have in the past devised many means for insuring the democratic administration of controls. Among these might be mentioned local rationing boards, the decentralization of price control, the elaborate procedures for adjustment of appeals under price control, and the representation of diverse interests before the Requirements Committee that administered the Controlled Materials Plan. These devices were not perfect, and careful attention should certainly be given to these and other mechanisms for insuring justice and freedom under temporary controls.

The second danger which we are told threatens us is government regimentation of private business: It is argued that the larger the share of national resources at the disposition of the government, the less is the scope for free economic decisions by private citizens. Again, there can be no question but that we must guard against this danger. Government has no claim to a dominant role in fostering economic growth, nor are government servants possessed of unique insights and skills which would qualify them as the arbiters of the nation's business. In this study, however, we are concerned with problems which, of their essence, must be attacked primarily by the people collectively rather than as individuals. Individuals do not and cannot make effective decisions to arm against aggression by foreign nations or to explore space. They cannot provide massive aid to underdeveloped countries (although much more can be done by private enterprise to assist underdeveloped countries and our government should seek ways of encouraging private investment as a substitute for direct government aid).

Our models of potential expansion were designed to show what is economically feasible, not what the national objective should be.

It is necessary to determine what we can afford to spend on meritorious government programs, but their worth does not lie in our ability to pay for it. Every national program should (1) be held to the minimum scope necessary to achieve the given objective and (2) receive the minimum financial support necessary for its execution. In brief, each program should be administered economically and efficiently.

Longer-Run Reforms

Increased government spending on a large-scale program of national security will neither wreck our economy nor subvert our institutions. To the contrary, it will underwrite our commitments abroad, contribute to international stability and create that climate of confidence which fosters an increase of world trade. The costs are great, but our gains will be greater. Increased government spending is a means to this end—and to no other. The cynical notion that an increased arms budget should serve to head off a depression or ward off unemployment is the first cousin of Marxist theory. It has no place in the rational management of a free economy.

The preceding section has emphasized the need, in times of government expansion, to guard constantly against undue inflation, inefficiency and direct controls that are neither necessary nor temporary.

Are there, in fact, means of achieving national aims without expanding the role of government? By definition, the answer must be no. As noted above, this study addresses problems which are essentially national and governmental in their nature, although private enterprise plays an important role in civil defense and aid to underdeveloped areas. But the size of government and government expenditures can be kept within tolerable limits.

The net social cost, too, can be kept down. To the extent that the cost of public programs can be met out of additional income (which accrued to the national economy because of the budgetary increase) these public programs can be carried out without social cost, for government outlays create jobs for hitherto unemployed workers and start up idle machines. If, however, government-stimulated economic expansion has to be stoked by longer hours of work, then the social "cost," sacrificed leisure, is low indeed for the goals to be won.

Few will deny that a certain amount of lethargy, wastefulness and productive "fat" impair the workings of our economic system and its ability to compete internationally. Symptomatic is the increasing production of goods and services which the consumer either does not want or does not need; our proclivity for needless styling and obsolescence (annual modifications of automobile design being the handiest example); the rank complex of sales promotion, public relations, advertising, labor union featherbedding, farm subsidies and expense accounts—all include mischievous, wasteful practices which increase costs. A rising chorus of criticism deplores the steady deterioration of work discipline and sense of personal responsibility —in the federal bureaucracy, in corporation offices, on the assembly line, among the professions and in the university classroom. Undoubtedly, these phenomena reflect profound trends within our materialist culture which transcend the scope of economic analysis; but economic analysis cannot ignore them.

Anyone familiar with our political scene will stand in respectful awe before the difficulties which beset the enactment of sound national programs: the appropriation of funds; the passage of necessary tax bills; a debt ceiling hike. Yet these difficulties are relatively paltry when compared with the obstacles that stand in the way of improving the efficiency of the economy as a whole. We must sharpen both edges of the scissors. We must remove the sources of waste in our economy. The battle against waste is, indeed, the indispensable companion piece of any sustained effort nourished by large government expenditures. If the causes of waste are not corrected, waste begets waste. The spectacle of wasteful government, wasteful enterprise and careless labor undermines the moral support of national policy. Weakening of the moral fibre spawns abuses such as tax evasion and degeneration of national programs to mere subsidies for the greedy, the lazy and the inefficient.

Major objectives of long-run qualitative reforms should include: (1) a greater willingness of individuals and business firms to save more and invest more within a framework of expanded incentives; (2) a pattern of taxation, trade and regulatory policies more conducive to fostering competition, trade and the growth of capital; (3) legislation encouraging depreciation write-offs in key industries to promote the modernization and increase of producer durables; (4) wage, cost and price relationships consistent with expanded output and trade requirements; (5) reduction of unproductive overhead in the American economy; (6) a national patents policy which will encourage a steady flow of technological innovations and permit their full utilization by private industry to cut costs and improve quality all along the line.

The United States has achieved the "affluent society" in its postwar growth. Pursuit of the cult of personal consumption has been well nigh single-minded. While distribution of the fruits of affluence has been more egalitarian than in past history, it has not always been equitable. Too many prizes have gone to the most nimble in the competition for special privilege, where equity is no more than the fortuitious result of inequities offsetting one another.

Increasing reliance on the federal government for services of all kinds has meant inevitably increasing the tax rates—and the incorporation of special privileges into the tax laws. Under high levels of corporate taxation, the expense account, for example, becomes a cheap way for businesses to raise the compensation of individuals and an attractive way for individuals to accept additional compensation without incurring taxes. The expense account may not represent a large addition to production costs, and does not always (or perhaps not even most of the time) represent economically wasteful activity. Yet great is the temptation—and not a few succumb to it—to transform the expense account into a device for the avoidance of taxes, a form of institutionalized privilege detrimental to economic health.

Our income tax structure has in fact become a hodgepodge of special exemptions. Many preferential provisions may be proper and defensible on the grounds that they foster incentive, boost morale or promote beneficial types of activity (such as research). But their stipulations often tend to reflect the relative political strength of lobbies rather than the intrinsic merits of the groups and activities favored.

Whatever period of grace lies ahead, it is of the utmost importance that we use it wisely to resolve a central problem: to put our strategic programs on a pay-as-you-go basis. We can move toward this goal through the enactment of long overdue tax reforms.

Our present tax structure, last overhauled in the 1930's and then influenced by the notion that the public interest is truly safeguarded only when the profits of enterprise are vitiated by overtaxation, no longer jibes with the sophisticated insights of modern economics. More important still, it stunts rapid economic growth.

Clearly, the time has come to reform the tax structure as a whole, rather than patch it up with those bits and pieces which have no warrant other than political convenience. Revision of our tax system has been on the legislative agenda for a long time; but until now no significant steps in this direction have been taken. No one would argue that the task is politically easy, but tax reform holds one of the keys that will unlock our economic potential.

There is serious danger that further increases in the progression rate would have a deleterious effect upon the incentives of American citizens and consequently upon the growth rate of the national economy. Our present tax policy makes it more difficult to raise our growth rate, especially in the strategically important areas of industry. Basic tax rate reform, therefore, is a must of national fiscal policy during the next three years.

"Closing the loopholes" in our tax laws would add substantially to the sources of revenue. Appropriate measures will redound to the public good—provided they are carried out as part of a thorough overhauling of the tax edifice. Within the last decade, the list of exclusions, deductions, exemptions and special tax credits, many contrary to basic principles of tax equity, has grown steadily longer. The result has been a serious narrowing of the tax base. Thus, for example, the United States imposes rates ranging from 20 to 91 per cent on incomes—and manages to raise by the feat of arbitrariness a tax revenue that averages only 10 per cent of total income.[22]

Loopholes which encourage "legally dishonest" practices should be plugged immediately. The withholding system should be applied to dividends, and code provisions for reporting income from interest and other sources should be policed more effectively. Some of the preferential provisions and even some of the so-called loopholes in our tax laws (such as liberal interpretations of what constitutes capital gains or legitimate expenses) reflect the lawmakers'

[22] Testimony of Joseph Pechman of the Committee for Economic Development, Hearings on Income Tax Revision, House Committee on Ways and Means, 86th Congress, 1st Session, November-December, 1959, pp. 111-112.

dilemma: The Congress, while it feels compelled to subscribe *in principle* to the concept of progressive tax rates, must simultaneously build into the law ameliorative devices which, *in practice,* will prevent the stifling of initiative. Pending needed tax reforms of a more fundamental character, the retention of some of these devices will be essential to continued economic growth. But a general revision of our tax policy ought to move toward the inclusion of every dollar of income in the tax base. Ideally, all preferences ought to be eliminated except those which can be justified on grounds of strategic value.[23] The American tax system should be designed to raise revenue for the government and to advance our national strategic interests by fostering needed economic growth. It should have no other social purposes.

During the next decade, we shall depend mainly on economic growth for broadening our tax base. The growth of GNP will be more significant for the expansion of government revenue-raising capabilities than any efforts to incorporate into the tax base items which are now excluded or deductible (although we favor such efforts). If we achieve a growth rate of 5 per cent, the personal tax base alone would be augmented, during the next eight years, by $120 billion. But if we are to reach even this modest rate of growth in GNP and sustain a substantially higher rate in the vital sectors of industry, we must gear our tax policy to the requirements of economic growth in a free enterprise society.

Several experts who testified in the hearings on tax revision before the House Committee on Ways and Means in late 1959,[24] recommended that the progression rates on personal income be made less steep. William Fellner of Yale estimated that a 15 per cent rate reduction in each bracket would cost the government only about six billion dollars. This loss could be made up almost immediately in several different ways—by closing loopholes, policing unreported income more intensively or devising other types of taxes.

[23] What is required, of course, is equity, not strict equality. Individuals and firms will always have to be grouped in categories, and various distinctions will have to be drawn. Persons and business firms that fall in the same category should be accorded equal treatment.

[24] Among them were Joseph Sneed of Cornell University, Neil Jacoby of the University of California, William Fellner of Yale University, Roswell Magill, President of the Tax Foundation, and Joseph Pechman of the Committee for Economic Development.

Fellner himself proposed a 7 per cent tax on approximately 40 per cent of the national consumption expenditure, excluding foodstuffs, rent and other items that matter to low-income budgets. Such a tax would more than compensate for the revenues lost by lowering the progression rates. Meanwhile, the higher income brackets would be able to save more, thus augmenting the supply of venture capital—of which there is now a serious shortage.

It is not our purpose to suggest the specifics of tax reform. We are convinced, however, that any major addition to government revenues which may be deemed necessary during the next few years will necessitate levying higher consumption taxes. Higher income taxes probably will not materially raise the total "take." Taxes on consumption heighten the individual's sense of fiscal responsibility as he makes his spending-and-saving choices. In contrast, higher progression rates of taxation on income cut into money which would otherwise be saved and invested. This is a prime consideration today: Our population is expanding, and an average of fourteen thousand dollars must be invested in order to create a new job. At present, our high tax progression rates do not leave any "elbow room" for raising additional federal revenues quickly without dangerously weakening incentive. We conclude, therefore, that progression rates should be reduced and consumption taxes be raised.

Taxation of industrial corporations, too, stands in dire need of reform. The considerations that apply to the encouragement of individuals, hold *a fortiori* for corporations. The tax rate on reinvested profits ought to be reduced. Two particular changes in the tax code deserve immediate attention: (1) Industrial depreciation allowances should be liberalized. (2) The formation of new industrial firms should be eased by a reduction of the tax burden. A brief comment on each of these recommendations is in order.

The United States is today one of the most backward among the world's leading industrial nations in depreciation policies and practices. It is plagued by a high rate of obsolescence of basic productive equipment. About half of our machine tools and related productive items (nearly $100 billion worth in all) are outmoded. Worse still, unless we alter drastically our write-off policy, the obsolescence rate in the United States will become even steeper in the sixties. If we are to retain the technological leadership of the Free World, or even remain abreast of our industrial competitors, we must make adequate provision for replacement in the fullest sense of the word. This means that depreciation can no longer be carried over 33⅓ years when most modern machines become obsolete in about ten years or so. Britain, Sweden, Denmark, the Netherlands, Japan and Canada have all recognized this fact. It is essential that we too extend the meaning of "true costs" to cover the replacement of machinery not merely when it is actually worn-out but when it should give way to productive equipment of greater efficiency. Technological obsolescence is now more influential than wear and tear in world economic competition.

Our existing tax structure penalizes new industrial firms. Is the only lesson of economic history that we do not learn its lessons? Historically, it is not only the expanded operations and production innovations of existing large corporations but also the ventures—often unconventional and seemingly heedless ventures—of newly created businesses that foster economic growth. More than ever before, economic growth feeds on technological innovation. Memorable advances have been set in motion by the ingenuity of small enterprises. Tax policy, instead of impeding their efforts to establish a foothold in seemingly closed terrain, should give them their chance to grow. Reforms designed to encourage new ventures could be adopted with relatively little and only temporary loss of tax income. (Special credit mechanisms might also be used to advantage.)

But the strategic economic growth vital to America's future is not just a matter of uninhibited productive increases across the whole range of industry, without regard to quality. The strategic posture of the United States might be weakened by a prodigal rise in the output of basic industries, since most of the production gains might go into goods which satisfy superfluous consumer wants. Pious generalizations notwithstanding, the fate of the world will not be decided by a standard of living contest. The protracted conflict between the free and the slave states is essentially a power struggle. Its many dimensions are all measured in real power—military, industrial, psychological and ideological.

A prime desideratum, therefore, is tax reforms to insure growth in strategically significant industries. New firms will have to enter the field in metallics, intermetallics, electronics, nucleonics, plastics, ceramics, fuels, engines, machine tools and computers, to mention only a few of the more obvious industries. One avenue for promoting new enterprise in strategic fields might be new-firm tax exemption, perhaps for five years or so. A more reasonable alternative (to eliminate the inefficient) might be the allowance of additional rapid write-off privileges, including liberalized carry-forward provisions for any losses incurred in the early years. Congress made a start in this direction during 1959 by allowing a twenty-thousand-dollar equipment write-off for small business.[25]

Conclusions

A fully employed, purposive Soviet economy, bent on overtaking the U.S., appears, at present, to be gaining in the race. An underemployed United States, lacking a positive strategy, is lagging.

But the underemployment of the resources of the U.S. economy can be a source of strength. Our economy possesses the flexibility and reserves to support any and all strategies which lie in the national interest.

The United States and the Soviet Union are currently spending about equal amounts of resources on national security. The Soviet Union could increase this amount at the rate of about 6 per cent a year without changing the relative allocation of resources to security purposes. United States national security expenditures have been fairly constant in recent years, and actually have declined in relation to a rising GNP. If the United States were to hold constant its relative allocation of resources to government as a whole (20 per cent of GNP), an additional seven or eight billion dollars annually could be devoted, by 1964, to national security purposes.

[25] There are precedents galore for granting special tax privileges to certain industries. An outstanding example was the "Tax Amortization" program of the World War II and Korean War periods. "Certificates of Necessity" were issued to private firms making investments in support of military programs. These certificates permitted rapid write-offs of the investment during the period in which the investors could be sure that there would be a requirement for the product, thus insuring them against the risk of cessation of government demand once the plant was built. But special amortization privileges, which may be necessary for designated defense industries, should not be construed as a substitute for a general liberalization of depreciation allowances for American industry as a whole. Only with an across-the-board improvement in efficiency can we strengthen our total international competitive position, reduce outward-flow pressures on our gold supply, strengthen the dollar as the Free World's major currency reserve, and maintain a modernized technological capacity for meeting all international contingencies.

This might be enough to "sharpen the cutting edge" of our defenses, but would not suffice to keep pace with the Soviet Union if the latter continued heavy allocations to military and other security purposes.

A bolder program, restoring the relative allocation to government of the Korean period (24 per cent), could provide, by 1964, almost forty billion dollars of additional resources. This should outdistance the best efforts which the Soviet Union can make without abandoning other programs, such as increasing the standard of living of its people. In contrast, such an American effort would probably significantly increase the rate of growth in our economy's private sector. In all probability the United States could perform this amazing feat without imposing stringent direct controls.

If the United States chose to allocate to government functions as large a part of the national product as does the Soviet Union, it could more than treble its expenditures, adding some $95 to $100 billion annually. The United States could reach this level by 1964, devote almost one-third of its resources to government purposes and still keep our economy growing at the average rate of 1945 to 1960.

The unused resources of the American economy are enormous. They can be put to work, far short of an "all-out" war effort, to match and outdo Soviet economic performance. There is no magic in the high rate of increase in Soviet industrial productivity. The United States can attain the same rates and stay ahead of the Soviet Union, if necessary, by a factor of two to one. The United States can take on the Soviet Union in any form of economic competition; as a matter of fact, the United States has the means and more to challenge Soviet competition. A really serious arms race could break the back of the Soviet economy. Nor could the Soviets meet sustained competition in foreign trade or economic assistance to the underdeveloped countries. If the resources, actual and potential, of Western Europe are added to those of the United States, the superiority of the West becomes overwhelming. It seems we have nothing to fear but our fears, oddly alloyed with complacency.

The above discussion has steered clear of advocating any particular program. Every program must be screened carefully and submitted to searching national debate. It should be measured by one yardstick only: its contribution to national security. If it measures up, promises to achieve its objective and has been intelligently planned, then—and only then—does it deserve public support.

In the light of the facts, we can repose our faith in the abiding vigor of the most powerful economy the world has ever known. If we place our trust in the basic values of our people and our free institutions, for which we have fought wars in the past and for which we now fight a Cold War at the ever-present risk of a hot and terrible one, we will pay the economic price of our security as a matter of course. The argument that to do so will bankrupt us is economically fallacious and a poor excuse for inaction.

CHAPTER 11 STRUCTURE FOR STRATEGY

Communist successes owe much to organizational skill. Many competent observers of American national security policy have questioned the efficacy, in the face of this highly organized communist challenge, of our machinery for making and implementing decisions in the area of national security. They ask, for example, have existing mechanisms of government provided a comprehensive approach to the problems of national security policy and the means and methods of their solution? Have these mechanisms succeeded in the vital functions of co-ordinated execution and review of operations? Finally, have the responsible cabinet officials devised dynamic national security policies and projected these policies into the future in a manner which capitalizes fully on available national resources?

Our present National Security Council and its substructure derive directly from the State-War-Navy Co-ordinating Committee (later the State-Army-Navy-Air Force Co-ordinating Committee) established in 1944.

Ferdinand Eberstadt, in a report in 1945 to the Secretary of the Navy, James Forrestal, first proposed the establishment of a National Security Council. Subsequently, President Truman submitted to Congress a proposal for a new Organization for National Security. Congress promulgated the National Security Act of 1947. President Truman fostered its development and growth, and used it in the development of some of his most important foreign policies.

Upon his election, President Eisenhower proceeded to reconstitute the National Security Council, principally by adding to its supporting structure. He created the post of Special Assistant to the President for National Security Affairs, transformed the Senior National

Security Staff into the Planning Board, added to the National Security Council permanent staff, created the Operations Co-ordinating Board and expanded the participation of civilian consultants in the policy-formulation process. (See opposite page for graphical chart of the National Security Council. A description of the 1960 structure of the National Security Council can be found in Appendix B.)[1]

From the establishment of the National Security Council in 1947 to the present day there have been repeated adaptations in our governmental structure for handling national security. The search for a better structure continues. Soviet successes in foreign affairs, military weapons development, propaganda, space exploration and scientific discovery have triggered an ever more insistent and wider demand for improvement in our national security policy-making machinery.

In July, 1959, the Senate unanimously authorized its Committee on Government Operations to establish a Subcommittee on National Policy Machinery. This Subcommittee was not to concern itself with questions of substantive policy or to pass judgment on the manner in which America was waging the Cold War. Rather it was to study the effectiveness of the federal government's organization and procedures. Although good policy-making machinery can never substitute for good leadership, the Senate nevertheless elected to devote considerable attention to the former.

There is both dissatisfaction and impatience with the present national security structure of the government. The dissatisfaction stems from the increasing number of setbacks to our national prestige which have occurred during the last few years. The impatience is directed at the pedestrian pace of our procedures for interagency co-ordination, which do not enable us to respond effectively to the more flexible, aggressive Soviet initiatives.

If, as we have argued in these pages, we are locked in a struggle for survival, then the first task of our government is to organize or reorganize its functions so that its structure in its parts and as a whole responds to the requirements of the all-encompassing protracted conflict. We must test the federal structure by the following basic criteria and principles:

[1] This statement is excerpted from the report *Organizing for National Security* prepared for the Committee on Government Operations, United States Senate, and its Subcommittee on National Policy Machinery, Washington, 1960.

Organizational Structure of the National Security Council

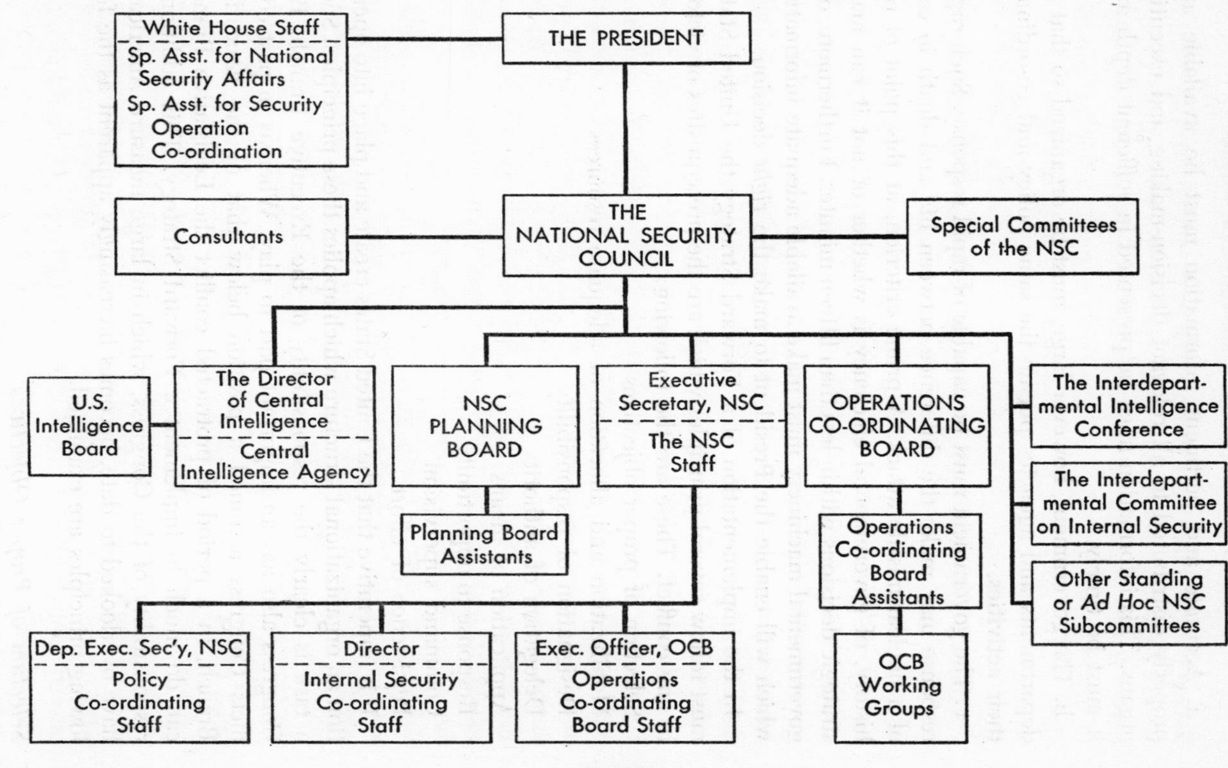

CHART 7

a. Accurate and pertinent information must be available and properly distributed to all relevant decision-making and executive organs. This information must be presented in sufficient depth and it must be timely.

b. The government, however large, must be organized so that all departments and agencies pursue the same policy and co-ordinate their activities.

c. The government must be capable of rapid response. Such rapid response may make the difference between life and death in case of a nuclear-missile attack. A prime criterion, at this point of our history, of governmental efficiency is whether or not it can make strategic decisions within less than fifteen minutes. Furthermore, our governmental machinery must make available adequate information which will enable the President to make the *right* decision.

In the implementation of a Forward Strategy the United States must follow several principles which are the prerequisites of victory in any conflict. These are the following:

Selection of proper objectives
Mobilization and allocation of adequate resources
Designation of responsibility
Delegation of authority
Application of means
Response to opportunity
Command supervision
Persistence of effort

It is imperative that the United States create and place into operation an organizational structure which applies these principles. Such a task is clearly the responsibility of the Executive Branch. But Congress also has an important part to play. Whereas in past conflicts Congress assumed a position below that of the Executive Branch, in a period of protracted conflict the Legislative Branch can do much to implement a Forward Strategy. This additional responsibility of the Congress, which in large measure Americans have overlooked to date, becomes increasingly apparent as the following principles are examined.

Selection of Proper Objectives

U.S. national objectives are officially expressed in National Security Council documents. The "Basic National Policy" paper is reviewed annually by the Council. Classified "Top Secret," it is distributed on a limited basis throughout the Executive Branch. It is the matrix for all subsequent policy planning.

What are the key elements of this national policy? They are fourfold: first, to avoid the catastrophe of general war; second, to weld an allied coalition whose combined strength prevents any further communist expansion; third, to maintain an efficient military establishment, armed with the most modern weapons, capable of deterring or defeating armed aggression anywhere in the world; and fourth, to sustain a sound, vigorous domestic economy. The problem which the United States faces today is not the absence of clear-cut objectives or basic national policy. The problem is how to put this policy to work.

Avoiding war does not mean avoiding conflict. The very presence of two such opposing political systems as democracy and communism on the same stage and in the same act of history makes a continuous state of conflict inevitable. American officials charged with the conduct of national security affairs must take into account not only our long-term objectives, but also the changing currents of history which rarely flow along channels of our choice. Thus, the daily direction of national affairs requires adherence to our principles and at the same time the flexibility of mind to recognize the varying human forces which operate to shape the future of the world. While no one can halt or reverse these forces, they are, nevertheless, susceptible to varying degrees of manipulation. They can often be influenced so that they contribute toward the ultimate attainment of U.S. national objectives. The combination of the intuitive power of recognizing these forces and the art of influencing them is what is so often lacking in our efforts to achieve our basic objectives.

Specifically, it is as we move from these broad national goals to more limited U.S. objectives applicable to geographic regions or countries about the world that we find serious deficiencies. These regional or country objectives as stated in NSC documents tend to be entirely too general to provide useful guidance for our officials in the field. They lack the direct contributory relationship to the achievement of our national objectives that an "intermediate objective" on the battlefield has to the eventual capture of the final objective. They are formulated primarily on the basis of "living with" the situation as it exists, rather than of attempting to turn social, political or economic forces in a specific region or country to the advantage of our over-all political and strategic goals. It is imperative, therefore, that the two principal departments of the government, State and Defense, take prompt steps to insure that "intermediate" regional and country objectives are developed which will contribute directly and specifically to our national global objectives. If this relationship were recognized and applied during the deliberations of both the National Security Council and its supporting Planning Board, the conduct of a national Forward Strategy would inevitably be pursued more aggressively and with far greater success than we have had in the past.

Needless to say, specific programs tailored for particular countries must be related to a long-term campaign for winning the current struggle. We reiterate that victory in the protracted conflict implies the extension of freedom to all peoples who desire it. However, in addition to this general statement of policy provided by the National Security Council and the specific country plans previously alluded to, we will need to develop specific operational programs to enable those charged with weighing our efforts to determine whether or not we are in fact moving forward.

Our intelligence has a vital role to play in the selection of national objectives. By their very nature, national objectives reflect a balance between domestic aims and resources, on one hand, and an estimate of external conditions. Intelligence is a crucial component of our structure for strategy. The Central Intelligence Agency acts as co-ordinator for the other members of the intelligence community (the intelligence arms of State, the Army, Navy and Air Force) in making progress evaluations. But the Agency, although it produces considerable intelligence of its own, has only limited power to reconcile evaluations. National intelligence estimates are prepared under Central Intelligence Agency supervision by the same kind of inter-departmental staff-operator system that prevails in the National Security Council structure as a whole. Its assessor functions thus suffer from the same handicaps of parochial presentation.

The intelligence effort contains three major parts: the collection of raw data; the evaluation of information made up of fact, opinion or hunches; and the presentation of the intelligence forecast to the policy-maker. The U.S. has all the information it needs regarding the noncommunist world. Our evaluation of trends is growing increasingly more sophisticated—although we have failed to anticipate some important Cold War developments. Policy-makers, it seems, have sometimes ignored the message given to them by intelligence experts. For example, the extent of Castro's commitment to communism was known well in advance of the fall of Batista. It was blandly dismissed. The excuse given for this sorry tale is that Castro "betrayed" the Revolution.

We have never displayed an outstanding capacity for or interest in analyzing what we need to know for the formulation of long-range policies. During the early days of the Cold War, the inexperience of America's intelligence community was, perhaps, a valid excuse for this deficiency. But this no longer is sufficient explanation for our frequent failure to anticipate the dynamics of political change, which often render outmoded our elaborate attempts to forecast political trends.

America's military intelligence, as distinct from many of her civilian agencies, has a clearly defined mission: to monitor and assess the military capabilities of foreign nations, and then seek to determine the intentions of their leaders. Unfortunately, the swift march of technology, combined with the restrictions imposed by the Iron Curtain, calls for a more complete picture of what we need to know before we can begin to search for the relevant data, let alone interpret them.

Our intelligence mechanism limits its forecasting of political trends and developments to the "facts" of a supposedly immutable situation. Discovery of the possibilities for changing this situation through U.S. action should be a part of the same process of analysis. Admittedly, to do this is to court the charge of usurping the job of the policy-maker. Yet, there is a sharp difference between policy-making and the assembly of the facts and prospects which would offer the policy-maker the range of possibilities from which he may make his selection. The view of the future and the view of what we might do to create the future to our liking need not necessarily conflict.

We cannot build defenses against the unknown nor can we exploit Soviet vulnerabilities and weaknesses without an accurate understanding of the basic forces and factors which pertain to a particular situation. We need, therefore, a net evaluation apparatus which can integrate data and can project a total picture of our relative strengths and weaknesses vis-à-vis the communist bloc. Only on the basis of such a comprehensive and continuing balance sheet can we measure the weight and impact of "new factors," such as technological innovations or political developments. And only in the light of this total picture can sound objectives be selected and effective strategy be devised and executed.

Mobilization and Allocation of Adequate Resources

Victory in any form of conflict generally goes to the side which succeeds in applying the greatest effort, at the most vulnerable spot of the opponent, at the right time. This in turn requires a mobilization of resources, a continuing and accurate assessment of the situation and of the resources being expended to achieve our national ends, and a technique for the rapid, flexible application of the national potential at the crucial moment.

Examining the problem of mobilization of resources, the question immediately arises, "Mobilization for what?" The answer here is "Mobilization for protracted conflict." Had the political realities of the post-World War II world been understood fully during the brief period when the United States, as a result of its monopoly of atomic weapons, was clearly supreme in all aspects of national power, we might have devised and pursued a program designed to achieve the early destruction of communism. But the opportunities and freedom of action that existed in those brief years of 1945-1952 are gone. Now the problem is fraught with greater urgency, demands greater effort and requires greater courage.

This book and its preceding volume have sought to make clear, in general terms, the nature of the conflict and to outline a conceptual strategy for waging it. This chapter, in turn, focuses on the governmental organization for the implementation of such a strategy. In considering the problem of mobilization of industrial and technological resources, it becomes immediately apparent that there is no mechanism within the Executive Branch for a meaningful assessment of requirements and for the comparison of these requirements with existing means. During World War II, the War Production Board performed this function insofar as the immediate requirements of the battlefield were concerned. When the WPB was abolished in 1945 and the country turned its full attention to expediting the reconversion to civilian production, no effort was made to transfer to another agency the job of reconciling requirements for protracted conflict with the means available. For the American people, once the shooting stopped, the conflict was over.

The Eisenhower Administration intuitively recognized, in the course of its efforts to make the NSC machinery more effective, that there was a need to assess requirements in terms of available means and to allocate existing resources where they would do the most good. Unfortunately, however, the solution devised was to put a "price tag" on every NSC policy paper. The "price tag" made our responsible officials examine more critically the many proposals which pour in constantly from the field. It also made the men in the field realize that their proposals could not completely ignore the competing requirements of other projects from other areas of the world. But this process did not allow for the very essential requirement to *price simultaneously the results of inaction or of half-measures*. Consequently, the policy-makers were presented with only one side of the coin: the cost of doing something—not the cost of inaction.

Foreign policy decisions formulated against this background are usually dulled and blunted by the determined resistance of the budgeteers. It is no criticism of them to point out that they earn their daily bread by holding expenditures within certain predetermined fiscal limits which were established on the basis of criteria having little reference to the struggle for predominance in world affairs between the U.S. and the U.S.S.R. Rather, it is a criticism of a system of policy-making which permits the "fiscal tail" (Budget and Treasury) to wag the "operational dog" (State and Defense).

By failing to price the results of inaction, policy-makers find themselves confronted with only two possible solutions. One is to cut essential programs—which patriotic budgeteers are reluctant to do; the other is to "stretch out" the programs to the point where, through lack of vitality, they provoke the criticism rather than the support of the governments we are seeking to assist. Under such procedures there is no incentive to seek ways in which additional funds can be raised to meet essential requirements over and above the arbitrarily selected budgetary norm.

In World War II, the cost of inaction or economic lethargy at home was measured in terms of defeat in military campaigns and in lives lost on the battlefield. An agency of the government, the War

Production Board, was charged with *meeting* the nation's wartime requirements through expanded production, priorities of economic effort, and the reduction of nonessential industrial activities. Certainly, when the successful implementation of a Forward Strategy may determine whether or not we continue as a free society, this country cannot afford to be without some governmental organization charged with the responsibility of *providing* the means to meet our essential national security requirements. We cannot long afford to fashion national policy in an environment which tends to stint on the resources required for victory; we cannot go on "stretching out" essential programs to the point where they no longer serve the purposes for which they were conceived and we cannot continue to ignore the "price tag" of inaction.

Some persons are anxious to "strengthen" the National Security Council machinery and attempt to force all decisions in the security area through the Council. It is debatable whether major budget decisions in the security area should be made through the National Security Council machinery or through the normal budget process. Both the National Security Council and the Bureau of the Budget have power only to the extent that the President follows their advice. It is no secret that in recent years the President personally determined the Department of Defense budget, with the Budget Bureau acting in an advisory and fact-finding capacity. Obviously, under our system the President should have the maximum flexibility in determining with whom and under what circumstances he will attempt to reach decisions on questions of defense, which falls within his powers as Commander in Chief of the armed forces. He is completely free to use the National Security Council, the budget process, or just an *ad hoc* meeting in his office with selected top officials.

Any increase of resources for national security involves either a change in national fiscal policy or convincing evidence that a larger share of our present budget should go into security programs. Changes in the policy-making machinery itself offer little prospect for increasing the funds available for national security.

The enormous and unused mobilization capacity of the U.S. represents our strongest weapon. The preceding chapter disposes of the popular misconception that we would go "bankrupt" by a greater response to the communist challenge. We refuse to believe that the Soviet economic system and decision-making capabilities are superior to those of the democracies. If we recognize the existence of a protracted conflict we must meet our opponents on *every* ground, including fiscal commitment. If the way to win this conflict is through the conduct of a Forward Strategy, then we must be prepared to assume the responsibility and launch a program for the adequate development and utilization of our national resources. It is clear that our National Security Council must receive a policy support more extensive than it has received in the past from the Bureau of the Budget and the Treasury Department. It must not only price the programs; it must price the results of the lack of programs. Machinery is needed within the Executive Branch to maintain a useful inventory of the resources available for protracted conflict, to assess their adequacy in meeting national security requirements, to provide a "cost accounting" and to recommend measures for providing additional means from the net growth of our expanding economy.

The United States can improve its organizational capabilities for economic policy-making and use its fiscal-monetary powers to improve its performance in the pervasive struggle. Initial steps to establish a "high command of economic strategy" began with the National Security Resources Board (later merged with Civil Defense as the Office of Civil and Defense Mobilization). The older Industrial College of the Armed Forces wisely sought to integrate military and civilian programs. But these efforts fall short of creating an organization that can deal systematically and swiftly with the kind of perplexing economic strategy problems which we face in the sixties.

Crash wartime mobilization of raw materials, plants and manpower became obsolete with the nuclear age. Today's task is nothing less than a thorough overhauling of our financial and fiscal management in time of so-called peace. Governmental agencies dealing with taxation currency exchanges, and internal and external credit, are widely dispersed. They are as far from being integrated in an organic scheme as are the institutions of our free market system. Chaos reigns in the field of monetary policy: Powerful governmental agencies for the creation of credits do not work in close co-operation with either the Federal Reserve Bank or the Treasury (e.g., both the Commodity Credit Corporation and the Federal National Mortgage Agency market vast amounts of securities and thus exert considerable influence over the money supply). Similarly, the Defense Department intervenes forcefully and not always considerately in the national economy through its expenditures and contracts. Of all the governmental agencies, the Bureau of the Budget comes closest to exercising some sort of general integrating function, but its charter compels it to take an essentially negative position. The extent to which the Director of the Budget holds a veto power over our national strategy is a justifiably serious matter for debate.

Our financial-fiscal management might well be reorganized: (a) The anachronistic concept of budgetary planning limited to a one-year time span should be revised.[2] (b) Central monetary control should be strengthened through a more vigorous use of the Federal Reserve Board's powers to regulate reserve requirements, rediscounting, open market operations and credit. (c) An Economic Strategy Staff (a genuine staff body, not an interagency co-ordinating committee) should provide the President with an independent source of detailed advice on the formulation of co-ordinated policies for the Bureau of the Budget, the Treasury Department, the Federal Reserve Board, the mortgage agencies, and the line departments which control expenditures for national security.

Consideration might well be given to establishing an Assistant Secretary of Defense for National Resources, an Assistant Secretary of the Treasury for National Security and an Assistant Secretary of State for National Resources. These functionaries might meet together with the chairman of the Office of Civilian Defense Mobilization and the Director of the Budget as a cabinet for economic mobilization. Their mission would be to propose the requisite actions to

[2] It would be very helpful if the federal budget could be presented in such a form that businessmen could determine from it just what the government expects to spend in various directions. At present, the budget is based upon the concept of administrative accounting. It shows what each department or agency will spend, but it does not tell the businessman how the government intends to spend its total annual outlay so that he can plan to expand and innovate accordingly. Important administrative and organizational considerations should not be allowed to dominate the budget format. The budget should also contain a section in which governmental spending activities are packaged so that their full impact upon the American productive system can be comprehended. This requires that: (a) the current budget be compared with those of the previous year or two; (b) the time span be drawn between outlays for capital investment, maintenance and operating costs, and research and development. The case for improvement in the budgeting process is argued by the RAND Corporation's David Novick and G. H. Fisher in "The Federal Budget as a Business Indicator," *Harvard Business Review*, May-June, 1960, pp. 64-72.

the National Security Council to provide the resources needed to achieve our national goals.

These reforms do not necessitate any drastic legislative overhauling of the Executive Branch, delegation of authority or revolutionary new grants of power. A sufficient statutory basis for an efficient integration of strategic-economic policy exists in laws already on the books (e.g., the Full Employment Act and the Defense Mobilization Act). In brief, these suggested reforms simply call for a more vigorous and imaginative use of powers already vested in the Executive in strict accord with our principle of constitutional government.

In Chapter 4 we presented the profound influence which the *technological factor* is having both on the world-wide systemic revolution and on the conduct of protracted conflict. Now we turn to the problem of mobilizing our technological resources.

Many responsible and knowledgeable persons in the Executive Branch, the Congress and the private sector are preoccupied with not only the operation of the aggregate technological effort but also the management and organization of the uses of technology. More than one solution to the problem of making the most of technology is workable.[3]

At present, the U.S. lacks an up-to-date inventory of the technological situation. A better system is needed for gathering technological data and transmitting them for wider utilization. Although many agencies as, for example, the Defense Department, the Atomic Energy Commission, the National Science Foundation and the

[3] While avoiding premature proposals, one can assert that the eventual organizational solution should provide for: a credible superiority in the protracted conflict; application of science and technology to the needs and aspirations of the open, the free society; conditions that are conducive to intelligent decision-making; and pursuit of science for science's sake; methods of communicating available knowledge effectively.

A proposal has been mooted for establishing an Executive Department of Science and Technology. The *service* aspect of technology is susceptible to "departmentalizing" just as certain of the established federal departments manage services as well as goods or people.

What is needed most, however, is a firmer and fuller grasp on technology at the level where strategy is formulated and directed. This greater awareness must be infused corporately, so to speak, in the mechanisms for the execution of strategy. It is a matter of lesser importance whether or not this task should be entrusted to a new agency. Looking at the mechanisms already at hand, it seems that improvement of the managerial function of technology at the higher echelons requires few, if any, additional resources.

Smithsonian Institution, engage in technological data-gathering, reporting and analysis, the information thus gained is not being fed into one center responsible for the estimate of the technological situation as a whole. It might prove desirable to establish an agency, or, at least, assign responsibility for dealing with (a) technological management, (b) research and (c) net evaluation of our technological situation in relation to that of the communist bloc and with respect to our principal industrialized allies.

A major contribution the U.S. could make to the security and welfare of all free peoples and to its own power would be the development of more effective and liberal programs for the exchange of technological information and skills within the Free World. An excellent device is the establishment, here and abroad, of study centers and of clearinghouses of ideas. A co-ordinated effort to reap mutual benefits accruing from the cross-fertilization of ideas would bring large tangible gains to our allies as well as ourselves and would break down many barriers that now impair the workings of the Free World coalition. Such teamwork could open novel approaches to international economic development. Above all, it would strengthen the Free World's capacity to wage a successful Forward Strategy.

The Committee on Government Organization, created in response to the urging of the Hoover Commission, provides the appropriate place for examining the organizational structure for technology. The Committee on Government Organization should be charged to carry out this task with the advice and assistance of the President's Assistant on Science and Technology. The following principal departments and agencies should collaborate with the Committee on Government Organization: the Secretary of Defense, the Secretary of State, the Director of OCDM, the Secretary of the Treasury, the Chairman of the Atomic Energy Commission, and representatives of Congressional committees concerned with technological matters.

Summary reports, culled from the information available to the government, should impart to laymen in lay language a general view of the technological situation. Similarly, as daily and monthly intelligence reports and national estimates are circulated to our key decision-makers, so technological bulletins, over-all estimates and summaries should be issued to keep decision-makers abreast of developments.

Although the Special Assistant on Science and Technology has direct access to the President, and presumably can exercise broad managerial functions over the entire span of technology, he is merely an observer at meetings of the National Security Council. Pending more definitive solutions, the Office of the Special Assistant should be raised in stature and adequately staffed to fulfill the functions which its present charter assigns to it.

The technological aspects of national security should be taken hold of more firmly—and by proper institutional provisions—under the cognizance of the National Security Council and should be integrated into strategic concepts and national security policies and programs in just as orderly and deliberate a manner as are military, foreign policy, economic and fiscal considerations. The Department of Defense as the principal "user" of technological resources should have a special voice in their allocation and control and should not be once or twice removed from technological decisions that are vital to its mission.

Designation of Responsibility

In theory, the President, through the Secretary of State, transmits guidance and authority to his various ambassadors throughout the world for the conduct of American foreign relations in the country to which they are individually accredited. The ambassador, in turn, implements policy through the "Country Team." This body is composed of representatives of all U.S. governmental agencies operating in the country concerned. Generally it includes, in addition to the ambassador who acts as chairman, the head of the U.S. Operations Mission (ICA), the senior representative of the U.S. Information Agency, the local Treasury representative, the senior CIA representative, the Chief of the Military Assistance Advisory Group, and, where U.S. armed forces are stationed in the country, the representative of the unified commander for the area.

The Country Team operates on the basis of instructions from Washington. In the nation's capital, however, the proliferation of procedures required prior to any action, the mushrooming of interagency boards, *ad hoc* committees, study groups, special assistants and special consultants, all serve to fragment decisions and water down directives. Furthermore, bureaucratic confusion cloaks the actual authors of national policy to the point where it is practically impossible to place responsibility for establishing any specific policy upon any individual or group of individuals. As a result, a premium is placed on inaction, and the prompt response so sorely needed is rarely made.

This situation results in "slippage" in the issuance of instructions. This "slippage," which seriously hampers the development of sound tactics for waging the Cold War, stems from various causes. Sometimes it is lack of wholehearted support within a particular department for a particular NSC policy or for the Operations Co-ordinating Board's co-ordinating instructions. Such reluctance to accept the Board's decision can be expressed indirectly in various ways. For example, the wording of the department's instructions to its field representatives can be made ambiguous; the instructions themselves can be delayed in transmittal; or, in extreme cases, directives can be countermanded through private correspondence giving guidance as to the department's interpretation of the official instructions.

Sometimes "slippage" is a direct result of the vagueness of the NSC policy itself. The translation of a broad national directive into specific instructions to be issued to the field is primarily the responsibility of the OCB members. The degree of success of this whole operation of policy implementation is a measure of the wisdom and statesmanship of the individual senior OCB members working together as a team.

Unfortunately, because of "slippage," the interdepartmental differences which exist in Washington are reflected on a smaller but no less intense scale in the field. Consequently, the Country Team's battles are not all with our enemies—many of them are internal to the embassy. Internal disputes can in large measure be reconciled by the leadership of an able ambassador. However, no two ambassadors use the Country Team in the same way. The effectiveness of the Country Team varies with the personality of the ambassador, the magnitude of the various departmental programs in the country concerned, and the personalities and team spirit of the individual members.

In the larger embassies, as a general rule, the Country Team meets together informally on a regular basis. When specific OCB instructions are received, the ambassador evaluates their importance and urgency and decides whether or not to hold a special meeting. Up to the present, Country Team meetings have been used more as a means of exchanging information on the progress of the separate departmental programs than as staff meetings to co-ordinate and direct the future efforts of all the field representatives toward specific tactical goals. Of course, the whole concept—and operation—of the OCB–Country Team combination is relatively new, and time, experience and good will are necessary before we can properly evaluate its operation under the stress of continuous conflict.

One of the principal factors which detracts from the effective implementation of national policy is the internal organization of the U.S. government agencies for the management and direction of programs in regions of the world. No two agencies operate on the same basis. Except for the military, organizational structure or resources are rarely related to the existing enemy threat. The federal government would do well to examine the Department of Defense organization of unified military theaters as a pattern for other agencies to follow. It is specifically designed to conduct operations through a chain of command which assigns responsibility unequivocally.

The President, as Commander in Chief, gives instructions through the Secretary of Defense and the Joint Chiefs of Staff to his Unified and Specified Commanders who are in charge of joint military forces deployed in specific military theaters throughout the world. These commanders, in turn, are authorized to establish subordinate unified commands. Basic to the concept of a subordinate command is (1) the delegation of command authority and (2) a forward deployment of the subordinate command's headquarters. Delegation of authority is designed to permit prompt reaction to changes in the tactical situation encountered in the field. Forward deployment places the command in closer touch with events in the area of immediate concern.

In the conduct of national policy abroad, the Department of State still holds that no regional authority can be interposed between the ambassadors and the Secretary of State and the President. This concept hampers effective implementation of a Forward Strategy. The Department of State continues to adhere to its tradition of reserving decision-making authority to Washington. Ambassadors, as personal representatives of the President abroad, report directly to the Secretary of State, not to or through any intermediate regional official. True, there are assistant secretaries in the department who have regional responsibility, but these responsibilities are strictly those of staff advisors to the Secretary. Assistant Secretaries have little if any delegated policy authority and, by virtue of their location in Washington, are as remote from the regions which they monitor as the Secretary is himself. The proposition of interposing between the Secretary and his ambassadors in the field a forward representative of the Secretary has been studied on several occasions by the department. Tentative experiments toward this end have been tried in Europe in connection with NATO and with our unsuccessful efforts to encourage the establishment of an EDC. However, the power and personal prerogatives of ambassadors are jealously guarded. In the present circumstances, it would require a distinguished diplomat with tremendous personal prestige to achieve any real co-ordination of effort among the several ambassadors in a given area.

This fundamental difference in organizational structure between State and Defense has prevented serious consideration of the interposition of regional officials designated by the President to exercise authority within a given geographic area. The "slippage" in the issuance of departmental instructions to Country Team representatives; the inability of the Team to react to rapidly changing events; and the difficulties of co-ordinating military, economic, psychological and other programs in any given country may be traced directly to the tremendous gap which divides the departments in Washington and the Country Team in the field.

To overcome this obstacle, appropriate world-wide adaptations in the military theater command structure should be made where necessary to establish identical geographical areas of responsibility for both the senior regional official and the theater commanders. Once this were done, the twenty-one or more supporting government agencies, departments and intelligence organizations might be induced to adopt a similar, parallel regional grouping of their overseas responsibilities.

In establishing standard regional areas, applicable to all departmental operations abroad, consideration would be given necessarily to the existing Free World alliance structure, so that our national efforts could be most effectively co-ordinated with those of our allies. Regional alliances already in being generally have been formed on a geographic basis best suited to meet the enemy threat in the area. It would certainly be unwise for the proposed standard regional areas to cut across already established allied groupings such as NATO, SEATO, CENTO and the OAS. The guiding principle should be to match up U.S. governmental organizations overseas so that the allocation of geographic areas of responsibility of all agencies would be identical.

Delegation of Authority

Once a clear-cut chain of command has been established from the President through regional officials down to the ambassadors in the various countries throughout the world, then we will have provided the governmental machinery needed to make the "field" responsive to policy direction from Washington. Now we must determine how we can help the "field" find ripostes to the opportunities and threats which events and the local communist organizations create almost daily. Put another way, the problem is how to assist the ambassador and the Country Team in winning the tactical battles against communism.

There was a time when an ambassador represented the United States in accordance with what he thought best for his country in accordance with his own philosophy of America's ultimate destiny in world history. Then the very nature of communications was such that the appointment of an ambassador carried with it not only a public expression of confidence in his judgment, but also an actual delegation of authority from the President to act as his personal representative to the country to which he was accredited. Now, our modern communications work against the decentralization of authority and virtually strip the ambassador of any opportunity to exercise his own judgment or to initiate, on his own responsibility, actions which may be urgently needed to win the Cold War in his area.

The irony here is that while these modern communications make it possible to send long, important messages to Washington which are delivered to the responsible officials within a matter of hours, we still are subject to the inevitable delays inherent in a large bureaucracy. The net result is that the combination of superlative communications with a ponderous bureaucracy accomplishes an almost total stifling of initiative in the field. Foreign service officers often refer even the most minute or detailed questions back to the department. Given the facilities for communications, why, when the "buck" can be passed back to Washington, risk making a mistake and thereby jeopardizing one's future?

What is the result of these rigid procedures? The U.S. ambassador becomes little more than a messenger for the "desk officer" in the State Department. And who is this key official, one may ask. Invariably, he is a foreign service officer, far less experienced than the ambassador. If he has had one tour of duty in the country he supervises, he is fortunate. How does he form his judgments? By reading the cables from the embassy, the foreign broadcast clips, the local newspapers which he receives weeks late by diplomatic pouch, and the various intelligence bulletins which flood the Executive Branch. These latter documents plagiarize so freely from one another that the desk officer's net intellectual take is an incestuous blending of all these highly speculative sources. What little local political insight the ambassador is able to glean from his personal contacts, from conversations with officials of the party in power (in some areas, it is considered "counterproductive" to become acquainted with the opposition, or to try to understand their point of view), from an occasional trip away from the capital, and from reading the local press, is compressed into carefully drawn cables placed before the Washington desk officer for his evaluation and preparation of a draft reply. This reply, admittedly, is extensively "co-ordinated" within the department and cleared with the responsible regional official—perhaps even with the Department of Defense (i.e., a similar junior desk officer)—but by then the tactical situation which gave rise to the original cable has often been lost in the frenetically industrious process of Washington bureaucracy.

The net result is that we lose out and will continue to lose out, in the small but important daily conflicts with the communists. We lose because the ambassador is no longer the "commander in the field" he once was, before modern communications made him a dignified messenger. We lose because the conduct of the battle is not responsive to the changing tactical situation, since the judgment of the U.S. ambassador regardless of his competence or initiative now means so little, being emasculated through the bureaucratic process which refers decisions back to the far distant "desk officer."

The authors are aware that in Washington there continues to be a lack of agreement as to whether the ambassador really represents the President or is merely an employee of the State Department. If he represents the President, no one has yet been able to figure out a fully acceptable arrangement in Washington for backstopping the ambassador. The problem is further complicated because the domestic agencies now operating overseas have provisions in their laws for preventing the President or his representative from exercising the kind of control over them that we have suggested.

The notion of a chain of command running from the President to the Secretary of State to the ambassadors must mesh with the fact that negotiations with other countries involve not only contacts at the country level but also with their local embassies in Washington, at the UN and at other international organizations. Yet the challenge remains to clear away the underbrush so that the ambassadors can do a better job of *implementing* agreed policies and programs.

How can this situation be remedied? First, the ambassador should be given more personal responsibility. He must, when the tactical situation requires, make more decisions on his own without prior reference to Washington. Second, as the representative of the President in the field, he must assume control of his local resources. This he can do by taking charge of his Country Team and by making it function in accordance with his own plan. Through personal leadership, he must persuade the individual departmental or agency representatives who make up his Country Team to exercise the initiative and judgment required to work together in the interest of the job to be done, rather than in the interest of maintaining that compartmentalization which is the bane of all progress in Washington. Here, fortunately, the pressures resulting from a steady series of setbacks to U.S. prestige throughout the world are forcing a new *modus operandi* on the departmental representatives in the field. As a result, there is a steady increase of co-ordination of programs, day-to-day operations and prior planning. Ambassadors are beginning to devote more of their personal time to Country Team operations as a whole, as contrasted to the supervision of separate and distinct departmental programs.

Two specific steps could facilitate the operation of the Country Team. The first is an organizational improvement designed to make procedures of the Country Team more businesslike. What appears to be needed is, in military terminology, a "chief of staff for plans." However the job is handled administratively, the ambassador should be able to rely on a senior assistant who could supervise and co-ordinate on a full-time basis the Country Team programs.

The second step, which is closely related to the first, would be the ambassador's participation in the formulation of Country Team plans. Conceivably these would include: (1) an annual master plan based on NSC and OCB policies; (2) limited objective plans designed to accomplish specific tasks assigned to the Country Team by Washington or by the ambassador himself; and (3) contingency plans.

All of these greatly needed changes can be introduced by the Executive Branch under existing legislative authority. The development of techniques for contingency planning requires no formal directive to the responsible departments. What it does require, however, is an appreciation of the need for such planning and the willingness to expend the necessary effort to prepare practical contingency plans. The appointment of regional officials is predicated upon a revision of the State Department's traditional conception of the direct and personal relationship between the Secretary and his ambassadors. And finally, the ambassador himself can tighten Country Team operations regardless of action taken in the two other areas. All he needs is a willingness to assume responsibility, a capacity for hard work and dynamic leadership and the moral, intellectual and personal stature to do what his mission demands.

Application of Means

We have already discussed the allocation of adequate national resources. The problem which must now be considered is the transformation of these resources into weapons systems appropriate to all aspects of the struggle with communism. The term "weapons system" is used here in its broadest context. It includes not only the military means for the entire spectrum of armed conflict, from general war to counterguerrilla or riot control operations, but also the economic, political and psychological means for carrying forward a strategy designed ultimately to secure our victory.

The communist bloc, for its part, has at its disposal means of extraordinary variety. They range from the Sputnik and the megaton-armed ICBM at one end of the scale, to indigenous communist parties, controlled from Moscow, on the other. Experts who have studied resources available to the Kremlin and analyzed the communist techniques for their employment, generally conclude that at the root of, and basic to, the communists' success has been their organizational skill. The communists themselves assess organization as their greatest single element of strength. The importance of this element is obvious since the communists regard their relationship to the rest of the world as one of continuous and irreconcilable conflict, requiring an organizational capacity comparable to that which democratic states marshal only in times of war and crisis.

We have already examined the military field. In the political arena, we have seen that our organization for political action is geared to antiquated theories and methods. We have yet to understand fully the techniques of revolution, of subversion, of mob instigation and control which are the routine of communist usage. In general, the tremendous strength and ability of our country is either underestimated, dissipated or withheld. Co-ordination of the elements of our national effort in forward areas is hampered by interagency strife and by an insistence upon the detailed direction of day-to-day operations from Washington, rather than from advanced regional headquarters, where policy-makers would be far better attuned to the realities and opportunities in their immediate areas of responsibility.

There is no agency or organization responsible for the active conduct of psychological warfare or propaganda. True, there are the USIA[4] and VOA, but these are more often engaged in "public relations" than in waging a psychological battle against the communists. Consequently, our many assets in the psychological struggle—continuing streams of refugees who have both contacts and resources in communist-controlled areas, anticommunist groups of political orientations varying from extreme right to extreme left, official and unofficial international organizations—are rarely utilized in a systematic manner for any specific national purpose.

One conclusion which emerges from the foregoing discussion is that our current programs must be tailored to accomplish specific national objectives and must be adequate to accomplish these objectives. Our top policy-makers have generally accepted the term "scientific breakthrough." They recognize that in specific areas of scientific or technical development, the withholding of resources may indefinitely postpone the day when the scientific threshold is crossed and the

[4] United States Information Agency; the VOA—Voice of America—is its radio broadcasting arm.

breakthrough achieved. Here the axiom of "penny wise, pound foolish" is well understood. In the field of political action, however, there seems to be no appreciation of an analogous "political breakthrough." As a result, the tendency throughout the U.S. bureaucracy is to inch along in the direction of our national objectives rather than make the selective application of adequate means *at the time when conditions are ripe for achieving the desired political breakthrough* and thereby realizing a key national objective.

In military strategy, the functional suitability of weapons systems should be the criterion for the determination of appropriate means. The examination of our current military posture from this point of view is long overdue. It has been thirteen years now since the Joint Chiefs of Staff were forced to face up to the central problem of the roles and missions of the Services. It is obvious that weapons developments, both in the U.S. and the Soviet Union, make imperative a re-examination of this problem.

In psychological warfare and propaganda, the criteria must be the adequacy of our governmental organization to conduct operations in this field and the effectiveness of our national effort when compared with that of the communists. Any review based on such criteria will inevitably reveal the surprising fact that no governmental organization exists for this specific purpose. The Voice of America and USIA, under the direct supervision and control of the Department of State, have not been permitted to engage actively in the rough and tumble of ideological conflict with the communists. State Department guidance is desirable *provided* the decision is made to wage an effective propaganda campaign. Until we are organized, trained and willing to engage in this intellectual "body contact" with the communists, we will never be able to give motivation or impetus to student or labor movements, or to control mob political action. Events in Japan, Korea and Italy illustrate the dynamism of the communist effort to upset the normal procedures of representative government. The U.S., sooner or later, must get off the sidelines and get out on the playing field. In this case, the playing field is not diplomatic receptions or international conferences. It is in the universities and labor unions. It requires tough, trained professionals to win this kind of battle.

In the economic field, we cannot but play for long-range stakes. But our initiatives must be guided by a more attentive consideration of the current political reactions of our friends and allies. At the least, our economic aid programs must be carried out in such a way that our enemies and critics do not fare better than our loyal supporters.

In the political field, we should be responsive to opportunities as they occur. All who have examined U.S. policies since the end of World War II have acknowledged to varying degrees that we react to communist initiatives rather than move forward under the steam of our own programs in a manner befitting the leader of the Free World.

Response to Opportunity

But we must not become overly preoccupied with the organizational solution. Our greatest deficiencies are not so much that the organizational structures are wrongly drawn, but that the men who occupy the slots are sometimes wrongly motivated, lack initiative, are inadequately trained, and are so hemmed in by procedures that imagination cannot be brought into play.

Another fundamental deficiency in our government's efforts to implement its policies abroad has been its seeming inability to cope with and exploit the rapidly changing situations which confront us throughout the world. This may be attributed to two main causes: first, the failure to develop a technique for contingency planning at the national level; and second, the lack of central control facilities from which the daily operations inherent in the protracted conflict can be monitored and directed. The term "planning" may here be misleading. The drawing of plans may indeed be futile, while a firm grasp on contingency situations may be an indispensable preparation for concrete and rapid action once the need arises. The obstacles to contingency planning are those which unfortunately are endemic to the Washington scene. But they stem primarily from conflicting philosophies regarding the conduct of international relations. This basic conflict is amplified further by the usual occupational hazards of governmental bureaucracy, particularly interdepartmental rivalry, reluctance to explore the unorthodox and, finally, the ever-present risk of a press "leak" during the policy-making process.

At the crux of the problem are long-standing differences on the day-to-day conduct of foreign affairs which have long existed between the Departments of State and Defense. These two departments entertain widely divergent views as to the feasibility of contingency planning. The Department of Defense has consistently pressed for a greater degree of contingency planning, while the Department of State has shied away from this approach, preferring a "play it by ear" solution. Repeatedly Defense, on behalf of our military commanders abroad, has asked State for guidance for positive action should this or that specific situation arise. But State generally has been reluctant to allow itself to be drawn into what it felt might be premature policy decisions. The answer, the foreign service officers told their frustrated opposite numbers in the Pentagon, would always depend on the "situation then obtaining."

As indicated above, there are two points of view on contingency planning. Military staffs are entirely familiar with the purpose of contingency planning. However, military problems are reasonably clear-cut and generally can be reduced to a manageable number of practical solutions. This is possible because certain immutable factors, such as time, space, geography, logistic, etc., tend to confine or restrict the number of courses of action open to the enemy. This does not mean that the enemy always does exactly what he is expected to do. It would be pure coincidence if that were the case. However, when military forces are disposed to meet the various contingencies which have been foreseen, they are usually capable of handling any unexpected variations the enemy may inject.

The extension of this technique of contingency planning into the political field is more difficult. In the first place, the limiting factors are seldom the same type of physical realities—time, space, logistics—that govern military planning. Instead they include human factors which are difficult to isolate and define. Thus the number of foreseeable contingencies is greatly multiplied and the job of the planners becomes increasingly complicated. Secondly, in a military operation a commander knows in advance what resources he has immediately available to counter the enemy's moves. On the political battlefield, however, this is seldom the case. The resources available, and even the alternative courses of action open to consideration, usually have "strings" on them. Specifically, advance notification, and frequently clearance, is often required from Congress or our allies before we can counter communist moves. This, of course, greatly increases our reaction time and invariably puts our government at a disadvantage.

It appears almost impossible to get any real forward planning in Washington which is based on solid research and which can gain the attention necessary for its consideration and implementation. More external research can probably be justified in this area. However, it is difficult to identify those bureaus which can backstop such research and assure that key officials pay attention to it in the Executive Branch. Part of the problem is our continuing reluctance to think in terms of strengthening specific regimes of foreign governments. The idea of "noninterference" is so deeply rooted in our thinking that we are reluctant to undertake the forward planning necessary to assure the future political and social stability of the government with which we have to deal.

What frequently is lacking is the development of concrete programs of action to go into effect when an anticipated change in government takes place (e.g., a nation achieves independence or a government is overthrown). There are scattered attempts at forward planning of this sort today, but undoubtedly they could benefit from more centralized direction and top-level support.

Within the Executive Branch there is a decided difference of opinion as to the feasibility of thinking through in advance how to meet potential Cold War challenges. Although Department of Defense representatives admit that many contingencies are difficult to anticipate, they also claim that there are many having a high probability of occurrence and for which we should therefore plan. They concede that even in such predictable cases there are many unknown factors. Nevertheless, they argue, the unknown factors can be narrowed down to the point where useful planning can begin. If several unknowns involved are critical, it may be necessary to study the contingency in question under two or three sets of assumptions.

The problem facing the United States is to develop a system to accomplish this vital contingency planning efficiently. Given a group of competent individuals from the various departments, all sincerely willing to give this procedure a fair trial, there is no question that a great improvement can be made in our conduct of the Cold War. The very process of considering important contingencies and of agreeing on realistic sets of assumptions which apply in each case would be a major step forward. It would help bring the thinking of the various government departments together, thus automatically providing for more effective interagency co-ordination. And even more important, careful consideration of these contingencies would often serve as an indispensable preparation for rapid action once the need arose. It would also point the way to actions which, if initiated promptly, could very well prevent the contingency from ever arising.

It is generally accepted that the communist leaders are conducting a highly co-ordinated form of protracted conflict on a global scale. Seemingly isolated moves, are, therefore, related to one another as parts of a wider campaign. Similarly, for all our faults, the U.S. is attempting to meet this challenge, in conjunction with our allies, on a world-wide basis. End results of high-level policy decisions are difficult to foresee. They have a way of producing the most unexpected repercussions as the ripple of U.S. actions spreads out from Washington. Similarly, policy decisions in Washington produce political reactions throughout the communist bloc. The same is true in reverse when policy decisions are made in Moscow. Yet, despite this continuing, complicated interrelationship of action and reaction, little effort is being made in either State or Defense at the departmental level to view the world, so to speak, as a panorama of change.

How can we enable our responsible officials to respond promptly to the opportunities or threats which result from the continuing interaction of the communist and Free World societies?

First of all it is necessary to place our responsible officials in a truly operational environment. This requires a radical revision of the present committee procedures for interdepartmental co-ordination of governmental operations. Their efforts should be focused on the solution of the Cold War problems created by U.S. and communist initiatives. In short, they must be given a sense of urgency which is sadly lacking today.

The officials responsible for the supervision of day-to-day operations should be relieved from a considerable responsibility for policy formulation. One major defect in our present organizational structure is the tendency prevalent among operational officials to stray into discussions of policy. Only too frequently they seek a new policy for every new operational situation. As a result, they fail to take the vigorous actions which are required to carry out existing directives. The ensuing debate is based, more often than not, on an inadequate understanding of the basic policy itself. It is, therefore, largely "academic" and serves primarily as an excuse for inaction.

A third requirement is to provide the responsible officials with an up-to-date, comprehensive picture of the scope and nature of U.S. and Soviet operations throughout the world. Only by setting their tasks in a global perspective can they appreciate the relationship between the programs which they manage in one part of the world and those their colleagues conduct in another. It is one of the ironies of our time that, notwithstanding the vast machinery for co-ordination in Washington today, there is no place in the U.S. government where one can find the results of both U.S. and communist programs presented side-by-side. Bits and pieces of the picture are available in the various departments and agencies throughout Washington and can be obtained in a haphazard fashion by attending the continuous round of briefings conducted for our harried high officials.

Coping with the protracted conflict involves estimating the facts about tremendously complicated affairs. What are the opportunities? What are the risks? What kind and level of forces do we need to handle the risks? What are our present capabilities? There is need for a way of showing what the answers are and for comparing the different answers with each other. There is need, also, for a way of showing the effects of a change in any one set of factors. For the most part, only the method of narrative description has been used to state the involved, interrelated, and delicate components of each set of estimates.

A device is needed which permits key officials to see each of the key parts of the global picture by itself and each part in relation to the others. The establishment of a "Presidential Operations Center" would permit the government to focus better on winning the Cold War. A comprehensive visualization of the protracted conflict could be made possible by establishing a focal point for bringing together all pertinent information and presenting it in a form which would permit evaluation. The Presidential Operations Center would incorporate visual devices (closed circuit TV, films, viewgraphs) to enable the person or persons being briefed to grasp a variety of changing factors at one time, thus making it possible to see more readily a composite picture of U.S. operations focused on a critical situation, or to measure a progressing or retrogressing position. These devices would provide measuring tools, as well as check lists and time schedules. Policy goals would be spelled out in measurable achievement stages. Negative reports would be noted as clues to necessary action.

Hostile action in each region or country would be portrayed on a comparative basis with U.S. effort so that the effort might be made responsive to shifts. A picture of other Free World action and indigenous action and progress would be presented. The total Free World effort picture is a requisite in evaluating our own part, and the long-range goals are tied to indigenous progress.

The Presidential Operations Center would be equipped to give a more intimate, flexible progress—or lack of progress—picture on a week-to-week basis, as well as graphical presentation of the attainment or non-attainment of limited or long-range objectives. Spot reports discussed orally, using the background of familiar maps and a situation board, keep a situation alive and relate the specific incidents to the general picture.

The Presidential Operations Center would enable the key officials to evaluate the degree of an achievement of U.S. objectives in a given country with a greater degree of accuracy. They would be alerted about dangerously adverse efforts in the situation, and could take all the measures to cope with them. Of course, in the turbulence of the protracted conflict, mistakes will occur and opportunities will be missed. A consistent record of achievements should provide a basis for recognition and promotion; similarly, a record of consistent setbacks brought about through temerity and/or inaction could provide a basis for removing or replacing officials who persistently fail in their mission. The Presidential Operations Center would cut through the techniques practiced by any bureaucracy for avoiding decisions involving a high degree of risks. Somehow or other, personal responsibility must be re-established in the government, and the men who have the courage of their convictions to act, and who have proven successful, must be identified and supported. If this were done, we would soon create a corps of "great captains" for directing the global struggle.

Another valuable role of such a Center would be to serve as a mechanism for ensuring the execution of an operational decision.

The Center would assist responsible officials to keep abreast of changing circumstances, such as communist actions requiring additional countermeasures or new American initiatives. By thus monitoring each situation as it developed, the Center would encourage an intelligent, co-ordinated, continuous command supervision over U.S. programs abroad. This, in itself, would be a major step forward in the conduct of the Cold War. Today, the closest approach to any truly *co-ordinated* command supervision is the Operations Co-ordinating Board Reports.

Undoubtedly, the mere establishment of a presidential Operations Center in itself is not a guarantee for expediting the actual conduct of governmental operations abroad. Important operational decisions require careful consideration by the departmental staffs; no amount of communications and electronic gear or fancy techniques of presentation can change procedures which are the product of many years of experience or alter the statutory responsibilities of the individual departments. Finally, organization is not nearly so important as sound judgment. Even though these reservations are plausible in the light of past experiences, they need not—unless we choose to let them—inhibit the adoption of improved methods.

Any device which will reduce the time key officials must spend to keep abreast of world events will permit that much more study and reflection. With such an integrated background of the relative strengths and weaknesses of the two contestants in today's conflict, it should be possible to weigh the impact of crucial new factors, including unexpected political, technological or economic developments. Only against such a background can an effective U.S. Forward Strategy be devised and applied.

One final but essential function which a Presidential Operations Center should perform would be the periodic testing of our plans for coping with both political-military and political contingencies. Various war-gaming devices can be used by the Pentagon for testing military plans. The concept of "operation alert" for checking our civilian defense preparations can likewise be expanded. With regard to political contingencies, consideration should be given to forming a simulated communist command group manned by people with a demonstrated grasp of communist ideology, communist strategic doctrines and operational techniques. These people would be given the opportunity to "test" our own programs, so that gaps and deficiencies could be identified, insofar as humanly possible, prior to putting any given plan into action. Testing would obviously not pick up all the flaws in our planning, but it should improve the efficiency of American operations many fold.

Command Supervision

"Command supervision" is the process of ascertaining that all elements involved in the execution of a plan are carrying out their parts as originally conceived. It has three important functions: (1) to insure that responsible officials in the field fully understand the instructions under which they are operating; (2) to determine the effectiveness of these officials in carrying out their assigned missions; and (3) to provide the personal leadership necessary to any plan or strategy before it can have impetus and meaning.

The lack of command supervision contributes, in many cases, to a repetition at the country level of all the internecine quarrels which rend the bureaucracy at home. Thus, the ambassador as well as other agency officials are judged more by their ability to fulfill to the letter the instructions they receive from their home offices than they are for their ability to work together as members of a team to defeat the communists.

The President can exercise command supervision through personal visits to foreign capitals. These are usually so hurried, and so taken up with direct discussions with heads of state, that he has little opportunity to inspect at firsthand the effectiveness of the U.S. programs in the area. Instead, he must rely on the primary means at his disposal, the OCB reports which are submitted to him periodically through the NSC. Most of the troubles issue from the manner in which these reports are compiled and processed. They originate as progress reports from field missions and commands, generally quite detailed and balanced. These detailed reports are then processed by "working groups," and it is here that there sets in the same diluting process described earlier in connection with policy recommendation and directives. Each department and agency member is naturally anxious to present the performance of his department and its field representatives in the most favorable lights. Facts that mar this idyllic picture are gradually weeded out or watered down. By this system, performers in effect become appraisers of their own performances—a practice analogous to a banker writing his own examiner's report.

Current procedures provide that these reports are *not* to be forwarded to the NSC and the President unless they recommend a change in existing policy or unless a "significant development" justifies such action. Consequently, the President is isolated from the changing political scene unless an extraordinary crisis requires re-examination of the entire U.S. policy in the country concerned.

The fact that the whole reporting process tends to emasculate itself clamors for corrective action. The need remains for a clear-cut chain of command and review from the President all the way down to his Country Team, i.e., a true system of command supervision.

The ambassador, while nominally the head of the Country Team, has little real authority over the representatives of the agencies centered in Washington, who administer programs in "his country." Therefore, he cannot be held fully responsible for the success or failure of U.S. policy in his particular country. The high-level Washington officials, who visit foreign capitals, rarely carry with them any concise idea of the national objectives with regard to the country they have descended upon. On the contrary, they are much more concerned with protecting their own programs from any attempts at local controls that might possibly encroach on their prerogatives. In other words, these visits serve to reinforce the departmental lines of authority rather than to give impetus to our national effort.

Communication and co-operation between the Executive and Legislative branches in broad policy areas are far from smooth and mutually rewarding. In Congress, power is dispersed among many standing committees, and frictions over prerogatives generate more heat than light in the discussion of national security and foreign affairs legislation. This circumstance weakens the ability of Congress to co-operate effectively with the Executive Branch.

No committee of Congress deals with a range of policy remotely comparable to that embraced by the National Security Council.

The nature of the links that might exist between Congress and the Executive Branch, and, especially, the Bureau of the Budget and the National Security Council in the key areas, raises special difficulties. The latter are arms of the Executive Branch. Many proposals have been made to permit a responsible Congressional group to get at the heart of those issues that make up the body of a forward strategy.

Congress, not having access to Executive Branch reports, has established its own procedures. These include Congressional reports prepared by a committee or its individual members upon their return from inspection trips abroad. The quality of such reports fluctuates widely depending upon the background and knowledge of the committee members themselves. The Mansfield Reports on Vietnam are excellent examples of objective reporting. Unfortunately a good many Congressional reports fall short of so high a standard, being devoted to partisan briefs, or to stoking the never-ending feud between the Executive and Legislative branches of the government.

Congress has at command the General Accounting Office reports. These, while useful for administrative purposes, are written by junior civil servants who have little direct knowledge of the rationale behind the programs which are being carried out. Their viewpoint is narrow, being concerned almost exclusively with the financial aspects of the operations of the United States agencies. These reports, unfortunately, are almost totally unrelated to national objectives or even to the effects of programs in one country on those in adjacent countries of the same region.

Persistence of Effort

Central to any Forward Strategy must be the thesis that there is no substitute for victory. The growing tendency within certain elements of the U.S. public to accept conditions short of victory must be reversed. This can be done only through strong and courageous leadership by the Administration. The public cannot be continually fed statements which convey too often the impression that all is well.

In time of war, responsible leaders are required to achieve their objectives. Unless every forward commander carries out his part of the military operation the entire effort may come to nought. In a hot war, failure of a commander to achieve his objectives is usually corrected by his prompt replacement. It is time the U.S. gave serious consideration to applying this same "demand for victory" to its responsible officials in the diplomatic and political fields. Admittedly, evaluation of the degree of success with which an ambassador or a chief of mission accomplishes U.S. political objectives in a specific country is more complex than the evaluation of whether or not a military commander has taken specific geographic objectives. However, if our aims are not achieved in the Cold War, U.S. interests may be jeopardized every bit as much as they would be through lack of aggressive leadership in a hot war.

Measures must be taken to develop procedures to evaluate the success or failure of ambassadors. Ambassadors are in effect the commanders in chief in the country to which they are accredited. There is too much at stake to judge their performance on any criterion other than ultimate success. If they cannot carry out the national objectives in the country to which they are assigned, the proper corrective action is not so much to modify or rewrite the national objective, but rather to replace the official concerned with one who is prepared to stake his personal reputation on his ability to carry out his orders.

Future historians, reviewing the first half of the twentieth century, may well conclude that the Korean armistice marked the beginning of a significant change in American national character. From that time on, America seemed to accommodate itself more and more to a world position moving toward second place. Meanwhile, the communists have moved steadily toward making their claims stick: communism is the wave of the future; time is on their side, and ultimately they will "bury us." It cannot be reiterated too strongly that the precondition of any national Forward Strategy must be the cultivation of the American people's "will to win." All public statements by responsible officials, all policies, all actions must be examined in the light of this axiom. If they deviate from it, that can only serve to detract from U.S. national objectives. Let us turn to the crucial factor of official evaluation of public opinion in influencing U.S. policy and strategic actions.

The Free World governments, including that of the United States, have increasingly persuaded themselves that one or the other strategy or policy cannot be used because public opinion would be opposed or critical. Our decision-makers appear bewitched by a somewhat naive understanding about the true nature of public opinion, its measurement and its significance. They ignore or cavil at the fact that "public opinion" might be another term for psychological warfare waged by the enemy against us, designed to scotch the making of positive decisions. Genuflections before the altar of public opinion are frequently the reverence paid by timid officials to their own preference for ambiguity and evasion.

If public opinion is to be regarded as a significant factor in our decision-making, we should have more effective means to determine its content at any given time with greater precision. There is not *one* public opinion but *at least two* basic types, namely, the public opinion of those who want the United States to extend freedom and that of those who seem to care little if our opponents win. This being the case, the strategic decision would then have to be made whether we want to humor *both* opinions at the same time; or, if this should prove to be impossible, whether we take the first type of public opinion for granted and work on the second one, in the hope that we might modify public opinion in between; or whether we should devote our main efforts to strengthening the public opinion of those who are basically committed to the struggle for a Free World victory. If our own public opinion reposes in the confidence of victory, its very poise will eventually sway the vacillating elements and rally them to the support of a Forward Strategy.

The other question is as to whether a strategic decision which will provide lasting benefits to the Free World should be postponed or abandoned for the sake of temporary and perhaps spurious advantages of psychological gamesmanship. Strategy is a serious business and cannot be conducted as if it were a popularity contest. Some bad strategic decisions will be popular and some good ones will be unpopular. Invariably, whenever a strategic decision-maker wanted to please the crowds, he was defeated in battle—a truth which any reader of Plutarch should understand. Actually, the successful strategist is he who makes the necessary military and conflict decisions *and* gains public support precisely because he convinces the public that his decisions are sound.

Obviously, these simple relationships are complicated by intellectual time-lags, public emotions, secrecy, incomprehension of the strategic problems, multiple propaganda campaigns, election requirements, press coverage and a host of other factors. Nevertheless, the principle stands. *The cult of public opinion has gone beyond the bounds of reason.*

The policy-makers should always bear in mind that: (a) the general public does not deeply care about strategy, and hence has little opinion about it; (b) the general public tends to accept the easy solution of the demagogue but, if properly informed, will make the sacrifices demanded by a Forward Strategy; (c) public opinion does not emerge spontaneously but is created; (d) the demagogue humors public opinion as he finds it. He pays it court by offering easy solutions to hard problems. Democratic leadership should take public opinion into account and *mold it to support what must be done.* The conscientious statesman, if he does not succeed in his endeavor, does what his conscience tells him to do; when he must act, he accepts the risk of unpopularity, and hopes that time will bear him out.

Specific structural changes in our national security organization are an immediate task of American leadership. In this chapter our purpose has been to point up the need for the overhauling of our structure for strategy and to suggest directions in which changes might be made.

The communists have been more successful than we in specific areas of strategy and tactics of the Cold War. Their success has not been achieved because we are inferior in intelligence and cleverness; rather, they have developed a superior technique for political warfare and for the management of conflicts which they themselves initiate and foster. The Kremlin for decades has practiced the refinement of political strategy, propaganda agitation techniques and organizational manipulation.

Many Americans still cling to illusions regarding the nature of their enemy and fail to recognize our struggle with the communist world for what it is: a war in which the ultimate stake is national survival. Our reluctance to recognize the efficiency of the novel forms of aggression developed by the communists has obscured the necessity for making some basic changes in our present approach to national security to cope with this new type of warfare. As Abraham Lincoln declared in his message to Congress on December 1, 1862, "The dogmas of the quiet past are inadequate for the stormy present. The occasion is piled high with difficulty and we must rise with the occasion. As our case is new, so we must think anew and act anew. We must disenthrall ourselves and then we shall save our country."

CHAPTER 12 SURMOUNTING THE CRISIS

The United States and the Free World are confronted by a deadly challenge. Within less than a generation the cause of freedom and the prestige and influence of the United States have been progressively so weakened that the West-at-bay is no longer a figure of speech but a precise statement of a real condition. This is the overarching and staggering fact of the early sixties. Nothing illustrates better how our situation has worsened than the fact that, while at the beginning of the past decade we were fighting the forces of communism ten thousand miles away, in 1960 the Soviet Union and China were in the process of establishing a protectorate over Cuba, some ninety miles off the coast of Florida.

Not all the victories of the Cold War have gone to the communists. The fabulous economic recovery of Western Europe, sparked by the Marshall Plan, confounded the dogmatic predictions of the communists. The creation of NATO, backstopped by American deterrent power, barred Western Europe and the Mediterranean to Soviet military penetration. Each step forward on the road to the economic integration of Western Europe and European political cooperation has been a defeat for the communists, who tried with every means at their disposal to sabotage European unity. American intervention in the Lebanon and the Formosa Straits defied successfully communist nuclear blackmail. In the Middle East, communist incursions have collided at various places with the countervailing forces of Arab nationalism. In Western Europe, the communist parties have been troubled by a decline in paying membership and the defection of intellectuals. American science and technology have recovered some of the ground lost in the competition for leadership in rocketry and space exploration. It would be strange indeed if the Soviet Union, which forty years ago started virtually from scratch industrially and suffered immense damages in World War II, had been able to draw abreast of Western economic and technological development. It would be even more remarkable if the Soviet Union —which, without Western aid, would have been crushed by Nazi power, did not possess before the 1950's operational atomic weapons, and until a few years ago had not a ruble to spare for foreign investment and economic assistance—had by now gained a conclusive military-technological advantage over the combined power of the Western Allies and held the world economy at its mercy. The bases of the Free World coalition still ring the communist bloc; the bulk of the world's trade is still done by the North Atlantic peoples; and since the fall of China no major nation of the Free World has disappeared behind the Iron Curtain. Yet does it follow from the respective record of Western and Soviet performance in the Cold War that the "tide has turned"? It does not. The very fact that the communists have managed to build up their present formidable power position while they were militarily and economically inferior by a broad margin to the Western powers should give us cause to ponder this extraordinary phenomenon. The margin is no longer so broad and is getting all the time thinner. The "ebb and the flow" should, by now, be an understood characteristic of communist strategy. Thus far, the tide has been coming in stronger after every period of ebbflow. The operational advantage in the contest, which is literally a contest for the future of man upon this earth, is shifting to the side of communism. This slippage of power opens a period of mounting concern for America and her associates and a time for great decisions.

The unsure response of the Western powers to repeated communist-instigated crises and the ever-resurgent hopes of Western democracies for a magic formula for peace bespeak the drift of the Western mood at the threshold of the sixties—the decade considered by the Soviets as the most crucial operational period in their history. The Soviets, beset by the internal contradictions of the communist world, may try to finish us. Our defeat will free their hands for settling "domestic" issues. Communist ideological vulnerabilities and the latent antagonism among the peoples of the communist bloc argue persuasively for the Kremlin to adopt a course of action that will insulate the communist experiment from interference from outside. There is, last but not least, the problem of Kremlin succession. The present generation of Russian communist leaders must seek to bring about a decisive change in the balance of power in order to harvest the fruits of victory. They may have left, at best, only ten years to do the job. For the very dynamics of the power struggle within the communist orbit accelerate the momentum of communist strategy. The communists, if they want to remain standing, must seek to keep us off balance—to cause us to fall.

Thus far, subsurface tensions have not openly cracked the unity of the communist bloc. Its solidarity-in-action is not matched by the Western Alliance, not to speak of the Free World as a whole. The communist states still act within a framework of a common ideology, they share a common purpose—and benefit from the flagrant disunity of the West. The communists agree, if they agree on nothing else, on despoiling their divided opponents. They are likely to smother their own differences, at least until the West leaves them free to quarrel over the loot. Communist strategy has successfully exploited the divisive tendencies within the Free World; Western strategies for exploiting the schisms and rivalries within the communist world are either ineffective or nonexistent.

Neither our people nor our government, nor for that matter the free peoples in general, have agreed on the basic nature of the communist threat. Lacking this consensus, they cannot agree on a common plan for meeting it.

History has cast the United States in the role of leader of the Free World and its principal defender against the communist bid for world domination. The difficulty of that role is matched only by the reluctance of the American people to assume leadership. Little in American history has prepared us for a protracted conflict of unpredictable length and indeterminate outcome. Americans like to think of other peoples as friendly neighbors. They find it difficult to grasp the mentality of the communists, for whom conflict is a way of life.

To defeat the enemy we must know him. To understand the nature and workings of the strategy of protracted conflict is an indispensable step toward meeting the challenge of communist imperialism. What will be the likely gambits of communist strategy in the sixties? Tactical surprises and technical novelties notwithstanding, communist strategy will, in all likelihood, conform to a familiar pattern. Nothing in the objective historic situation calls for its fundamental reorganization. It has been a successful strategy. Hence we can assume that it will be the same mixture as before—only more so—and that it will be applied with greater effectiveness. Its sinews—a vast continental base, increasing productive power, expanding knowledge, tight organization and general ideological consistency—will, on the whole, grow stronger. There is no reason to believe that, barring defeat in war, any of these strengths will suffer a substantial decline. We may assume that, as long as present trends in the Free World continue, communist power will grow not only absolutely but, far more important, relatively.

Communist strategy will be aimed at completing the world revolution, i.e., the world-wide expansion of communist domination at the rate at least of its advance during the last fifteen years. In the light of past achievements, this is not altogether an unreasonable objective. Specifically, communist strategy will be directed at the dissolution of the American alliance systems and the ejection of the American-led coalitions from Western Europe, the Middle East and the Far East. To guess at the communist schedule of priorities is a hazardous game. Yet it is likely that the principal, if not the first, objective of the communist strategic plan is the neutralization of Germany followed by the break-up of the various European agencies of integration; the next target might well be the neutralization of Japan and reduction of the American base system off the coast of China. Depending on developments, this sequence can, of course, be reversed.

While these transactions are being closed, the communists can turn simultaneously their energies to the domination of the Middle East, the subversion of Africa south of the Sahara and of Latin America.

The very shrinkage of the geographical area and economic markets controlled by the United States and Western Europe will, as the communists must surmise, constitute a compelling argument for Western surrender. When the isolation of the Atlantic Community—or what is left of it—will have been completed, the global prizes worth mortal combat will have passed into communist hands. Communist territorial expansion is spearheaded—and may soon be superseded—by the constant growth of communist technological and military power. In a total war of desperation, the West can wreak massive vengeance upon its tormentor, even if it cannot retrieve its over-all losses. But this threat cannot be relied upon to impress the Soviets with the ultimate futility of their strategy. Only an American Forward Strategy can halt the communist assault.

The principal techniques of communist strategy throughout 1960-1970 will still be nuclear blackmail, divisive diplomacy, subversion, propaganda and increasingly selective economic warfare backed by economic aid, offers of trade and dumping.

That in the near future the communists may prefer to apply these limited techniques of conquest—techniques short of a direct military assault on the continental United States—should not obscure the totality of the communist threat. Military and nonmilitary techniques are interrelated and mutually supporting. Indeed, nonmilitary means may ease the application of military means, including total nuclear war—just as the specter of "nuclear holocaust" eases the application of nonmilitary means. The communists might be tempted, within the next few years, to achieve and exploit missile superiority and to inflict upon the United States the military or psychological *coup de grâce*. Assuming even that the United States and the Soviet Union will be locked in a shifting nuclear stalemate—which appears to us a highly unlikely contingency—the communists could still expect to gain considerable advantages from their superiority in limited war capabilities and means of nonmilitary warfare. In any case, the communists bank heavily on Western inertia and illusions, Western moral erosion, anti-Western tendencies throughout Asia and Africa and eventual paralysis in the West itself.

We have sought to define the principles of a dynamic grand strategy that will advance our national interests and those of the Free World. It is incumbent upon our civilian and military statesmen in partnership to design and pursue an effective grand strategy that peoples at home and abroad will understand and support.

At present, we are dissipating much of our incomparable national power through defensive measures taken in counteraction to calamities which timely action on our part might have prevented. This is the heart of our strategic problem. Unless and until the U.S. discards strategic concepts that are passive or, at best, reactive, our choice will be confined to two equally disastrous alternatives: (1) to keep on living in a fool's paradise and to let ourselves be drained slowly of our strength or (2) to risk the holocaust of nuclear destruction. Is it too much to ask of ourselves that our range of choice be wider?

It has been argued throughout these pages that the main goal of the U.S. should be—for its own sake and the sake of mankind—the extension of freedom. The American experience does not furnish a simple panacea for the troubles of our age. For that matter, no national experience offers a nostrum for the conflicts inherent in the human condition. But the lessons of our history, sharpened by the rub of international conflict, point to the highroad which leads toward a better life for all peoples, that they may develop in responsible freedom as part of a world community.

How can the U.S. discharge its obligation to mankind and itself? The answer seems to lie in a paradoxical strategy that will engage us deliberately in a variegated range of "warfare" over an indefinite period for long-term political objectives. Our efforts should be always harnessed to the pursuit of prudent measures; toward limiting, but not to shrinking from, risk; and toward the positive, the creative solution.

To be sure, there is no way to guarantee that the use, especially a bolder use, of the several instruments of power will not lead to graver consequences than intended. This uncertainty is greatest in respect to the use, when all other instruments have failed, of armed force. But lacking the demonstrable capability for the measured employment of power in all its aspects, including military force, the art of statesmanship is reduced to an idle exercise in rhetoric. Rhetoric has its place in international politics, but neither clever arguments nor noble sentiments are substitutes for power.

The difficulies in arriving at the "right" strategic decisions and solutions, and pursuing them with vigor, are evident. Yet, if the United States and its Free World associates will husband their available resources and apply them wisely and courageously in pursuit of reasonable aims, the future could be theirs. The great danger lies in apathy: Will we rouse ourselves in time to cope with the treacherous currents and turns in the swelling stream of international crisis? Will we do what must be done to insure our survival as a nation and, beyond that, the survival of our way of life, indeed, of our civilization? That we have the capability to act effectively in our self-interest is incontrovertible. Whether the United States does act in its true self-interest in the next few years depends on its will to act and hence its will to sacrifice.

Principles of Forward Strategy

The principles of a Forward Strategy for the United States must be derived from the following propositions:

1. The priority objective of any American grand strategy is, by a broad margin, the preservation and enhancement of our political system rather than the maintenance of peace. The attainment of this objective may or may not be predicated on the establishment of compatible systems all over the world, but it certainly is predicated on the maintenance or establishment of compatible free systems in *some* key parts of the world. All other objectives, such as increased social welfare and continuing economic progress, while interrelated with the primary objective, are of secondary importance. Historically, democracies have proved to be short-lived. In the light of the unprecedented dangers which now beset human freedom, it behooves us to think through the weaknesses of the democratic system and to overcome them. Perhaps the root weakness of democracy is reluctance to gauge the full measure of the perennial and ever-recurring threat to its very existence—the very precariousness of freedom. It is because of this deficiency of will that democracies cavil at taking the steps *in time* that will insure their defense in the moment of supreme peril. The very existence of so aggressive and dynamic a force as communism imperils the survival of democracy everywhere. Woodrow Wilson's celebrated dictum carries today a meaning far deeper than his generation could read into it: To make the world safe *for* democracy is to make it safe for the continuing growth of the individual and freedom. The American system, in particular, can survive and grow only in a world that is safe for the pursuits of peace. It is upon this premise that American strategy must rest.

2. Our philosophy of international relations must be based on the self-evident axiom that utopias are, by definition, unattainable. Societies will not conform to our vision of perfection, certainly not on a global basis, and most assuredly not in the near future. For we live in permanent crisis. This permanent crisis poses a permanent threat to the political and physical survival of any

"system." There are no quick and easy answers to this problem; its solution will engage a far larger part of our national resources than we now set aside for the pursuit of our foreign policy and national security objectives. The argument that the permanent threat to our existence can be fought by limiting our initiatives to programs for better education, higher living standards and improved international co-operation for world economic development is not only fallacious but also dangerously deceptive. It detracts attention from the hard solutions which our continuing survival demands.

3. Alliances are an integral part of our security system. But alliances will not lighten our burden. Unless our intrinsic strength improves, defection will inevitably thin the ranks of our allies. Our own strength is the most convincing pledge of our loyalty to friends and allies. Our military programs are the hard core of our alliance systems and Free World security. We do not hold with the comfortable assumption that economic assistance to the underdeveloped countries can be a satisfactory alternative to military and alliance programs. The idea that help to the underdeveloped countries will by itself insure Free World stability and security is a flagrant form of Fabianism applied on an international scale. Unless incorporated in a stronger security system, a policy hitched primarily to the idea of world economic growth will drain our own resources and, in the bargain, might strengthen the hands of those factions in the underdeveloped countries who look upon us with cupidity, if not with hatred. This would be inescapably true if aid to underdeveloped countries were accompanied by a reduction in our over-all power posture, i.e., if world-wide economic growth were conceived of as a *substitute* for power. Programs of economic development redound to our benefit only if they are fitted as secondary elements into an integrated system of strategy. Such an integrated system must be designed to deal with *all* techniques of conflict. If the over-all strategic system is bereft of its hard core, the willingness and ability to wage conflict in all its dimensions, the supplementary efforts will dissipate scarce resources and fall short of their intended purposes. At the very heart of the communist strategic system lies the will and the commitment to permanent conflict. For example, the Soviets, in their programs for the economic development of the Asian and African countries, have not displayed either outstanding ad-

ministrative skill or a deep insight into the processes of change in underdeveloped societies. They have, however, a doctrinal framework for relating all their policies. Strangely, their over-all grasp on historical process enables them to fit change in transitional societies into a larger scheme, the remaking of the world order. Soviet policies thus appear more sensitive than ours to revolutionary change, i.e., social revolution and systemic revolution.[1] In brief, it is the strategic concept that must inform techniques of policy and not the other way around.

4. If strategy were just a matter of systematic procedures and orderly schemes for mastering predictable events, no campaign mounted by a resource-rich contender would ever have been lost. In the main, strategy, rather than being predetermined, is a more or less crude attempt at keeping one jump ahead of the contingent: "*On s'engage et puis on voit.*" ("You join the issue and then you see.") Long-range plans provide the necessary frame for purposeful action. But in addition to devising long-range programs and concepts, strategy threads together numerous *ad hoc* responses to concrete situations. Furthermore, execution of the long-range programs hinges on many subsidiary decisions which are in the nature of responses to unforeseen challenges or objective difficulties. However sound our long-range programs may be, the day-by-day decisions (and, in particular, the responses to crisis situations) are crucial. When the chips are down, an instant of equivocation can reduce the most elaborate and foresighted strategy to gibberish. Strategy is inseparable from the willingness to take risks and deny the enemy a guarantee of immunity in case he desists from a particular aggression. If it is our purpose to combat communism, then it follows that our overriding objective is not to preserve peace at all costs, but to destroy the aggressive power of communism. In approaching specific problems we should ask: Does the decision hurt the enemy or put him under pressure or at least compound his decision-making problems? Does it hasten his demise, or help to replenish his capabilities for waging international conflict? Firmness—hardness—of decision should not be mistaken for continuously rattling the saber.

[1] "Thus, in working single-mindedly for their political goals, the Soviets have been able to offer the peoples of the newly emergent countries the vision of not only a new society at home, but also a place in a new international community." Lucian W. Pye, "Soviet and American Styles in Foreign Aid," *Orbis*, (Summer, 1960), p. 172.

A sense of measure and moderation is the leaven of all constructive undertakings. But without the willingness to use force and without the sacrifice which the use of force as well as the prevention of war entails, no major international crisis ever has been settled short of appeasement or surrender.

5. We cannot concur with the interpretation of democracy as a system which is too flaccid to allow for the making of firm decisions. Vigorous public debate and high national morale, the spirit of sacrifice and the strength of motivations are all elements of our political system. Our political system is basically sound, but it must be stripped for action and, in part, reorganized so it is equal to its dangerous tasks in a dangerous environment. It would be foolish to pretend that, in a crisis in which societies are pitted against societies, the collective will is not a decisive element. Our collective will is weak, partly because our grasp on the meaning of the challenge has been weak—and because we persist in emphasizing the products of our system to the detriment of the system itself. Well-being flows from freedom and order. But by fastening our attention on the good things of life we cannot preserve the political conditions under which we have prospered.

6. The fundamental decision before us is whether we should accept the communist concept of coexistence in one form or the other or bring about the final defeat of communism. If we choose the latter course, we must decide whether we should bank on the defeat of communism by such fortuitous circumstances as internal erosion or revolution or whether we should extend ourselves to achieve this objective. We must decide whether a passive, expectant strategy might actually delay the demise of communism while hastening our own. And, lastly, we should decide why we really want to defeat communism. Is it because we wish to replace one "economic order" with another? Or do we seek to disestablish a particular political system, raze the intellectual prison camp of communism and help the peoples within the communist bloc to obtain self-government? Or do we stake our policies on the belief that communism, despite its present hostility, might be a more tractable opponent than a possible successor system—assuming that we live long enough to see that successor?

Shorn of all ideological connotations, our policy must be based upon the premise that we cannot tolerate the survival of a political system which has both the growing capability and the ruthless will to destroy us. We have no choice but to adopt a Catonic strategy. Cato the Censor was not the most lovable of men. No man who, in and out of season, chooses to propound a discomforting truth can gain popularity. If we are to triumph in the protracted conflict, we have to face what it means to have implacable enemies who, in turn, deem us to be *their* implacable enemies. We have to cultivate those dour virtues which alone sustain a people in mortal combat. To equate democracy with vapidity of spirit and the indulgence of the flesh is an unforgivable insult to democracy. Freedom is not a marginal luxury. Of all forms of government, democracy should be the one best fitted to inspire men with the sense of what they owe to one another and to themselves. But, if the communists prove to have more courage, a stronger will, a more steadfast spirit, a clearer intellectual insight into conflict in the nuclear age, they obviously are the better men and deserve to win—and probably will.

A *Summation*

Within the framework of the foregoing principles, let us review the salient issues raised in this book.

The world is in the midst of a great systemic revolution—military, technological, economic, social, psychological, political and ideological. This revolution confronts mankind with a fundamental structural crisis. Because of the existence of the two irreconcilable power centers, the revolution could issue into a universal catastrophe.

The communists espouse a dynamic plan of protracted conflict, the outcome of which is to be world domination by the communist elite and destruction of that freedom of man that ennobles our civilization. Protracted conflict as waged by the communists runs the full spectrum of the exercise of power. This spectrum of conflict includes the possibility of all-out nuclear war to bring the contracted conflict to a swift and decisive conclusion.

The Free World, tenuously led by the U.S., has not fully perceived the all-encompassing nature of protracted conflict and consequently has failed to pursue courses of action that would thwart the communist threat. Furthermore, the Free World has been laggard in awakening to the manifestations of the systemic revolution—the collapse of the "old order," the wave of rising expectations sweeping across the lands of the underprivileged peoples, the explosive growth of populations and the meteoric onrush of technology. In a word, the U.S. and the Free World are failing to meet the challenges of the systemic revolution, which would be immense even if they were not aggravated by the communist threat.

The many great forces at work in the world are locked so intensely in struggle that the future of all mankind is at stake for the first time in history. The basic conflict over the question as to whether all mankind shall live henceforth under tyranny—for however long—or under freedom could be decided one way or another within the next decade.

America and her associates, their commitments to the cause of freedom notwithstanding, have failed to rally their moral and material strength sufficiently to enhance and extend freedom and make it prevail over tyranny. We have not unambiguously accepted the fact that the battle is already engaged. We have comported ourselves in the world struggle in a manner that is essentially passive, reactive and defensive. We act as if time were on our side, when the evidence points to the contrary.

In the protracted conflict, the aspirations of the communist elite have been fulfilled far beyond the reach of their material power. The phenomenal growth of communist power and the naïveté and opportunism of many Free World elites obscure the real issue of tyranny versus freedom. The forces of tyranny and inhumanity are gaining in relative power over the forces of the free and open societies. More specifically, communist power is reaching a point where its integrated and manifold instruments of protracted conflict may achieve the triumph of communist tyranny.

Only by bold and sustained action can the U.S. and the Free World emerge the victor in this deadly struggle. There is a burning need for the restatement of the free peoples' common ideal of human progress under freedom, for concerted action to check and reduce the spread of communist totalitarianism, and for the advancement by mutual endeavor of the well-being of mankind.

The situation calls for certain changes in the organizational structure of the Free World nations, separately and collectively. Specifically, the reorganization of the free international community must issue from a reappraisal of those attributes of national sovereignty which have been outmoded, at least in the West, by the 150 years' advance from the age before steam to the age of space explorations.

The U.S., the leader of the Free World, offers mankind a vision more alluring than the communist counterfeit. The success of the American experiment and the universal ideas it embodies hold out to all men the prospect of growing in freedom. We can offer experience in evolutionary social, political and economic growth. We extend to all who seek to wrest a new polity from the turmoil of the systemic revolution the principle of federation as a means of creating the new political community of free men upon the foundation of the nation-state.

It is a truism to say that no people can be forced to be free or exhorted to make sacrifices which they do not believe are necessary. The great stumbling block to positive American action is not only American affluence but, above all, the intellectual euphoria that it engenders. In history, political systems usually were destroyed by their foes after their own leadership groups had committed intellectual suicide. Can a prosperous, easygoing people be aroused to their own defense? Can it master intellectually the discipline and sacrifice required for survival? This perhaps is the central question which this book must leave unanswered. In the last resort, the answer is given—as it has always been given in history—by the unique response of the living.

A national strategy for the next decade that measures up to the great issues of our times calls for an increase in effort and expenditure of resources. The impact on our way of life of sustained national effort may not be a cheerful prospect. A decision to launch our people on a more positive and expensive course is not an easy one to make. The psychological gap between the present order and the requisite national effort is difficult to bridge for any national leader. But this is precisely what he must do.

Actually, the gap between present levels of effort and the requirements of the next decade may not be so difficult to close as one might think. The American people have always met a genuine challenge when it was put to them squarely. Conversely, the record is replete with instances of national erosion in response to pusillanimous leadership. The potentialities of the American people should not be underestimated. We believe they will do what has to be done provided they are given the opportunity.

Public support requires education of the public by the responsible leaders, and trust by them in the people. Education in national strategy calls for patient and persistent effort. This is *the* task of leadership.

There never was a time in our history more propitious for great leadership than now. We face a challenge beyond historic precedent. At no time before has mankind faced such staggering possibilities, both for good and for evil.

What is the leadership we seek—who are leaders who can convince our people that firmness and not timidity will lead to our goal? We need leadership for mastering crisis, not for conducting debate. A leader may fully command the art of persuasion, but he must eventually demonstrate a readiness to close discussion, make a decision, stand by it and, if need be, carry it through under difficulties and against the protests of those who cannot be persuaded. He who by temperament and natural inclination believes that compromise solutions, or solutions voluntarily concurred in by all concerned, are inherently best; he who seeks to obtain general understanding of, and sympathy for, his views as a prerequisite for action may be a successful tactician in a limited field, but he does not fit the role of international leader in times of accelerating world crisis.

The great leader conquers the awful loneliness, which imprisons the holder of supreme power, by inner certitude and faith in a good cause from which springs the power of decision. Aloofness and righteousness are inseparable from leadership. These unlovable and unsociable attributes are basically alien to the character of contemporary civilization. Many of those, therefore, who call for "U.S. leadership" do not recognize or, at least, are unwilling to admit the objectionable and repugnant elements in the very concept of leadership.

That we do consider these elements repugnant and objectionable is a symptom of high civilization and genuinely humanitarian trust in the dignity and equality of men who live with one another on a basis of free consent and free co-operation. But modern man feels entirely insecure, if not within the United States, then certainly in the world at large. Whatever our own predilections, the burden to provide certainty and thus security for the world that is still free does lie overwhelmingly on our shoulders. We cannot impose this burden on the shoulders of others, more exposed and less powerful than ourselves. We try to obtain universal consent and agreement for policies and actions. We feel more at ease if we scatter our bounty over the lands of the needy and desist from exploiting our potential power. But in a crisis of such magnitude as the one the world faces now, this reluctance to lead appears also as an unwillingness to accept ultimate responsibility and as an attempt to lighten the terrible load by sharing responsibility with those who simply cannot bear it.

It would be both erroneous and ridiculous to assume that by embracing the role of a true "leader" the U.S. would become virtually free to choose its policies according to its whims and *without* regard for other free peoples. In a very important respect, in fact, true leadership would fix our position more firmly and narrowly: The corollary of our right to guide and to prescribe a course would be our duty to protect and support our friends even where our specific interests do not coincide. How, otherwise, can we make credible our pledge to stand at their side in the hour of need?

The writing of this book has been a sobering task. The conclusions we have reached about the world struggle are grim. The strategies we propose are not easy ones to accept or follow. If they were, there would be no need for a book about them—nor, for that matter, for any national strategy at all. Then things would take care of themselves. Unfortunately, we are confronted by an opponent who sees to it that the "normal" processes of history shall not remain normal. Our lot is conflict. History brings us "not peace but a sword." Will our hands grasp it?

In his *Life of Mark Antony*, Plutarch quotes Plato's *Gorgias* to the effect that there are four sorts of flattery. The four flatteries are the four counterfeit arts which profess to do good to men's bodies and souls and in reality only gratify their pleasures. "The legislator's place is thus usurped by the sophist, that of the judge by the rhetorician, while the physician is supplanted by the purveyor of luxuries and the teacher of bodily discipline by the adorner of the person." In this crisis those who wishfully pursue counterfeit policies and strategies gain their adherents by thousands of flatteries. To abstain from flattery and accept unpopularity when need be is the statesman's down payment on his right to his place in the history of mortal crisis—on his right to lead free men in times like ours.

APPENDIX A

This Appendix is to provide the reader with a fuller analysis of the question of potential U.S. economic growth at higher levels of governmental expenditure. In Chapter 10, where this analysis was summarized, it was asserted that during the Korean War period, i.e., from 1950 to 1953, government expenditures for goods and services[1] rose by almost $50 billion. (The figures in this Appendix will all be given in terms of 1959 prices or "1959 dollars.") (See Table I.)

GNP rose in the same period by $60 billion or $10 billion more. Thus, GNP rose 5 per cent a year, and the resources remaining after the government took its share of the GNP were adequate to permit gross private expenditure (GPE) to rise more than 1 per cent a year from 1950 to 1953. Personal consumption, the largest part of GPE, actually rose almost 3 per cent a year, or more than 1 per cent per capita, as the real curtailment occurred in the sector of private investment. During this period, government expenditures rose from about one-seventh to almost a quarter of GNP.

The above figures are conservative. Measured from 1949 to 1953, GNP rose at 6 per cent a year instead of 5 per cent, and private

[1] We shall talk throughout of government expenditures for goods and services rather than total expenditures and the related government budgets. We are concerned here with resources, i.e., "goods and services," as they are used in national product and income accounting. The familiar government budgets include large amounts of so-called "transfer payments," such as Social Security, debt service and most agricultural program payments. Transfer payments loom large in the familiar government budgets and expenditure data, but they have no direct bearing on the volume of resources used and the output produced each year.

TABLE I

The Korean Build-up

	1950	1953	Average Annual Increase
	(Billions of 1959 Dollars)		(%)
Government Expenditures	54	101	23
Federal	26	70	39
State and Local	28	31	2.7
Gross Private Expenditure (GPE)	303	313	1.1
Gross National Product (GNP)	357	414	5.0
Government Expenditure/GNP[2]	15.1%	24.4%	

expenditures rose at 5 per cent annually, instead of only 1 per cent. Let us note that 1949 was a recession year. Furthermore, anticipation of the effect of increased government expenditure led the private sector greatly to increase its expenditures in the last six months of 1950, before federal expenditures started to climb.

The three-year build-up period, 1950-1953, appears an appropriate sample. Three years is a reasonable minimum in terms of the required lead-times for planning and for actual procurement of the "longest lead" items such as new plant (*cf.* also the World War II experience).

Direct controls were instituted, following the World War II experience. As it turned out, these controls were largely unneeded. However, adoption of controls was undoubtedly a correct decision in 1950 and 1951, for no one knew how serious the emergency would prove.

World War II Experience

Now let us look at the World War II patterns (Table II). In the three years from 1941 to 1944, federal and total government ex-

[2] Computed in current dollars, the figures would be 13.7% for 1950 and 22.7% for 1953. The prices of goods and services purchased by government have risen more rapidly than the prices of purchases by the private sector. These are the percentages which would be required to represent the same relative allocation of real resources today.

penditures rose by some 125 billion 1959 dollars, but total GNP rose only $90 billion (10 per cent per year, nevertheless). This time, we do find gross private expenditure curtailed. Private consumption continued to rise, even on a per capita basis, except in 1942. All of the impact was absorbed in the investment sector, in which private domestic investment was deferred and the total was held below 50 per cent of prewar levels. Moreover, there occurred a shift from a net export to a net import position, i.e., a decline in "net foreign investment."

TABLE II

The World War II Build-up

	1941	1944	Average Annual Increase (%)
	(Billions of 1959 Dollars)		
Government Expenditures	58	183	47
Federal	37	166	65
State and Local	21	17	−7
Gross Private Expenditure (GPE)	210	174	−6
Gross National Product (GNP)	267	357	10
Government Expenditure/GNP[3]	21.7%	51.3%	

By 1944, the proportion of government expenditure was more than 50 per cent. Somewhere between the almost 25 per cent of Korea and the 51 per cent of World War II, there appears to be a point beyond which government activities cannot be expanded rapidly (within three years) without temporarily cutting into the private sector.

Sources of Wartime Growth

In both wars, the economy drew primarily on new workers, that is, net additions to the labor force. Despite the fact that World War II followed a depression and Korea a recession, in each case more new workers were hired than number of unemployed rehired (Table III).

[3] Computed in current dollars, the corresponding figures are 19.7% for 1941 and 45.6% for 1944. See explanation in Footnote 2.

TABLE III

Sources of Wartime Growth

	Korea	World War II
	(Per cent per Annum)	
Employment		
New Workers	2	3.33
Re-employment	1	2.66
Total	3	6
Productivity/Employee*		
Increased Hours	0	3
Productivity/Man-hour	2	1
Total	2	4
Total (Real Gross National Product)	5	10
Productivity/Employee	4	9
Productivity/Man-hour	2	6

* If Armed Forces Are Excluded

In times of an expanding economy, the labor force, of course, also expands. In the wartime years housewives, early retired workers and young people, normally outside the labor market, swelled the employed ranks.

In each war, productivity per employee accounted for two-fifths of the production growth. In World War II, however, this was mainly a matter of increased hours of work, which went up about 10 per cent, from roughly forty-four to forty-eight hours. This yielded a 3 per cent increase in output, with another 1 per cent coming from increased productivity per man-hour. Some very real gains in productivity, from technological improvements and changes in the "product mix" as we shifted to higher-value war goods, are obscured by the tremendous shift of manpower into the armed forces. Considering productivity of civilian employees only, productivity per man-hour actually rose by about 6 per cent a year, against 2 per cent during the Korean period.

Sources of Growth in the Sixties

Since the war, as remarked earlier, GNP in constant prices has been rising about 3.5 per cent a year (Table IV). Of this, rising employment has accounted for 1.1 per cent. The remainder of 2.4 per cent is increased productivity per employee, which is the net sum of a decline in the work week and a somewhat larger rise in productivity per hour. Bureau of Labor Statistics projections for the early sixties show an average annual rise of 1.75 per cent in the labor force. Employment will also rise at 1.75 per cent if the unemployment ratio remains at 5 per cent. Productivity may be assumed to rise at 2.75 per cent—the rate from 1946 to 1955—a most conservative assumption for the sixties in the light of the research and development boom and the large plant and equipment investments in the fifties, factors which may reasonably be expected to pay off in productivity gains. Reduction of unemployment to 4 per cent would permit the same gains with the 2.4 per cent productivity growth rate of 1946-59.

These increases in employment and productivity make 4.5 per cent a conservative estimate—but not a prediction—of reasonable growth in the next few years.

Let us now consider expanded government programs at two levels: the first, of the order of the Korean effort and probably not requiring direct controls, and the second program large enough to be comparable to the Soviet relative allocation and requiring temporary controls of the Korean sort (Table IV).

TABLE IV
Current and Feasible Growth Rates
(Per cent per Annum)

		Minimum	Expanded Programs		
	Current	Prosperity in 60's (A)	No Controls (B)	Mild Controls (C)	World War II Pattern
Employment	1.1	1.75	2.50	3.5	6
Productivity/Employee	2.4	2.75	3.25	3.5	4
Total (Real Gross National Product)	3.5	4.50	5.75	7	10

Under the conditions of increased demand postulated in the first case, at least another 0.75 per cent of annual increase in employment may be anticipated as the labor force increases and unemployment begins to be cut back. A modest additional .5 per cent annual increase in productivity gives a 5.75 per cent annual growth rate, or probably about that of the Soviet Union.

With the stimulus of an even larger program, there might well be as much as 3.5 per cent annual growth in employment, with unemployment declining to 2-3 per cent, and 3.5 per cent annual increase in productivity per man, assuming that the decline in average hours is temporarily halted. Even 3.5 per cent seems conservative in the light of the technological backlog available and of the increase in the average work week (not the standard work week) which might be anticipated. These factors would give an annual growth rate of 7 per cent, which is higher than most estimates of Soviet growth.

Potential by 1964

On the basis of these projections of the sources of growth, we have constructed "models" of the 1964 economy (Table V). The use of the year 1964 allows the minimum three years for build up, assuming 1961 to be a year of decision. The estimated 1960 pattern is used as a base.

From the end of the Korean program through 1959, federal government expenditures in real dollars actually declined by 1 per cent a year, as the budget was held almost constant and inflation took its toll. State and local government expenditures, which were held down somewhat by government controls during Korea, have since that time risen at about 5.5 per cent per annum, in response to the familiar demands of increased school age population, suburbanization and highway use. On the assumption that these requirements will continue, the 5.5 per cent rate is used for all models in the 1960's. Federal and state and local rates add up to a net increase of 1.4 per cent a year for all government expenditures. We take GNP to have been rising at 3.5 per cent per year for the whole period since 1946, since it seems necessary to average out the distortions introduced by the Korean controls. Private outlays, GPE, have been rising at only 2.8 per cent since World War II, while the government share has risen from a low of 12 per cent in 1947 to

TABLE V

U.S. Potential by 1964

(Dollar Figures in Billions of 1959 Dollars—Percentages Are Average Annual Changes Except Last Line)

	(1960) Estimated	Recent Trends	Minimum Prosperity (A)		Expanded Gov't. No Controls (B)		Programs With Controls (C)		World War II Pattern	
			PROJECTIONS TO 1964							
	$	%	$	%	$	%	$	%	$	%
Government Expenditures	101	1.4	120	4.5	150	10.4	210	20.1	355	38
Federal	55	−1.1	63	4.5	93	14.0	153	29.1	317	56
State and Local	46	5.5	57	5.5	57	5.5	57	5.5	38	−7
Gross Private Expenditures (GPE)	404	2.8	482	4.5	482	2.7	449	2.7	355	−6
Gross National Product (GNP)	505	3.5	602	4.5	632	6.9	659	6.9	710	10.3
Government Expenditure/GNP	(20%)		(20%)		(24%)		(32%)		(50%)	

20 per cent in 1959 and 1960 (even though the latter figure reflects a decline from the 1953 peak.)

In Model A, government expenditures are assumed to keep pace with the rest of the economy, i.e., we continue to devote one-fifth of our resources for 4.5 per cent growth (see the estimate of Table IV). Let us note that federal expenditures increase only by 3.5 per cent per year, or the same rate as the base period growth rate of the economy as a whole.

Model B is drawn to the scale of the Korean-level-of-effort, with almost a quarter of the economy devoted to governmental activities. By 1964, this means $150 billion, or $93 billion for the federal government alone. (Note that this is a rise from $54 billion, not from the $80 billion figure of the federal budget, since we are talking here only of purchases of goods and services, not of total budgets, which include transfer payments, interest, etc., which do not directly affect real resources). On the very conservative assumption that gross private expenditure grows no faster than the 4.5 per cent to which we might all like to become accustomed, total growth would be 5.8 per cent. Controls would probably be unnecessary, since GPE could be permitted to rise faster than 4.5 per cent.

In Model C, almost a third of the national product is devoted to government. This is roughly comparable to the Soviet allocations, but represents more than twice as much in resources available for government programs. By 1964, $210 billion would be available for government functions—over $150 billion for the federal government.

In the final column of Table V, the World War II figures are recapitulated, simply as a frame of reference.

In Model C we see a real need for temporary direct controls along the Korean lines to contain the private economy, which under this kind of stimulus would otherwise tend to burst its bonds and to pre-empt some items needed by government. It is only in this program that we see evidence of inflationary pressures during the build-up, requiring containment by direct controls, over and above the judicious fiscal and monetary policy assumed to accompany each program. The models are in "constant" 1959-dollars, and reflect the tremendous real expansion of goods which would be available to control inflation. It is not assumed that there will be no inflation, but simply that needed and sustainable growth must take precedence as an objective over attempts to control inflation rigidly.

In Model C the total GNP growth rate is almost 7 per cent and GPE is still rising at 2.7 per cent, or almost the rate to which we have become accustomed since the war. We are not talking about sacrifice, except perhaps in the illusory sense of making people give up what they would like to have but have never had. Models B and C, far from being austerity programs, provide for private expenditure growth rates which bracket the probable rate of consumption growth in the Soviet Union.

It is likely that the principal impact of direct government controls would be the curtailment of private investment and the deferment of some building of new plant and equipment for from one to three years during the rapid build-up of government expenditures. Under some types of armament programs, it might prove necessary to cut back the production of automobiles and other consumer durables. But the chief impact would be on investment, not consumption, so that the growth of 2.7 per cent a year calculated for GPE in Model C is an underestimate of the growth in private consumption.

These models have been designed to show the "worst case." Should 1961 prove a year of national decision, should it be the national purpose to close the missile gap, to erect a more imposing armed defense, to support large-scale development of the underdeveloped half of the world, to press the exploration of outer space, to strengthen the economy for longer-run competition by raising the level of education, further increasing the highways, urban renewal, water supply or antipollution programs—the models show what could be done for the most rapid feasible build-up of these programs. The three-year lead-time is based on the experience in the two historical precedents, which showed it to be the minimum lead-time which allows for the taking of steps necessary to appropriation, obligation and expenditure of moneys and the construction of new plants and the start-up of production.

Any large programs are easier to undertake if we allow more time for their completion. Thus, if the feasibility of a given program within three years is demonstrated, its feasibility within a longer period is already established.

But what of the levels of government activity after the build-up has been completed? Obviously, we do not contemplate the continued growth of government expenditures at the rates shown. But it is equally clear that the resources of the country as expressed in terms of labor force and productivity would be adequate to go on supporting for an indefinite period the levels of government expenditures reached in our models in the year 1964. If government expenditures grew no further (or actually declined), continued growth of the private sector would mean that the government share would once more decline, when measured as a percentage of GNP. Even if the total government expenditures continued to grow at the same rate as the rest of the economy, as postulated in Model A for the years up to 1964, the growth of labor force and productivity indicated in Table IV, Column 2, would be adequate to support continued expansion of the economy at 4.5 per cent. This might also be feasible without strain at the level of growth implied in Model B, that is, almost 6 per cent per annum.

APPENDIX B

The National Security Council

STATUTORY FUNCTIONS OF THE COUNCIL

1. The National Security Act of 1947, as amended, established (title I) the National Security Council, the Central Intelligence Agency, and the Office of Defense Mobilization, and (title II) the Department of Defense. By section 2 of Reorganization Plan No. 1 of 1958 (effective July 1, 1958), the Office of Defense Mobilization and the Federal Civil Defense Administration were consolidated to form a new agency in the Executive Office of the President, to be known as the Office of Civil and Defense Mobilization; by section 4 of the reorganization plan, the functions of the Director, Office of Defense Mobilization, with respect to being a member of the National Security Council, were transferred to the Director, Office of Civil and Defense Mobilization. Since 1949, the National Security Council has been a part of the Executive Office of the President.

2. Title I of the act, titled "Co-ordination for National Security," states the function of the Council: "to advise the President with respect to the integration of domestic, foreign, and military policies relating to the national security so as to enable the military services and the other departments and agencies of the Government to co-operate more effectively in matters involving the national security."

3. Title I of the act further states the duties of the Council: (1) "to assess and appraise the objectives, commitments, and risks of the United States in relation to our actual and potential military power, in the interest of national security, for the purpose of making recom-

mendations to the President in connection therewith"; (2) "to consider policies on matters of common interest to the departments and agencies of the Government concerned with the national security, and to make recommendations to the President in connection therewith"; (3) to perform "such other functions as the President may direct, for the purpose of more effectively coordinating the policies and functions of the departments and agencies of the Government relating to the national security"; and (4) from time to time to "make such recommendations and such other reports to the President as it deems appropriate or as the President may require."

4. Title I of the act also establishes the Central Intelligence Agency "under" the Council and provides that it functions "under the direction of" the Council.

CONCEPT OF COUNCIL OPERATIONS

5. The following basic concepts govern the operations of the National Security Council and, as appropriate, the Council's Planning Board and Operations Co-ordinating Board:

a. To deal only with issues affecting national security.

b. To be advisory to the President in his determination of national security policy and to the responsible departments and agencies in their implementation of such policy.

c. To seek to integrate domestic, foreign, and military policies so as to enable government agencies to co-operate more effectively in national security matters.

d. To assist, according to Presidential direction, in co-ordinating policies and functions of government agencies relating to the national security.

e. To be concerned with both our actual and our potential military power.

f. Not to be limited to areas of agency agreement; on its own initiative, to seek out areas of agency conflict or omission to act, so as to present alternative or new courses of action for executive decision.

COUNCIL STRUCTURE

6. The National Security Council operates through the following mechanism:

a. The Council itself:

(1) Periodic meetings of the Council.
(2) Special committees, *ad hoc* committees, and consultants.

b. The Council subsidiary organization:
(1) The Planning Board.
(2) The Operations Co-ordinating Board.
(3) The NSC staff.
(4) Interdepartmental Intelligence Conference:
Director, Federal Bureau of Investigation, Chairman;
Assistant Chief of Staff, Intelligence, U.S. Army;
Director of Naval Intelligence;
Director of Special Investigations, U.S. Air Force;
(NSC representative on Internal Security—adviser.)
(5) Interdepartmental Committee on Internal Security:
First Assistant, Internal Security Division, Department of Justice, Chairman;[1]
Administrator, Bureau of Security and Consular Affairs, Department of State;
Director, Office of Domestic Programs, Department of Defense;
Assistant General Counsel, Treasury Department;
(NSC representative on Internal Security—adviser.)
(6) Other special and *ad hoc* committees.

c. The Joint Chiefs of Staff: "Principal military advisers" to the Council.

d. The Central Intelligence Agency: "Intelligence adviser" to the Council.

CURRENT COUNCIL PROCEDURES

A. Existing Presidential instructions

7. The Council mechanism aids the President in formulating and co-ordinating national security policy. In that area, it functions in accordance with the instructions which he gives from time to time. His current instructions include:

a. The Council should be the channel through which recommendations for national security policy reach the President for his decision.

[1] The Chairman is designated by the President from the membership of the committee after consultation with the Attorney General.

b. Except as directed by the President, matters to be considered by the Council should insofar as possible deal with the making or alteration of broad policies—either policies for the future or policies immediately required by currently developing events—and with reports on the progress of carrying out approved policies. The Council should not concern itself with interagency conflicts not involving policy considerations.

c. The Council is a corporate body, composed of individuals advising the President in their own right rather than as representatives of their respective departments and agencies. Their function should be to seek, with their background of experience, the most statesmanlike solution to the problem of national security, rather than to reach solutions which represent merely a compromise of departmental positions. The same concept is equally applicable to advisory and subordinate groups, such as the Joint Chiefs of Staff, the NSC Planning Board, and the Operations Co-ordinating Board; although the members of the latter two Boards are responsible also for stating the views of their respective departments and agencies.

B. Membership of the Council

8. Statutory members: The present statutory members are: the President; the Vice President; the Secretary of State; the Secretary of Defense; the Director, Office of Civil and Defense Mobilization.

9. Participant members: In addition to statutory members, the President invites such other officials of the government to participate as members in Council activities (including attendance at Council meetings) as his convenience and the agenda items at a particular meeting make desirable—

a. Regular participant members: for all Council activities until the President otherwise determines. (Currently, the Secretary of the Treasury, and the Director, Bureau of the Budget.)

b. Special-request members: for all agenda items which are the subject of official interest to their responsibilities, until the President otherwise determines. (Currently, the Attorney General, the Chairman, Atomic Energy Commission, and the Administrator, National Aeronautics and Space Administration.)

c. *Ad hoc* members: for any agenda item which the President may determine (for example, the Secretary of Commerce; the Chairman, Council of Economic Advisers).

10. Advisers, observers, staff: In addition to statutory and participant members, there are in attendance at each Council meeting the following persons who do not formally participate as Council members:

a. Advisers:

The Chairman, Joint Chiefs of Staff.

The Director of Central Intelligence.

b. Observers:

The Assistant to the President.

The Deputy Assistant to the President.

The Director, USIA.

The Undersecretary of State for Economic Affairs (as co-ordinator of the mutual security program).

The Special Assistants to the President for Foreign Economic Policy and for Science and Technology.

The White House staff secretary.

c. Staff:

Special Assistant to the President for National Security Affairs.

Special Assistant to the President for Security Operations Coordination.

Executive Secretary, NSC.

Deputy Executive Secretary, NSC.

11. Persons without executive responsibilities to the President are not invited to sit as participant members.

12. Consultants: In order to bring to the Council deliberations a fresh, frequently changing nongovernmental point of view and to gain public understanding of national security problems through the use of private citizens of stature, from time to time the President appoints one or more consultants as informal advisers to the Council. As a general rule, such consultants appear at a Council meeting only to present and discuss their report. . . .

OFFICERS OF THE COUNCIL

14. The President is Chairman of the National Security Council.

15. Two special assistants, appointed by the President on the White House staff, assist the President in the operation of the Council mechanisms. Neither has status as a participant member of the Council.

a. The Special Assistant for National Security Affairs is the principal supervisory officer of the National Security Council and serves as Chairman of the Council's Planning Board and the OCB.

b. The Special Assistant for Security Operations Co-ordination serves as Vice Chairman of the OCB.

16. There is an Executive Secretary (provided by statute) and a Deputy Executive Secretary of the National Security Council, appointed by the President. Under the supervision of the Special Assistant for National Security Affairs, the Executive Secretary is the head of the NSC staff, acts for the special assistant in his absence (including acting as Chairman of the Planning Board), and advises and aids him in the performance of his duties.

17. There is within the staff of the National Security Council an executive officer and a deputy executive officer of the Operations Coordinating Board. The executive officer is appointed by the President and, as the head of the OCB staff, is responsible to the Board for assisting it in the performance of its functions. He works under the general direction of the Board, and advises and aids the Chairman, Vice Chairman and Board members in the performance of their duties as members. He acts as Chairman of the OCB assistants.

The executive officer provides staff support as required for the Special Assistant for Security Operations Co-ordination.

NSC PLANNING BOARD

18. The functions of the NSC Planning Board, as the principal policy formulating body of the Council, are as follows:

a. To anticipate and identify problems and situations affecting the security objectives, commitments, and risks of the United States, and initiate action to provide the required analysis and draft policy statements for the consideration of the Council.

b. To facilitate the formulation of policies, during the process of drafting policy recommendations, by marshaling the resources of the respective departments and agencies; by identifying the possible alternatives; by endeavoring to achieve acceptable agreements; by discussing differences; by avoiding undesirable compromises which conceal or gloss over real differences; and by reducing differences to as clearly defined and narrow an area as possible prior to reference to the Council. . . .

20. Each Planning Board member or adviser is appointed by the

President upon nomination by the head of the department or agency and approval by the Special Assistant for National Security Affairs. He has the stature and ability which meet the standard required for Assistant Secretary. While his work with the Board is his principal responsibility, he continues to be sufficiently in the stream of activity in his department or agency as to be capable of representing its views.

21. Policy papers submitted by the Planning Board for Council consideration are presented, except in unusual cases, in uniform format, and include: A concise statement of the general considerations on which the policy recommendations are based; a succinct statement of recommended policy objectives; a fuller statement of recommended major policy guidance; and a summary indication of financial implications.

22. The Planning Board is assisted in the drafting of papers by the NSC Board assistants, who meet as required under the chairmanship of the Director of the Planning Board secretariat and attend all Planning Board meetings.

OPERATIONS CO-ORDINATING BOARD

A. Functions

23. Executive Order No. 10700[2] states the Board's functions as follows:

"In order to assist in the effective coordination among certain agencies of certain functions relating to the national security and to provide for the integrated implementation of national security policies by the said agencies, there is hereby established within the structure of the National Security Council the Operations Coordinating Board, hereinafter referred to as the Board, which shall report to the National Security Council." (Sec. 1(a).)

"The President having approved any national security policy after receiving the advice of the National Security Council thereon, the Board shall (1) whenever the President shall hereafter so direct, advise with the agencies concerned as to (*a*) their detailed operational planning responsibilities respecting such policy, (*b*) the coordination of the interdepartmental aspects of the detailed operational plans developed by the agencies to carry out such policy,

[2] Dated Feb. 26, 1957; effective July 1, 1957.

(*c*) the timely and coordinated execution of such policy and plans, and (*d*) the execution of each security action or project so that it shall make its full contribution to the attainment of national security objectives and to the particular climate of opinion the United States is seeking to achieve in the world, and (2) initiate new proposals for action within the framework of national security policies in response to opportunity and changes in the situation. The Board shall perform such other advisory functions as the President may assign to it and shall from time to time make reports to the National Security Council with respect to the carrying out of this order." (Sec. 2.)

"Nothing in this order shall be construed either to confer upon the Board any function with respect to internal security or to abrogate or restrict in any manner any function vested by law in, or assigned pursuant to law to, any agency or head of agency (including the Office of Defense Mobilization[3] and the Director of the Office of Defense Mobilization)." (Sec. 5)

B. Membership

24. Members designated by Executive order:

a. The Undersecretary of State for Political Affairs, representing the Secretary of State.

b. The Deputy Secretary of Defense, representing the Secretary of Defense.

c. The Director of Central Intelligence.

d. The Director, U.S. Information Agency.

e. The Director, International Co-operation Administration.

f. One or more representatives of the President, as designated by the President.[4]

25. The Board has a Chairman and Vice Chairman, each of whom is designated by the President from among its members[5]. . . .

[3] Consolidated with the Federal Civil Defense Administration to form the Office of Civil and Defense Mobilization, pursuant to Reorganization Plan No. 1 of 1958.

[4] Currently the Special Assistant to the President for Security Operations Co-ordination; the Special Assistant to the President for National Security Affairs.

[5] (The President's Special Assistant for National Security Affairs was designated chairman on January 13, 1960.)

D. Board assistants

30. Each member of the Board (other than a Presidential representative) is assisted in his responsibilities by a Board assistant. The Board assistants: (*a*) Meet as a group under the chairmanship of the OCB executive officer to review papers to be considered by the Board, and to assist the Board in carrying out agreed action programs; and (*b*) act within their respective agencies to insure staff support of their principals in OCB matters.

E. Standing committees and ad hoc *working groups*

31. OCB projects are usually referred to an appropriate OCB standing committee or an ad hoc working group, of agency personnel having operating responsibilities, plus an OCB staff member. Its functions are to assure that: (*a*) Interagency matters are fully coordinated; (*b*) approved courses of action are planned and carried out; and (*c*) the Board is kept informed through adequate reporting of the status of its assignments.

SELECTED BIBLIOGRAPHY

The following books, studies and articles represent a diversity of interpretations and analyses of the major problems treated in *A Forward Strategy for America.* The reader who seeks to broaden his knowledge will find in these sources a wealth of additional information, much of which reflects the thinking of the authors of this volume and some of which presents differing approaches to the major problems confronting the United States in its foreign policy.

Chapter III—Building the Free World

BIERI, ERNST. "An Atlantic Dialogue in Bruges," *Orbis,* I (Winter, 1958).

CHAMBERLIN, WALDO. "The North Atlantic Bloc in the U.N. General Assembly," *Orbis,* I (Winter, 1958).

KOHN, HANS. "The Atlantic Community and the World," *Orbis,* I (Winter, 1958).

———."The Difficult Road to Western Unity," *Orbis,* III (Fall, 1959).

The Nature of Foreign Policy and the Role of the United States in the World. Prepared at the request of the Committee on Foreign Relations, U. S. Senate. Washington: U. S. Government Printing Office, 1959.

The Operational Aspects of U. S. Foreign Policy. Maxwell Graduate School of Citizenship and Public Affairs, Syracuse University. Prepared at the request of the Committee on Foreign Relations, U. S. Senate. Washington: U. S. Government Printing Office, 1959.

POPPER, KARL R. *The Open Society and its Enemies.* Princeton: Princeton University Press, 1950.

SCHUMAN, ROBERT. "The Atlantic Community and Europe," *Orbis,* I (Winter, 1958).

SPAAK, PAUL-HENRI. "The Atlantic Community and NATO," *Orbis,* I (Winter, 1958).

STRAUSZ-HUPÉ, ROBERT, COTTRELL, ALVIN, J., and DOUGHERTY, JAMES E. *American-Asian Tensions.* New York: Praeger, 1956.

STRAUSZ-HUPÉ, ROBERT and HAZARD, HARRY W. (eds.) *The Idea of Colonialism.* New York: Praeger, 1958.

STRAUSZ-HUPÉ, ROBERT. "Protracted Conflict: A New Look at Communist Strategy," *Orbis,* II (Spring, 1959).

———. "World in Revolution," *Saturday Evening Post,* Vol. 232 (August 15, 1959).

Chapter IV—The Technological Factor

CONANT, JAMES. *Harvard Case History in Experimental Science.* Cambridge: Harvard University Press, 1959, 2 vols.

HART, HORNELL. "Technological Acceleration and the Atomic Bomb," *American Sociological Review,* II (June, 1946).

JEWKES, JOHN. *Sources of Invention.* New York: St. Martin's Press, 1958.

JOHNSON, ELLIS A. "Crisis in Science and Technology and Its Effect on Military Development," *Operations Research,* VI (January-February, 1958).

KLEIN, BURTON H. "A Radical Proposal for Research and Development," *Fortune* (May, 1958).

National Security—The Military Aspect. Rockefeller Fund, January, 1958.

"Perspectives on Government and Science," *The Annals of the American Academy of Political and Social Science,* Vol. 327 (January, 1960).

POKROVSKY, G. I. (translated by Raymond L. Garthoff). *Science and Technology in Contemporary War.* New York: Praeger, 1959.

POPPER, KARL R. *Logic of Scientific Discovery.* New York: Basic Books, 1959.

Possible Nonmilitary Scientific Developments and Their Potential Impact on Foreign Policy Problems of the United States. Stanford Research Institute. Prepared at the request of the Committee on Foreign Relations, U. S. Senate. Washington: U. S. Government Printing Office, 1959.

SILK, LEONARD S. *The Research Revolution.* New York: McGraw-Hill, 1960.

SINGER, CHARLES, HOLMYARD, E. J., and HALL, A. R. (eds.). *A History of Technology.* New York: Oxford University Press, 1954, 5 vols.

VUCINICH, ALEXANDER. *Soviet Academy of Sciences.* Stanford: Stanford University Press, 1956.

Chapter V—Military Strategy, Power and Policy

ACHESON, DEAN. "The Illusion of Disengagement," *Foreign Affairs,* XXXVI (April, 1958).

———. "NATO and Nuclear Weapons," *New Republic* (December 30, 1957).

AMME, CARL H. "Psychological Effects of Nuclear Weapons," *U. S. Naval Institute Proceedings,* LXXXVI (April, 1960).

ARON, RAYMOND. *On War.* Garden City, New York: Doubleday Anchor Books, Inc., 1960.

BRODIE, BERNARD. *Strategy in the Missile Age.* Princeton: Princeton University Press, 1959.

CANNELL, ROGERS. "The Active Role of Passive Defense," *Stanford Research Institute Journal,* III (Fourth Quarter, 1959).

COTTRELL, ALVIN J. "Military Security and the New Look," *Current History,* XXXVIII (April, 1960).

COTTRELL, ALVIN J., *et al.* "A New Strategy for Europe," *Yale Review,* XLVII (Autumn, 1957).

DE HUSZAR, GEORGE B. (ed.). *National Strategy in an Age of Revolutions.* New York: Praeger, 1959.

Developments in Military Technology and Their Impact on United States Strategy and Foreign Policy. Washington Center of Foreign Policy Research, Johns Hopkins University. Prepared at the request of the Committee on Foreign Relations, U. S. Senate. Washington: U. S. Government Printing Office, 1959.

DINERSTEIN, HERBERT S. *Soviet Strategic Ideas, January 1960,* Research Memorandum 2532. Santa Monica, California: The RAND Corporation, February, 1960.

———. *War and the Soviet Union.* New York: Praeger, 1959.

FURNISS, EDGAR S., JR. *American Military Policy: Strategic Aspects of World Political Geography.* New York: Rinehart, 1957.

GARTHOFF, RAYMOND L. *The Soviet Image of Future War.* Washington: Public Affairs Press, 1959.

———. *Soviet Strategy in the Nuclear Age.* New York: Praeger, 1958.

GAVIN, JAMES M. *War and Peace in the Space Age.* New York: Harper, 1958.

GORDON, LINCOLN. "NATO in the Nuclear Age," *The Yale Review,* XLVIII (March, 1959).

HAHN, WALTER F., and NEFF, JOHN C. (eds.). *American Strategy for the Nuclear Age.* Garden City, New York: Doubleday, 1960.

ATKINSON, JAMES D. "Unconventional Warfare."

BALDWIN, HANSON W. "Limited War."

COTTRELL, ALVIN J. and HAHN, WALTER F. "Needed: A New NATO Shield."

FOSTER, RICHARD B. "Values, Power and Strategy."

JOHNSON, ELLIS. "The Lead-Time Problem and Technological Waste."

KAHN, HERMAN. "The Nature and Feasibility of War and Deterrence."

LOOSBROCK, JOHN F. "Strategy on Trial."

WILLIAMS, Commander RALPH E., JR. "Security through Sea Power."

WOHLSTETTER, ALBERT. "The Delicate Balance of Terror."

HALPERIN, MORTON H. *Nuclear Weapons and Limited War.* Cambridge: Center for International Affairs, Harvard University, July, 1960.

HOAG, MALCOLM. "Interdependence for NATO," *World Politics,* XII (April, 1960).

KAHN, HERMAN. "The Nature and Feasibility of War and Deterrence," *Stanford Research Institute Journal,* III (Fourth Quarter, 1959).

KING, JAMES E., JR. "The Military Conflict: Limited or Guerrilla Warfare." Address delivered at the Defense Strategy Seminar, National War College, Washington, D. C., 1960.

KISSINGER, HENRY A. "Arms Control, Inspection and Surprise Attack," *Foreign Affairs,* XXXVIII (July, 1960).

———. *Nuclear Weapons and Foreign Policy.* New York: Harper (for the Council on Foreign Relations), 1957.

KNORR, KLAUS (ed.). *NATO and American Security.* Princeton: Princeton University Press, 1959.

LIDDELL HART, B. H. *Deterrent or Defense.* New York: Praeger, 1960.

MIKSCHE, F. O. *The Failure of Atomic Strategy.* New York: Praeger, 1959.

OSGOOD, ROBERT E. *Limited War: The Challenge of American Strategy.* Chicago: University of Chicago Press, 1957.

POSSONY, STEFAN T. *A Century of Conflict.* Chicago: Regnery, 1953.

SCHELLING, THOMAS C. *Strategy of Conflict.* Cambridge: Harvard University Press, 1960.

The Soviet Union and the NATO Powers: The Military Balance. London: The Institute for Strategic Studies, 1960.

STEEL, JOHN, with the assistance of HERMAN KAHN. "Civil Defense is Possible," *Fortune* (December, 1958).

STRAUSZ-HUPÉ, ROBERT. "Is NATO Expendable?" *U. S. Naval Institute Proceedings,* LXXXIII (September, 1957).

———. "A Policy for the West," *Yale Review,* XLVI (Autumn, 1956).

TAYLOR, MAXWELL D. *The Uncertain Trumpet.* New York: Harper, 1960.

TURNER, GORDON B., and CHALLENER, RICHARD D. (eds.). *National Security in the Nuclear Age: Basic Facts and Theories.* New York: Praeger, 1960.

WOLFERS, ARNOLD (ed.). *Alliance Policy and the Cold War.* Baltimore: Johns Hopkins Press, 1959.

Chapter VI—Economic Framework of Strategy; and Chapter X—Strategy of Ways and Means

The Budget and Economic Growth. Statement by the Research and Policy Committee of the Committee for Economic Development, April, 1959.

Comparisons of the United States and Soviet Economies. Papers Submitted by Panelists Appearing Before the Subcommittee on Economic Statistics, Joint Economic Committee, Congress of the United States, Parts I and II. Washington: Government Printing Office, 1959.

Comparisons of the United States and Soviet Economies. Hearings before the Joint Economic Committee of the Congress, November, 1959. Washington: Government Printing Office, 1960.

DE JOUVENEL, BERTRAND. "American Policy and the Free World Economy," *Orbis,* III (Fall, 1959).

Economic, Social, and Political Change in the Underdeveloped Countries and Its Implications for United States Policy. Center for International Studies, Massachusetts Institute of Technology. Prepared for the Committee on Foreign Relations, U. S. Senate. Washington: Government Printing Office, 1960.

EISNER, ROBERT, HOEBER, FRANCIS P. and RILEY, RODERICK H. *Potential for Expansion of U. S. National Security Programs: A Study of Economic Feasibility.* Prepared for Stanford Research Institute, 1960.

HAHN, WALTER F. and NEFF, JOHN C. (eds.). *American Strategy for the Nuclear Age.* Garden City, New York: Doubleday, 1960.

BROWNLEE, JAMES F. "The Defense We Can Afford."

GARNER, ROBERT L. "Private Enterprise: America's Best Export."

PETERSON, HOWARD C. "Soviet Economic Growth and United States Policy."

ROSTOW, WALT W. "The Stages of Economic Growth."

TRUDEAU, Lieutenant General ARTHUR G. "The Economic Threat of Soviet Imperialism."

WOLFERS, ARNOLD. "Military or Economic Aid: Questions of Priority."

HOOVER, CALVIN B. *The Economy, Liberty and the State.* New York: Twentieth Century Fund, 1959.

National Objectives and the Balance of Payments Problem. Statement by the Research and Policy Committee of the Committee for Economic Development, 1960.

NOVE, ALEC. *Communist Economic Strategy: Soviet Growth and Capabilities.* Washington: National Planning Association, 1959.

RANDALL, CLARENCE B. *The Communist Challenge to American Business.* Boston: Little, Brown, 1959.

ROWEN, HENRY. *National Security and the American Economy in the 1960's.* Study Paper No. 18 Prepared for the Joint Economic Committee Study of Employment, Growth and Price Levels. Washington: United States Government Printing Office, 1960.

SALVADORI, MASSIMO. *The Economics of Freedom.* Garden City, New York: Doubleday, 1960.

SCHLESINGER, JAMES R. *The Political Economy of National Security.* New York: Praeger, 1960.

Significant Issues in Economic Aid to Newly Developing Countries. Staff Paper Prepared by the International Industrial Development Center, Stanford Research Institute. Menlo Park, California, 1960.

Soviet Economic Penetration of the Middle East. A Special Study Prepared at the request of Senator Hubert H. Humphrey by the Legislative Reference Service of the Library of Congress. Washington: U. S. Government Printing Office, 1959.

Statement Developed by the Princeton Conference on the Balance of Payment of the United States. Stanford Research Institute; Center for International Studies, Massachusetts Institute of Technology; Center of International Studies, Princeton University; Foreign Policy Research Institute, University of Pennsylvania, November 16, 1959.

TRIFFIN, ROBERT. *Gold and the Dollar Crisis.* New Haven: Yale University Press, 1960.

Worldwide and Domestic Economic Problems and Their Impact on the Foreign Policy of the United States. Study Prepared by the Corporation for Economic and Industrial Research, Inc. at the request of the Committee on Foreign Relations, U. S. Senate. Washington: U. S. Government Printing Office, 1959.

Chapter VII—The Diplomatic Arm of Strategy

ACHESON, DEAN. *Power and Diplomacy.* Cambridge: Harvard University Press, 1958.

BALL, MARGARET M. *NATO and the European Union Movement.* New York: Praeger (for the London Institute of World Affairs), 1959.

BARNETT, A. DOAK. *Communist China and Asia: Challenge to American Policy.* New York: Harper, 1960.

BUCHAN, ALISTAIR. *NATO in the 1960's.* London: Institute for Strategic Studies, 1960.

BULLARD, SIR READER (ed.). *The Middle East: A Political and Economic Survey.* 3rd ed. New York: Oxford University Press, 1958.

COTTRELL, ALVIN J. "NATO: Cornerstone of U. S. Foreign Policy," *Current History,* XXXIX (September, 1960).

DEUTSCH, KARL, *et al. Political Community and the North Atlantic Area.* Princeton: Princeton University Press, 1957.

FIFIELD, RUSSELL H. *The Diplomacy of Southeast Asia, 1945-1958.* New York: Harper, 1958.

Foreign Policy Research Institute, University of Pennsylvania. "A Study of United States Military Assistance Programs in Underdeveloped Areas," Annex C, *Supplement to the Composite Report of the President's Committee to Study the United States Military Assistance Program.* Washington: U. S. Government Printing Office, 1959.

The Formulation and Administration of United States Foreign Policy. Brookings Institution. Prepared at the request of the Committee on Foreign Relations, U. S. Senate. Washington: U. S. Government Printing Office, 1960.

GOLDSCHMIDT, WALTER (ed.). *The United States and Africa.* New York: Columbia University Press (for the American Assembly), 1958.

HAAS, ERNST B. *The Uniting of Europe: Political, Social and Economic Forces, 1950-1957.* Stanford: Stanford University Press, 1958.

HAHN, LORNA. *North Africa: Nationalism to Nationhood.* Washington: Public Affairs Press, 1960.

KERTESZ, STEPHEN D. and FITZSIMONS, M. A. *Diplomacy in a Changing World.* Notre Dame: University of Notre Dame Press, 1959.

KISSINGER, HENRY A. "Force and Diplomacy in the Nuclear Age," *Foreign Affairs,* XXXIV (April, 1956).

———. "Reflections on American Diplomacy," *Foreign Affairs,* XXXV (October, 1956).

———. *A World Restored.* Boston: Houghton Mifflin, 1957.

KNORR, KLAUS. *NATO and American Security.* Princeton: Princeton University Press, 1959.

LAQUEUR, WALTER Z. *The Middle East in Transition.* New York: Praeger, 1958.

———. *The Soviet Union and the Middle East.* New York: Praeger, 1959.

LIEUWEN, EDWIN. *Arms and Politics in Latin America.* New York: Praeger (for the Council on Foreign Relations), 1960.

MATTHEWS, HERBERT L. (ed.). *The United States and Latin America.* New York: Columbia University Press (for the American Assembly), 1960.

NIEMEYER, GERHART. "NATO's Strength and Weakness," *Orbis,* II (Spring, 1959).

PALMER, THOMAS W., JR. *Search for a Latin American Policy.* Gainesville: University of Florida Press, 1957.

Regional Development for Regional Peace: A New Policy and Program to Counter the Soviet Menace in the Middle East. Washington: Public Affairs Institute, 1957.

RITNER, PETER. *The Death of Africa.* New York: Macmillan, 1960.

STRAUSZ-HUPÉ, ROBERT, and HAZARD, HARRY W. (eds.). *The Idea of Colonialism.* New York: Praeger, 1958.

THAYER, CHARLES W. *Diplomat.* New York: Harper, 1959.

THAYER, PHILIP W. (ed.). *Tensions in the Middle East.* Baltimore: Johns Hopkins Press, 1958.

U. S. Foreign Policy—Africa. Program of African Studies, Northwestern University. Prepared at the request of the Committee on Foreign Relations, U. S. Senate. Washington: U. S. Government Printing Office, 1959.

U. S. Foreign Policy—Asia. Conlon Associates Ltd. Prepared at the request of the Committee on Foreign Relations, U. S. Senate. Washington: U. S. Government Printing Office, 1959.

U. S. Foreign Policy—Middle East. Staff Study Prepared for the use of the Committee on Foreign Relations, U. S. Senate. Washington: U. S. Government Printing Office, 1960.

U. S. Foreign Policy in the U.S.S.R. and Eastern Europe. Columbia-Harvard Research Group, Columbia University. Prepared at the request of the Committee on Foreign Relations, U. S. Senate. Washington: U. S. Government Printing Office, 1960.

U. S. Foreign Policy in Western Europe. Foreign Policy Research Institute, University of Pennsylvania. Prepared at the request of the Committee on Foreign Relations, U. S. Senate. Washington: U. S. Government Printing Office, 1959.

ZURCHER, ARNOLD J. *The Stuggle to Unite Europe, 1940-1958.* New York: New York University Press, 1958.

Chapter VIII—Psychological Operations

BARNETT, FRANK R. "Disengagement or Commitment?" *Orbis,* III (Winter, 1959).

DAUGHERTY, WILLIAM E., in collaboration with MORRIS JANOWITZ. *A Psychological Warfare Casebook.* Baltimore: The Johns Hopkins Press (for Operations Research Office), 1958.

DJILAS, MILOVAN. *The New Class: An Analysis of the Communist System.* New York: Praeger, 1957.

FERREUS. "The Menace of Communist Psychological Warfare," *Orbis,* I (April, 1957).

HAHN, WALTER F. and NEFF, JOHN C. (eds.). *American Strategy for the Nuclear Age.* Garden City, New York: Doubleday, 1960.

BARNETT, FRANK R. "What Is To Be Done?"

COTTRELL, ALVIN J. and DOUGHERTY, JAMES E. "The Larger Strategic Vision."

HOOVER, J. EDGAR. "The Appeals of Communism."

JONAS, ANNE M. "Changes in Soviet Conflict Doctrine."
KINTNER, WILLIAM R. "The Orchestration of Crisis."
NIEMEYER, GERHART. "The Ideological Core of Communism."
POSSONY, STEFAN T. "Communist Psychological Warfare."
SARNOFF, DAVID. "A Political Offensive against Communism."
WOLFE, BERTRAM D. "Communist Vulnerabilities."

HANNON, STUART L. "Diplomacy and Propaganda." Unpublished address, University of Dublin, 1959.

———. "Propaganda of Coexistence." Unpublished address before World Affairs Council of Northern California, Asilomar, California, 1960.

Ideology and Foreign Affairs. Center for International Studies, Harvard University. Prepared at the request of the Committee on Foreign Relations, U. S. Senate. Washington: U. S. Government Printing Office, 1960.

KOESTLER, ARTHUR. *Darkness at Noon*. New York: Macmillan, 1940.

KRAEMER, FRITZ G. A. "What U. S. Propaganda Can and Can't Be." *Stanford Research Institute Journal,* III (Fourth Quarter, 1959).

LINEBARGER, PAUL M. A. *Psychological Warfare*. Washington: Infantry Journal, 1948.

PETROV, VLADIMIR. "Wither Soviet Evolution?" *Orbis,* III (Fall, 1959).

POSSONY, STEFAN T. "Ideologies and Beyond," Washington, 1955 (Unpublished monograph).

———. "Words that Divide the World," *Saturday Evening Post,* Vol. 233 (July 9, 1960).

STRAUSZ-HUPÉ, ROBERT. "Why Russia is Ahead in Propaganda," *New York Times Magazine* (September 27, 1959).

The United States Through the Eyes of Soviet Tourists. Staff Report, Subcommittee to Investigate the Administration of the Internal Security Act and other Internal Security Laws of the Committee on the Judiciary, United States Senate, 86th Congress. Washington: U. S. Government Printing Office, 1960.

Chapter IX—Security Through Arms Control

Control and Reduction of Armaments. Final Report of the Committee on Foreign Relations, Subcommittee on Disarmament, Report No. 2501, 85th Congress. Washington: Government Printing Office, 1958.

DYSON, FREEMAN J. "The Future Development of Nuclear Weapons," *Foreign Affairs,* Vol. 38 (April, 1960).

FELD, BERNARD T., *et. al. The Technical Problems of Arms Control*. New York: Institute for International Order, 1960.

HAHN, WALTER F., and NEFF, JOHN C. (eds.). *American Strategy for the Nuclear Age*. Garden City, New York: Doubleday, 1960.

KISSINGER, HENRY A. "Disarmament: Illusion and Reality."
WOLFE, THOMAS W. "Soviet Strategy of Disarmament."

Khrushchev's Strategy and its Meaning for America. A Study presented by the Subcommittee to Investigate the Administration of the Internal Security Act and Other Internal Security Laws of the Committee on the Judiciary, United States Senate, 86th Congress, 2nd Session. Prepared by the Foreign Policy Research Institute, University of Pennsylvania. Washington: U. S. Government Printing Office, 1960.

KISSINGER, HENRY A. "Arms Control, Inspection and Surprise Attack," *Foreign Affairs,* Vol. 38 (July, 1960).

MATTESON, ROBERT T., and ELIOT, GEORGE FIELDING. "Prospects for Disarmament: Two Views," *Orbis,* Vol. II (Fall, 1958).

MELMAN, SEYMOUR (ed.). *Inspection for Disarmament.* New York: Columbia University Press, 1959.

MURRAY, THOMAS E. *Nuclear Policy for War and Peace.* New York: World, 1960.

"Nth" Country Problem and Arms Control, The. A Statement by the NPA Special Project Committee on Security Through Arms Control and a Technical Report by W. Davidson, M. Kalkstein, and C. Hohemser. Washington: National Planning Association, 1960.

SCHELLING, THOMAS C. "Surprise Attack and Disarmament," *Bulletin of the Atomic Scientists,* Vol. XV (December, 1959).

STRAUSZ-HUPÉ, ROBERT. "The Disarmament Delusion," *United States Naval Institute Proceedings,* Vol. 86 (February, 1960).

STRAUSZ-HUPÉ, ROBERT. *et al. Protracted Conflict.* New York: Harper, 1959.

Technical Aspects of Detection and Inspection Controls of a Nuclear Weapons Test Ban. Joint Committee on Atomic Energy. Washington: U. S. Government Printing Office, 1960.

Chapter XI—Structure for Strategy

DUFFIELD, EUGENE S. "Organizing for Defense," *Harvard Business Review,* XXXVIII (September-October, 1958).

FELD, M. D. "Information and Authority: The Structure of Military Organization," *American Sociological Review,* XXIV (February, 1959).

HITTLE, J. D. "Military Planning at the Seat of Government," *U. S. Naval Institute Proceedings,* LXXXIII (July, 1957).

HUNTINGTON, SAMUEL P. "Strategic Planning and the Political Process," *Foreign Affairs,* XXXVIII (January, 1960).

KINTNER, WILLIAM R. "Organizing for Conflict: A Proposal," *Orbis,* II (Summer, 1958).

———. "Progress in Defense Organization," *Journal of Public Law,* IX (Spring, 1960).

KINTNER, WILLIAM R., in association with COFFEY, JOSEPH I. and ALBRIGHT, RAYMOND J. *Forging a New Sword.* New York: Harper (for American Project Series, Center of International Studies, Massachusetts Institute of Technology), 1958.

KISSINGER, HENRY A. "Strategy and Organization," *Foreign Affairs,* XXXV (April, 1957).

KNOX, DUDLEY W. "Development of Unification," *U. S. Naval Institute Proceedings,* LXXVII (December, 1950).

LEE, GUS C. "The Organization for National Security," *Public Administration Review,* IX (Winter, 1949).

LIVINGSTON, J. STERLING. "Decision-Making in Weapons Development," *Harvard Business Review,* XXXVI (January-February, 1958).

MANSFIELD, HARVEY C. "Civil-Military Relations in the United States," *Current History,* XXXVIII (April, 1960).

MARWALD, ALEXANDER. "The German General Staff: A Model of Military Organization?" *Orbis,* III (Spring, 1959).

MOSHER, FREDERICK C. *et al.* "Decision-Making in Defense: The Role of Organization," *Public Administration Review,* XVIII (Summer, 1958).

OREM, HOWARD E. "Shall We Junk the Joint Chiefs of Staff?" *U. S. Naval Institute Proceedings,* LXXXIV (February, 1958).

PROBERT, JOHN R. "Pentagon Reorganization: Phase III," *U. S. Naval Institute Proceedings,* LXXXI (January, 1955).

United States Senate, Committee on Government Operations. *Organizing for National Security: The Department of State, the Policy Planning Staff, and the National Security Council.* Hearings before the Subcommittee on National Policy Machinery, 86th Congress, 2nd Session (May 26, June 17 and 27, 1960).

———. *Organizing for National Security: The Executive Office and Public Support.* Hearings before the Subcommittee on National Policy Machinery, 86th Congress, 2nd Session (June 28 and July 1, 1960).

———. *Organizing for National Security: The National Security Council and the Departments of State and Defense.* Hearings before the Subcommittee on National Policy Machinery, 86th Congress, 2nd Session (June 2, 6, 10, 13 and 14, 1960).

INDEX